plant sciences

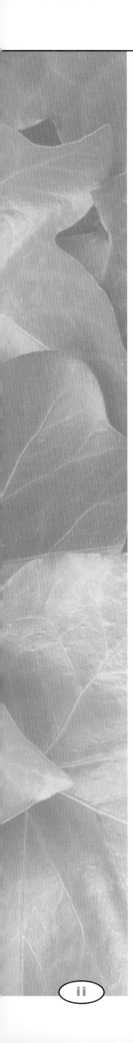

plant sciences

VOLUME 2
Co–Gy

Richard Robinson, Editor in Chief

Macmillan Reference USA
an imprint of the Gale Group
San Francisco • London • Boston • Woodbridge, CT

Macmillan Reference USA   Gale Group
1633 Broadway   27500 Drake Rd.
New York, NY 10019   Farmington Hills, MI 48331-3535

Printed in Canada
1 2 3 4 5 6 7 8 9 10

Library of Congress Cataloging-in-Publication Data
Plant sciences / Richard Robinson, editor in chief.
     p.   cm.
Includes bibliographical references (p.).
ISBN 0-02-865434-X (hardcover : set) — ISBN 0-02-865430-7 (vol. 1) —
ISBN 0-02-865431-5 (vol. 2) — ISBN 0-02-865432-3 (vol. 3) —
ISBN 0-02-865433-1 (vol. 4)
    1. Botany—Juvenile literature.   2. Plants—Juvenile literature. [1.
       Botany—Encyclopedias.] I. Robinson, Richard, 1956-
QK49.P52 2000
580—dc21
00—046064

Preface

Someone once said that if you want to find an alien life form, just go into your backyard and grab the first green thing you see. Although plants evolved on Earth along with the rest of us, they really are about as different and strange and wonderful a group of creatures as one is likely to find anywhere in the universe.

The World of Plants

Consider for a minute just how different plants are. They have no mouths, no eyes or ears, no brain, no muscles. They stand still for their entire lives, planted in the soil like enormous drinking straws wicking gallon after gallon of water from the earth to the atmosphere. Plants live on little more than water, air, and sunshine and have mastered the trick of transmuting these simple things into almost everything they (and we) need. In this encyclopedia, readers will find out how plants accomplish this photosynthetic alchemy and learn about the extraordinary variety of form and function within the plant kingdom. In addition, readers will be able to trace their 450-million-year history and diversification, from the very first primitive land plants to the more than 250,000 species living today.

*Explore further in Photosynthesis, Light Reactions and Evolution of Plants

All animals ultimately depend on photosynthesis for their food, and humans are no exception. Over the past ten thousand years, we have cultivated such an intimate relationship with a few species of grains that it is hardly an exaggeration to say, in the words of one scientist, that "humans domesticated wheat, and vice versa." With the help of agriculture, humans were transformed from a nomadic, hunting and gathering species numbering in the low millions, into the most dominant species on the planet, with a population that currently exceeds six billion. Agriculture has shaped human culture profoundly, and together the two have reshaped the planet. In this encyclopedia, readers can explore the history of agriculture, learn how it is practiced today, both conventionally and organically, and what the impact of it and other human activities has been on the land, the atmosphere, and the other creatures who share the planet with us.

*Explore further in Agriculture, Modern and Human Impacts

Throughout history—even before the development of the modern scientific method—humans experimented with plants, finding the ones that provided the best meal, the strongest fiber, or the sweetest wine. Naming a thing is such a basic and powerful way of knowing it that all cultures have created some type of taxonomy for the plants they use. The scientific understanding of plants through experimentation, and the development of ra-

tional classification schemes based on evolution, has a rich history that is explored in detail in this encyclopedia. There are biographies of more than two dozen botanists who shaped our modern understanding, and essays on the history of physiology, ecology, taxonomy, and evolution. Across the spectrum of the botanical sciences, progress has accelerated in the last two decades, and a range of entries describe the still-changing understanding of evolutionary relationships, genetic control, and biodiversity.

✳Explore further in Ecology, History of; Biodiversity; and Phylogeny

With the development of our modern scientific society, a wide range of new careers has opened up for people interested in plant sciences, many of which are described in this encyclopedia. Most of these jobs require a college degree, and the better-paying ones often require advanced training. While all are centered around plants, they draw on skills that range from envisioning a landscape in one's imagination (landscape architect) to solving differential equations (an ecological modeler) to budgeting and personnel management (curator of a botanical garden).

✳Explore further in Curator of a Botanical Garden and Landscape Architect

Organization of the Material

Each of the 280 entries in *Plant Sciences* has been newly commissioned for this work. Our contributors are drawn from academic and research institutions, industry, and nonprofit organizations throughout North America. In many cases, the authors literally "wrote the book" on their subject, and all have brought their expertise to bear in writing authoritative, up-to-date entries that are nonetheless accessible to high school students. Almost every entry is illustrated and there are numerous photos, tables, boxes, and sidebars to enhance understanding. Unfamiliar terms are highlighted and defined in the margin. Most entries are followed by a list of related articles and a short reading list for readers seeking more information. Front and back matter include a geologic timescale, a topic outline that groups entries thematically, and a glossary. Each volume has its own index, and volume 4 contains a cumulative index covering the entire encyclopedia.

Acknowledgments and Thanks

I wish to thank the many people at Macmillan Reference USA and the Gale Group for their leadership in bringing this work to fruition, and their assiduous attention to the many details that make such a work possible. In particular, thanks to Hélène Potter, Brian Kinsey, Betz Des Chenes, and Diane Sawinski. The editorial board members—Robert Evans, Wendy Mechaber, and Robert Wallace—were outstanding, providing invaluable expertise and extraordinary hard work. Wendy is also my wife, and I wish to thank her for her support and encouragement throughout this project. My own love of plants began with three outstanding biology teachers, Marjorie Holland, James Howell, and Walt Tulecke, and I am in their debt. My many students at the Commonwealth School in Boston were also great teachers—their enthusiastic questions over the years deepened my own understanding and appreciation of the mysteries of the plant world. I hope that a new generation of students can discover some of the excitement and mystery of this world in *Plant Sciences*.

Richard Robinson
Editor in Chief

Geologic Timescale

ERA	PERIOD		EPOCH	STARTED (millions of years ago)
Cenozoic: 66.4 millions of years ago–present time	**Quaternary**		Holocene	0.01
			Pleistocene	1.6
	Tertiary	**Neogene**	Pliocene	5.3
			Miocene	23.7
		Paleogene	Oligocene	36.6
			Eocene	57.8
			Paleocene	66.4
Mesozoic: 245–66.4 millions of years ago	**Cretaceous**		Late	97.5
			Early	144
	Jurassic		Late	163
			Middle	187
			Early	208
	Triassic		Late	230
			Middle	240
			Early	245
Paleozoic: 570–245 millions of years ago	**Permian**		Late	258
			Early	286
	Carboniferous	**Pennsylvanian**	Late	320
		Mississippian	Early	360
	Devonian		Late	374
			Middle	387
			Early	408
	Silurian		Late	421
			Early	438
	Ordovician		Late	458
			Middle	478
			Early	505
	Cambrian		Late	523
			Middle	540
			Early	570
Precambrian time: 4500–570 millions of years ago				4500

Contributors

Miguel Altieri
University of California, Berkeley

Sherwin Toshio Amimoto
Redondo Beach, CA

Edward F. Anderson
Desert Botanical Garden, Phoenix, AZ

Gregory J. Anderson
University of Connecticut

Mary Anne Andrei
Minneapolis, MN

Wendy L. Applequist
Iowa State University

Rebecca Baker
Cotati, CA

Peter S. Bakwin
National Oceanic and Atmospheric Administration

Jo Ann Banks
Purdue University

Theodore M. Barkley
Botanical Research Institute of Texas

Ronald D. Barnett
University of Florida

Patricia A. Batchelor
Milwaukee Public Museum

Hank W. Bass
Florida State University

Yves Basset
Smithsonian Tropical Research Institute

Stuart F. Baum
University of California, Davis

Gabriel Bernardello
University of Connecticut

Paul E. Berry
University of Wisconsin-Madison

Paul C. Bethke
University of California, Berkeley

J. Derek Bewley
University of Guelph

Christopher J. Biermann
Philomath, OR

Franco Biondi
University of Nevada

Richard E. Bir
North Carolina State University

Jane H. Bock
University of Colorado

Hans Bohnert
Nara Institute of Science and Technology

Brian M. Boom
New York Botanical Garden

David E. Boufford
Harvard University Herbaria

John L. Bowman
University of California, Davis

James R. Boyle
Oregon State University

James M. Bradeen
University of Wisconsin-Madison

Irwin M. Brodo
Canadian Museum of Nature

Robert C. Brown
Iowa State University

Leo P. Bruederle
University of Colorado, Denver

Robert Buchsbaum
Massachusetts Audubon Society

Stephen C. Bunting
University of Idaho

John M. Burke
Indiana University

Charles A. Butterworth
Iowa State University

Christian E. Butzke
University of California, Davis

Kenneth M. Cameron
New York Botanical Garden

Deborah K. Canington
University of California, Davis

Vernon B. Cardwell
American Society of Agronomy

Don Cawthon
Texas A & M University

Russell L. Chapman
Louisiana State University

Arthur H. Chappelka
Auburn University

Lynn G. Clark
Iowa State University

W. Dean Cocking
James Madison University

James T. Colbert
Iowa State University

Daniel J. Cosgrove
Pennsylvania State University

Barbara Crandall-Stotler
Southern Illinois University

Donald L. Crawford
University of Idaho

Thomas B. Croat
Missouri Botanical Garden

Lawrence J. Crockett
Pace University

Sunburst Shell Crockett
Society of American Foresters

Richard Cronn
Iowa State University

Anne Fernald Cross
Oklahoma State University

Rodney Croteau
Washington State University

Judith G. Croxdale
University of Wisconsin

Peter J. Davies
Cornell University

Jerrold I. Davis
Cornell University

Elizabeth L. Davison
University of Arizona

Ira W. Deep
Ohio State University

Nancy G. Dengler
University of Toronto

Steven L. Dickie
Iowa State University

David L. Dilcher
University of Florida

Rebecca W. Doerge
Purdue University

Susan A. Dunford
University of Cincinnati

Frank A. Einhellig
Southwest Missouri State University

George S. Ellmore
Tufts University

Roland Ennos
University of Manchester

Emanuel Epstein
University of California, Davis

M. Susan Erich
University of Maine

Robert C. Evans
Rutgers University

Donald R. Farrar
Iowa State University

Charles B. Fenster
Botanisk Institutt

Manfred A. Fischer
University of Vienna, Austria

Theodore H. Fleming
Tuscon, AZ

Dennis Francis
Cardiff University

Arthur W. Galston
Yale University

Grace Gershuny
St. Johnsbury, VT

Peter Gerstenberger
National Arborist Association, Inc.

Stephen R. Gliessman
University of California, Santa Cruz

J. Peter Gogarten
University of Connecticut

Govindjee
University of Illinois, Urbana-Champaign

Linda E. Graham
University of Wisconsin, Madison

Peter H. Graham
University of Minnesota

Michael A. Grusak
U.S. Department of Agriculture, Children's Nutrition Research Center

Gerald F. Guala
Fairchild Tropical Garden, Miami

Robert Gutman
Athens, GA

Charles J. Gwo
University of New Mexico

Ardell D. Halvorson
U.S. Department of Agriculture, Agricultural Research Service

Earl G. Hammond
Iowa State University

Jeffrey B. Harborne
University of Reading

Elizabeth M. Harris
Ohio State University Herbarium

Frederick V. Hebard
American Chestnut Foundation

Steven R. Hill
Center for Biodiversity

J. Kenneth Hoober
Arizona State University

Roger F. Horton
University of Guelph

D. Michael Jackson
U.S. Department of Agriculture, Agricultural Research Service

William P. Jacobs
Princeton, NJ

David M. Jarzen
University of Florida

Roger V. Jean
University of Quebec

Philip D. Jenkins
University of Arizona

Russell L. Jones
University of California, Berkeley

Lee B. Kass
Cornell University

George B. Kauffman
California State University, Fresno

Jon E. Keeley
National Park Service

Dean G. Kelch
University of California, Berkeley

Nancy M. Kerk
Yale University

Alan K. Knapp
Kansas State University

Erich Kombrink
Max-Planck-Institut für Züchtungsforschung

Ross E. Koning
Eastern Connecticut State University

Thomas G. Lammers
University of Wisconsin, Oshkosh

Mark A. Largent
University of Minnesota

Donald W. Larson
Columbus, OH

Matthew Lavin
Montana State University

Roger H. Lawson
Columbia, MD

Michael Lee
Iowa State University

Michael J. Lewis
University of California, Davis

Walter H. Lewis
Washington University

Douglas T. Linde
Delaware Valley College

Bradford Carlton Lister
Rensselaer Polytechnic Institute

Margaret D. Lowman
Marie Selby Botanical Gardens, Sarasota, FL

Peter J. Lumsden
University of Central Lancashire

Lynn Margulis
University of Massachusetts, Amherst

Wendy Mechaber
University of Arizona

Alan W. Meerow
U.S. Department of Agriculture, Agricultural Research Service

T. Lawrence Mellichamp
University of North Carolina, Charlotte

Scott Merkle
University of Georgia

Jan E. Mikesell
Gettysburg College

Orson K. Miller Jr.
Virginia Polytechnic Institute

Thomas Minney
The New Forests Project

Thomas S. Moore
Louisiana State University

David R. Morgan
Western Washington University

Gisèle Muller-Parker
Western Washington University

Suzanne C. Nelson
Native Seeds/SEARCH

Robert Newgarden
Brooklyn Botanic Gardens

Daniel L. Nickrent
Southern Illinois University

John S. Niederhauser
Tucson, AZ

David O. Norris
University of Colorado

Lorraine Olendzenski
University of Connecticut

Micheal D. K. Owen
Iowa State University

James C. Parks
Millersville University

Wayne Parrott
University of Georgia

Andrew H. Paterson
University of Georgia

Jessica P. Penney
Allston, MA

Terry L. Peppard
Warren, NJ

John H. Perkins
The Evergreen State College

Kim Moreau Peterson
University of Alaska, Anchorage

Peter A. Peterson
Iowa State University

Richard B. Peterson
Connecticut Agricultural Experiment Station

D. Mason Pharr
North Carolina State University

Bobby J. Phipps
Delta Research Center

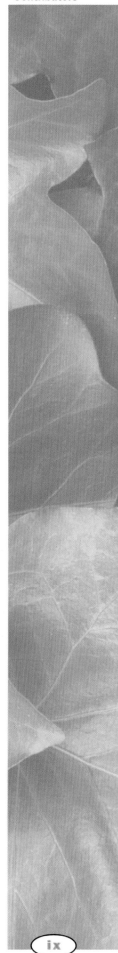

Janet M. Pine
Iowa State University

Ghillean T. Prance
The Old Vicarage, Dorset, UK

Robert A. Price
University of Georgia

Richard B. Primack
Boston University

V. Raghavan
Ohio State University

James A. Rasmussen
Southern Arkansas University

Linda A. Raubeson
Central Washington University

A. S. N. Reddy
Colorado State University

Robert A. Rice
Smithsonian Migratory Bird Center

Loren H. Rieseberg
Indiana University

Richard Robinson
Tuscon, AZ

Curt R. Rom
University of Arkansas

Thomas L. Rost
University of California, Davis

Sabine J. Rundle
Western Carolina University

Scott D. Russell
University of Oklahoma

J. Neil Rutger
*U.S. Department of Agriculture,
Dale Bumpers National Rice
Research Center*

Fred D. Sack
Ohio State University

Dorion Sagan
Amherst, MA

Ann K. Sakai
University of California-Irvine

Frank B. Salisbury
Utah State University

Mark A. Schneegurt
Witchita State University

Randy Scholl
Ohio State University

Jack C. Schultz
Pennsylvania State University

Hanna Rose Shell
New Haven, CT

Timothy W. Short
*Queens College of the City
University of New York*

Philipp W. Simon
University of Wisconsin-Madison

Garry A. Smith
Canon City, CO

James F. Smith
Boise State University

Vassiliki Betty Smocovitis
University of Florida

Doug Soltis
Washington State University

Pam Soltis
Washington State University

Paul C. Spector
*The Holden Arboretum, Kirtland,
OH*

David M. Spooner
University of Wisconsin

Helen A. Stafford
Reed College

Craig Steely
Elm Research Institute

Taylor A. Steeves
University of Saskatchewan

Hans K. Stenoien
Botanisk Institutt

Peter F. Stevens
University of Missouri, St. Louis

Ian M. Sussex
Yale University

Charlotte A. Tancin
Carnegie Mellon University

Edith L. Taylor
University of Kansas

Thomas N. Taylor
University of Kansas

W. Carl Taylor
Milwaukee Public Museum

Mark Tebbitt
Brooklyn Botanical Gardens

Barbara M. Thiers
New York Botanical Garden

Sean C. Thomas
University of Toronto

Sue A. Thompson
Pittsburgh, PA

Barbara N. Timmermann
University of Arizona

Ward M. Tingey
Cornell University

Alyson K. Tobin
University of St. Andrews

Dwight T. Tomes
Johnston, IA

Nancy J. Turner
University of Victoria

Sarah E. Turner
University of Victoria

Miguel L. Vasquez
Northern Arizona University

Robert S. Wallace
Iowa State University

Debra A. Waters
Louisiana State University

Elizabeth Fortson Wells
George Washington University

Molly M. Welsh
*U.S. Department of Agriculture,
Agricultural Research Service*

James J. White
Carnegie Mellon University

Michael A. White
University of Montana

John Whitmarsh
*University of Illinois, Urbana-
Champaign*

Garrison Wilkes
University of Massachusetts, Boston

John D. Williamson
North Carolina State University

Thomas Wirth
*Thomas Wirth Associates, Inc.,
Sherborn, MA*

Jianguo Wu
Arizona State University

Table of Contents

plant sciences

Coastal Ecosystems

An ecosystem is an interacting **community** of organisms and their non-living physical environment occupying a certain place and time. Coastal ecosystems occupy the margins of the land and the sea. There are many different types: salt marshes, mangrove swamps, sand dunes, seagrass meadows, coral reefs, kelp forests, tidal flats, rocky **intertidal**, maritime forests, and coastal heathlands. All are heavily influenced by some combination of saltwater, ocean waves, currents, and ocean breezes, though not necessarily all of these.

community a group of organisms of different species living in a region

intertidal between the lines of high and low tide

Components of Coastal Ecosystems

The major interactions of organisms and their environment in coastal ecosystems include energy transfer and cycling of materials. These involve several functional groups of organisms. Plants and algae are the major primary producers, that is, organisms that produce their own food through the process of photosynthesis. They use the energy from the sun and the nutrients washed down to the coast from the surrounding land or brought to the coast by the ocean.

The plants living in constant or periodic contact with ocean water are called halophytes ("salt plants"). They must have special adaptations to be able to thrive because saltwater is toxic to most plants.

Plants and algae are the bases of the coastal food chain. They may be consumed by **herbivores**, such as insects or geese that feed on salt marsh grasses, snails that consume seaweeds on rocky shores, or fish that graze on tropical seagrass beds. Except for the intertidal marshes and mangrove swamps, the place of insects in coastal ecosystems is minor, their ecological role being replaced by crustaceans (such as crabs, shrimp, lobsters, and beach fleas) and mollusks (snails, clams, mussels, etc.) All these, in turn, may become food for carnivores, such as birds (shorebirds, waterfowl, hawks, etc.) or fish. Many animals living in coastal ecosystems do not feed directly on plants or other animals but feed on **detritus**, nonliving plant material that may contain a large amount of bacteria and fungi. The bacteria and fungi that **colonize** particles of detritus act to break down this material to simple chemical compounds that can be recycled.

herbivore an organism that feeds on plant parts

detritus material from decaying organisms

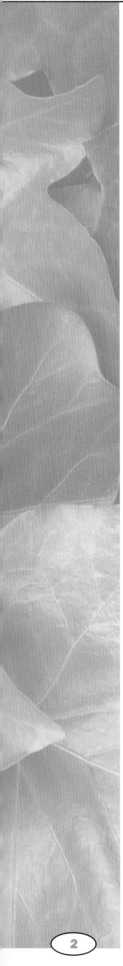

The rich underwater ecosystem of a mangrove swamp on Palawan Island in the Philippines.

Coastal versus Terrestrial Ecosystems

Coastal ecosystems differ from terrestrial ones in several significant ways. The ocean contributes to the exchange of materials, bringing nutrients and removing waste products. In terrestrial ecosystems, the exchange of materials between organisms and their environment does not involve this major mediating agent.

The dominant types of producer organisms in terrestrial ecosystems are plants. In coastal ecosystems they include plants, macroalgae (seaweeds), and phytoplankton (unicellular algae). Seaweeds reach their greatest level of diversity and productivity in coastal ecosystems.

Estuaries

An estuary is a semienclosed body of water where freshwater meets the sea. Typically located at the mouth of rivers, estuaries have characteristics of both fresh and marine habitats and serve as a vital ecological link between the two realms. One of the major factors that determines the place where different organisms can live within an estuary is the gradient of salt concentration, that is, the salinity. The upper reaches of the estuary are most influenced by the river and therefore may be almost completely freshwater. As one moves downstream the influence of the sea becomes increasingly dominant. The salinity of the water gradually increases until at the mouth of the estuary, it is similar to that of the surrounding coastal ocean.

There are daily changes in the movement of water and the salinity profile within an estuary. At high tide the estuary is flooded with higher salinity seawater, and at low tide the river water may dominate and the flow is in a downstream direction. Seasonal changes in response to times when greater rainfall and snowmelt wash down the rivers also strongly influence the estuary.

Another characteristic of estuaries is the salt wedge. Since saltwater is more dense than freshwater, the saltwater tends to underlie the river water where the two meet. Thus the surface water of the estuary is usually much fresher than that at the bottom.

These changes in salt concentration within the estuary present a real challenge to plants and animals. They not only have to be salt tolerant, but they also have to be able to tolerate changes in salinity, thus estuaries have their own unique species that differ from those of wholly freshwater or marine habitats. Those few plants that have been able to adapt to life in the estuaries, such as seagrasses, salt marsh plants, and different types of algae, are often extremely productive because having adapted to tolerate the stresses of changing salinities, growing conditions are ideal. Intertidal plants, such as salt marsh grasses and mangrove trees, submerged sea grasses, and algae, are constantly moist with a steady supply of nutrients coming from the sea or the river. As a result, estuaries are among the most productive ecosystems on Earth in terms of the amount of organic matter produced by plants and algae. Estuaries are home to abundant fish, bird, and invertebrate populations, which take advantage of this tremendous plant and algal productivity. Many species of ocean fishes, including a number that are commercially important, spend their juvenile stages in the relative safety of estuaries where the abundance of life sustains their growth to adulthood.

Located at the end points of watersheds, estuaries are often sites where pollutants accumulate and thus the estuaries are very sensitive to human activities. Pollutants generated in the watershed and transported downstream by rivers tend to settle out once they reach estuaries. Thus estuaries serve as barometers of the health of entire watersheds.

Coastal Dunes

Coastal dunes are an unstable, shifting habitat whose very structure is a product of ocean currents, winds, and storms. Currents and waves along the shore deposit sand on the beach, then winds shape the sand into series of small hills that often gradually migrate inland to be constantly replaced

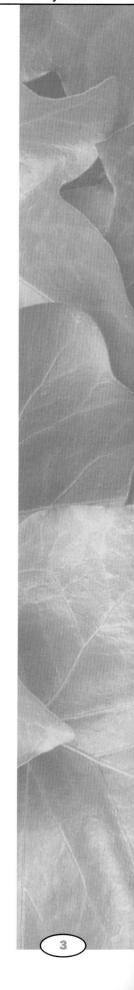

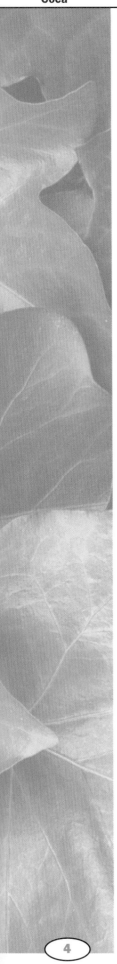

at the beachfront by new dunes. Winter storms may completely reshape the landscape, blowing holes in the dunes closest to the ocean and starting the process over.

Sand is unstable, which is why dunes can achieve a maximum stature of only several hundred feet. Dune plants have to be able to tolerate life in shifting sands where water rapidly **percolates** through the soil and out of the reach of plant roots. Plants that grow on sand dunes must be able to tolerate harsh, desert-like conditions where, as any beachgoer who has walked barefoot on hot sand will attest, there is no shade and daytime temperatures can be extremely hot. Dune plants have a lot in common with desert plants, in which fresh water loss and overheating are real problems. Thus many are **succulent** or have thick **cuticles** on their leaves and deeply sunken **stomata** to prevent water loss. These same kind of adaptations are found in cacti and other desert plants.

The roots of some dune plants play a role in stabilizing sand dunes, helping to shape the nature of this ecosystem. Beach grass is particularly notable in this regard and is often planted deliberately by people to keep dunes in place. The rapidly growing network of roots produced by beach grass penetrates deep into the dune, lending structural support that can keep the dune in place except under the most severe coastal storms. Beach naupaka, a shrub, is valued the same way on Hawaii and other Pacific islands. A dune initially covered by these stabilizing plants is ripe for colonization by other plants, thus the original plant colonizers set the stage for a successional cycle. SEE ALSO Aquatic Ecosystems; Halophytes.

Robert Buchsbaum

Bibliography

Bertness, Mark. *The Ecology of Atlantic Shorelines.* Sunderland, MA: Sinauer Associates, 1999.

Carson, Rachel. *The Edge of the Sea.* Boston: Houghton-Mifflin, 1979.

Teal, John, and Mildred Teal. *Life and Death of the Salt Marsh.* Boston: Little Brown, 1969.

Valiela, Ivan. *Marine Ecological Processes*, 2nd ed. New York: Springer-Verlag, 1995.

Coca

Coca plants are the only natural source of the alkaloid cocaine and related compounds. For several thousand years, the leaves of the coca plant have been used by South American Indians as a mild stimulant, a remedy for medical problems, and for ritualistic or religious purposes. Coca chewing reduces hunger and increases endurance. It also eases the nausea, dizziness, and headaches associated with altitude sickness and relieves the symptoms of various stomach ailments. From **pre-Columbian** times coca has been an integral part of Andean cultures, and the commerce of coca leaves is still a legal and accepted practice in Peru and Bolivia.

The extraction and purification of cocaine hydrochloride from coca leaves, first accomplished in the mid-1800s, yields a drug with very different pharmacological effects than those associated with traditional coca chewing. Recreational use of cocaine produces a quick sense of euphoria

percolate to move through, as a fluid through a solid

succulent marked by fleshy, water-holding leaves or stems

cuticle the waxy outer coating of a leaf or other structure, providing protection against predators, infection, and water loss

stomata openings between guard cells on the underside of leaves that allow gas exchange

pre-Columbian before Columbus

Leaves and fruit of the coca plant.

and heightened awareness. Its use became widespread in the United States and elsewhere in the 1970s. It has since resulted in profound economic and sociological impacts both in the South American countries where it is grown and refined as well as in countries worldwide where it is consumed.

Coca leaves can be harvested several times a year from two shrubby species of the genus *Erythroxylum*. *Erythroxylum coca* has two varieties, the main one occurring along the lower slopes of the Andes in Ecuador, Peru, and Bolivia, and a lesser-known variety called ipadu in the lowlands of the upper Amazon basin. This is the species grown most intensively for cocaine extraction. *Erythroxylum novogranatense* is a related species that differs slightly in its chemical composition and leaf and floral features. This species, which grows naturally from northern Peru to Colombia, is part of the original formula of Coca-Cola® and is still used today as a flavoring in the popular soft drink (but only after the cocaine is first extracted from the leaves).

In traditional use, coca leaves are dried before they are chewed, and to increase the release of alkaloids, small amounts of lime are added to the **quid** of masticated leaves. In lowland Amazonia, where the alkaloid content is generally lower, a fine powder is made from the leaves and mixed with leaf ashes before being made into a quid. To extract cocaine from coca leaves, a large volume of leaves is required, and they are first soaked and mashed in a series of solvents such as kerosene and sulfuric acid and neutralizers like lime, which results in the **precipitation** of a crude cocaine paste. To produce purified cocaine hydrochloride from the paste, more controlled laboratory conditions are required, using reagents such as acetone, ether, and hydrochloric acid.

Cocaine is most often inhaled through the nostrils, but it can also be smoked as a paste or as crack cocaine, or even freebased using an organic solvent. All of these chemically concentrated forms of cocaine have proven to be highly addictive. From the local growers to the paste producers to the clandestine laboratories, then through the international and local drug distribution networks, cocaine demands a high street price and forms the

quid a wad for chewing

precipitation falling out of solution

illicit illegal

basis of a multibillion-dollar **illicit** economy. SEE ALSO ALKALOIDS; MEDICINAL PLANTS; PSYCHOACTIVE PLANTS.

Paul E. Berry

Plowman, T. "Botanical Perspectives on Coca." *Journal of Psychedelic Drugs* 11 (1979): 103–117.

———. "The Ethnobotany of Coca (*Erythroxylum* spp., Erythroxylaceae)." *Advances in Economic Botany* 1 (1984): 62–111.

Coevolution

When two kinds of organisms exert natural selection on each other so they influence each other's evolution, they are undergoing coevolution. Any two organisms may exert selective pressure on each other. **Herbivores** exert selection on plants favoring the evolution of defenses, and plant defenses exert selection on herbivores to overcome them. Competitors exert selection on each other favoring superior competitive ability. Pollinating insects exert selection on flowering plants to provide attractants and rewards, and plants exert selection on pollinators for superior pollination service. This reciprocal natural selection is the core concept in coevolution. It may produce ongoing evolutionary "warfare," in which the participants constantly change their weapons or tools, or it may produce a relationship that benefits both participants. When the outcome is beneficial to both, it is called mutualism.

herbivore an organism that feeds on plant parts

In 1964 entomologist Paul Ehrlich and botanist Peter Raven suggested that these reciprocal changes in physical, chemical, or behavioral traits could be great enough to generate new species. Theoretically, as selection favors changes in each partner, the altered partner could differ from its ancestor enough to become isolated as a new species. For example, if a plant gains protection from its parents' enemies (disease or insects) by producing novel defenses, and if this protection is lost by sharing genes with the parental plant types, then selection should eventually eliminate mating between these two types, resulting in two species where before there was one. Natural selection may then favor enemies capable of colonizing the new plant species, with subsequent reproductive isolation and the formation of additional enemy species. New enemy and plant species are thus formed. Ehrlich and Raven claimed that coevolution may be the major kind of interaction generating the diversity of species on land. While many scientists are skeptical of that statement, the evidence of coevolution is all around us, and many fascinating relationships in nature have arisen from it.

Evidence of Coevolution

Most plants and animals experience natural selection from many sources at once. So it seems unlikely that one organism would be the sole or even the primary selective influence on another. Nonetheless, there are good examples of tightly coevolved relationships (the two participants have a highly specialized interaction). In these cases, the selective advantages gained by responding to one source of selection (the other participant) must outweigh many other factors.

For example, butterflies in the cabbage butterfly family (Pieridae) feed primarily on plants in the cabbage family (Brassicaceae). Members of the cabbage family (cabbage, broccoli, mustards) all share a common set of chemical defenses, called glucosinolates, that are found in very few other plant families. Species in the cabbage butterfly family are capable of feeding on these **toxins** without harm. According to the coevolutionary view, a mutation long ago in a cabbage ancestor provided that plant with the ability to make glucosinolates, which allowed it to escape the pests plaguing its glucosinolate-free ancestors. But soon natural selection favored butterflies with mutations allowing them to feed on glucosinolates, and these butterflies were able to eat the new plants. Additional mutations in the plants produced new glucosinolates, protecting those plants but selecting for butterflies that could overcome the new chemistry, and so on. In the coevolution scenario, the ability to produce glucosinolates and stepwise responses to evolving enemies resulted in the cabbage family as well as the cabbage butterfly family. If we were to draw cladograms, or evolutionary trees, for co-evolved insects and their host plants, they would be near-mirror images, since each chemical change and **speciation** event among the plants should have produced one in the insects, and each change in the insects should have produced one in the plants.

toxin a poisonous substance

speciation creation of new species

Factors Inhibiting Coevolution

Closely matched trees are said to be concordant, an indication of coevolution between two sets of organisms. Scientists have thus far found few concordant trees involving plants and insects, for at least four reasons. First, it is very difficult to construct such trees, especially for insects, because the fossil record (and even current knowledge about insect diets) is so incomplete. Diets are not preserved in the fossil record. Second, insect and plant evolution are influenced by many things. Most plants are attacked by many different kinds of enemies, and a single defense is unlikely to work equally well against all. And insect success is dependent not only on food, but on weather, escape from predators and disease, and other factors. So plants may not be the single greatest influence on insects or vice versa.

Third, these selective factors interact. The **susceptibility** of insects to predators, parasites, and disease is also influenced by plant defenses, sometimes in a direction opposite to the way chemistry influences growth and reproduction. For example, gypsy moths grow larger and produce many more eggs when feeding on aspen leaves than on oak. But they are killed readily by a viral disease when they feed on aspen and are protected by oak leaves. So there are conflicting selective forces acting on the insects. The net result is that gypsy moth caterpillars do not distinguish between oaks and aspens consistently. Similarly, plant defenses against their own diseases sometimes inhibit production of defenses against herbivores. This would make coevolution between plants and herbivores very unlikely.

susceptibility vulnerability

Fourth, herbivores usually do not exert enough selection to favor major changes in the plants. They rarely consume more than a small fraction of their plant food and seldom kill plants outright. Compared with other factors, like obtaining water, nutrients, and light, herbivores are seldom the strongest evolutionary influence on plants. Similarly, competitors infrequently exert the kind of influence on plant neighbors that would produce

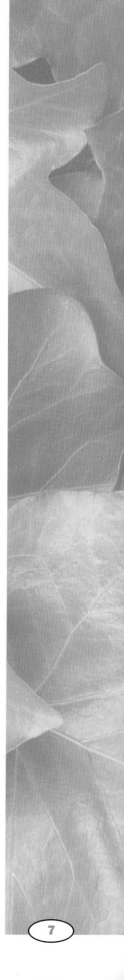

FIGS AND FIG WASPS

More than nine hundred species of figs (*Ficus*) are pollinated by figs wasps (family Agaonidae) in relationships that exhibit closely coevolved characteristics. The hollow fig inflorescence is formed by a swollen flower receptacle (base) and is lined inside with flowers that go through five stages:

1. **Prefemale,** in which the fig is closed to wasps as flowers develop;

2. **Female,** in which tiny wasps crawl inside the inflorescence through a special pore and lay eggs in the mature flowers;

3. **Interfloral,** during which wasp larvae develop inside some female flowers while others produce seed;

4. **Male,** in which male flowers mature, producing pollen, while the new generation of wasps emerges from female flowers. Female wasps mate, collect pollen, and exit through escape holes bored by males; and

5. **Postfloral,** in which seeds ripen, and the fruit becomes attractive to animals that disperse it.

The escaped females invade new fig flowers on other trees, repeating the cycle. The figs provide specialized flowers in which the wasps lay eggs, sacrificing these as a reward, and the timing of male and female flower production is designed to match the wasps' development. The wasps are specifically adapted for life in the fig, and cannot lay eggs or feed anywhere else. Usually only one wasp species can live in one fig species. A natural consequence of this system is that the figs we eat contain some of the minute wasps that do not escape.

coevolutionary patterns. Plants exhibit adaptations to competition, including growth responses to the green light reflected from neighbors, and perhaps the production of chemicals toxic to competitors (allelopathy). But there are few, if any, clear cases of mutual adaptation among plant competitors.

But diseases do kill plants frequently and so exert strong selection on plants favoring defense responses specific to the attacking microbe. Scientists have documented many gene-for-gene interactions between plants and **pathogens** in which a single gene difference between two plants can determine susceptibility to a given microbe. A single gene difference between two microbes can determine which can successfully attack a given plant. One can clearly see evidence of coevolution in these cases, where plants have responded to pressure from microbes with successive genetic and biochemical modifications and the microbes have responded in kind to those changes. A few similar examples do exist for plants and insects, in plant species (e.g., conifer trees, parsnips) with defenses strongly influenced by genes (and less by environment) and insects that can kill them.

Mutually Beneficial Coevolution

Perhaps the most striking examples of coevolution involve mutualisms, in which the participants have exerted selection that makes their relationship increasingly beneficial to each of them. In mutualisms natural selection has favored traits in each participant that strengthen or improve the relationship and its benefits. These interactions contrast with those described above, in which each organism participates at the other's expense.

For example, insects and other animals that transfer pollen among flowers (pollen **vectors**) provide a crucial service to the plant while receiving a reward, usually nectar and pollen itself. Because it is disadvantageous for a plant's pollen to be deposited on the flower of another species, natural selection has favored the evolution of traits to reduce these "errors," usually by narrowing the range of species attracted and moving pollen. For example, flowers may produce nectar guides, patterns that reflect ultraviolet wavelengths, making them visible only to certain insects. Others may provide a long, tubular entrance accessible only to night-flying moths with long tongues. The length of a flower's corolla tube is often matched to a particular moth having the same tongue length. This ensures that the pollen will be carried only to other flowers with the same tube length, presumably of the same species. Some flowers provide necessary resources for specific insects, such as oils needed to cement a bee's nest or for mating purposes. In each case, there presumably has been a series of evolutionary changes in the flower (such as corolla tube length) that exerted selection-favoring changes in the pollen vector (tongue length, for example), fine tuning the interaction to mutual benefit.

The evolution of mutualism provides opportunities for deception. For example, many species of orchids produce colorful flowers and odors but provide no reward. They depend on mistakes made by inexperienced bees to get their pollen onto a vector. To ensure that a mistake pays off, the orchid is constructed so that any visiting bee necessarily carries away the pollen in sticky packets called pollinia deposited on its body. The flower is constructed so that when the bee makes a second mistake the pollinium is removed and deposited on the stigma of the second flower. Pollen transfer

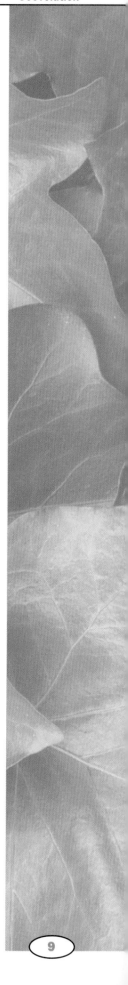

A parasitic fig wasp (*Torymidae*) inserting its ovipositer into a fig (*Ficus capensis*).

has to be efficient; terrestrial orchids in temperate North America may only be visited once in a decade.

Some tropical orchids improve their chances of being visited by producing volatile chemicals that are collected by certain bees and used as mating signals. Some orchids may produce an odor that mimics a bee's mating signal, attracting bees that are then disappointed in finding no mate, but carry away a pollinium. In more elaborate coevolved interactions the orchid flowers actually look like a female bee or wasp, with which males attempt to mate. In yet others the flower resembles a male bee, and territorial males attack it. In these latter situations, the pollinia are deposited on the bee when it contacts the flower to mate or fight. All of these deceptive floral adaptations produce a very dependable relationship between the plant and insect (pollinator constancy), but at the insects' expense.

Plants may form mutualisms with potential enemies as well. A limiting step in the nitrogen cycle is the capture of inorganic nitrogen from the air and its incorporation into organic forms plants can use. Bacteria have developed this ability, called nitrogen fixation, and are a critical link in this cycle. Legumes and some other plants have formed associations with certain bacteria, particularly the genus *Rhizobium*, in which the bacteria live in swellings, or nodules, on the plant roots. But since many bacteria are enemies (pathogens) of plants, plants and *Rhizobium* have had to reach a coevolved

pathogen disease-causing organism

vector carrier, usually a carrier who is not affected by the thing carried

accommodation. Through coevolution, they have developed a specialized interaction that depends on manipulating expression of each other's genes. *Rhizobium* produces signals that turn off plant defense responses and identify it as friendly to the plant. Host plants produce chemical signals that turn on genes in the bacteria that produce signals directing the plant root to produce a nodule. The bacteria then invade the nodule, where the plant provides necessary nutrients in return for nitrogen. It is clear that this relationship has evolved from a battle between enemies, host and pathogen, to a mutualism.

Unanswered Questions

Scientists are divided about how many species have been shaped by coevolution. Several important questions need to be answered before this issue will be resolved. If insects exert relatively little pressure on plants, how often would plant defenses change? Do insects make mistakes in selecting plants as food or **oviposition** sites? If not, how do they ever begin feeding on a new plant type? How great a change is necessary to provoke a response in the coevolutionary partner; for example, how much change in the shape of an orchid is necessary to provide improved visitation by an insect? And how can we evaluate the importance of the coevolutionary partner versus other factors that influence the evolution of plants, animals, and microbes? SEE ALSO EVOLUTION OF PLANTS; INTERACTIONS, PLANT-FUNGAL; INTERACTIONS, PLANT-PLANT; INTERACTIONS, PLANT-VERTEBRATE; POLLINATION BIOLOGY.

Jack C. Schultz

oviposition egg-laying

Bibliography

Price, Peter W. *Insect Ecology.* New York: John Wiley & Sons, Inc. 1997.

Schoonhoven, L. M., T. Jermy, and J. J. A. van Loon. *Insect-Plant Biology.* London: Chapman and Hall, 1998.

Thompson, John N. *The Coevolutionary Process.* Chicago, IL: University of Chicago Press, 1994.

———, and John J. Burdon. "Gene-for-Gene Coevolution Between Plants and Parasites." *Nature* 360 (1992): 121–25.

Coffee

The coffee plant is a woody shrub native to the understory of the forests of east Africa. The genus responsible for this caffeine-loaded beverage is *Coffea*, to which taxonomists assign between twenty-five and one hundred distinct species. Some 80 percent of the world's coffee comes from *Coffea arabica* L., known as arabica coffee on the global market. Most of the remaining world trade features *Coffea canephora* Pierre ex Froehner, commonly known as robusta coffee. Robustas have about twice the caffeine content found in arabicas.

Coffee belongs to the family Rubiaceae, a commercially important family that provides the drugs quinine (*Cinchona* spp.) and ipecac (*Psychotria ipecacuanha*), as well as the sweet-scented ornamental known as *Gardenia augusta*. Like many woody species growing in a forest setting, coffee has a vertical stem with horizontal branches. The **lateral** branches become progressively longer the farther away they are from the **apical meristem**, giving the shrub an overall pyramidal or Christmas-tree shape.

lateral side

apical meristem the growing tip of a plant

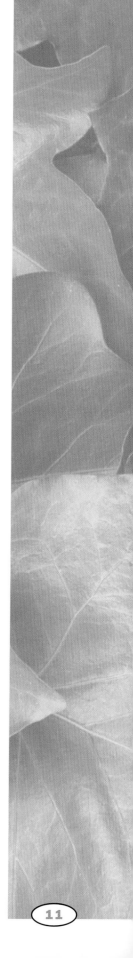

A worker looking for mature coffee beans on a plantation in Java, Indonesia.

Shiny, waxy, dark green leaves occur in opposite pairs. They are elliptical in shape with distinctly visible veins. The underside of leaves, like other species in the family, shows small cavities (domatia) at the midrib/lateral vein junctions. While the function of these domatia remains a mystery, some investigators believe they might serve as "houses" for mites or ants.

Coffee flowers are small, fragrant, white structures with five to nine narrow petals. Flowering usually comes about ten days after the first rain ends the dry season. A blanket of frostlike **inflorescence** and its associated perfume can envelope a large estate for two days before the flowers start to fade. Pollination by bees, wasps, and flies leads to fruit set. The fruit, called a cherry or berry, is actually a **drupe** that turns dark red (or yellow in some varieties) when ripe. It usually contains two seeds (the beans) surrounded by a sweet mucilage.

inflorescence an arrangement of flowers on a stalk

drupe a fruit with a leathery or stonelike seed

Distribution of Coffee Cropping Systems

Coffee production occurs within the confines of the tropics, girdling Earth some 23.5° latitude north and south of the equator. As a mountain-loving shrub, *C. arabica* does best in the temperate climatic regimes associated with high tropical altitudes. Most coffee zones have temperature ranges from 17° to 25°C. But wherever coffee grows close to subtropical latitudes (as in southern Brazil) or in extremely high mountain regions, frost threatens the harvest from time to time. Minimum rainfall for a profitable crop is 1,200 to 1,500 millimeters per year. Excessive **precipitation** (greater than 2,500 millimeters per year) or windy conditions **impede** production by hampering pollination or fruit set.

precipitation rainfall

impede slow down or inhibit

World production of coffee in 1998 exceeded 6.4 million metric tons, harvested on lands covering more than 10.7 million hectares (an area equivalent in size to Guatemala or Bulgaria). Coffee exports derive from more than fifty countries. Though native to east Africa, coffee production has found a solid base in the New World (the Western Hemisphere), where Brazil, Colombia, Mexico, and the Central American countries account for

59 percent of global exports (of all coffees—arabicas and robustas combined). Brazil is the single-largest exporter. Other important producing countries include Ecuador, Peru, and Papua New Guinea for arabicas, and Indonesia, Ivory Coast, Uganda, and Vietnam for robustas.

From Tree to Cup

Processing of coffee beans into the morning habit many people know as having a cup of coffee begins with the harvest. The relatively short interval in which most beans mature requires the mobilization of a large workforce. Men, women, and children alike participate in this annual event. During peak harvest, a family of six might pick 400 to 600 pounds of beans. For every 100 pounds of freshly picked "cherries," workers receive on average the equivalent of $3.33. Once picked, the cherries may be processed in one of two ways: the wet or washed method, in which water is used to wash, ferment, and rewash the beans; or the dry or natural method, in which the fresh bean is left to dry in its husk. The preferred method for the U.S. palate is the wet method.

Once washed and sun dried on patios or in large cylindrical tumbler-dryers (in areas where rain prohibits patio drying), the beans are milled by machines that remove the final thin parchment. Beans are normally dried to about 11 percent moisture content, which inhibits fermentation or molding of the commodity in shipment. Once milled and dry, the gray-green or bluish beans are ready to travel the world to wherever they are to be roasted. The 100 pounds picked for $3.33 mentioned previously, can, if it is quality coffee, fetch anywhere from $6 to $9 per pound in the specialty coffee shops of the United States.

Coffee quality (its taste or "cup quality," as the experts call it) depends upon a host of factors, including soil, climate, altitude, and processing. The best-quality coffees come from mountainous regions where high standards in processing are consistent. The slow growth at higher elevations produces a harder bean, a highly prized quality on the world market. But locale is only one part of the quality equation. Processing plays a critical role in the final product, which means that coffee grown in the best environmental conditions can be transformed into a mediocre commodity if not processed correctly.

Consequences of Different Cultivation Practices

As an understory shrub native to east Africa, *C. arabica* is evolutionarily suited to shade conditions. Many coffee growers today—the majority of whom cultivate small plots in poor rural areas—produce their coffee beneath the shade of taller trees. This traditional, forestlike system, while technically an artificial or managed forest, provides an array of what ecologists call ecological services. The foliage cover intercepts heavy tropical rainfall, lessening its impact upon the soil. The leaf litter generated by the canopy provides a mulch layer that further helps to protect the soil, and gradually decomposes into the soil, recycling the nutrients contained in the leaves and other debris. Shade trees with deep roots draw nutrients from lower soil layers into the system. And a diverse mix of plant species creates a relatively stable ecological system with little need for chemical inputs such as synthetic fertilizers or pesticides.

The shade canopy often includes tree species that are nitrogen-fixing **legumes** (e.g., *Inga* spp., *Albizia* spp., *Gliricidia* spp., etc.), fruit trees such as citrus species, avocados, or bananas, and species that yield precious hardwood (e.g., *Cordia* spp.). This agroforestry management strategy provides noncoffee products that can be used by the farm family or sold on local markets.

legumes beans and other members of the Fabaceae family

Recent changes in production, encouraged by the late-twentieth-century gains in basic grain crops such as corn, wheat, and rice, have changed the coffee landscape in many countries. Higher plant density (number of individual plants per hectare), the use of high-yielding varieties, and the introduction of an array of agrochemicals (fertilizers and pesticides) now characterize a growing number of farms. These changes are often accompanied by a reduction or total elimination of shade trees. In many Latin American countries, fear of the disease known as coffee leaf rust (*Hemileia vastatrix*) and of its spreading in the shaded environment of traditional systems has fueled the transformation from shade to sun or nearly shadeless systems. The objective is to increase yield (production per unit area).

The goal of increased yields is certainly laudable, but it ignores the total production of both coffee and noncoffee products obtained from a traditional, shade coffee system. Noncoffee products such as fruits and firewood, for instance, can represent upwards of 20 percent of a farm's annual income. When shade trees are removed completely or greatly reduced in number, a farmer becomes much more dependent upon the volatile international price of coffee—a position few peasant farmers can afford.

Aside from the socioeconomic impact of changes related to production, there are also some environmental consequences. Obviously, the benefits afforded the soil from the forestlike setting are reduced or lost along with the shade cover. Moreover, recent research shows that shaded coffee lands can play a role as a refuge for biodiversity. Birds use shade coffee lands similar to the way they use natural forests. The important features of the shade are the species diversity of the shade trees (the different types of shade trees) and the structural diversity of the shade trees (the height and layers of the canopy). In fact, from ornithological work conducted in Mexico, Guatemala, and Peru, we now know that coffee managed in a way that maximizes the species and structural diversity of the shade component harbors a bird community as diverse as that found in natural forests in the same region. SEE ALSO AGRICULTURAL ECOSYSTEMS; ALKALOIDS; ECONOMIC IMPORTANCE OF PLANTS; PSYCHOACTIVE PLANTS.

Robert A. Rice

Bibliography

Dicum, Gregory, and Nina Luttinger. *The Coffee Book: Anatomy of an Industry.* New York: New Press, 1999.

Smithsonian Migratory Bird Center. "Coffee Corner." [Online] Available at http://www.si.edu/smbc.

Wrigley, Gordon. *Coffee.* New York: Longman Scientific and Technical/John Wiley and Sons, 1988.

College Professor

The career of college professor is based on a commitment to lifelong learning. Most college professors in the plant sciences have earned a Ph.D., a degree signifying expertise in a specialized subject area such as agronomy, plant pathology, or molecular biology. An individual wishing to become a professor typically completes four years of college, usually majoring in biology or a related area such as botany, biochemistry, or genetics, and receives a bachelor's degree. This is followed by additional college courses, usually over a four- to six-year period, that result in the Ph.D.

specimen object or organism under consideration

College professors typically have duties involving teaching, research, and service. Most professors teach several courses during the academic year. Some may be introductory courses having hundreds of students, while others may be advanced courses having only a few. Some courses are taught in the classroom where the professor may lecture or lead discussions. Other courses are taught in the laboratory or on field trips, where the professor teaches students to collect **specimens**, operate instruments, make observations, and analyze data. Associated with teaching are related activities such as meeting with students during office hours, preparing lectures, writing exams, and grading student work. In addition, most professors in the plant sciences are expected to do research. This may involve conducting experiments in the laboratory or field, collecting specimens throughout the world, analyzing data using the computer, writing results for publication in professional journals, and working in the library to learn about the work of others. Finally, most professors are expected to perform services such as advising students, serving on college committees, participating in national organizations that focus on teaching or research, and serving as a resource person at the community, state, or even global level.

In the United States, the college professor may work in a community college, a four-year college, or a university. In a community college, a professor's emphasis is on teaching. In a four-year college, the emphasis is usually on a combination of teaching, research, and service. In a university, an institution consisting of several colleges, the emphasis is usually on research.

When a person with a Ph.D. is hired, it is usually at the rank of assistant professor, a temporary position lasting approximately six years. At the end of this period, based on the person's accomplishments in the areas of teaching, research, and service, he or she is promoted to associate professor and receives tenure, a condition that provides employment for life. Based on continuing accomplishments, an associate professor may be promoted to full professor. In 1999 the average annual salary for assistant professors was approximately $42,000, for associate professors $51,000, and for full professors $65,000.

Regardless of academic rank and where employed, college professors frequently mention the ability to interact with students as one of the greatest rewards of their profession. In addition, they enjoy the freedom to conduct research on topics of their own choosing, to make discoveries that contribute to scientific knowledge, and to generally participate in a lifelong learning experience. SEE ALSO AGRONOMIST; FOOD SCIENTIST; PHYSIOLOGIST; SYSTEMATICS, PLANT; TAXONOMIST.

Robert C. Evans

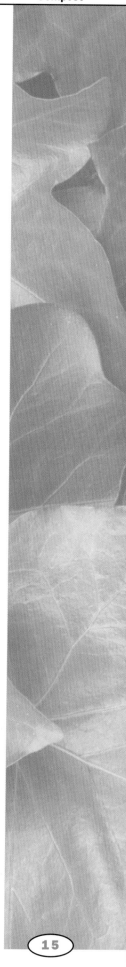

Bibliography

American Association of University Professors. "Ups and Downs: Academic Salaries Since the Early 1970s." *Academe* 85, no. 2 (1999): 26.

U.S. Department of Labor. Bureau of Labor Statistics. *Occupational Outlook Handbook, 1998–1999.* Washington, DC: U.S. Government Printing Office, 1998.

Compost

Compost refers to a biological process that uses any one of several methods to speed up the decomposition of raw organic matter, usually by piling, aerating, and moistening. It is also the crumbly, nutrient-rich product of this process.

Composting is an important means of recycling organic wastes to return their nutrients to the soil, where they become available to plants. Composting reduces or eliminates problems with odors and water pollution from raw waste products such as livestock manure and slaughterhouse and food-processing wastes. Many cities compost yard wastes in order to conserve scarce landfill space. High-temperature composting methods also kill weed seeds and **pathogens,** turning a potentially expensive health hazard into a valuable resource. The resulting product contains balanced soil and plant nutrients, including trace minerals, and is rich in beneficial microbes that further improve the soil's ability to nourish plants. Composed primarily of **humus,** compost also conditions the soil, making it easier to work and improving its drainage, **aeration,** and nutrient holding capacity.

pathogen disease-causing organism

humus the organic material in soil, formed from decaying organisms

aeration introduction of air

Almost anything that was once alive or is a waste product of a living organism can be composted. Dry, bulky materials, including wood products such as sawdust and newspaper, as well as straw, cornstalks, and leaves, contain a high proportion of carbon relative to nitrogen. Materials that are wet, heavy, and smelly, such as manure, grass clippings, and fish wastes, are usually high in nitrogen relative to carbon. Both types of materials should be combined in a ratio of about thirty parts carbon to one part nitrogen to promote thorough decomposition. Mineral powders such as rock phosphate can be added to compost as a source of trace elements, which can also be supplied by organic materials such as seaweed and bonemeal. Microbial cultures and worms are sometimes used to improve compost activity. Large quantities of fats or oils, as well as toxic or synthetic materials, should not be added to compost.

Compost requires enough air and moisture to provide optimum conditions for microbial activity. Turning compost to incorporate more air will speed decomposition, generating higher temperatures. Compost can be finished in anywhere from two weeks to a year, depending on climate, what kinds of materials are used, and how often it is turned. Finished compost has a spongy texture and earthy fragrance, and its original ingredients are no longer identifiable.

Compost can be used as a fertilizer and soil conditioner on any scale, from houseplants to large farms. It contains a good balance of essential plant nutrients in a stable form that will not leach away in the rain, and

A garden compost pile.

can be applied at any time of year without danger of burning plants. Compost can be included in potting soil, spread on lawns, worked into garden beds, side-dressed around trees and perennials, and added to transplant holes. Compost is often used to stimulate growth of new vegetation on land that has been strip-mined or badly eroded. Compost tea can give growing plants a quick boost, and is known to suppress certain plant diseases because of its beneficial microorganisms. Organic farmers rely on compost to build soil fertility and recycle nutrients. SEE ALSO AGRICULTURE, ORGANIC; FERTILIZER; SOIL, CHEMISTRY OF; SOIL, PHYSICAL CHARACTERISTICS OF.

Grace Gershuny

Bibliography

Gershuny, Grace. "Compost: Gardener's Gold." *Start with the Soil.* Emmaus, PA: Rodale Press, 1993.

Hanson, Beth, ed. *Easy Compost: The Secret to Great Soil and Spectacular Plants.* Brooklyn, NY: Brooklyn Botanic Garden, 1997.

Martin, Deborah, and Grace Gershuny, eds. *The Rodale Book of Composting: Easy Methods for Every Gardener.* Emmaus, PA: Rodale Press, 1992.

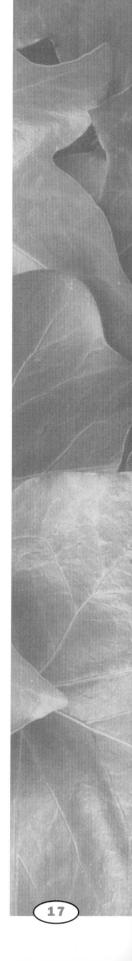

Coniferous Forests

Coniferous forests are dominated by gymnosperm trees such as pines, spruces, and firs. Conifers were the first plants to evolve seeds. Gymnosperms (from the Greek words *gymnos*, meaning "naked," and *sperma*, meaning "seed") have seeds exposed to the environment on cones. In most species, male and female cones occur on the same tree, but the *Juniperus* (juniper) and *Taxus* (yews) genera have species with separate male and female trees. Male cones are smaller than female cones and produce pollen in the springtime. The larger female cones are able to be fertilized only when they are young and often unnoticeable. Most conifers rely on wind to carry their beautiful and diversely shaped pollen grains to the female cone.

The phylum Coniferophyta is organized into two orders. Older classification schemes included a third, Ginkgoales, containing only one species (*Ginkgo biloba*); more recent classification schemes now place *Ginkgo* into its own phylum, Ginkgophyta. Coniferales, with five families and over six hundred species, including the species most often identified with coniferous forests, is the most populous order. Some of the world's most remarkable plants are found in Coniferales. Bristlecone pine (*Pinus aristata*) can live to be over six thousand years old; coastal redwoods (*Sequoia sempervirens*) grow to be over one hundred meters tall; and Monterey pine (*Pinus radiata*) is one of the most productive timber species. The Taxales order contains two families and over thirty species but is best known for the poisonous yew (*Taxus*) genus.

Conifer Leaves

Most conifers are evergreen, meaning that they maintain green leaves, usually needles, year-round. Needles exist in all families. Scalelike leaves often obscuring the woody portion of the shoot exist in the Cupressaceae, Podocarpaceae, and Taxodiaceae families. The Podocarpaceae family contains the only broadleaf conifers. Two genera, the celery pine (*Phyllocladus*, found in the Southern Hemisphere) and the Japanese umbrella pine (*Sciadopitys*), do not contain true leaves and instead carry out photosynthesis using specially adapted shoots.

In climates with mild, wet winters and warm, dry summers, drought adaptations and the ability to conduct photosynthesis all winter give evergreen conifers a distinct advantage over deciduous **angiosperms**. In the boreal forest, conifers succeed due to a combination of factors. First, growing seasons are short and conifers are able to begin photosynthesis with a full canopy as soon as temperatures warm. Second, because needles last from two to ten years, conifers need to replace fewer leaves each year than deciduous trees. Since leaves require large amounts of nutrients, nutrient-poor areas (such as the boreal forest and the southeastern United States) are often dominated by conifers. Third, conifers are more able to resist periodic drought stresses common in the boreal forest. Finally, in climates where temperatures dip below -45°C, conifers can survive where angiosperms cannot.

Nearly all conifers are evergreen but there are four deciduous genera: *Larix*, *Pseudolarix*, *Metasequoia*, and *Taxodium*. The *Larix* and *Pseudolarix* (common name larch) live in the boreal forest. In addition to possessing

angiosperm a flowering plant

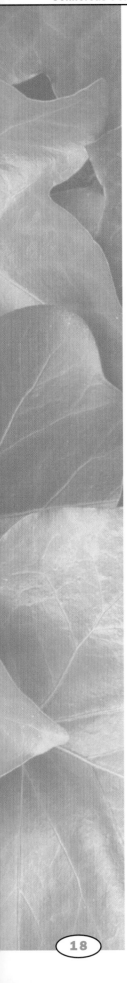

Western larches change to autumn yellow amid evergreen fir trees in Washington's Wenatchee National Forest.

good cold-resistance, larches have high photosynthetic rates, flush early in the spring, and use nutrients very efficiently. *Metasequoia*, the dawn redwood, grows well on damp sites. *Taxodium*, the swamp cypress, grows in standing water in the southeast United States and parts of Mexico.

Distribution of Coniferous Forests

Coniferous forests exist in many climates around the world. The Podocarpaceae family is distributed in tropical and subtropical climates in South America and Southeast Asia. Small areas of southern Chile and western Argentina have coniferous *Araucaria* species living with evergreen broadleaf species. Mexico and Central America have pine forests in high elevation mountain ranges. Western North America and Japan support one million square kilometers of coastal coniferous rain forests. With nearly sixteen million square kilometers, the northern latitude boreal forests contain the vast majority of coniferous forest area. The Eurasian boreal forest begins in Scandinavia and extends east in a widening band all the way to the Kamchatka Peninsula in eastern Russia. The forest reaches its northernmost boundary at 73°30′N in Siberia but is usually found no farther north than

68°N. In North America, the eastern boreal forest ranges from 45°N to 55°N; the western forest extends from 55°N to 69°N. Forested areas called **subalpine** forests cover about three million square kilometers in the U.S. Rocky Mountains, mid-elevation areas in the Himalayas, and other temperate mountain ranges.

subalpine a region less cold or elevated than alpine (mountain top)

Coniferous Forests in the United States and Canada

U.S. and Canadian coniferous forests follow a general rule found worldwide: as temperatures cool, species diversity declines. In Alaska and northwestern Canada, the boreal forest is primarily composed of black spruce (*Picea mariana*), white spruce (*Picea glauca*), and larch (*Larix laricinia*). Farther south and in isolated warm northern areas, aspen and birch intermingle. In central Canada, lodgepole pine (*Pinus contorta*), jack pine (*Pinus banksiana*), and balsam fir (*Abies balsamea*) appear. East of the Great Lakes, red pine (*Pinus resinosa*), eastern white pine (*Pinus resinosa*), oaks, and maples are common.

The Rocky Mountains resemble the boreal forest but are distinguished by the presence of subalpine fir (*Abies lasiocarpa*). Engelmann spruce (*Picea engelmannii*) replaces black and white spruce. In the central Rockies, drier regions of the northern Rockies, and high elevations of the southern Rockies, Douglas-fir (*Pseudotsuga menziesii*) and ponderosa pine (*Pinus ponderosa*) are common. In the southern Rockies, Engelmann spruce remains at higher elevations. Piñon pine (*Pinus edulis*) and Rocky Mountain juniper (*Juniperus scopulorum*) occupy the grassland-forest boundary. Trembling aspen exists throughout the Rocky Mountains.

The temperate rain forest, stretching along coastal North America from northern California to southern Alaska, contains western red cedar (*Thuja plicata*), Douglas-fir, Pacific silver fir (*Abies amabilis*), Sitka spruce (*Picea sithcensis*), and hemlock (*Tsuga heterophylla*). Redwoods (*Sequoia sempervirens*) indicate the southern limit of the temperate rain forest. The giant sequoia (*Sequoia gigantea*), one of the largest trees in world, grows well on the western Sierras in California.

Plant-Animal Interactions

Most conifers do not rely on insects, birds, or mammals to distribute their seeds and therefore have fewer readily observable examples of plant-animal interactions than flowering plants. Nonetheless, insects, birds, and mammals maintain strikingly diverse interactions with the coniferous trees in their habitat.

With few exceptions, insects in conifer forests are pests. Moths and butterflies are highly destructive, as are spruce budworms. All coniferous forests have some level of insect infestation. Vigorous forests use sap and other compounds to defend themselves against insects and are rarely catastrophically damaged. Forests in decline as a result of fire suppression or improper management are much more susceptible to insect outbreaks.

Birds in coniferous forests eat seeds and sometimes inadvertently help to plant trees. The Clark's nutcracker, for example, collects seeds from whitebark pine (*Pinus albicaulis*) and limber pine (*Pinus flexilis*) and brings them to nesting areas up to 45 kilometers away. The birds collect more seeds

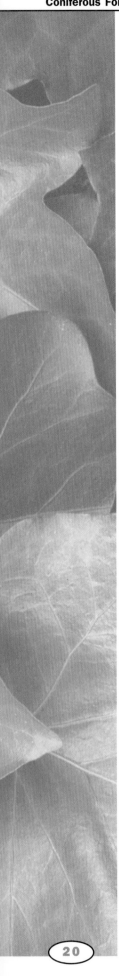

than they eat and the leftovers germinate. Insect-eating birds such as chickadees, nuthatches, and woodpeckers help to control insect populations. Owls and hawks live in coniferous forests and many, such as the spotted owl, use dead coniferous trees for nesting sites.

Mice and squirrels are the most common mammals in the coniferous forest. During the summer, these animals eat buds, berries, seeds, and even bark. Squirrels plan ahead for winter by collecting cones. As with birds not all the seeds are eaten, and some germinate into new trees. Deer, elk, mountain lions, bears, and other large mammals found in coniferous forests do not consume significant amounts of seeds or foliage. By chewing completely around a tree, porcupines interrupt the flow of sugars from leaves to roots. They are the only mammal besides humans known to kill coniferous trees.

Natural and Human-Managed Coniferous Forests

Coniferous forests exist along a gradient from purely natural to purely human created. The boreal forest, because it is so inhospitable and often contains commercially undesirable trees, contains the largest natural coniferous forests. Wildfires, insect outbreaks, and other disturbances are usually uncontrollable in remote boreal forests. In these forests, there is a variety of tree and undergrowth species; abundant animal, insect, and microbial life; and a natural fire cycle.

For most of the twentieth century the U.S. Forest Service pursued a policy of total fire suppression. Without fire, open stands of ponderosa pine were invaded by dense thickets of Douglas-fir and lodgepole pine. Insect outbreaks became common and fuels began to accumulate on the forest floor. Unmanageable and devastating fires such as the 1988 Yellowstone National Park fire caused a shift in public and scientific opinion; forest managers began to reincorporate fire through controlled burns and forests are now beginning the long process of regaining their natural relationship with fire.

ecosystem an ecological community together with its environment

In plantation forests, timber companies are interested in producing the maximum possible amount of commercial timber, not maintaining a diverse forest community. Many areas are planted with a single species at the same time. Conifers such as Monterey pine and slash pine (*Pinus caribaea*), because they grow straight and quickly, are popular plantation trees. The lack of species diversity and geometrical forest arrangement make plantations very different from natural or partially managed forests. Plantations do not support diverse **ecosystems** nor are they are desirable for recreation. Society, however, has a large demand for forest products and maximizing plantation production reduces the need to exploit other forests. SEE ALSO BIOME; CONIFERS; DECIDUOUS FORESTS; ECOLOGY, FIRE; FORESTER; FORESTRY; GINKGO; SEQUOIA; TREES.

Michael A. White

Bibliography

Archibold, O. W. *Ecology of World Vegetation.* London: Chapman and Hall, 1995.

Johnson, Edward A. *Fire and Vegetation Dynamics: Studies from the North American Boreal Forest.* New York: Cambridge University Press, 1992.

Larsen, James Arthur. *The Boreal Ecosystem.* New York: Academic Press, 1980.

Perry, Jesse R., Jr. *The Pines of Mexico and Central America.* Portland, OR: Timber Press, 1991.

Pielou, E. C. *The World of Northern Evergreens*. Ithaca, NY: Comstock Publishing Associates, 1988.

Rushforth, Keith D. *Conifers*. New York: Facts on File, 1987.

Shugart, Herman H., Rik Leemans, and Gordon B. Bonan. *A Systems Analysis of the Global Boreal Forest*. New York: Cambridge University Press, 1992.

Smith, William K., and Thomas M. Hinckley, eds. *Ecophysiology of Coniferous Forests*. San Diego: Academic Press, 1995.

———, eds. *Resource Physiology of Conifers: Acquisition, Allocation, and Utilization*. San Diego: Academic Press, 1995.

Conifers

Conifers are the largest, most widespread, and most economically important group of gymnosperms (nonflowering seed plants), including about 630 species divided into six or seven families. Conifers are the oldest extant group of seed plants, dating back to more than 280 million years in the fossil record. Some of the current families and genera have long fossil records; for example, remarkably well-preserved and modern-appearing cones of the genus *Araucaria* dating to 160 million years ago have been discovered, and a well-preserved fossil pine cone dating to 130 million years ago can be compared directly with cones of living pine trees.

Conifer Diversity

All conifers are woody plants, mostly trees or sometimes shrubs. Typical conifers such as members of the pine, cypress, and araucaria families are recognized by their woody seed cones, with flattened or shield-shape cone scales arranged spirally or in pairs or **whorls** around a central axis. The woody-coned conifers usually have winged seeds that are dispersed by wind and gravity. Other important groups of conifers such as the yew family, junipers, and most of the podocarp family have their seed cones reduced to one- or few-seeded fleshy structures that are dispersed by birds. Conifer seed cones range from less than 1 centimeter in length to up to 50 centimeters long and may be quite massive in some species of pines and araucarias.

whorl a ring

Most conifers are evergreen, but a few genera (notably bald cypress, dawn redwood, and larch) shed their leaves during the winter. The majority of conifers have narrow, needle-shaped leaves, arranged in spirals or sometimes in pairs, or are found in tightly clustered whorls on short branches. Pines are unusual in having their leaves extremely tightly clustered in needle clusters (fascicles) with almost no stem elongation between the leaves. Some conifers have their leaves very reduced and scalelike (most of the cypress family), while subtropical to tropical conifers in the podocarp and araucaria families may have the leaves flattened and are relatively broad.

Conifers include some of the longest-living, tallest, and most massive trees in the world. Bristlecone pines from the southwestern United States are among the longest living individual trees in the world, having been dated from tree rings to more than five thousand years in age. Sequoias are among the tallest trees in the world, reaching more than 110 meters in height, while the related giant sequoia reaches 106 meters in height and up to 11 meters in diameter. Large and ancient **specimens** of conifers are featured attrac-

specimen object or organism under consideration

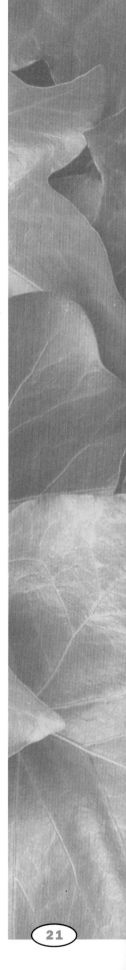

21

SELECTED CONIFER GENERA

Common Name	Generic Name	Family of Species	Number of Species (approximate)	Geographic Range	Economic Uses
Pine	*Pinus*	Pine	110	Northern Hemisphere	Timber, paper, resins, ornamentals
Spruce	*Picea*	Pine	40	Northern Hemisphere	Timber, paper, ornamentals
Fir	*Abies*	Pine	50	Northern Hemisphere	Timber, paper, resins, ornamentals
Hemlock	*Tsuga*	Pine	10	Eastern and western North America, eastern Asia	Timber, paper, ornamentals
Douglas-fir	*Pseudotsuga*	Pine	6	Western North America, eastern Asia	Timber, paper
Juniper	*Juniperus*	Cypress	50	Northern Hemisphere	Wood, pencils, flavorings, ornamentals
Cypress	*Cupressus*	Cypress	13	Western North America, Eurasia	Ornamentals
Bald cypress	*Taxodium*	Cypress	2	Eastern United States to Central America	Timber, ornamentals
Sequoia	*Sequoia*	Cypress	1	California to southern Oregon	Timber, ornamentals
Yew	*Taxus*	Yew	10	North America, Eurasia	Ornamentals, medicinal alkaloids
Araucaria	*Araucaria*	Araucaria	18	South America, South Pacific	Timber, ornamentals
Podocarpus	*Podocarpus*	Podocarp	95	Southern Hemisphere, northern to eastern Asia, Mexico, Caribbean	Timber, ornamentals

tions in national parks in many parts of the world, most notably sequoias and giant sequoias in California, alerce (*Fitzroya*) in Chile and Argentina, and kauri (*Agathis*) in New Zealand.

Conifer Distribution

Conifers are important forest components in many areas of the world, and members of the pine family are especially abundant in cool to cold-temperate and mountainous areas of the Northern Hemisphere, where such genera as pines, spruces, firs, and hemlocks often form dense forests. Junipers and pines are also very abundant trees in semiarid environments of the Northern Hemisphere such as the Great Basin region of the western United States. Pines are the most widely distributed genus of trees in the Northern Hemisphere and are also especially widely planted as timber trees in both hemispheres.

Several genera of conifers with only a single living species of very restricted distribution were once much more widespread in the fossil record and have been termed "living fossils." These include the dawn redwood (*Metasequoia*) from China and the sequoia and giant sequoia from California. Another remarkable genus, *Wollemia* (from the araucaria family), was known only as a fossil from Australia until 1994, when a living plant of this species was discovered growing in a remote canyon area near Sydney, Australia.

Economic Uses

Conifers are extremely important economically as sources of lumber and other wood products, and are also widely planted as ornamental trees and shrubs. The most important sources of softwood lumber in the world are

A giant alerce tree dwarfs a man near Puerto Montt in the Lake District of southern Chile.

trees in the pine family, especially species of pine, spruce, larch, and Douglas-fir, which are widely used for dimensional timber for building construction and boat building, and for general construction uses such as utility poles, doors, and cabinetry. These woods are also widely used for plywood and veneer and as sources of wood pulp for paper and cardboard and other modified wood products, such as charcoal. Southern yellow pines, such as slash pine and loblolly pine, are widely grown in their native southeastern United States as sources of lumber and pulp, while the Monterey pine from coastal California is now widely planted as a commercial timber tree in the Southern Hemisphere. Douglas-fir (*Pseudotsuga menziesii*) is a particularly important timber species in the northwestern United States and Canada. Several species of pines are tapped or cut and steam-distilled for stem resins, which are used as commercial sources of turpentine, tar oils, rosin, and pitch. Wood of the Norway spruce and white spruce has also been prized for constructing musical instruments such as violins, and the light, strong wood of Sitka spruce has been used for aircraft construction. The attractive reddish-colored wood from species of the cypress family, such as the sequoia, is quite weather- and decay-resistant and is highly prized for building construction, decks, fences, and other outdoor uses. Wood of the western red cedar (*Thuja plicata*) has been heavily used for weather-resistant roof shingles. Fragrant wood from junipers has natural insect-repellent properties and is used for moth-resistant cedar closets or chests. Wood of juniper and incense cedar has been commonly used to make pencils.

Many species of conifers are grown as ornamentals, and a wide variety of cultivated shrub forms have been selected for garden use from members of the yew and cypress families, including several species of yew, juniper, cypress, and golden cypress (*Chamaecyparis*). Conifers from a number of genera are prized as ornamental trees, of which some particularly attractive examples are the blue spruce (*Picea pungens*), the Himalayan cedar (*Cedrus deodara*), and the Norfolk Island pine (*Araucaria heterophylla*). Several species of firs and pines are commercially grown and cut as Christmas trees, and young plants of the subtropical Norfolk Island pine are grown for indoor use as living Christmas trees. Several species of pines from Eurasia and North America are highly esteemed as sources of oil-rich edible seeds (pignoli or pine nuts). Cones of *Juniperus communis* (juniper berries) are used as flavorings in cooking and provide the aromatic flavoring of gin, whose name is derived through the Dutch *jenever* from the name of juniper. Recently, bark and leaves of several species of yews have become important as the source of taxol and related alkaloids, which disrupt the process of cell division and are used in the treatment of several types of cancer. SEE ALSO CONIFEROUS FOREST; EVOLUTION OF PLANTS; FORESTRY; GYMNOSPERMS; SEQUOIA; TREES; WOOD PRODUCTS.

Robert A. Price

Bibliography

Dallimore, W., A. Bruce Jackson, and S. G. Harrison. *A Handbook of Coniferae and Ginkgoaceae*, 3rd ed. New York: St. Martin's Press, 1967.

Judd, Walter S., Christopher S. Campbell, Elizabeth A. Kellogg, and Peter F. Stevens. *Plant Systematics: A Phylogenetic Approach.* Sunderland, MA: Sinauer, 1999.

Richardson, David M., ed. *Ecology and Biogeography of Pinus.* New York: Cambridge University Press, 1998.

Rushforth, Keith D. *Conifers.* London: Christopher Helm, 1987.

Cordus, Valerius

German Botanist
1515–1544

Valerius Cordus was an early sixteenth-century German botanist who advanced the study of pharmacology by studying botany in a newly observant way. Born in 1515 as the son of botanist Euricus Cordus, Valerius Cordus was introduced to botany at an early age. He trained with his father and with an uncle who was an apothecary (druggist). In the early 1500s, plants were the main source of medicines used to treat human ailments, and the study of medicine required knowledge of botany. Cordus not only learned botany rapidly from his family, but made brilliant botanical observations of his own. He received his bachelor's degree at the age of sixteen in Marburg, Germany, and went on to study at Wittenberg University. He gave several lectures and wrote a number of important works that were published after

Valerius Cordus.

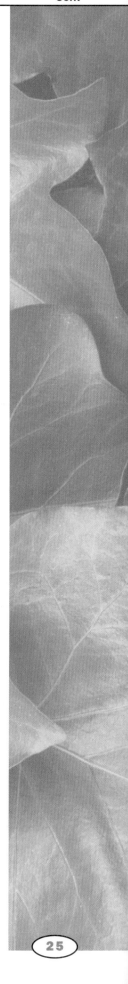

his death. Unfortunately, Cordus died of fever in Italy in 1544 at the age of twenty-nine.

By the time of his death, Cordus was already well respected, known for his inventiveness in teaching botany. Rather than relying on just the standard botany in older texts, he made a point of lecturing using examples from his own fieldwork. It was his keen attention to detail in the field that allowed Cordus to write one of the first systematic accounts of herbal and botanical knowledge. Regarding herbals, Cordus gave each plant a full and clear description so that it might be identified without the use of illustrations. He followed a pattern in his descriptions, which was not often the case with other herbals at that time. He included information about the plant stems and leaf arrangements, the structure of the flowers and the time of flowering, and details about the fruits of the plants—and was able to do this despite a lack of descriptive botanical terminology. Cordus included details about the number and types of parts in the flowers and tried to give information about the appearance, smell, and taste of the plants, as well as where they might be found, in an attempt to minimize confusion and mistakes in naming and using herbs at the time. He included information in his works about the ways to derive medicines from the plants he described. After his death, his text became the standard for pharmacy in Germany.

Cordus's attention to detail helped him make great strides in plant taxonomy. Many of his observations and techniques anticipated work done hundreds of years later. Using flower parts to describe and classify plants is still an important taxonomic technique. SEE ALSO CANDOLLE, AUGUSTIN DE; MEDICINAL PLANTS.

Jessica P. Penney

Bibliography

Morton, A. G. *History of Botanical Science.* New York: Academic Press, 1981.

Reed, H. S. *A Short History of the Plant Sciences.* New York: Ronald Press Company, 1942.

Cork

Anatomically, cork is a secondary tissue formed from a specialized **lateral meristem** located in the stems and roots of woody gymnosperms and **angiosperms**. The tissue develops from a ring of meristematic cells (the cork cambium or phellogen) located beneath the outer surfaces of the tree, and to the outside of the vascular cambium. The cells that form from the cork cambium are specialized, in that their cell walls contain a high proportion of suberin, a fatty material that **impedes** the movement of water. As cells derived from the cork cambium continue to grow, they eventually die when mature, not unlike the development of xylem cells from the vascular cambium. The result of this process is that the stem (trunk) or root of the tree develops a waterproof covering, generally known as bark. During active phases of tree growth, bark protects the tree from excessive water loss due to the suberized cork cells it contains. Additionally, bark provides a measure of physical protection from direct damage of the tree's trunk by nonliving structures (such as rocks), animals, and humans. In some trees that

lateral away from the center

meristem the growing tip of a plant

angiosperm a flowering plant

impedes slows down or inhibits

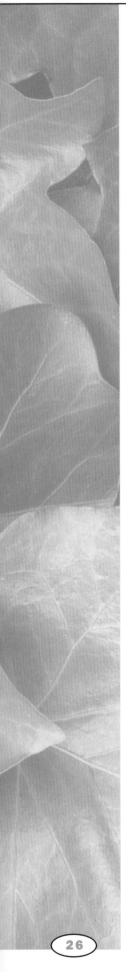

Cork strippers harvest the cork of a large cork oak in Portugal.

abrasion wearing away through contact

occur in habitats prone to frequent fires (e.g., savannas, certain coniferous forests), the bark is extremely important to protect the tree against heat damage by providing a layer of thermal insulation between the lateral meristems (vascular cambium and cork cambium) and the outside environment. The insulation properties are due to the cellular structure of cork; the spaces inside the dead cells are filled with air, and this provides resistance to heat flow through the cork.

Several other physical characteristics make cork a unique material. Cork is inherently resistant to **abrasion** and can withstand very high pressures of compression without suffering physical damage. When the pressure is released, the cork returns to its original shape and is seemingly unaffected by the structural changes of compression. Due to the air in its cell spaces, cork is also a lightweight buoyant material, floating easily on water and resisting waterlogging due to its suberized cell walls.

The properties of cork derived from the bark of certain trees has been used by humans for thousands of years. Specifically, the outer bark of the cork oak, *Quercus suber* (family Fagaceae), is the species upon which commercial cork production is dependent. The cork oak is native to the Mediterrannean region of southern Europe, and is grown commercially in Portugal and Spain. It is an evergreen oak species, and individual trees have been reported to be in cultivation and are harvested for their bark for periods of 150 years or more.

Production and Harvest

The first cutting of cork oak trees takes place when the trees are between fifteen and twenty-five years old, and produces virgin cork, which is of lesser quality than the cork that develops in the years following the initial cutting. While removing the bark/cork layer, harvesters must avoid damaging the cambial layers beneath the accumulated outer tissues. The first cutting (virgin) cork is not discarded. Some virgin cork is used in the horticultural industry as a growing **substrate** for epiphytic plants, such as bromeliads, orchids, and certain ferns. The waterproof nature of the virgin cork, as well as its rough surface and resistance to decay, provides a long-lasting, natural medium onto which the epiphyte's roots may attach. The virgin cork is also ground up into small pieces, mixed with fillers, adhesives, and other materials to be manufactured into a variety of materials. Subsequent strippings of cork harvests are done at eight to ten year intervals. Each successive stripping causes the production of better quality cork in the next harvest. The trees do not seem to be negatively affected by this harvesting practice when done by experienced cork cutters.

substrate the physical structure to which an organism attaches

Processing

Once the cork has been removed from the trees, the material is washed in water to remove debris and to keep the cork supple for further processing. It can be flattened into sheets and is generally cut to uniform thickness. Depending upon which product is being manufactured, the order of cutting and sizing the pieces may vary. Bottle stopper corks, such as those used by the wine industry, must be of excellent quality and have the properties of uniformly small cell size, uniform suberization and water repellancy, and favorable properties of resiliency. In use, the wine cork is compressed into the neck of the bottle, where it expands and provides an airtight seal; the wine bottle must be stored on its side to keep the liquid wine in contact with the cork in order for the cork to remain moist and maintain the seal. Some wines stored in this manner are useable for over one hundred years. Certain wine experts also feel that over time, the cork imparts certain subtle and desirable characteristics to the flavor of some wines.

Uses

In addition to the familiar uses of cork to close bottles of beverages, cork has a wide range of other uses by humans. It has historically been used as soles of shoes since Grecian and Roman times. Its buoyancy characteristics have been exploited for use as floats for fishing nets, buoys, flotation ballast in small boats, decoys, life preservers, fishing lures, and bobbers for line fishing. Prior to the development of specialized plastics, cork was used in the manufacture of artificial limbs due to its favorable structural characteristics, carvability, and light weight. It also has been used extensively in the preparation of wall coverings and flooring, as cork may have favorable acoustic characteristics, such as the ability to absorb sound, thus reducing noise. In addition, the sealing and insulating properties of cork are used by the automotive and other industries for the manufacture of gaskets. Cork is also frequently found as the surface material in bulletin boards as a prepared composition veneer material made from ground cork particles (often from the first-cut virgin cork, or from lower quality cork harvests). It is used for

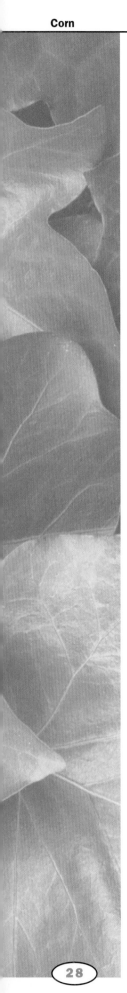

this application because of its self-healing properties when tacks, staples, or other items are pushed through it and are then removed. Cork is a renewable plant-derived resource and despite advances in wood technology, it continues to be grown, harvested, and used in a way similar to its production and utilization hundreds of years earlier. SEE ALSO ALCOHOLIC BEVERAGES; ECOLOGY, FIRE; TREES; WOOD PRODUCTS.

Robert S. Wallace

Bibliography

Constantine, Jr., A. *Know Your Woods.* New York: Albert Constantine and Son, Inc., 1969.

Simpson, B. B., and M. C. Ogorzaly. *Economic Botany: Plants in Our World*, 2nd ed. New York: McGraw-Hill Inc., 1995.

Corn

Corn, Indian corn, or maize is one of three grasses that account for almost half of all human calories consumed. The seed of these grasses are called cereals and each developed in a distinct part of the world: corn in the Americas, specifically Mexico/Guatemala (where its name is derived from the Arawak-Carib word *mahiz*, when Christopher Columbus first encountered the grain on the island of Cuba), and wheat and rice in the Old World. Corn was and still is the most important food plant for the indigenous people of the Americas. Its cultivation stretched from the Gaspé Peninsula of eastern Canada to Chile in South America. It is grown from sea level to elevations of ten thousand feet in the Andes.

Origin of Corn

Most of the corn grown in the developed world is from improved **hybrid** seed while subsistence farmers plant mostly open-pollinated farmer-selected varieties called landraces. There are approximately three hundred landraces of corn, each with its own geographic/climatic zone where it is most productive. Even commercial hybrid corn in the United States belongs to a recognized landrace, which is called Corn Belt Dent.

Three distinct views on the origin of corn exist within the scientific community: 1) corn evolved from an extinct wild corn, 2) corn evolved from its closest relative, teosinte, and 3) corn evolved after hybridization of either wild corn or teosinte with a more distant relative in the genus *Tripsacum*. During the 1960s there was widespread support for the idea of wild corn as the ancestor of the **domesticated** form. In contrast, in the 1980s the theory holding greatest currency was that of teosinte as the **progenitor** of corn. Recent research suggests that *Tripsacum* has had a role.

Although there are distinctly different hypotheses regarding the ancestry of corn, all agree on the basic circumstances surrounding its origin. The **ecosystem** that gave rise to corn had almost frost-free, seasonally dry winters alternating with summer rains, and highland (above 1,500 meters). Sometime between 5000 and 3000 B.C.E., corn appeared in Mesoamerica (Mexico and Guatemala), most probably along the western **escarpment** of south central Mexico in an arc within five hundred kilometers of present-day Mexico City. This location also describes the major area occupied by the closest relatives of corn, both annual and perennial teosinte, and nu-

hybrid a mix of two species

domesticate to tame an organism to live with and to be of use to humans

progenitor parent or ancestor

ecosystem an ecological community together with its environment

escarpment a steep slope or cliff resulting from erosion

A farmer checks an ear of corn for ripeness at harvest time in Merti, Kenya.

merous species in the genus *Tripsacum*. Corn and teosinte are unique among the grasses because the male and female flowers are borne in separate structures: the ear, or female seed-bearing cob, is carried half way down the stem while the male central spike, or tassel, is at the top of the stem. In the early stages of domestication the ear was small (one to three centimeters) yielding no more than fifty small, hard, popcornlike seeds. Archaeological corn remains, from cave sites dating back to 3000 B.C.E. in Tehuacán, Mexico, match the above description perfectly. In contrast, modern corn yields a massive ear (25 to 30 centimeters) producing more than 750 seeds. This modern corn plant is unable to disperse its seed because of the unique husk and cob structure where the seed do not fall free at maturity as in all wild plants. Humans must harvest, shell, and plant the seed for maize to exist.

Modern Corn

Modern corn is a single species, *Zea mays*, with five kinds of seeds based primarily on the storage starch of the **endosperm**. The earliest corns were popcorn types with a hard protein rind that held moisture in the starch, and when heated they exploded. Seeds that have a soft starch are called flour corns; sugary varieties are called sweet corn, which are often eaten immature when the sugar content is highest relative to starch; hard-starch varieties are called flint corn; and dent corn, which is intermediate between flour and flint, has a characteristic small dent or dimple at the top of the kernel. Dent corn is the most common form grown in the Corn Belt of the United States (accounting for one-half of the world's total production, valued at fifteen bil-

endosperm the nutritive tissue in a seed, formed by fertilization of a diploid egg tissue by a sperm from pollen

lion dollars). On commodity markets it is called #2 yellow dent. Much of this goes into animal feeds or is used in the chemical and processing industries.

Corn seed is used industrially to make ethyl, butyl, or propyl alcohol; acetaldehyde; acetone; glycerol; and acetic, citric, or lactic acids by fermentation then distillation. Wet milling produces zein, a protein used to make polyurethane, corn starch, and specialty corn products such as high fructose corn syrup (widely used as a sweetener and replacement for sucrose or cane sugar in candies and baked and processed foods).

In the Americas (excluding the United States and Canada) corn is the mainstay of the diet and the preferred cereal. This is also true for east Africa, south Africa, and regions around the Mediterranean and southeastern Europe. More than half of the dietary calories in both Guatemala and Kenya are accounted for by corn alone. In Mexico corn is eaten in tortillas (an un-leavened, griddle-toasted flat bread), tamales (dough steamed in corn husks and often stuffed with meat and chilies), *atole* (roasted, ground corn flour beverage) or *elotes* (roasted or steamed ears). In the southern United States it is consumed as grits (boiled, cracked endosperm from which the bran and embryo or germ have been separated), hominy (entire kernels soaked in lye, then washed and boiled). Corn on the cob and corn chips are eaten nationwide. Cornflakes, invented in the United States, are made from toasted rolled grits; they started the boxed cold cereal breakfast a century ago. Popcorn is both an ancient form of consuming corn and a modern one as it comes freshly popped from the microwave. In Andean countries corn is fermented by first a salivation process to convert starch to sugar and then fermentation by yeast to produce *Chicha. Pombay* beer is made from corn in Africa; whiskey made from corn is called bourbon whiskey.

Corn kernels or seeds are much larger than either rice or wheat but on a per-weight basis the three supply approximately the same energy as measured in calories. Corn has less protein than wheat and is deficient in the essential amino acids tryptophan and lysine. In the ancient civilizations of Mesoamerica this deficiency never appeared because corn and beans were eaten together and the combination formed a complementary protein supplying all the essential amino acids. Only when corn alone forms a major part of the diet, as in diets of poverty, do we see malnutrition. The corn kernel, especially the germ or embryo, is rich in oil and the grain is a good source of the B vitamins except for niacin. The low content of niacin can lead to the deficiency disease pellagra, historically prevalent in the South until the 1930s and still common in parts of Africa where corn is consumed. Corn grain is an outstanding feed for pigs, cattle, and chickens; the entire

silage livestock food produced by fermentation in a silo

plant cut up and made into **silage** is a major food for milk cows. Americans consume much more corn as pork, beef, eggs, and milk than we do from corn products directly. Corn is the largest harvest in the United States and the most valuable crop, but it is also Mexico's most significant gift to the world. SEE ALSO AGRICULTURE, HISTORY OF; AGRICULTURE, MODERN; ECONOMIC IMPORTANCE OF PLANTS; FERTILIZER; GRAINS.

Garrison Wilkes

Bibliography

Mangelsdorf, Paul C. *Corn: Its Origin, Evolution and Improvement.* Cambridge, MA: Harvard University Press, 1974.

Purseglove, J. W. *Tropical Crops: Monocotyledons.* London: Longman, 1972.

Wallace, Henry A., and William L. Brown. *Corn and Its Early Fathers*, rev. ed. Ames, IA: Iowa State University Press, 1988.

Weatherax, Paul. *Indian Corn in Old America*. New York: Macmillan, 1955.

Cotton

Four species of cotton are grown for commercial fiber (lint) production. *Gossypium arboreum* L. and *Gossypium herbaceum* L. are grown in Africa and Asia. These produce lint of inferior quality. *Gossypium barbadense* is grown commercially in limited parts of the world and produces a lint of excellent quality, long and strong, that is used in high-quality garments. It is difficult to produce and is grown in limited quantities. *Gossypium hirsutum* is grown on most of the world's cotton acreage, producing a good quality fiber that is shorter and has less fiber strength than *G. barbadense*. The United States, India, China, Brazil, and Australia are major producers.

Cotton is unique since the fiber is an extension of cells of the seed coat instead of being derived from other plant parts, as flax and the other fiber crops are. Each cotton fiber is actually a single cell and is nature's purest form of cellulose. Unlike synthetic fibers, which are made from petroleum, cotton is a renewable resource. The fiber is used in textiles, high-quality paper, cellophane, and plastics. The seed and fiber (seed cotton) are harvested and processed in a gin where the fiber is removed from the seed. The seed

Farm machines harvest cotton in a Mississippi field.

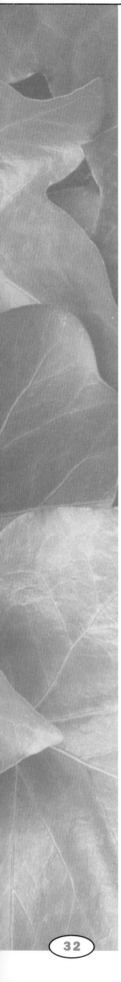

Puffs of cotton grow on the stem of a cotton plant in Mississippi.

is sold for livestock food for ruminant animals such as cattle. Seed is also processed to produce cottonseed oil for cooking and the meal is used as a source of protein for livestock. The fiber is graded for trash content, color, length, strength, and coarseness and generally sold to textile mills.

Before the invention of the cotton gin, the lint was so expensive due to the labor required to remove the lint from the seed that cotton garments were only for the very wealthy. With the invention of the gin, cotton became affordable for everyone. Cotton is a very labor-intensive crop. Slave labor was the principal means of production in many areas until more of the production steps were mechanized.

The cotton plant is a perennial tree that is grown as an annual plant since it is easily killed by freezing weather. The perennial nature of the plant makes it very difficult to grow. The crop can grow too large under good conditions and growth must be controlled with chemicals. The crop in many areas is killed with chemicals in order to facilitate harvest before adverse winter weather develops. Many of the production areas have serious insect problems requiring the use of several applications of insecticide. These prob-

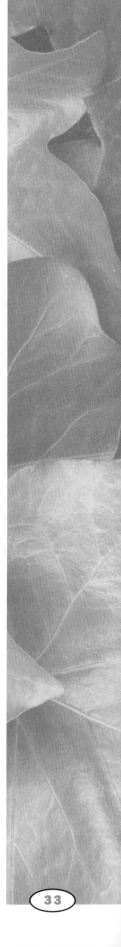

lems made cotton one of the first plants to be a candidate for genetically engineered (manmade) insect-resistance genes to be incorporated in order to reduce the use of insecticides. The engineered resistance has been a tremendous success.

A specialty market exists for organically grown (produced without use of chemicals) cotton and naturally brown or green-colored lint. A very small acreage of organically grown cotton is being produced; production, however, is difficult due to severe weed and insect problems. Lint that is naturally white, brown, or green can be produced. The colored lint eliminates the need for artificial dyes. SEE ALSO AGRICULTURE, MODERN; ECONOMIC IMPORTANCE OF PLANTS; FIBER AND FIBER PRODUCTS.

Bobby J. Phipps

Bibliography

Kohel, Russel J., and Charles F. Lewis, eds. *Cotton.* Madison, WI: American Society of Agronomy, 1984.

Mauney, Jack R., and James McD. Stewart, eds. *Cotton Physiology.* Memphis, TN: Cotton Foundation, 1986.

Cotyledon   *See Dicots; Monocots; Seeds.*

Creighton, Harriet

American Botanist
1909–

Harriet Baldwin Creighton is a geneticist who helped prove that genes are located on chromosomes. She was born in Delevan, Illinois, on June 27, 1909. She attended Wellesley College in Massachusetts and received her Bachelor of Arts degree in 1929. That year she matriculated at Cornell University as a botany graduate student and a laboratory assistant in botany. At that time Barbara McClintock, who later became a top American plant geneticist and Nobel Prize winner in medicine in 1983, was an instructor at Cornell. The two women immediately became friends and began working together on an important genetic problem: since the beginning of the twentieth century, **cytologists** theorized that chromosomes carried and exchanged genetic information to produce new combinations of physical traits, but cytological evidence to prove their hypothesis was lacking.

cytologist a scientist who studies cells

McClintock had bred a special strain of corn (*Zea mays*) with a ninth chromosome that produced a waxy, purple kernel. In the spring of 1930, Creighton and McClintock planted the kernels from this strain. That summer they fertilized the silks with pollen from a plant of the same strain that did not have either waxy or purple kernels. Once the ears were harvested in the fall, Creighton and McClintock found that some of the kernels were waxy and purple and others had inherited one trait or the other—either waxy or purple—but not both, indicating that the two genes had become separated.

When Creighton and McClintock examined the chromosomes of the new kernels under a microscope they saw that the chromosomes had crossed-over, or exchanged segments. They thus proved that genes for physical traits are carried on chromosomes. This process is extremely complex, and cytol-

ogists had been working to understand it for more than thirty years. Creighton and McClintock were the first to provide cytological evidence in plants that proved corresponding segments of genetic material on the chromatids of homologous chromosomes are able to cross over during meiosis. They published their remarkable findings in the Proceedings of the National Academy of Sciences, "A Correlation of Cytological and Genetical Crossing-over in *Zea mays*."

Creighton completed her Ph.D. in botany at Cornell in 1933. She went on to teach at Connecticut College as assistant professor of botany in 1934 where she remained for the next six years. In 1940 she accepted a position as an associate professor of botany at Wellesley College in Massachusetts. Creighton's professional career is graced with many distinguished honors. She was twice a Fulbright Lecturer, once in genetics and plant **physiology** at the University of Western Australia and the University of Adelaide in 1952 and 1953, and again in genetics at the University of San Antonio Abad, Peru in 1959 and 1960. Creighton was the first female secretary of the Botanical Society of America (1950–54); she also served as vice president in 1955 and president in 1956. In addition Creighton was a fellow of the American Association for the Advancement of Science (AAAS) where she served as vice president of the Botanical Sciences Section in 1964. Throughout her professional career, she continued to work in the field of plant genetics; much of her research focused on problems of heredity in corn, but her later research sought to investigate the "mad begonia," *Begonia phyllomania*, with its strange growth patterns, which Creighton believed might hold important clues for cancer researchers. She retired from Wellesley College in 1974. SEE ALSO CORN; MCCLINTOCK, BARBARA.

Mary Anne Andrei

physiology the biochemical processes carried out by an organism

Bibliography

Creighton, H. B., and B. McClintock. "A Correlation of Cytological and Genetical Crossing-Over in *Zea mays*." Proceedings of the National Academy of Science, 17 (1931): 492–97.

McGrayne, Sharon Bertsch. *Nobel Prize Women in Science: Their Lives, Struggles, and Momentous Discoveries.* New Jersey: Carol Publishing Group Edition, 1998.

Cultivar

Horticultural plants of the same species that are distinctive enough to be given a name are called cultivars, which is short for "cultivated variety." A cultivar can be distinguished from other similar cultivars by some combination of characters, including appearance, color, taste, size, and pest resistance. Although the terms variety and cultivar are used interchangeably, cultivar is not the same as a botanical variety, which is a taxonomic category below the species level that can apply to both wild and cultivated plants.

According to rules for naming plants, cultivar names must be in modern languages and not italicized. The first letters are capitalized and the name is either preceded by the abbreviation cv. (cultivar) or is put in single quotes. For example, a commonly grown yellow tomato is *Lycopersicon esculentum* cv. Yellow Pear and a popular type of sweet corn is *Zea mays* 'Silver Queen.' Cultivar names can follow generic, specific, or common names.

New cultivars are usually developed from either wild ancestors or established cultivars through selective breeding, a process that has been ongoing since the domestication of plants. Desired traits can also arise through mutations and plant viruses. Modern technologies of cloning and tissue culture that allow plants to be **propagated** vegetatively have added greatly to the number of such cultivars now produced. SEE ALSO BREEDING; HORTICULTURE; ORNAMENTAL PLANTS; SPECIES; TAXONOMY.

Sue Thompson

propagate to create more of through sexual or asexual reproduction

Curator of a Botanical Garden

The curator of a botanical garden is the person who oversees the operation of the entire facility. He or she is involved in all aspects, including collection, preservation, and education. The successful curator of a botanical garden will have the opportunity to develop major plant collections. Unique plant collections may be obtained through plant expeditions or by exchanges with other botanical institutions and collectors. Field collecting is encour-

Brian M. Lamb, a botanical specialist and the curator of the Alameda Botanical Gardens in Gibraltar, clears water lilies from a pond.

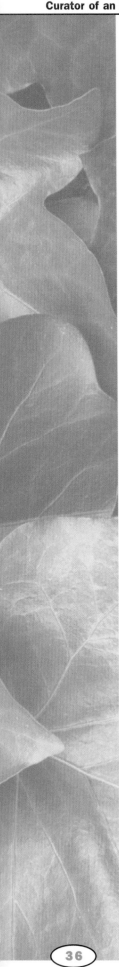

aged and the curator must have travel flexibility. A curator will interact with a talented staff and will meet interesting colleagues from many perspectives.

The curator is responsible for the maintenance, development, and control of all collections, including living collections and herbarium and spirit-preserved collections. The curator is also responsible for periodic review and maintenance of garden design in the context of an overall plan. Specific duties include:

accession a plant that has been acquired and cataloged

- overseeing periodic review of live plants for damage or disease and general health, taking appropriate measures for improved health
- overseeing periodic inventories to assess losses as well as to guide new acquisitions
- overseeing periodic review of plant labels and making needed repairs or replacements
- maintaining databases for all plant **accessions**, preferably linking both preserved and living collections
- reviewing the development of the garden facilities both to assure the well-being of the collections and to plan for growth
- periodically reviewing the health of herbarium collections, guarding against damage by insects

specimen object or organism under consideration

- seeing that loans of **specimens** to and from institutions are handled in a professional manner
- periodically checking specimens preserved in spirits for loss of fluid, topping vials when necessary
- interacting with the garden director and administrative staff to assure adequate staffing and resources for collections management.

The curator is expected to work among both spirit- and herbarium-preserved specimens as well as inside greenhouses and on the grounds and should be able to lift fifty pounds.

The successful curator must demonstrate a love of living plants, plant collections, and people, as well as have expertise in living and preserved collections management. Computer skills in database management, word processing, and grounds collections management through computer-aided programs are required. A master's degree in the organismal plant sciences is preferred, with emphasis on both botany and horticulture. Salary range is commensurate with experience. Salary advancement is accomplishment-based with annual reviews. SEE ALSO BOTANICAL GARDENS AND ARBORETA; CURATOR OF AN HERBARIUM; HERBARIA.

Margaret D. Lowman

Curator of an Herbarium

An herbarium is a collection of preserved plants used for research. The job of a curator of an herbarium is to coordinate the growth of the herbarium while preserving the past collections. Depending on the size of a facility the curator may supervise a small or large staff, thus the salary range is great:

approximately $25,000 to $80,000 or more per year. A curator also assists herbarium users and researchers and conducts her/his own research. Most curators of large herbaria have doctorate degrees, but in smaller herbaria the position may require only a master's degree. Degrees required are related to some branch of botany, most commonly plant systematics.

The curator oversees the selection of **specimens** to be placed in the collection. Specimens are selected for their quality and completeness. The curator knows the contents of the general collection in the herbarium, and selects specimens that add new information. She/he also chooses specimens that are used in specific studies, called voucher specimens.

specimen object or organism under consideration

Those who process new specimens are trained by the curator to mount the collections on herbarium paper, to prepare them for accession into the herbarium, and to file the specimens. Sheets must be carefully mounted with a label that contains the collector's information, and then a number (called an accession number) is stamped on each sheet. The plant is sterilized and filed. The filing must be done carefully, as a misfiled plant may not be seen again for years until it is accidentally found. At university herbaria, student workers are hired to assist in all of the herbarium functions, and that is how many interested people get their introduction to an herbarium and get their first botanical job experience.

Often the information on an herbarium sheet is entered into a computer database. This information is kept in the herbarium for visitors and users, and increasingly such information is being posted on Web sites. Searchable databases may subsequently be linked with similar databases from other herbaria and accessed by any computer.

Visitors and users of the herbarium may include the public, researchers, students, or representatives from public agencies trying to solve problems or accurately enforce laws and regulations. The curator is both a botanist and public servant who has knowledge of the local plants. He/she must try to confidently identify specimens brought to the herbarium, including those that are not in ideal condition. Accurate identification is a skill that takes time to develop. The curator is knowledgeable about the literature available, reads new articles as they are published, and acts as a librarian who is able to direct people to the resources they need to find answers to their questions.

Herbaria both borrow and lend specimens so that researchers working at specific herbaria can study them. The borrowed specimens are treated carefully, kept in herbarium cabinets, and before the sheet is returned a small label (called an annotation label) is attached describing the study or naming the specimen. Herbaria also exchange duplicates of specimens so that other facilities can have more complete collections.

Herbarium curators usually have their own research projects. Often the curator becomes a specialist and publishes papers on her/his research. Publications from an herbarium inform the rest of the botanical world that the herbarium is active and is the location of expertise. The curator is also an administrator, determining the needs of the herbarium and budgeting money to effectively accomplish the herbarium's mission. The scope of this responsibility is varied from herbarium to herbarium. Herbaria may be associated with universities or museums, publicly or privately funded, or a com-

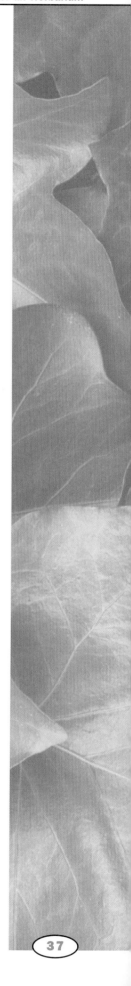

bination of both. Many changes are coming to herbaria as science finds new information and paths of research. An herbarium curator is at the center of many and varied disciplines, protector of a historical asset, and a growing resource. Curators of herbaria are generally dedicated people who are fascinated by their jobs. SEE ALSO TAXONOMIST.

Philip D. Jenkins

Bibliography

Benson, Lyman D. *Plant Classification*, 2nd ed. Lexington, MA: D.C. Heath and Company,1979.

Bridson, Diane, and Leonard Forman. *The Herbarium Handbook*, 3rd ed. Kew, UK: Royal Botanic Gardens, 1998.

Cyanobacteria

morphological related to shape

phylogenetic related to phylogeny, the evolutionary development of a species

lineage ancestry; the line of evolutionary descent of an organism

eukaryotic a cell with a nucleus (*eu* means "true" and *karyo* means "nucleus"); includes protists, plants, animals, and fungi

anoxic without oxygen

Cyanobacteria are a **morphologically** diverse group of photosynthetic prokaryotic microorganisms that form a closely related **phylogenetic lineage** of eubacteria. Historically, cyanobacteria were classified with plants and called blue-green algae, although true algae are **eukaryotic**. Cyanobacteria appear early in the fossil record with some examples approximately 3.5 billion years old. Stromatolites are large, often fossilized colonies of cyanobacteria that build up layer upon layer. Cyanobacteria contributed to the conversion of Earth's atmosphere from an **anoxic**-reducing environment to one rich in oxygen. Commonly studied genera include *Anabaena, Lyngbya, Microcystis, Nostoc, Oscillatoria, Synechococcus,* and *Synechocystis.*

Marine and freshwater aquatic environments (including aquaria) are rich in cyanobacteria, either free-living, in biofilms, or in mats. Cyanobacterial species (*Microcystis* or *Oscillatoria*) that produce compounds (e.g., microcystins) toxic to humans and animals are sometimes associated with large-scale blooms in aquatic systems. Curling crusts on soils are often due to cyanobacteria. Pioneer communities on bare rock surfaces often include cyanobacteria or lichens, the latter existing as symbiotic associations of cyanobacteria and fungi. Cyanobacteria are found in extreme environments, including hot springs, desert sands, hypersaline ponds, and within the rocks of dry Antarctic valleys. Urban cyanobacteria are found as biofilms on concrete, brick buildings, and wooden fences.

filamentous thin and long

prokaryotes single-celled organisms without nuclei, including Eubacteria and Archaea

organelle a membrane-bound structure within a cell

polymer a large molecule made from many similar parts

nanometer one-millionth of a meter

Cyanobacteria are morphologically diverse, including unicellular and **filamentous** forms (branched and unbranched). Some filamentous species produce specialized cells including heterocysts, trichomes, hormogonia, and akinetes. As **prokaryotes**, cyanobacteria lack a nucleus and membrane-bound **organelles**. Photosynthetic thylakoid membranes and polyhedral bodies (carboxysomes) are visible using an electron microscope. Cyanobacteria may contain gas vacuoles, polyphosphate granules, and inclusions of cyanophycin, a nitrogen storage **polymer**.

A distinguishing feature of cyanobacteria is their photosynthetic pigment content. In addition to chlorophyll *a*, cyanobacterial thylakoids include phycobilin-protein complexes (phycobilisomes) containing mixtures of phycocyanin, phycoerythrin, and allophycocyanin, which give cyanobacteria their characteristic blue-green coloration. Phycobilisomes harvest light at wavelengths (500 to 650 **nanometers**) not absorbed by chlorophylls. Most

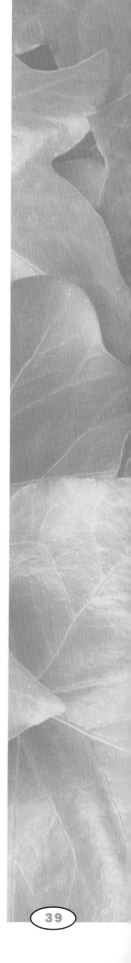

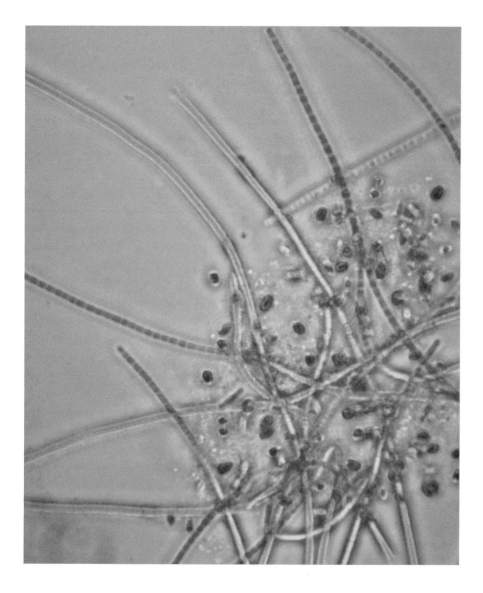

Anabaena, a genera of cyanobacteria, greatly improve crop yields when cultured in the soil of rice paddies.

cyanobacteria perform oxygenic photosynthesis like higher plants. A few species perform anoxygenic photosynthesis, removing electrons from hydrogen sulfide (H_2S) instead of water (H_2O). There is a general dependence on carbon dioxide as a carbon source, although some cyanobacteria can live **heterotrophically** by absorbing organic molecules. The reductive pentose phosphate pathway predominates for carbon assimilation, as cyanobacteria have an incomplete tricarboxylic acid (Krebs) cycle.

Many species of cyanobacteria fix atmospheric dinitrogen (N_2) into ammonia (NH_3) using nitrogenase, an **enzyme** that is particularly sensitive to the presence of oxygen. In filamentous cyanobacteria, such as *Anabaena* and *Nostoc*, certain cells differentiate into heterocysts (thick-walled cells that do not photosynthesize), in which nitrogen fixation occurs under reduced oxygen concentrations. Cyanobacterial nitrogen fixation produces bioavailable nitrogen compounds that are important in nitrogen-limited aquatic ecosystems and plays an important role in global nitrogen cycling.

No other group of microbes participates in as many symbioses as cyanobacteria, including extra- or intracellular relationships with plants,

heterotroph an organism that derives its energy from consuming other organisms or their body parts

enzyme a protein that controls a reaction in a cell

progenitor parent or ancestor

chloroplast the photosynthetic organelle of plants and algae

fungi, and animals. This phenomenon, coupled with the plantlike photosynthesis of cyanobacteria, suggests that cyanobacteria were the **progenitors** of **chloroplasts**. Endosymbiotic theory holds that ancestral eukaryotic cells engulfed the ancient cyanobacteria that evolved into modern plastids. Better candidates may be prochlorophytes, oxygenic photosynthetic bacteria that contain chlorophyll *a* and *b* and form an evolutionarily related group with cyanobacteria and plastids. SEE ALSO AQUATIC ECOSYSTEMS; ENDOSYMBIOSIS; EUBACTERIA; NITROGEN FIXATION; PHOTOSYNTHESIS, CARBON FIXATION AND; PHOTOSYNTHESIS, LIGHT REACTIONS AND; WETLANDS.

Mark A. Schneegurt

Bibliography

Carr, N. G., and B. A. Whitton, eds. *The Biology of Cyanobacteria*. Berkeley and Los Angeles: University of California Press, 1982.

Cyanosite: A Webserver for Cyanobacteria Research. [Online] Available at http://www-cyanosite.bio.purdue.edu/index.html.

Fogg, G. P., W. D. P. Stewart, P. Fay, and A. E. Walsby. *The Blue-Green Algae*. London: Academic Press, 1973.

Cytokinins *See Hormones.*

Darwin, Charles

English Naturalist
1809–1882

Charles Darwin was probably the most influential scientist of the nineteenth century. He is best known for his revolutionary ideas that species transmute, or evolve, by means of the primary mechanism of natural selection, ideas he set forth in his great work *On the Origin of Species* in 1859. This work shaped intellectual, political, and philosophical attitudes of the nineteenth century and fundamentally transformed humanity's understanding of its origins in terms of natural rather than supernatural causes. Though deemed controversial, his ideas continued to hold sway through the twentieth century. For these reasons, he is generally regarded as not only one of the great figures of the history of science, but also one of the great figures of the western intellectual tradition.

Early Life and Background

Charles Robert Darwin was born on February 12, 1809, in Shrewsbury, England, into a wealthy, distinguished family. His paternal grandfather was Erasmus Darwin, a physician who delved into many subjects, including poetry, and who made one of the early statements in support of **transmutation**, or the belief that species are changeable and not fixed. His father was Robert Waring Darwin, an equally successful physician, who practiced in Shrewsbury. His mother was Susannah Wedgwood, the daughter of the industrialist potter Josiah Wedgwood.

Charles Darwin's education began at home, largely through the efforts of his older sisters who took the place of his mother when she died prematurely. He was eventually sent to a local day school, and in 1818 he entered

Charles Darwin.

transmutation change from one form to another

Shrewsbury School, one of the great English public schools of the nineteenth century. Though a poor student, Darwin developed a keen interest in natural history at a young age, and spent many of his leisure hours collecting insects and plants.

In 1825 Darwin enrolled at Edinburgh University with the intent of studying medicine. He was unsuccessful in his formal studies and developed a distaste for surgery. Two years later, he gave up his medical aspirations and left Edinburgh for Cambridge University, where he intended to study theology in the hopes that he could lead the respectable life of a country vicar. He failed to perform adequately in his formal studies, however. His one true interest remained in natural history, an interest that was encouraged by the professor of botany at Cambridge, John Stevens Henslow (1796–1861). Darwin became so enamored of this mentor that he came to be known as "the man who walks with Henslow." Another important influence on Darwin at this time was the professor of geology, Adam Sedgwick (1785–1873). Though Sedgwick provided the only formal training in science that Darwin was to receive, it was Henslow who provided directive influence in Darwin's life after he recommended him to the Admiralty, which was preparing a survey expedition to chart the coastline of South America. Darwin was to serve as companion to the captain, Robert FitzRoy, on the H.M.S. *Beagle*. On occasion he was to serve as ship's naturalist. The five-year voyage of the *Beagle*, beginning on December 31, 1831, and ending on October 2, 1836, was to prove the pivotal experience in shaping Darwin's subsequent scientific work. Darwin returned to England much altered from his experiences. He had not only matured during the voyage, but also distinguished himself with his superb collections, so much so that he became the center of attention in scientific circles.

Scientific Work, 1831–59

While aboard the H.M.S. *Beagle*, Darwin was struck by the diversity of life that he encountered and how beautifully adapted it was to diverse environments. As he traveled up and down the eastern coastline of South America he was especially interested in the geographic distribution of plants and animals that appeared to replace each other. More importantly, he was taken by the fact that extinct fossils in the area closely resembled living forms of related species, and that the flora and fauna on oceanic islands bore a striking similarity to the nearest continental landmass. He became particularly interested in the distribution of the flora and fauna of a string of recently formed volcanic islands known as the Galapagos, after the unique species of tortoises that are found there. Darwin noticed that each island in the group had an entirely unique flora and fauna. He also noticed that the species bore a striking resemblance to the species on the nearest continental landmass, the western part of South America. With insights from British geologist Sir Charles Lyell (1797–1875), who espoused a **uniformitarian** rather than a **catastrophist** geological theory, the weight of this geographic evidence suggested to Darwin that species had not been independently created. They had instead slowly diverged from preexisting species as they came to **colonize** new habitats and as they adapted to new ecological **niches**.

uniformitarian the geologic doctrine that formative processes on Earth have proceeded at the same rate through time since Earth's beginning

catastrophism the geologic doctrine that sudden, violent changes mark the geologic history of Earth

colonize to inhabit a new area

niche the role of an organism in its habitat, involving the whole variety and ecological relationships of which it is a part

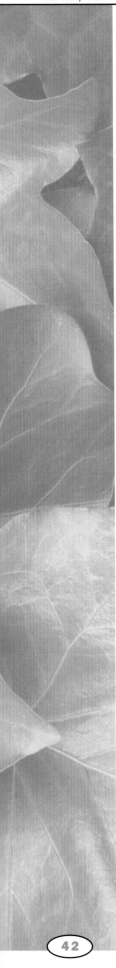

Although Darwin had recognized this geographic pattern, he did not have an explanation or a mechanism for how the flora and fauna were able to adapt themselves to their respective environments. The mechanism of evolution occurred to him only after his return to England and after he had been able to sort through his collections. The decisive moment came two years after his return while he was reading English economist Thomas Malthus's *An Essay on the Principle of Population* (1798). In this famous essay, Malthus had noticed that human populations, if left unchecked, had the tendency to double each generation. In other words, their pattern of growth was exponential. But Malthus also noted that resources necessary to sustain populations increased at a much slower rate, or arithmetically. To Malthus, this meant one thing: that at some point members of the population were subjected to strong competition for those resources, and that such events as war, disease, and famine were natural ways to keep the population in step with available resources. Darwin realized that this principle could just as easily apply to populations of animals and plants. In the competitive struggle for existence, Darwin added, those individuals who bore favorable characteristics would be more likely to survive to reproduce. They in turn were more likely to transmit these favorable characteristics to their offspring. Given enough time, subsequent generations of their offspring would depart from the parental types. Given more time, Darwin added, they would diverge even further from their ancestral types, eventually leading to new species. This principle of divergence strengthened and supported what Darwin called his theory of descent with modification by the mechanism of natural selection. It is what accounted for the origin of species.

Although he had formulated his theory between 1837 and 1838—now recognized as the critical period for Darwin's intellectual development—Darwin did not set these ideas formally on paper until 1842 in a rough sketch, and in 1844 in what is called his historical essay. He showed this short manuscript only to his close friend, the young botanist Joseph Dalton Hooker (1817–1911). Instead of publishing his theory, Darwin continued his research into the late 1850s, hoping to collect enough evidence to support what he knew to be a very controversial theory. Between 1837 and 1859 Darwin therefore engaged in a number of research projects intended to lend support to his theory, including some botanical studies to understand adaptation.

After formulating his theory, Darwin's plan was to collect data carefully from workers around the world to fortify his theory. In particular he was interested in both plant and animal breeding practices, which had been created by artificial selection, a form of selection through human intervention. He became especially interested in pigeon breeding, a popular hobby for Victorians, because it clearly demonstrated the stunning range of variation possible through artificial selection.

In 1839 Darwin married his first cousin, Emma Wedgwood, and in 1842 the couple left London to settle in the nearby village of Downe. There Darwin could escape from the bustle of the city and devote himself fully to his research. The quiet country environment removed from society was also important to Darwin, who began to suffer from an unknown illness, which sometimes left him incapacitated. Only a select group of scientists had access to him. By the 1850s, the inner circle of Darwin's friends, in addition to Hooker and Lyell, included a young morphologist, Thomas Henry Huxley (1825–1895), who became Darwin's intellectual defender.

Publication of *On the Origin of Species*

Darwin's peaceful existence was shattered in 1858 when he received a letter from a young naturalist named Alfred Russel Wallace (1823–1913). Wallace had been exploring the Malay Archipelago in Southeast Asia. Darwin faced the contents of the letter with mixed feelings: Wallace had reproduced much of Darwin's secret theory, leaving Darwin to face a possible priority dispute. At the advice of the inner circle, Darwin and Wallace published their work jointly in the *Journal of the Linnaean Society* in 1858. Darwin used the push from Wallace to complete a longer account of his theory, and included evidence he had gathered not only from his own observations and experiments, but also from his correspondence with naturalists and breeders from around the world. Darwin intended this work to be merely an abstract of his longer theory, but the published book was over four hundred pages. Its full title in the first 1859 edition was *On the Origin of Species or the Preservation of Favored Races in the Struggle for Life*. The book appeared in bookstores on November 24, 1859, and promptly sold out on the first day. It was to go through six editions.

Darwin's life was permanently changed as the theory that Huxley named "evolution" became a topic of heated debate. It was criticized on the scientific front because it failed to provide an adequate theory of heredity and because blending theories of heredity, popular at the time, would have led to a dilution of favorable characteristics. This problem was addressed only after Darwin's death by the rediscovery of Gregor Mendel and his theory of heredity in 1900. Another problem was the age of Earth, which was thought to be about four hundred million years old, an insufficient amount of time to account for the slow, gradual process that Darwin envisioned. This problem was solved after the discovery of radioactivity in the late nineteenth century that, when included in calculations, increased the age of Earth to nearly five billion years, an estimate of time long enough to account for evolution. Yet another difficulty was the fact that Darwin had no direct proof for a process that took place over a long stretch of time. Darwin knew this, and predicted that it would take some fifty years to accumulate enough evidence to support this theory. This was in fact provided beginning in 1920s with the example of industrial melanism in the peppered moth, *Biston betularia*.

More difficult to resolve were the theological and philosophical questions that followed from the mechanism of natural selection. Even though Darwin had only one line on human evolution in the book, the theory implied that humans were subject to the same mechanistic process as plants and animals. Mechanistic and materialistic, natural selection also challenged the argument for God's existence from design and led to a nonpurposive view of the world. To some, like the poet Alfred, Lord Tennyson, a competitive nonpurposive view of nature implied that it was "red in tooth and claw."

Despite a storm of controversy over the mechanism, the fact of evolution was rapidly accepted by scientists. Only after the mechanism of heredity was understood and only after the science of genetics was integrated with

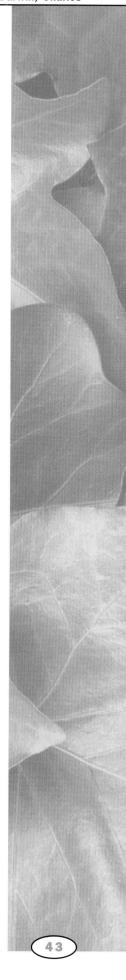

natural history was the debate over the mechanism of natural selection extinguished. This did not take place until the interval of time between 1920 and 1950 and was part of the event called the *evolutionary synthesis*.

Botanical Work

From the start, plants figured prominently in the development of Darwin's ideas of evolution by means of natural selection. Examples from the plant world abound in *On the Origin of Species* and *Variation of Plants and Animals Under Domestication* (1868). Not only were plants easily studied and bred, but they showed a stunning assortment of adaptive features. They were to prove one of Darwin's favorite objects of study, becoming the basis of no less than seven books, most of which appeared in the latter part of Darwin's life.

Darwin's first book on plant evolution was titled *Fertilization in Orchids* (1862). He chose to study orchids because of the range of adaptations they displayed with respect to fertilization. Darwin recognized that these elaborate adaptations served to facilitate cross-pollination by insects such as bees. For this reason, cross-pollinated plants had flowers with bright colors and fragrant nectaries to attract bees and other insects, while wind-pollinated plants, which did not have to attract insect pollinators, had flowers with little or no color.

Darwin also observed that plants that seemed to have one or few flowers had the tendency to be hermaphrodites, having flowers of both sexes on the same plant. Bigger trees with a large number of small flowers, however, usually had flowers of only one sex. To Darwin, this implied that flowers had adapted mechanisms to ensure cross-pollination. This likely increased the variability, and also increased the vigor of the offspring. Darwin performed numerous experiments to understand the manner in which cross-pollination took place in plants and to understand the adaptive function of increased variability. In the process he noted the phenomenon of heterosis, or **hybrid** vigor, in the progeny of cross-pollinated plants. He also began to unravel the adaptive functions of sexual reproduction.

hybrid a mix of two species

Darwin's work in pollination mechanisms appeared in two books. The first was *Effects of Cross and Self Fertilization* (1876), which was followed by *Different Forms of Flowers on Plants of the Same Species* (1877).

twining twisting around while climbing

Darwin was also interested in the adaptive functions of climbing plants. He found that the phenomenon of **twining**, or the differential bending of plants in a clockwise or counterclockwise manner around an object, permitted young or weak plants to raise themselves higher up off the ground. This maximized exposure to air and sunlight in a relatively short time, and without the costly and time-consuming investment of woody supportive structures. The various means used by plants to climb were explored in his book *Climbing Plants* (1875). The mechanisms by which this and other plant movements took place was explored in *Power of Movement in Plants* (1880). In this book Darwin explored plant tropisms, or the manner in which plants were able to grow toward light. He determined that the stem bends toward the light because of differential growth rates: the illuminated side grew more slowly than the unilluminated side so that shoot tips appeared to bend toward the light. He postulated the existence of a substance that was diffused

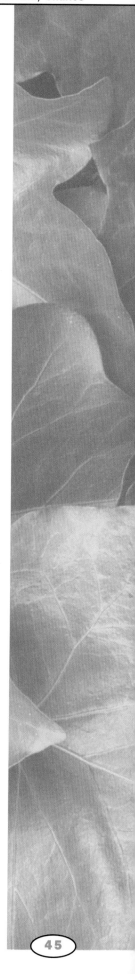

from the apex downward that affected growth rates. These investigations anticipated the existence and action of plant hormones.

Darwin then directed his attention to other types of movements in plants, including mechanisms for prey capture in insectivorous plants such as the sundew, *Drosera rotundifolia* (1880). After detailed observation and experimentation, Darwin concluded that carnivorous plants had acquired the ability to live in nitrogen-poor soil with little or no root structure by feeding on prey. In addition to developing sensory apparatus to detect and capture prey, plants had also developed a digestive system capable of breaking down proteins. Most of these observations, including experiments with the sundew plants, were the focus of his book *Insectivorous Plants* (1875).

Darwin's last book relating to plants was a work with a strangely ecological theme: the action of worms in turning up soil. After experiments that ran for more than fifty years, Darwin postulated that earthworms played a vital ecological role: they fed on dead leaves and other organic matter and excreted this back into the soil. In so doing, earthworms served to aerate the soil and recycle vital nutrients. These results, including quantitative estimates of how much soil was processed by earthworms, were included in *The Formation of Vegetable Mould Through the Action of Worms* (1881).

Darwin's botanical work is notable for its detailed observations and simple, elegant experiments. These were performed in the confines of Darwin's backyard or at greenhouses at his home in Downe. Despite the fact that some of these are now classic experiments reproduced by students the world over, they were judged harshly by the leading German plant physiologist of the late nineteenth century, Julius von Sachs (1832–1897). A revolutionary experimentalist who introduced powerful analytical laboratory methods to botanical science, launching the "New Botany," Sachs thought Darwin's naturalist tendency and simple backyard experiments to be antiquated and amateur. Nonetheless, Darwin's botanical work remains the cornerstone of his studies on variation and mechanisms of adaptation in plants and is significant for his keen insights.

The book on earthworms was published just six months before Darwin's death. Until his end, Darwin remained a productive scientist. Some of his most imaginative work was performed toward the end of his long life. His was a happy and productive life in a home filled with the voices of his ten children and numerous grandchildren. On his death in 1882, he received a rare honor for a scientist: he was given a state burial and was buried at Westminster Abbey. SEE ALSO CARNIVOROUS PLANTS; COMPOST; EVOLUTION OF PLANTS; EVOLUTION OF PLANTS, HISTORY OF; HOOKER, JOSEPH DALTON; MENDEL, GREGOR; ORCHIDACEAE; PHYLOGENY; SACHS, JULIUS VON; TROPISMS AND NASTIC MOVEMENTS.

Vassiliki Betty Smocovitis

Bibliography

Allan, Mea. *Darwin and His Flowers: The Key to Natural Selection.* New York: Taplinger, 1977.

Bowler, Peter J. *Charles Darwin: The Man and His Influence.* Cambridge, UK: Cambridge University Press, 1990.

Browne, Janet. *Charles Darwin: Voyaging,* Vol. 1. New York: Alfred A. Knopf, 1995.

de Beer, Gavin. "Charles Darwin." In *Dictionary of Scientific Biography, Vol. 3,* ed. Charles Coulston Gillispie. New York: Scribner's Sons, 1970.

Desmond, Adrian, and James Moore. *Darwin.* London: Michael Joseph, 1991.

Huxley, Julian, and H. B. D. Kettlewell. *Charles Darwin and His World.* New York: Viking Press, 1965.

Deciduous Forests

angiosperm a flowering plant

The temperate deciduous broadleaf forest (TDBF) is composed of broadleaf **angiosperm** trees like the oaks, maples, and beeches familiar to many Americans and Europeans. The forests exist best in moderate climates that are neither too hot nor too cold and neither too wet nor too dry. In addition to the temperate zone, deciduous forests are found in tropical and subtropical climates in open savannas and/or in closed forests. While there are roughly thirty families and sixty-five genera in the TDBF, variation in the precise definition and defined area of the forest make absolute numbers impossible. With thousands of species, the TDBF is a highly diverse biome.

North American Temperate Deciduous Broadleaf Forest

Worldwide, there are five major groups of TDBFs. Within each group, botanists define TDBFs by the species that tend to occur in a given area. These collections of species, together with their environment, are called associations. Eastern North America today contains the most extensive TDBF. The forest reaches from about longitude 95°W (just west of the Mississippi River) to the Atlantic coast and from 30 to 45°N, thereby forming a quadrant that includes most of the northeastern quarter of the United States. The eastern United States TDBF was almost completely deforested for agricultural purposes by 1850. At that time, land was opened for agriculture in the Mississippi valley, and many farms were abandoned. Pines grew well in the remaining grassy fields, but after a catastrophic hurricane in 1937, the TDBF grew back. Today, there is much more TDBF in the United States than there was one hundred years ago (though still less than before the arrival of European settlers).

There are nine generally recognized associations in the United States TDBF, each defined by differences in vegetation (see accompanying table). Though the species are representative of common dominants, many other species exist. TDBF associations are not completely separate. Many species, such as northern red oak and sugar maple, exist in more than one association. Nor are the boundaries between the associations sharp and easily identifiable. In particular, the Western Mesophytic association can be difficult to distinguish from its neighbors to the east (Mixed Mesophytic) and west (Oak-Hickory). Associations can change with time too. The Oak-Chestnut association is now almost completely devoid of chestnut, but many people still use the association name even though it is now mostly oak and maple. Association names in North America and elsewhere are most useful for distinguishing broad differences in forest type often associated with variation in soils, topography, and climate.

European, Asian, and South American Temperate Deciduous Broadleaf Forest

The European TDBF, stretching through most of Europe (except for very hot and cold areas) from the Atlantic Ocean to the Ural Mountains, is

TEMPERATE DECIDUOUS BROADLEAF FOREST (TDBF) ASSOCIATIONS IN THE UNITED STATES

Type of Association	Location	Common Species
Mixed Mesophytic	Unglaciated central Appalachian Mountains	White basswood (*Tilia heterophylla*), Carolina basswood (*Tilia caroliniana*), American basswood (*Tilia americana*), sugar maple (*Acer saccharum*), black maple (*Acer nigrum*), yellow buckeye (*Aesculus octandra*), northern red oak (*Quercus rubra*), white oak (*Quercus alba*), and eastern hemlock (*Tsuga canadensis*); transitional forest between Mixed Mesophytic and Oak–Hickory
Western Mesophytic	West of the southern Appalachian Mountains	White oak, yellow buckeye, white basswood, American beech (*Fagus grandifolia*), and sugar maple; dominant species highly variable
Oak–Hickory	Western boundary of the central and southern TDBF (western Missouri and Arkansas)	White oak, red oak (*Quercus borealis maxima*), black oak (*Quercus velutina*), bitternut hickory (*Carya cordiformis*), and shagbark hickory (*Carya ovata*); drought stress to the west is leading to increased grass cover and the eventual elimination of the TDBF in the Great Plains
Oak–Chestnut	Eastern Appalachian Mountains	Chestnut oak (*Quercus prinus*), northern red oak, and red maple (*Acer rubrum*); before 1904 this association was dominated by *Castanea dentata* (chestnut), but between 1904 and 1950 the chestnut blight killed virtually all mature chestnuts. *Castanea* was replaced by oaks, but the Oak–Chestnut association name is still used
Oak–Hickory–Pine	Piedmont region, southeastern Appalachian Mountains, mid-Atlantic states	Those in Oak-Hickory association with the addition of loblolly pine (*Pinus taeda*), shortleaf pine (*Pinus echinata*), Virginia pine (*Pinus virginiana*), longleaf pine (*Pinus palustris*), and Caribbean pine, also called slash pine and Jersey pine (*Pinus caribaea*); association similar to Oak–Hickory, and plantation forestry with coniferous species widely practiced
Southeastern Evergreen	Southern boundary of the TDBF (southern Arkansas through central Georgia)	Longleaf pine, slash pine (*Pinus elliottii*), loblolly pine, and shortleaf pine; transition between angiosperm and gymnosperm forest. Large oak stands exist, as well as limited areas of evergreen broadleaf trees (such as magnolia). Coniferous species dominate
Beech–Maple	South of the central Great Lakes	American beech, sugar maple, American elm (*Ulmus americana*), black walnut (*Juglans nigra*), white ash (*Fraxinus americana*)
Maple–Basswood	West of Lake Michigan	Sugar maple, American basswood, northern red oak, slippery elm (*Ulmus rubra*), American elm, and bitternut hickory; smallest association
Hemlock–White Pine–Northern Hardwood	Northern boundary of the TDBF (Canada and New England from the northern Great Lakes to Nova Scotia)	Sugar maple, American beech, yellow birch (*Betula alleghaniensis*), American basswood, red maple, aspen (*Populus tremuloides*), paper birch (*Betula papyrifera*), jack pine (*Pinus banksiana*), red pine (*Pinus resinosa*), eastern white pine (*Pinus strobus*), balsam fir (*Abies balsamea*), white spruce (*Picea glauca*), black spruce (*Picea mariana*), larch (*Larix lacricinia*), and northern white cedar (*Thuja occidentalis* and *Thuja canadensis*); largest association

the second-largest TDBF. Due to the moderating influences of the Gulf Stream, the TDBF exists as far as 60°N in northwestern Europe. Forests in Europe have been extensively modified by humans for more than two thousand years and are some of the most manipulated forests in the world. In the northern European TDBF, birch species are common, while in the middle European latitudes, beech (*Fagus sylvatica*) is widely distributed and commercially valuable. Towards the south, various oak and maple species abound. As in North America, much of the once-cleared TDBF is now regrowing. The European TDBF is replaced by drought-resistant shrubs and evergreen broadleaf trees in the south and the boreal coniferous forest in the north.

The last three TDBF areas are much smaller than the first two. East Asia, from 30° to 60°N and from central Japan to longitude 125°E in the northwest and longitude 115°E in the southwest, originally maintained very large forests. Today, even though the species mix is still very diverse, much of the East Asian forest outside of Japan is currently under **cultivation** and most existing forest fragments are protected refuges or in areas unsuitable for agriculture. Nearly all TDBF genera are present in East

cultivation growth of crop plants, or turning the soil for this purpose

47

Leaves of the sugar maple (*Acer saccharum*) provide rich hues of red during the autumn while birch and oak display brilliant orange and yellows.

Asia, especially China. The Near East between 35° and 45°N, including areas around the eastern Black Sea and mountainous regions in Iran and near the Caspian Sea, supports a diverse TDBF. Finally, a narrow strip of South America including southern Chile and Argentina contain TDBF. *Acacia caven* and seven *Nothofagus* species are also found there. In nearly all cases, the deciduous trees of South America occur in mixtures with evergreen broadleaf species.

Of the three major TDBFs, East Asia has by far the greatest diversity, followed by North America and Europe. East Asia was glaciated less severely than America and Europe, so most species were able to survive with little difficulty. In North America, the north-to-south orientation of major mountain ranges allowed species to migrate, and species diversity here is only slightly lower than in East Asia. In Europe, on the other hand, the east-to-west mountains caused the TDBF to be trapped by advancing glaciers. Many modern European TDBF species survived only in the Near East TDBF and migrated back after the glaciers retreated. Consequently, Europe has very low-species diversity.

Climate and Soils

TDBFs are generally restricted to a warm temperate climate with four identifiable seasons in which the average temperature of the coldest month is between 3 and 18°C and the average temperature of the warmest month exceeds 10°C. The length of the frost-free period ranges from 120 to over

250 days. **Precipitation** is year-round and averages between 80 and 200 centimeters per year. Snowfall can range from nonexistent in the southeastern United States to extremely heavy in northern habitats. Climates that are wet and warm all year are occupied by tropical forest consisting of broadleaf evergreen trees. As climates become drier, as occurs at the western edge of the Oak-Hickory association, drought stresses are too extreme for TDBF and grasses become dominant. To the north of the major TDBF, extreme cold, short growing seasons and poor soils favor evergreen coniferous forests. TDBF soils tend to be deep and fertile and, unlike some soils in the northern coniferous forest, do not freeze year-round. For this reason, TDBFs have historically been popular for agricultural use.

precipitation rainfall

Leaves and Phenology

Deciduous leaves are the most distinctive feature of the TDBF. In the fall, spectacular reds, oranges, and yellows produce breathtaking displays across the TDBF. Why does this occur? During autumn, as temperatures cool and days shorten, trees send hormonal signals to their leaves causing them to turn colors and fall off the branch. First, leaves form a barrier between the leaf and the branch, known as the **abscission** layer. At the same time, chlorophyll, the compound that gathers light for photosynthesis, begins to degrade in the leaf. Many of the nutrients in the leaf are sucked back into the tree for next year's leaves. Chlorophyll is responsible for the usual green leaf color: once it is gone, yellow and orange pigments that were there all along become visible. Some of the sugar in the leaves of oaks and maples may be converted into red colors. Once the leaf is totally shut down and no longer conducting any photosynthesis, the abscission layer becomes very brittle. Any small breeze can snap the leaf off at this point. In the spring, using carbon from special storage cells in the trunk, trees grow a new batch of leaves. In an evolutionary adaptation designed to maximize the amount of light received, shrubs and small trees growing in the understory will begin growth before the overstory.

abscission dropping off or separation

The study of any recurring biological cycle and its connection to climate is called phenology. Patterns of bird migration and insect outbreaks are examples of phenological cycles. For centuries, scientists have been studying phenology in the TDBF. In the deciduous forest, phenology refers to the timing of spring leaf growth and fall leaf drop and their relationship to climatic variation. Observational evidence has shown that TDBF phenology is highly sensitive to variation in weather. Warm springs will cause leaves to grow earlier, sometimes by up to as much as one month. Conversely, plants respond to a cold fall by dropping their leaves earlier. Phenological cycles in the forest are one possible indication that plants are responding to global warming. If temperatures are warming, the growing season should be getting longer. Most evidence between 1950 and 2000 suggests that the duration of the growing season has lengthened by several days in many forests. TDBF leaves are not only beautiful, they can also provide very useful scientific observations.

Plant-Animal Interactions

The TDBF supports rich plant-animal interactions in all three of the classic ecological relationships between two species or organisms: mutualism, commensalism, and antagonism.

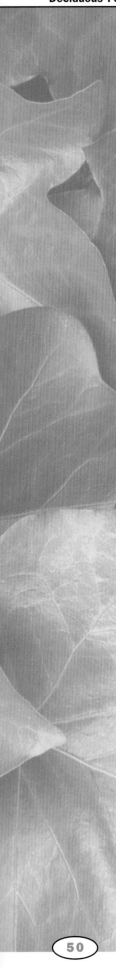

Mutualism. In a mutualistic relationship, both participants receive a benefit. Mutualisms are quite a bit like bargains or trades. In flowering plants, most pollination does not take place with wind. Pollen grains must be physically transported from the male stamen to the female stigma where the process of fertilization begins. In the past, angiosperms relied on the chance event that an insect would happen to brush against the stamen on one flower and then on the stigma of another flower. This was very inefficient and plants eventually evolved in such a way as to greatly increase the chances of successful pollination. While a few TDBF trees are wind-pollinated, most use nectar, a sweet sugary substance, to lure pollinators. While they eat the nectar, pollinators brush the stamen and collect pollen. When they visit a female flower, the pollinator brushes the stigma, transporting the pollen and beginning fertilization. Brightly colored flowers and vivid aromas also attract pollinators, as do ultraviolet markings on some flowers. In the TDBF, insects (especially bees) are the most important pollinators. Other pollinators in the TDBF include moths, butterflies, wasps, flies, and birds.

Commensalism. In a commensal relationship, one participant gains a benefit without harming the other. As in many forests, small mammals such as raccoons, squirrels, and mice as well as such birds as owls use trees for habitat in a commensal relationship. Some insects have evolved to look almost exactly like twigs or leaves. This makes it difficult for predators to locate them in the trees.

Antagonism. Organisms in an antagonistic relationship benefit at the expense of the other organism. Antagonistic relationships are common. Herbivory by insects, in particular the gypsy moth, can cause extensive damage to the TDBF. White-tailed deer and other ungulates eat leaves and can be the most destructive animals in the forest. In a response to browsing pressures, some trees have evolved leaves with distasteful **toxins**. The black-tailed deer, though, has developed special chemicals in its saliva to neutralize these toxins. In the future, it is likely that trees will evolve new defensive toxins. This process of back-and-forth evolution between **herbivores** and plants is an example of a process called coevolution.

toxin a poisonous substance

herbivore an organism that feeds on plant parts

Threats to the Temperate Deciduous Broadleaf Forest

Farming has historically represented the greatest threat to the TDBF. Today's TDBF has extensively regrown in the eastern United States, but in Europe and East Asia, the other two major areas, the forest is still highly fragmented. Species diversity fortunately tends to remain high even in highly scattered groups. Future regrowth can occur rapidly from these isolated or protected areas.

Fungal diseases are currently much more serious threats. Plants all over the world have fungal pests to which they are usually well adapted. Serious problems arise when these diseases are transported to forests that have no defenses. The chestnut blight, introduced to America from Europe in 1904, is the best-known example. In four decades, the chestnut blight eliminated a popular and valuable tree from an entire continent. Dutch elm disease reached the United States by 1930 and to date has killed millions of elms. Humans are almost always the cause of these introduced diseases. Fungi can easily store themselves on ships, cars, or trains. As global commerce increases, it is likely that humans will continue to accidentally introduce diseases into the TDBF. SEE ALSO BIOME; CHESTNUT BLIGHT; COEVOLUTION; CONIFEROUS FORESTS; DECIDUOUS PLANTS; DUTCH ELM DISEASE; FORESTER; FORESTRY; TREES.

Michael A. White

Bibliography

Archibold, O. W. *Ecology of World Vegetation.* London: Chapman and Hall, 1995.

Barnes, Burton V., and Stephen Hopkins Spurr. *Forest Ecology,* 4th ed. New York: Wiley, 1998.

Braun, Emma Lucy. *Deciduous Forests of Eastern North America.* Philadelphia: Blakiston, 1950.

Buchmann, Stephen L. *The Forgotten Pollinators.* Washington, DC: Island Press/Shearwater Books, 1996.

Foster, David R. "Land Use History (1730–1990) and Vegetation Dynamics in Central New England." *Journal of Ecology* 76 (1995): 135–51.

Kimmins, J. P. *Forest Ecology.* New York: Macmillan, 1987.

Menzel, Annette, and Peter Fabian. "Growing Season Extended in Europe." *Nature* 397 (1999): 659.

Myneni, Ranga B. "Increased Plant Growth in the Northern High Latitudes from 1981 to 1991." *Nature* 386 (1997): 698–702.

Röhrig, Ernst, and Bernhard Ulrich, eds. *Temperate Deciduous Forests.* New York: Elsevier, 1991.

Sayre, April Pulley. *Temperate Deciduous Forest.* New York: Twenty-First Century Books, 1994.

Deciduous Plants

A perennial plant that seasonally loses its leaves (and/or stems) is deciduous. This loss is typically related to water stress; for example, green portions of the plant are shed during the dry season. Dry does not have to mean no (or low) **precipitation**. It simply means that little water is available for the plant. Winter in some areas brings heavy snows; unfortunately, the ground water is frozen and unavailable for the plant. Most of the water lost by a plant occurs because of transpiration (evaporation through its leaves). By dropping its leaves during the dry season, deciduous plants are able to avoid dehydration.

precipitation rainfall

In colder climates, it is typically the reduction in both day length and temperature that cause the process to begin. In desert (or equatorial) regions, the winter (shortest days) is often the rainy season. Many plants in these areas do not develop leaves or aboveground portions until they have sufficient moisture. Loss of these portions is more closely associated with a decrease in moisture rather than a change in day length.

Whether caused by shorter day length, cooler temperatures, or decreased moisture availability, the process is the same. Environmental cues prompt the production of an important hormone, ethylene, which in turn induces the formation of an abscission zone. This zone is near the point of attachment of leaf (or stem) to the rest of the plant. The **abscission** zone is composed of two parts: the separation layer and the protection layer. The separation layer marks the area where the leaf will break away from the plant

abscission dropping off or separation

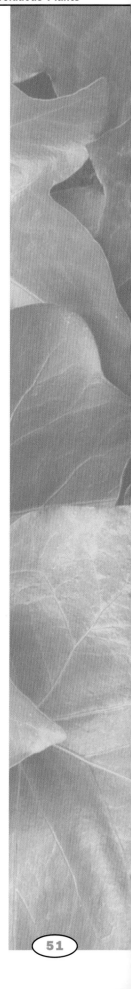

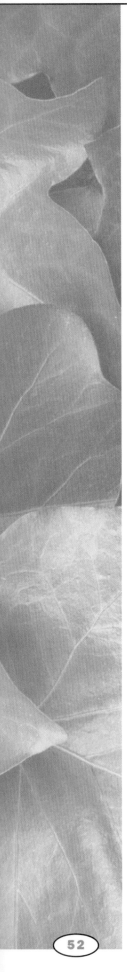

An oak tree in wintertime in the Shenandoah National Park in Virginia.

or abscise. The protection layer seals the wound left by the dropped leaf, protecting the plant from infection and moisture loss.

The formation of the abscission zone breaks many of the connections the leaf had with the plant. This causes a decrease in the amount of water available to the leaf, causing a consequent decrease in chlorophyll production. With the loss of chlorophyll, the other pigments in the leaf (anthocyanins and carotenoids) show through. The net result is the dramatic fall color changes seen in many deciduous forests.

Not all perennial plants are deciduous. Many are considered evergreen, since they retain their leaves throughout the year. Deciduous and evergreen plants can often be found in the exact same habitats growing next to one another. Each has its own adaptations to deal with seasonal water stress. For instance, some adaptations that evergreens have to deal with dry conditions include thick, waxy leaves, leaves with low surface area (conifer needles, for example), or water storage tissues (such as cacti).

There is a cost to dropping leaves, which is why some perennial plants are not deciduous. It can take a lot of nutrients from the soil to produce the

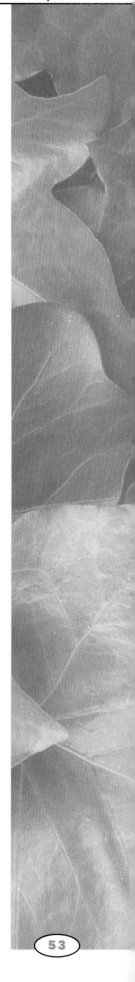

number of leaves produced in an average growing season. In areas where nutrients are plentiful, an annual leaf drop is not a problem. However, in areas with nutrient poor soils, dropping leaves may be very costly for the plant. The advantages of decreased water stress and the detriments of a seasonal loss of nutrients must be balanced to insure an evolutionarily stable strategy. SEE ALSO ANTHOCYANINS; CAROTENOIDS; CHLOROPHYLL; DECIDUOUS FORESTS; HORMONES; LEAVES; PIGMENTS; TREES.

Steve Dickie

Decomposers

Decomposers are the choppers, shredders, plowers, and dissolvers of the biological world. They break down tree leaves, dead flowers, grass blades, old logs in forests, and plant roots into small parts, and, finally, into carbon dioxide, water, and numerous basic chemical compounds in soils, water bodies, and sediments. Organisms involved in decomposition vary from earthworms that drag leaves into their burrows, chew up parts of the leaves, and pass them through their guts to microscopic bacteria that make the final breakdown of fragments into basic chemicals. Some decomposers are specialized and act most effectively on only, for example, oak leaves or maple seeds. Others decompose parts of many plant or animal remains that fall on the soil or into a stream or lake. Most decomposers are often not visible, but in some lawn areas, especially under deciduous trees, we can see little volcano-like earthworm mounds. Mushrooms in our gardens and forests are the visible parts of fungi that are decomposing plant and animal remains in the soil.

Decomposers are the ultimate recyclers of land and water **ecosystems**. As byproducts of their actions in breaking down organic matter, decomposers obtain (and release) nutrients and energy-yielding compounds. And decomposers leave behind simpler fragments for other decomposers along with simple forms of nitrogen, phosphorus, calcium, and other plant nutrients. Plant roots then can take up these nutrients to sustain new plant growth, and insects and other animals can eat the plants. So, the cycles continue. These cycles from plant organic matter, sometimes to animal tissues, then to decomposers and basic chemical compounds are essential to maintaining the world's ecosystems. Some of the residues of decomposition, and some byproducts of decomposer processes, serve to glue together mineral soil particles. This gives soils the **porosity** that allows roots to grow and water and air to enter and leave soils. These cycles maintain soil fertility in grasslands, forests, lakes, and agricultural lands.

ecosystem an ecological community together with its environment

porosity openness

Many decomposers are partners in interesting biological systems. Microscopic bacteria in the rumens—"first stomachs"—of cows decompose grass that cows eat and pass on more easily digestible substances to the real stomachs. Other bacteria in the gut "tubes" of earthworms partially decompose plant fragments, making elements and compounds available to the worms and yield nutrient-rich residues that are passed back into the soil. Some mushroom parts of wood-decomposing fungi are important foods for some insects and forest animals, including deer and small rodents. In some cases insects or animals then carry fungal parts or

Bacteria in earthworms' digestive tracts partially decompose plant fragments, yielding nutrient-rich residues that are passed back into the soil.

cultivation growth of crop plants, or turning the soil for this purpose

spores to other spots where they form new fungal decomposing systems. Many small insects and other arthropods are important first-stage shredders and partial decomposers of plant remains. In soils where such decomposers are excluded by intensive **cultivation** or excess chemicals, the natural recycling of organic matter is slowed down. This can lead to decreased soil fertility and plant growth; farmers or gardeners are then forced to add fertilizers or mulches. Good ecosystem stewardship includes keeping active populations of decomposers of all sizes to keep the systems productive. SEE ALSO BIOGEOCHEMICAL CYCLES; CARBON CYCLE; COMPOST; FUNGI.

James R. Boyle

Defenses, Chemical

herbivore an organism that feeds on plant parts

enzyme a protein that controls a reaction in a cell

All plants produce a diverse group of chemicals whose main function is to protect the plant against **herbivores** and diseases; these are the plant's chemical defenses. Many of these compounds seem to have no role in such core plant functions as growth and reproduction, and they are synthesized in unique pathways in the plant. As a result, they are often called secondary compounds or secondary metabolites. Others, including many **enzymes**, also have functions in growth, reproduction, and acquiring light or nutrients. Even though humans have exploited these plant products for thousands of years, it was not until the 1950s that scientists reasoned that these chemicals might be produced as defenses. While many plants have physical defenses such as thorns or spines, and some are just too tough to chew, those traits block feeding by large animals only, and do nothing against diseases. Chemical defenses are potentially effective against all of a plant's enemies. The study of how plants make, deploy, and benefit from chemical defenses is an important branch of chemical ecology.

Types of Chemical Defenses

Defensive chemicals are grouped into classes based on their structures and how the plant makes them. Some classes are very large and occur in all plants, while others are smaller and may occur in only one or two plant families or a few species.

It has been estimated that, overall, plants synthesize several hundreds of thousands of different secondary compounds. New ones are reported every day. Five groups are most common, diverse, or widespread: the alkaloids, cyanogenic glycosides, terpenoids, phenolics, and glucosinolates.

Alkaloids. There are more than ten thousand different alkaloids and relatives known from plants. Alkaloids are cyclic nitrogen-containing compounds. They are widely distributed among many higher plant families, where they are often produced in roots. Their activity in animals is diverse, but many interfere with **neurotransmitters**. When consumed, many alkaloids are **addictive**. Examples include caffeine (coffee), morphine (poppy), tomatine (tomato), nicotine (tobacco), and lupine alkaloids (**legumes**).

Cyanogenic Glycosides. **Cyanogenic** glycosides also contain nitrogen, bound with other carbons to a sugar. Certain plant and animal enzymes can remove the sugar, freeing hydrogen cyanide, which poisons the energy-producing mitochondria in all cells. Probably all plants can produce cyanogenic compounds, but they are most common in legumes (for example, bird's-foot trefoil) and the fruits of plants in the rose/apple family (Rosaceae); they have the odor of almonds.

Terpenoids. Terpenoids are the second-largest group of secondary compounds (fifteen- to twenty-thousand known). They are incredibly diverse in structure and activity, even though they all originally derive from a simple molecule called isoprene. Most monoterpenoids are **volatile** and comprise the characteristic odor of conifers and mints. Some volatile terpenes are produced only when the plant is wounded by an herbivore. They attract predators or parasites to the plant, which then kill the damaging herbivore; this is an indirect chemical defense because it acts via a third party (the predator or parasite). Sesquiterpenoids are the largest subgroup of terpenes and include gossypol from cotton and the sticky sap of plants in the family Asteraceae, such as lettuce and goldenrod. Triterpenoids include many extremely bitter compounds, including cucurbitacin from squashes and cucumbers; some are used as insecticides. Insects cannot synthesize cholesterol, the basis of their growth hormones, and must obtain the basic terpenoid skeleton from plants. But some plants produce steroids that act as insect hormones, disrupting insect development as a defensive ploy.

Phenolics. The most diverse and common secondary compounds are phenolics. Defined by possessing a benzene ring with one attached **hydroxyl**, an enormous number of structures can be called phenolic. Most of the more than twenty-five thousand known types of phenolics are good **antioxidants** and are frequently used as preservatives; in plants they prevent membrane **oxidation** and other types of oxidative damage. As defenses, various phenolics are distasteful, toxic, and inhibit digestion. When activated by light, coumarins in such plants as carrots and celery cross-link deoxyribonucleic acid (DNA) strands and halt cell division. The blue and red colors of most

neurotransmitter chemical that passes messages between nerve cells

addictive capable of causing addiction or chemical dependence

legumes beans and other members of the Fabaceae family

cyanogenic giving rise to cyanide

volatile easily released as a gas

hydroxyl the chemical group -OH

antioxidant a substance that prevents damage from oxygen or other reactive substances

oxidation the removal of electrons, or the addition of oxygen

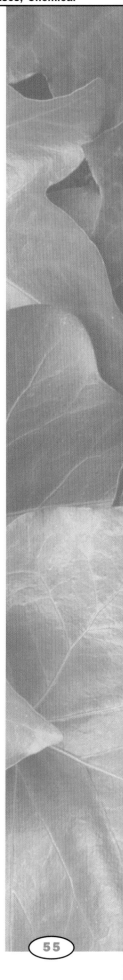

An insect on a California poppy (*Eschscholzia californica*). Poppies produce alkaloids, compounds that may interfere with neurotransmitters in the animals that ingest them.

flavonoids aromatic compounds occurring in both seeds and young roots and involved in host-pathogen and host-symbiont interactions

polymer a large molecule made from many similar parts

tannins compounds produced by plants that usually serve protective functions; often colored and used for "tanning" and dyeing

ionic present as a charged particle

hyphae the threadlike body mass of a fungus

flowers are provided by **flavonoids**, oaks and tea are rich in phenolic **polymers** called **tannins**, and the odor of wintergreen is a phenolic acid (methyl salicylate).

Glucosinolates. Glucosinolates comprise a small (one hundred) group of compounds containing both nitrogen and sulfur. They, too, are good antioxidants, but they are best known as repellents. They occur primarily in the cabbage family, where they provide the distinctive odor of those foods.

Many plant enzymes serve a defensive function. Some (such as oxidases) oxidize and activate secondary compounds; many phenolics and glucosinolates are much more defensive when this has occurred. Others produce toxic **ionic** forms of various molecules, called reactive oxygen species (ROS), which damage membranes, proteins, and DNA. Others produce signals that coordinate defense responses. Chitinases digest fungal **hyphae**, and other defensive enzymes can digest bacterial cells.

Inducible Defenses

While all plants produce some chemical defenses all the time, they also increase or alter chemical defenses when attacked by microbes or animals. These are called *inducible defenses*. Many things can induce chemical defenses, including wounding (for example, tearing), insect chewing, **pathogen** attack, and wind motion.

Induced responses to microbes can be very specific. A given plant geno-type (e.g., variety) can recognize and respond with specific defenses against particular microbe genotypes (e.g., bacterial strain) but may not respond to others. This ability has been exploited in breeding resistant crop plants and is called gene-for-gene resistance. Plants recognize potentially deadly mi-crobes by detecting unique proteins or other molecules on the pathogens' surface. The plant's recognition device, usually a protein, eventually acti-vates plant genes that encode the enzymes necessary to produce defensive chemicals. Phenolics and reactive oxygen species are produced at the point of infection, blocking microbial enzymes, killing microbes and the plant's own cells, and strengthening cell walls to prevent the spread of the infec-tion. These steps comprise a strategy for stopping the infection called pro-grammed cell death or apoptosis. The results appear as brown spots, or necrotic lesions, and the entire process from detection to lesion is called the hypersensitive response (HR). This approach to defense is shared with an-imal systems.

pathogen disease-causing organism

As HR proceeds, nearby plant cells produce signals that spread through the plant and generate **systemic** acquired resistance (SAR). A plant ex-hibiting SAR is resistant to the original pathogen as well as others. Even tissues not yet produced when the plant was first attacked are resistant once they appear. This effect superficially resembles immune responses in ani-mals. Scientists do not know with certainty what the signal is that circulates through the plant, but evidence indicates that it is probably not a protein, as it would be in animals. Candidates include carbohydrate cell wall frag-ments, phenolics (salicylic acid), plant growth hormones (e.g., abscisic acid), and electrical impulses. Many defenses are induced when genes' encoding defense-production mechanisms are activated in response to a complicated web of signals.

systemic spread throughout the plant

Salicylic acid is the chemical from which aspirin is made.

Plant responses to herbivores are not as well understood. Even small amounts of damage can induce plantwide defenses and systemic resistance. HR is not a usual component of wound responses, but signals emanating from the site of damage do produce systemic resistance. There is good evidence that a fatty acid product, jasmonic acid (JA), circulates through a wounded plant, inducing chemical defenses. In tomatoes a peptide, systemin, plays a similar role. Plant responses to herbivores is often less specific than to microbes, although different insects can induce the production of differ-ent volatile defenses from the same plant. A molecule (volicitin) related to JA has been found in the **regurgitant** of insects and triggers induced re-sponses. It appears that at least some plants can recognize their attacker via regurgitant or saliva chemistry, and induced defenses against herbivores are also probably often activated by altered gene expression.

regurgitant material brought up from the stomach

Effectiveness of Plant Defenses

While the physiological action of some plant chemical defenses is well established, and it is relatively easy to find plant chemicals that repel or poison animals or microbes, it is more difficult to demonstrate that chem-ical defenses benefit plants in nature, for three reasons. First, there has been repeated evolution of microbes and herbivores that can tolerate or detoxify plant defenses. Many of these plant pests can attack only the few plant species or even tissues to which they are adapted, but no plant

A woman cuts grooves into a rubber tree to extract the sap in Manguangiong, Yunnan Province, China. The compounds rubber and latex are made from the sap produced as defenses against wood-boring beetles.

lineage ancestry; the line of evolutionary descent of an organism

species is totally protected; there has been an evolutionary response to every plant defense. This dynamic process, in which two species (for example, plant and insect) influence each other's evolution reciprocally, is called coevolution.

Second, many scientists believe that producing defenses may be costly. Costs may include using materials (for example, sugars) for defense at the expense of growth or reproduction, a risk of poisoning one's self, or incompatibility with other life functions (for example, some nectars contain defensive chemicals and are toxic to bees). If so, then selection to reduce costs may counter selection for defense, leaving some plants vulnerable.

Third, the ability to produce defenses is constrained by the plant's genes and environment. If the mutations necessary to permit the development of a class of defenses (for example, alkaloids) has never arisen in a plant's evolutionary **lineage**, that defense—no matter how effective it might be—is not an option. And producing some defenses may be more difficult under some environmental circumstances. For example, low soil nitrogen can limit alkaloid production, and low light can restrict phenolic synthesis.

No plant is perfectly protected in nature, even if it is deadly to some enemies. Total plant protection must involve other forces acting together with the plant's own defenses. Employing extremely effective chemical defenses (pesticides) as the only plant protection produces resistant pests that

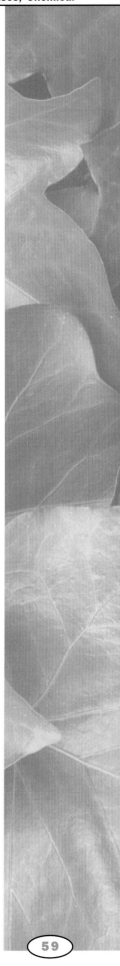

can tolerate and overcome them. This does not happen in nature; most natural plant systems are rarely decimated by pests. Many ecologists believe that in nature, plant protection derives from chemical defenses acting in combination with each other and with other pest control agents. For example, plant chemistry may help parasites or predators find and kill pests (indirect defense), or make pests more susceptible to their pathogens. Using more than one chemical defense at a time, and varying them through time, slows the rate at which a pest can evolve resistance. The complexity of nature is an important component of plant protection.

Human Use of Defensive Chemicals

Humans have exploited plant chemicals for thousands of years. Many uses derive directly from their defensive action. Nicotine was among the earliest of insecticides developed by humans, a practice that continues today with the isolation of antimicrobial and antiherbivore chemicals and eventual synthesis of **analogs**. Citrus chemistry is exploited as a mosquito repellent. Many antiseptic and antibiotic agents are derived from plants (e.g., terpenes in pine-scented cleaners).

analog a structure or thing, especially a chemical, similar to something else

The nervous system activity of some alkaloids has been exploited for recreational and religious drug use (opium, cocaine, nicotine, caffeine, and mescaline) and medicine (opium and codeine). The ability of some to block signal transmission at **neuromuscular junctions** makes them important in surgery as well as hunting tools (e.g., curare). Polyphenols have broad antimicrobial activity; they inhibit oxidative enzymes (e.g., cyclooxygenases) that cause disease, and their antioxidant characteristics are thought to prevent aging and some cancers. Much the same has been claimed for glucosinolates (cabbage family). More than 90 percent of the medicines prescribed in the twentieth century were originally plant derived, mostly involving presumed defensive chemicals. Human medicinal use of plants is based almost entirely on the action of defensive chemicals.

neuromuscular junction the place on the muscle surface where it receives stimulus from the nervous system

The quality of many foods derives from plant chemical defenses. **Tannins** are an essential flavor and color component of ripening fruits, wines, and chocolates. The distinctive flavors and aromas of plants in the citrus, cabbage, cucumber, and tomato families, among others, derive from their defensive chemistries. Apart from basic nutrition, food chemistry is largely the chemistry of plant defenses.

tannins compounds produced by plants that usually serve protective functions; often colored and used for "tanning" and dyeing

The cultural and industrial applications of plant defense chemistry are too numerous to list. Tannins preserve leather and were the original ink; plant phenols and carotenoids are important dyes; rubber and latex began as defenses against wood-boring beetles in rubber trees; jasmonic acid, a defensive signal, is the "queen of aromas" and is crucial to perfume formulation. SEE ALSO ALKALOIDS; ALLELOPATHY; COEVOLUTION; DEFENSES, PHYSICAL; FLAVONOIDS; INTERACTIONS, PLANT-FUNGAL; INTERACTIONS, PLANT-INSECT; INTERACTIONS, PLANT-PLANT; INTERACTIONS, PLANT-VERTEBRATE; PHYSIOLOGY; TERPENES; TRICHOMES.

Jack C. Schultz

Bibliography

Agosta, William C. *Bombardier Beetles and Fever Trees.* New York: Addison-Wesley, 1996.

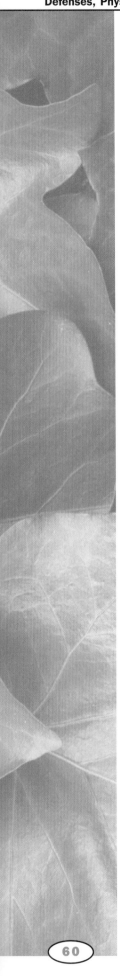

Karban, Rick, and Ian T. Baldwin. *Induce Responses to Herbivores.* Chicago: University of Chicago Press, 1998.

Price, Peter W. *Insect Ecology.* New York: John Wiley & Sons, 1997.

Schoonhoven, L. M., T. Jeremy, and J. J. A. van Loon. *Insect-Plant Biology.* London: Chapman and Hall, 1998.

Defenses, Physical

angiosperm a flowering plant

herbivore an organism that feeds on plant parts

taxa a type of organism, or a level of classification of organisms

Angiosperms and seed-bearing conifers provide a source of nutrients and habitat for large grazing mammals and birds as well as numerous species of insects and related arthropods. For many insect **herbivores**, the entire life cycle takes place on or within plant tissue. The evolutionary success of these plant **taxa**, the most conspicuous plants of our geological age, is due, in part, to their ability to adapt to a broad range of environments as well as their development of defenses against vertebrate and arthropod herbivores. Physical adaptations evolved by these vascular plants to defend against herbivores range from simple structural barriers to complex changes in anatomical form. Plant organs at which major defensive interaction with herbivores occurs include stems, leaves, and reproductive structures.

External Defenses

The leaves, stems, and aerial reproductive organs of vascular plants provide a large surface area and many opportunities for use as food or habitat by herbivores. Physical defensive adaptations are associated with plant color (controlled by tissue pigments, internal leaf structure, and the nature of the leaf surface), surface waxes, **pubescence**, the presence (or absence) of specialized glands, and anatomical adaptations involving plant shape and form.

pubescence covered with short hairs

Plant Color. Herbivorous insects sometimes use leaf and flower color as an aid in finding suitable host plants for food or for egg laying. Red foliage of cotton (*Gossypium*), cabbage (*Brassica oleracea*), and Brussels sprouts (*Brassica oleracea*, variety *gemmifera*) is discriminated against by the cotton boll weevil, imported cabbage worm, and cabbage aphid, respectively.

epicuticle the waxy outer covering of a plant, produced by the epidermis

desiccation drying

pathogen disease-causing organism

adhesion sticking to the surface of

Surface Waxes. The **epicuticle** of plant tissue is composed of surface waxes that protect against **desiccation** and often provide defense against insect attack and disease **pathogens**. Defensive waxes on plants of the mustard family (Cruciferae), such as cabbage, contain chemical compounds that repel pests such as flea beetles. The spatial orientation of waxy plates and rods on the leaves of resistant Brussels sprouts interferes with locomotion and **adhesion** by flea beetles. In some species of raspberry (*Rubus*), thick secretions of surface waxes act as a physical barrier by restricting aphids from successfully reaching the phloem with their sucking mouthparts.

Pubescence. Pubescence, the specialized epidermal hairs (trichomes) of vascular plants, plays an important physiological role in water conservation but also forms a physical barrier to use by herbivores and constitutes the last line of external defense. The sharp spines of cacti, the thorns of *Acacia*, wild rose (*Rosa*), raspberry, and the irritating hairs of stinging nettles (*Urtica*) create a painful barrier to grazing mammals and human interference. Trichomes that defend against insects and related arthropods also provide mechanical barrier protection, but some have evolved to entrap and immobilize these pests. Trichomes can interfere with insect adhesion and locomotion on the plant surface; trichomes rich in indigestible silica and lignin are nutritionally harmful and may **lacerate** the gut following ingestion. Highly specialized glandular trichomes can secrete substances toxic or repellent to insects through contact, ingestion, or inhalation. Although not defensive in the strict sense, glandular trichomes and **extrafloral** nectaries of carnivorous plants such as sundew (*Drosera*) secrete substances that not only entrap but aid in the digestion of prey arthropods.

Specialized Glands and Anatomical Adaptations. In many plant species leaves and flower buds bear nectar-secreting glands, probably to encourage visitation by ants or to attract pollinators such as bees. In cultivated cotton, adult moths of major pest species such as the cotton bollworm and pink bollworm are also attracted to the sugar-rich nectar. A wild species of cotton that lacks these glands has been used to breed nectarless varieties resistant to pest attack.

Some grain-producing plants such as corn (*Zea*) protect their seed by completely surrounding it with long and tight wrapper leaves (the husk) that interfere with penetration through the silk channel by corn earworm larvae. In cotton the flower bud is normally enclosed by three overlapping modified leaves (bracts), creating a moist, enclosed environment favored by the female cotton boll weevil for feeding and egg laying. In contrast, cotton varieties with the Frego bract condition are resistant because the narrow, twisted bracts create an exposed, unattractive environment for the weevil. An added benefit of the Frego bract trait is heightened weevil mortality resulting from greater exposure to weather extremes and natural enemies as well as improved penetration of pesticides applied by cotton farmers.

Internal Defenses

While the bark of woody perennials serves as a line of defense to most potential herbivores, some insects such as bark and ambrosia beetles can readily penetrate this barrier; their larvae feed just under the bark within the phloem tissue producing a distinctive pattern of tunnels often diagnostic for the species, for example, Dutch elm beetle. Feeding tunnels interfere with the normal transport of nutrients; disease pathogens introduced by the initial entry of the adult beetle further weaken the tree. Some species of conifers (*Pinus*) have evolved a form of hypersensitive response to bark beetle attack by increasing their production of oleoresin, effectively drowning or entrapping the insects within their brood chambers. Resin of resistant conifers is also characterized by high viscosity and rapid crystallization that further enhances its entrapping ability.

Another form of internal defense involves accelerated growth or replacement of damaged tissues to physically crush the invading pest (as in the case of cotton varieties resistant to the pink bollworm), or to restrict the passage of the invader through plant tissue, as occurs with galls produced by some plants in response to the entry of insects and mites.

Tissue strength and toughness are important internal defenses against the wheat stem sawfly, a significant pest of wheat (*Triticum*) in North Amer-

The protective star-patterned spines on the organ pipe cactus.

lacerate cut

extrafloral outside the flower

Tracks of a pine bark beetle in a cut log. While the bark of woody perennials serves as a line of defense to most potential herbivores, bark beetles can readily penetrate this barrier.

impede slow down or inhibit

abrasive tending to wear away through contact

ica. Larvae feed within the semihollow stems of the wheat plant creating tunnels that cause the stem to break or lodge, effectively reducing grain production. Some species of wild wheat have solid stems that **impede** the feeding and tunneling of sawfly larvae. This characteristic has been bred into modern wheat varieties to provide resistance to the sawfly. Other examples of plant breeders using wild relatives of crop plants to create barriers against tunneling insects by increasing the stiffness or toughness of stems include sugarcane (*Saccharum*) resistant to the sugarcane borer, zucchini squash (*Curcubita*) resistant to the squash vine borer, and rice (*Oryza*) resistant to the rice stem borer. In the case of rice, stems of resistant varieties have high levels of **abrasive** silica that causes accelerated wear of insect mouthparts, reducing feeding efficiency and limiting the number and length of tunnels within the stem. SEE ALSO CACTI; COTTON; DEFENSES, CHEMICAL; DUTCH ELM DISEASE; INTERACTIONS, PLANT-INSECT; INTERACTIONS, PLANT-VERTEBRATE; TRICHOMES.

Ward M. Tingey

Bibliography

Norris, Dale M., and Marcos Kogan. "Biochemical and Morphological Bases of Resistance." In *Breeding Plants Resistant to Insects,* eds. Fowden G. Maxwell and Peter R. Jennings. New York: John Wiley & Sons, 1980.

Tingey, Ward M., and John C. Steffens. "The Environmental Control of Insects Using Host Plant Resistance." In *Handbook of Pest Management in Agriculture,* 2nd ed., Vol. 1, ed. David Pimentel. Boca Raton, FL: CRC Press, 1991.

Deforestation

Deforestation occurs when the trees in a forested area are cut or destroyed faster than they can replace themselves. When too many trees are cut or destroyed, a very important element is taken from nature, making it difficult for the forest **ecosystem** to maintain a healthy balance in its natural cycle. The imbalance of the natural forest cycle threatens the humans, plants, and animals that depend on the forest for food, shelter, and protection. The loss of trees also causes negative effects on the natural cycles that affect water, soil, atmosphere, and weather.

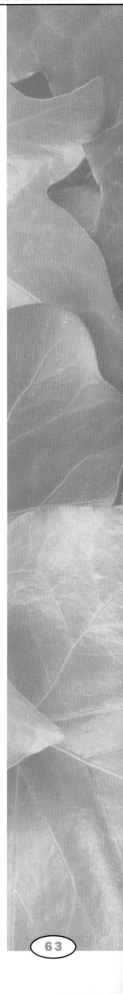

ecosystem an ecological community together with its environment

Why Does Deforestation Occur?

Deforestation can be a natural or manmade process. Natural deforestation is caused by changes in weather patterns during glacial periods, fires started by lightning, windstorms, floods, and volcanic eruptions. Forests often recover from natural deforestation.

Deforestation caused by humans often results in permanent deforestation. Even when humans were living as small bands of hunters and gatherers they were deforesting areas for hunting animals or to practice **swidden agriculture**, planting areas they had cleared and moving on after the soil was spent. Over time, population levels grew and areas of permanent agriculture were established, around which civilizations began to grow. These civilizations began intensely farming fields to meet the growing demand for food. As civilizations expanded, more land had to be cleared for fields and forests had to be cut to meet the demand for wood products. The stress on forested areas grew as pressure was exerted from both swidden and permanent agriculture. These stresses intensified in times of conflict as people were forced to use more marginal areas or to overcut forests to meet their needs.

swidden agriculture the practice of farming an area until the soil has been depleted and then moving on

The Industrial Revolution and the technology that came with it has allowed the world population to grow at an exponential rate and has helped bring about a different lifestyle, one based on consumerism and sustained economic growth. The end result is that the last remaining areas that still have extensive forest cover, especially tropical forests, are being cut to satisfy unsustainable human consumption patterns and economic growth models. At the turn of the twenty-first century, more than one-half of the forests that once covered the globe were gone, with much of the cutting occurring over the last decades of the twentieth century.

Effects of Deforestation

The effects of deforestation can be both local and global. In the local forest ecosystem, trees, water, soil, plants, and animals are all dependent on one another to keep healthy. When trees are cut this natural balance is upset and the important functions that trees perform such as holding the soil in place, protecting groundwater, and providing food and shelter for plants and animals cannot take place. Overcutting forests and the disruption of the forest ecosystem are causing erosion of soil, the drop in **water tables**, loss of biodiversity as plant and animal species become extinct, loss of soil fertility, and the silting up of many water bodies. When the process continues for a long period of time or over a large area there can be total environmental collapse. Parts of the world that are now desert, such as Syria, Iraq, and Lebanon, were once covered with healthy forests.

water table level of water in the soil

Deforestation, slumping, and soil erosion in Papua New Guinea's Star Mountains caused by a combination of mining and heavy tropical rainfall.

hydrological cycle movement of water through the biosphere

transpiration movement of water from soil to atmosphere through a plant

precipitation rainfall

desertification degradation or dry lands, reducing productivity

Globally the effects of deforestation are more difficult to see. Forests play an important part in the greater natural cycles that make and affect the weather and that clean the air in our atmosphere. They keep the **hydrological cycle** healthy by putting water back into the atmosphere through **transpiration**, making clouds and rain. They also capture carbon dioxide produced by the burning of fossil fuels from the atmosphere, replacing it with oxygen and thus reducing the risk of global warming. If too many forests are cut these important functions cannot be carried out. The result could be less rain, higher temperatures, and more severe weather patterns in many regions of the world.

Local and global effects of deforestation are beginning to have devastating consequences. Some areas in West Africa, for example, are already feeling the effects of lost **precipitation**, higher temperatures, and increased **desertification**. Other areas, like Venezuela, have experienced devastating floods due to treeless slopes being unable to catch the rain from heavy storms, sending it rushing into valleys. All of these problems impact the environment, but they also take a heavy toll on humans.

Alternative Strategies to Deforestation

There are several things that can be done to decrease deforestation and to offset its negative effects. Many communities are trying to reduce the

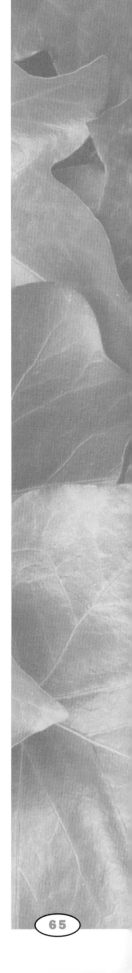

burden placed on forests by instituting recycling programs and by using alternative materials like plastics in place of wood. In business, companies have begun to use wood products that come only from certified renewable forests that are carefully managed to ensure that they are cut in a sustainable way. Alternative methods of agriculture, such as agroforestry and **permaculture**, promote the use of trees and the diversification of crops to reduce the stress placed on forests by large-scale agriculture. Protecting forests by creating parks and reserves is another strategy to keep forest resources intact. For those areas that are already devastated, great efforts are being made to replant once-forested lands with native species.

Other efforts are aimed at changing our ideas about the value of forests. Economists are now trying to calculate the true value of the forest as an ecosystem and the benefits it gives as a whole, not only the value of cut logs. This reevaluation will help us make more informed choices about how we use forest land. All of these efforts have helped reduce the burden on the forests, but cutting continues unsustainably. Without the cooperation of all humans to create alternative strategies to deforestation, it will continue with terrible results for the health of our planet. SEE ALSO BIOME; CONIFEROUS FORESTS; DECIDUOUS FORESTS; DESERTIFICATION; ECOSYSTEM; FORESTRY; HUMAN IMPACTS; RAIN FORESTS.

Thomas Minney

Bibliography

Bryant, D., D. Nielsen, and L. Tangley. *The Last Frontier Forests: Ecosystems and Economics on the Edge.* Washington, DC: World Resources Institute, 1997.

Eisenberg, E. *The Ecology of Eden.* New York: Vintage Books, 1998.

Global Forest Watch. *Forests of the World.* [Online] Available at http://www.globalforestwatch.org.

Hodge, I. *Environmental Economics: Individual Incentives and Public Choices.* London: MacMillan Press Ltd., 1995.

New Forests Project. [Online] Available at http://www.newforestsproject.com.

Ponting, C. *A Green History of the World: The Environment and the Collapse of the Great Civilizations.* New York: Penguin Books, 1991.

Timberlake, L. *Only One Earth.* New York: Sterling Publishing Company, Inc., 1987.

Dendrochronology

Trees and other woody plants grow by covering themselves with a new layer of tissue every year. When seen in a horizontal section, such wood layers appear as concentric tree rings, familiar to anyone who has looked at a tree stump. Because tree growth is influenced by the environment, tree rings are then natural archives of past environmental conditions. For instance, trees grow less when climate conditions are less favorable, producing narrower rings. The study of past changes recorded by wood growth is called dendrochronology.

Besides determining tree age, dendrochronological information has been used in four major fields of scientific research:

- reconstruction of climatic factors that control average wood growth from year to year (such as **precipitation**, temperature, air pressure, drought severity, sunshine)

permaculture agricultural practices that avoid plowing and replanting (from "permanent agriculture")

precipitation rainfall

Southern yellow pine tree rings, natural archives of past environmental conditions.

- dating of abrupt events that leave permanent scars in the wood (fire, volcanic eruptions, earthquakes, insect defoliations, and hurricanes, for example)

- dating of archaeological wood (such as the pueblos of the American Southwest, churches, bridges, and paintings in Europe)

- the calibration of the radiocarbon time scale over the Holocene epoch, covering the last ten thousand years.

The application of tree-ring dating to archaeology is indeed closely linked to the development of dendrochronology as a modern science, a process that began in the early 1900s at the University of Arizona under the direction of Andrew Ellicott Douglass, an astronomer who first established and demonstrated the principles of tree-ring dating.

Most tree-ring samples consist of pencil-shaped cores drilled from the lower stem, allowing an estimate of wood growth without cutting the tree down. So-called increment borers used for coring allow for nondestructive sampling because they leave only a 5 millimeter-wide hole, and such small injury can be readily managed by a healthy tree. (As an analogy, extracting an increment core is likely to affect a mature tree's vigor as much as drawing a blood sample is likely to affect an adult animal's health.)

Dating and Cross-Dating

Tree-ring dating is the assignment of calendar years to each wood growth ring. This requires more than simply counting visible rings, because not every growth layer is always present or clearly noticeable, especially in very old trees. When only one or two trunk **radii** are available per tree, the chance of dating errors is greater than when examining entire cross-sections. To ensure dating accuracy, ring patterns from many different trees of the same species and location are matched with one another. This allows the creation of a master chronology for this location. This cross-dating exercise, which is similar in principle to matching fingerprints or deoxyribonucleic acid (DNA) sequences, is first done visually under a binocular microscope using 10 to 30 power magnification. Once a tree-ring sample has been properly **surfaced**, that magnification is high enough to distinguish individual wood cells. After measuring the thickness of each ring, cross-dating can be verified using specialized numerical procedures. While numerical cross-dating is based on alternating patterns of narrow and wide rings, visual cross-dating can incorporate other anatomical elements as well, such as the proportion and color of earlywood and latewood within individual rings.

Cross-dating has found other important applications in dendrochronology. Once a (master) tree-ring chronology is established, a wood sample from the same species and area can be accurately dated by matching its ring-width patterns against the master. This procedure is commonly used in archaeological and historical investigations to date wood material, **artifacts**, and structures. In addition, as wood samples from older living trees are cross-matched against those from historic and prehistoric times, the length of the master chronology can also be extended farther back in time, a process that has allowed the development of tree-ring chronologies for the last ten thousand years, over the entire Holocene epoch.

The final tree-ring chronology is derived from the combination of all tree-ring samples into a single, average time series, which summarizes short- and long-term historical patterns for that species and site. Tree growth varies on multiple time scales, from interannual to interdecadal, and various numerical methods have been proposed to preserve (or discard) this information in the final tree-ring chronology. Such methods are grouped under the term *standardization* in the dendrochronological literature, and they are intended to minimize changes in growth rate that are not common to all trees. For climatological reconstruction, the final tree-ring chronology is statistically calibrated against instrumental records of climate, such as precipitation and temperature, to identify the main climatic signals present in the tree-ring record. The relationship between tree growth and climate is then extrapolated back into the past, and climatic changes are estimated from the tree-ring chronology itself. Because of the long life of many tree species, dendrochronological records tell of climate conditions occurring each year over hundreds, sometime thousands, of years, whereas instrumental weather records are commonly limited to the last decades, and seldom exceed one hundred years.

Tree-ring chronologies have been developed from a number of species in all continents where trees exist. In the western United States, most tree-ring records are derived from conifers, because they are very common, reach

radii distance across, especially across a circle (singular = radius)

surfaced smoothed for examination

artifacts pots, tools, or other cultural objects

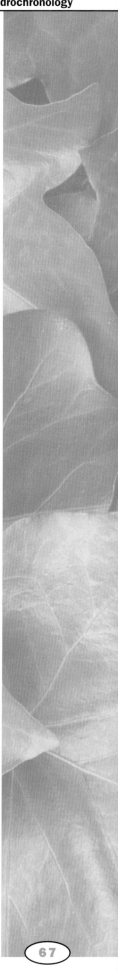

old ages, and, as softwoods, they are easier to sample than hardwoods. However, not all trees are equally suitable for dendrochronological studies. In temperate, high-latitude and high-elevation climates, wood growth is usually constrained to the warm season, and tree rings are easily recognizable. Cross-dating is easier when year-to-year variability of tree growth is higher, because this causes a greater number and degree of pattern differences in tree-ring series. When ring widths are less variable, common, climatically influenced patterns are more difficult to discern. Site conditions are therefore very important in dendrochronological studies because they affect tree-ring variability, which is an expression of the sensitivity of tree growth to climate. Other factors being the same, trees growing in difficult environments—on steep, rocky slopes, at the latitudinal or altitudinal edge of their natural range—attain greater age, grow more slowly, and show higher year-to-year changes than trees of the same species found in more **mesic** sites, on flat terrain, and/or deeper soils.

mesic of medium wetness

To date, tree-ring studies of tropical trees have been limited by the fact that wood growth layers are not visually identifiable, especially in species found at low elevations. Anatomical features and the lack of pronounced seasons allow wood growth in tropical lowlands to occur throughout or erratically during the year, making the identification of synchronous growth patterns among trees a difficult task. Even outside the tropics it is not always possible to reliably cross-date tree-ring patterns among individuals of the same species and site. A notable example is the world's tallest tree, the California coast redwood (*Sequoia sempervirens*), whose rings are not uniform around the stem. This causes different radii from the same tree to include a widely different number of rings, which prevents the development of a reliable tree-ring chronology. Such ring discontinuities are species specific and apparently unrelated to climate. SEE ALSO FORESTRY; PALYNOLOGY; RECORD-HOLDING PLANTS; TREES; WOOD ANATOMY.

Franco Biondi

Bibliography

Baillie, M. G. L. *Tree-ring Dating and Archaeology.* Chicago: University of Chicago Press, 1982.

Fritts, Harold C. *Tree Rings and Climate.* New York: Academic Press, 1976.

Nash, Stephen E. *Time, Trees, and Prehistory: Tree-ring Dating and the Development of North American Archaeology, 1914–1950.* Salt Lake City: University of Utah Press, 1999.

Schweingruber, Fritz H. *Tree Rings: Basics and Applications of Dendrochronology.* Boston: D. Reidel Publishing Co., 1988.

Stokes, Marvin A., and Terah L. Smiley. *An Introduction to Tree-ring Dating.* Tucson, AZ: University of Arizona Press, 1996.

de Saussure, Nicolas-Théodore

Swiss Botanist
1767–1845

physiology the biochemical processes carried out by an organism

Nicolas-Théodore de Saussure was one of the early founders of plant **physiology**. He introduced new and rigorous experimental methods to the study of plants, and his work helped to improve the science of botany.

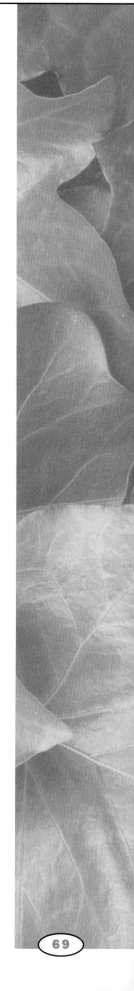

De Saussure was born in Geneva, Switzerland, on October 14, 1767. His father, Horace-Bénédict de Saussure (1740–1799), was also a scientist and he supervised his son's early experiments. Nicolas-Théodore accompanied his father on many expeditions to the tops of mountains to study the composition and density of air, and he made many weather and air measurements on these trips with his father in the Alps. This research led to his appointment as a professor of mineralogy and geology at the Geneva Academy.

At this time de Saussure had become interested in plant physiology, particularly in the way that plants use air. In 1804 he published his most famous work, *Recherches chimiques sur la végétation.* This collection of classic research papers introduced a new scientific method to the study of botany. His experiments were very carefully designed to address specific questions rather than to just make a series of observations. He also carefully controlled the experiments and repeated them to make sure his results were accurate. His detailed method of experimenting became the foundation for current plant science.

With this new scientific approach, de Saussure was able to demonstrate conclusively what others had long suspected. His first experiments concerned photosynthesis and respiration in plants. In one experiment, he enclosed plants in glass containers and used these containers to control the level of carbon dioxide available to the plants. After placing the plants in the light for a few hours, he measured changes in air composition in the containers and carbon accumulation in the plants. In this way, he showed that the plants had taken up the carbon dioxide and given off oxygen. In addition, he showed that carbon dioxide came from the air, not from water, as some other scientists believed. This and other similar experiments using different concentrations of oxygen and carbon dioxide and different light conditions helped him understand the basis of photosynthesis: that plants in the light are able to fix carbon in their tissues while giving off oxygen. He also correctly believed that plants used oxygen to respire in the same way as animals. He had first noted this need for oxygen in germinating seeds and plants grown in the dark. These beginning studies of respiration and photosynthesis and his later studies of plant nutrition became part of the new scientific study of plant physiology.

After this initial work, de Saussure went on to study the content of fruits and seeds and to use the ash of burned plants to examine other nutrients and minerals that plants required. Among other discoveries, he showed that plants take up nutrients from the soil selectively. His life work became a large survey of plant nutrition and, at the same time, it established a higher standard of plant scientific method. By the time de Saussure died in Geneva on April 18, 1845, he had received many honors and had become a member of many European scientific societies. SEE ALSO ATMOSPHERE AND PLANTS; HALES, STEPHEN; PHOTOSYNTHESIS, CARBON FIXATION AND; PHYSIOLOGIST; PHYSIOLOGY, HISTORY OF.

Jessica P. Penney

Bibliography

Morton, A. G. *History of Botanical Science.* New York: Academic Press, 1981.

Sachs, Julius von. *History of Botany,* tr. Henry E. F. Garnsey. New York: Russel and Russel, 1967.

sterile unable to support life

mitigation reduction of amount or effect

encroachment moving in on

Desertification

Human survival and prosperity are dependent ultimately on the productivity of the lands on which populations reside. In many parts of the world, however, previously productive lands have become less fertile or completely **sterile**, failing to meet the basic needs of local populations. Desertification has widely been recognized as one of the several major global environmental problems since the 1970s. According to the United Nations Environmental Programme, drylands that are susceptible to desertification account for more than one-third of the world land area and support more than 20 percent of the global human population. As the rapid growth of the human population continues, demands for resources from these fragile environments increase as well. Therefore, understanding the scope, causes, and mechanisms of desertification and developing sound and effective management and **mitigation** plans are extremely important for maintaining the ecological, socioeconomic, and political stability of both the dryland areas and the entire world.

Degradation and Loss of Productivity

The term *desertification* was first used by two French ecologists: L. Lavauden in 1927 and A. Aubreville in 1949, who then eyewitnessed the land degradation occurring in north and west Africa. Since then, more than one hundred definitions have appeared in the English literature. *Desertification* sometimes has been used interchangeably with *desertization*, which refers to desert **encroachment** into previously nondesert areas driven by human activities. A widely used definition for desertification is land degradation in arid, semiarid, and dry subhumid regions due to human activities and climate variations, which may lead to the permanent loss of land productivity. This definition was accepted at the United Nations Conference on Desertification in 1977, and later adopted by the Earth Summit, the United Nations Conference on Environment and Development in 1992, and the Intergovernmental Convention to Combat Desertification in 1994.

WORLD DISTRIBUTION OF DRYLANDS, 1996

Bioclimatic Zones	Extent (in thousands of square kilometers)	Percentage of World Land Area	P/PET Ratio*
Dry-subhumid land	12,947	9.9	0.45–0.65
Semiarid land	23,053	17.7	0.20–0.45
Arid land	15,692	12.1	0.05–0.20
Total drylands susceptible to desertification	51,692	39.7	
Hyperarid land (extremely harsh environment and thus not susceptible to desertification)	9,781	7.5	< 0.05
Total world dryland area	61,473	47.2	

* P is the mean annual precipitation, and PET is the mean annual potential evapotranspiration, which is a combined term for water lost as vapor from soil surface (evaporation) and from the surface of plants mainly via stomata (transpiration). P/PET ratio is also called aridity index (I) and is often used to classify bioclimatic zones. Smaller values of the ratio correspond to drier areas.

SOURCE: Data from United Nations Environmental Programme, 1992; adapted from H. N. Le Houérou, "Climate Change, Drought, and Desertification," *Journal of Arid Environments* 34 (1996): 133–85.

DESERTIFICATION EXTENT AND SEVERITY IN WORLD REGIONS, 1995

Region	Total Dryland Area (in thousands of square kilometers)	Desertified Area (in thousands kilometers)		
		Light and Moderate	Strong and Extreme	Total Area of Desertified Land
Asia	16,718	3,267	437	3,704
Africa	12,860	2,453	740	3,193
Europe	2,997	946	49	995
Australasia	6,633	860	16	876
North America	7,324	722	71	793
South America	5,160	728	63	791
Total	51,692	8,976	1,376	10,352

SOURCE: Data from D. S. G. Thomas, "Desertification: Causes and Processes." In *Encyclopedia of Environmental Biology*, Vol. 1, edited by W. A. Nierenberg (San Diego: Academic Press, 1995), 463–73.

Desertification may be viewed as the worst form of land degradation, the general process of declining soil fertility, impairing **ecosystem** structure and function, decreasing biodiversity, and diminishing economic viability. After an ecosystem is severely desertified, its full recovery may not be achieved even during relatively moist conditions without intensive rehabilitation efforts. Natural deserts, without human disturbances, are healthy and relatively stable ecosystems that support a variety of life forms—sometimes spectacular—like the saguaro in the Sonoran Desert. The simplistic view that desertification is a process that transforms nondesert lands into desert-like lands may thus be too superficial and misleading. Also, deserts do emerge independent of human activities, and the term *aridization* refers to this natural development of deserts through evolution of drier climates, which takes place much more slowly than desertification.

ecosystem an ecological community together with its environment

Causes of Desertification

Human abuses of the land (e.g., overcultivation, overgrazing, and **urbanization**) are the primary causes for desertification, whereas adverse climate variations (e.g., droughts) may accelerate or trigger the process. By drastically reducing or destroying vegetation cover and soil fertility, human activities can result in desertification without drought, but not vice versa. For example, overgrazing reduces both productivity and biodiversity of grasslands and can lead to a grassland-to-shrub land transition. Overcultivation completely destroys natural vegetation and can eventually exhaust soil resources. In both cases, human activities can transform drylands into unproductive wastelands through the processes of soil erosion (by wind and water), **salinization**, and **alkalinization**.

urbanization increase in size or number of cities

Desertification often is a result of the interactions between human and climate factors. Since human actions are tied to many social, economic, political, and environmental processes, the relative importance of major causes for desertification varies from one region to another. For example, the most dominant cause for desertification in China is overcultivation, but in north Africa and the Near East it is overgrazing. Besides droughts, global climate change may also affect desertification. Studies have suggested that global warming may reduce soil moisture over large areas of semiarid grasslands

salinization increase in salt content

alkalinization increase in basicity or reduction in acidity

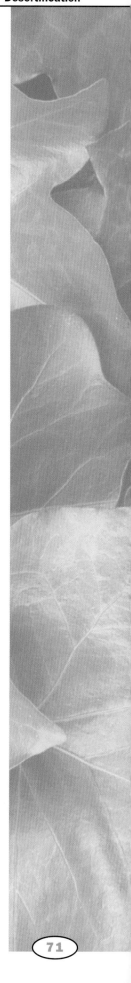

CAUSES OF DESERTIFICATION IN WORLD REGIONS, 1996

Regions or Countries	Overcultivation	Overstocking	Fuelwood Collection	Salinization	Urbanization	Other
Northwest China	45*	16	18	2	3	14
North Africa and Near East	50	26	21	2	1	–
Sahel and East Africa	25	65	10	–	–	–
Middle Asia	10	62	–	9	10	9
United States	22	73	–	5	N/A	–
Australia	20	75	–	2	1	–

* The numbers are in percentage of the total desertified area in the corresponding region.

SOURCE: Data from H. N. Le Houérou, "Climate Change, Drought, and Desertification," *Journal of Arid Enviroments* 34 (1996): 133–85.

and thus increase the extent of desertified lands in North America and Asia. The possible effects of climate change on desertification, however, seem much smaller than the impact of land use activities by humans.

Dry-subhumid, semiarid, arid, and hyperarid areas together form the world drylands, covering as much as 47 percent of the total land area. Dry forest, grassland, and shrub land ecosystems are found in drylands except in hyperarid land (the true desert), which experiences extreme dry conditions and usually seems lifeless (e.g., central Sahara and the Namib Desert of Africa, the Hizad on the Arabian Peninsula, the Taklimakan and Turpan Depressions in central Asia, and Death Valley in the United States). Desertification occurs primarily in all drylands except hyperarid lands because climatic and ecological conditions make them more susceptible to land degradation than more humid regions. It is hard for hyperarid lands to become more desertlike, and thus they are usually excluded from the consideration of desertification.

Desertification has been occurring at an astonishing rate over six continents. Most of the desertified lands are found in Asia and Africa, while the problem also has become significant in Europe, Australasia, North America, and South America. Approximately 25 percent of the irrigated land (3 percent of the drylands), 50 percent of the rain-fed cropland (9 percent of the drylands), and 75 percent of the rangeland (88 percent of the drylands) have been desertified to different degrees. Although the accuracy of estimating the exact extent and rate of desertification needs to be improved with the aid of advanced technologies such as satellite remote sensing and geographic information systems (computer systems for storing, retrieving, and manipulating spatial or geographic data), there is little doubt that extensive areas of the world's drylands have increasingly experienced some form of chronic land degradation since the early 1900s.

Desertification has affected more than one hundred countries and resulted in profound ecological, social, and economic consequences throughout the world. Combating desertification is an urgent and grand challenge facing humanity today. Global efforts and local solutions are both needed. Preventive and rehabilitation measures must be undertaken simultaneously based on scientific findings and socioeconomic considerations. SEE ALSO DESERTS; GLOBAL WARMING; HUMAN IMPACTS.

Jianguo Wu

Bibliography

Dregne, H. E., ed. *Degradation and Restoration of Arid Lands.* Lubbock, TX: International Center for Arid and Semiarid Land Studies, Texas Tech University, 1992.

———. "Desertification: Challenges Ahead." *Annals of Arid Zone* 35, no. 4 (1996): 305–11.

Schlesinger, W. H., et al. "Science and the Desertification Debate." *Journal of Arid Environments* 37 (1997): 599–608.

United Nations Environmental Programme. *World Atlas of Desertification.* London: Arnold, 1992.

Deserts

Desert **ecosystems** are characterized by an extremely arid, arid, or semiarid climate, low relative humidity, high air and soil temperatures, strong winds, high solar radiation, low **precipitation** levels, extended drought periods, soils low in organic matter, low net primary productivity, and a spatially patchy distribution of vegetation and soil resources. In them, water is the predominant controlling factor for most biological processes; precipitation is highly variable and occurs as infrequent and discrete events throughout the year; and precipitation events are highly unpredictable in both space and time. Desert ecosystems may be classified into three groups based on annual precipitation: extremely arid (less than 60 millimeters), arid (60 to 250 millimeters), and semiarid (250 to 500 millimeters). The plant communities of arid lands expand and contract in accordance with alternating wet and dry periods as well as with **anthropogenic** activities that contribute to desertification (also known as land degradation). While arid ecosystems occur on all continents in both hot and cold environments, this article will not focus on polar deserts.

Distribution of Deserts Worldwide

Earth's major deserts lie within the tropics of Cancer and Capricorn where stable, high atmospheric pressure creates an arid climate at or near latitudes 30°N and 30°S. Deserts are generally located in the interior of large continents. Continental deserts are separated from ocean moisture by large distances or **topographic** barriers, such as large mountain ranges, which create a rainshadow. Deserts may also be situated on the west coast of large continents adjacent to cold ocean currents, which draw moisture away from the land. Subtropical deserts, such as the Mojave Desert of California, lie within the latitudes of 30°N and 30°S. Cool coastal deserts, including the Peruvian Atacama Desert, occur where cold offshore currents generate high atmospheric pressure and large masses of dry air, which create arid conditions upon their descent. Rainshadow deserts, including the Great Basin Desert in the United States or the Gobi Desert in Mongolia, occur where a topographical barrier such as a mountain range interrupts the flow of moist oceanic air. As moisture-laden air masses travel inland, they are deflected upward on the windward side of a mountain range, lose their moisture, and descend as dry air masses on the leeward side of the mountains. Continental interior deserts, such as the Great Sandy Desert in Australia, occur far from marine moisture.

ecosystem an ecological community together with its environment

precipitation rainfall

anthropogenic human-made

topographic related to the shape or contours of the land

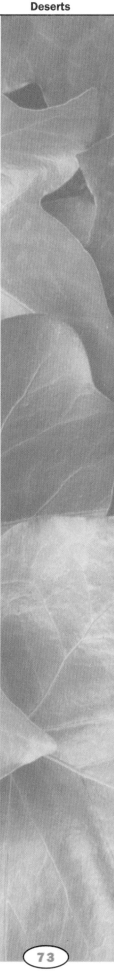

A desert plant community in Guadalupe Mountains National Park in Texas.

Plants in the Desert Environment

In order to understand the ways in which plants have adapted to arid lands, it is essential to consider the physical environment. Of all the abiotic constraints imposed on plant activity—high air temperatures, extremely high soil temperatures, high winds, intense solar radiation, and limited moisture—high temperatures and limited water are the two factors that severely limit plant growth. Summer air temperatures in the Sonoran Desert in Arizona may reach 40°C during the day but drop to 15°C at night. Soil temperatures may reach 80°C or higher. High temperatures generally are accompanied by strong winds in coastal deserts, such as the Atacama in South America and the Namib in Africa, as well as in continental deserts, including the Chihuahuan and Sonoran in the United States. As well as producing spectacular dust storms and dust devils (small whirlwinds containing sand or dust), wind also **abrades** and **desiccates** desert plants.

Water is the single-most limiting factor to the growth and productivity of desert vegetation. The highly sporadic nature of desert rainfall creates a pulse-reserve system of water and nutrient availability that influences many biological processes, especially plant productivity. In the Chihuahuan Desert of New Mexico, gentle winter rainfall penetrates deep into the soil profile and provides most of the moisture for the growth of perennial

abrade wear away through contact

desiccate dry out

shrubs, such as creosote bush and mesquite. In contrast, the high-intensity, brief summer thunderstorms provide minimal water for plant growth because most of the water runs off of the soil surface. Many plant species take advantage of rainfall immediately and grow rapidly following precipitation events, then slow their growth when soils dry and moisture once again becomes limiting.

Second only to moisture, the availability of soil nutrients, primarily nitrogen and phosphorus, limits plant productivity in deserts. Nitrogen is the key limiting nutrient in North American deserts, phosphorus is most limiting in Australian deserts, while nitrogen, phosphorus, and potassium are limiting in sand dune communities in Africa's Namib Desert. Soil nutrients and organic matter tend to be concentrated in the upper 2 to 5 centimeters of soil with the greatest amounts underneath the canopies of individual desert shrubs in "islands of fertility." These resource islands harbor greater concentrations of water, soil nutrients, and microorganisms than adjacent soils.

Certain plant species, such as creosote bush, are often referred to as nurse plants. Nurse plants effectively reduce high-incident solar radiation and high temperatures under their canopies and create ideal sites for seed germination and seedling growth. The concentration of limiting resources in islands of fertility or under nurse plants generates a spatially patchy distribution of vegetation across the desert. Competition for water maintains this spacing of plants. While this phenomenon has been most studied in U.S. deserts, it occurs in arid lands worldwide.

Desert Soils

Hot deserts exhibit generally similar soil types. Immature and alkaline with weakly developed **soil horizons**, desert soils are dry most of the year, and poor in soil organic matter, nitrogen, and phosphorus, but are rich in inorganic ions, carbonate, and gypsum. The main soil orders of hot deserts are Entisols, soils without well-defined layers that are formed from recently exposed rock, and Aridisols. Aridisols, exclusive to arid regions, contain two dominant suborders: Orthids and Argids. Orthids are young calcareous and **gypsipherous** soils with a caliche (or calcium carbonate hardpan) within 1 meter of the soil surface. The thickness of the caliche layer has been correlated with the size of creosote bush shrubs in Arizona's Sonoran Desert: the thicker the layer, the smaller the shrubs. Argids are older soils and lack the carbonate hardpan layer, but are clay-rich and may be good agricultural soils when water is available.

Plant Adaptations to the Desert Environment

Desert plant species show various physical, physiological, and phenological (timing of growth and reproduction) characters that enable them to survive and grow in arid, nutrient-limited environments. Some plants, such as summer and winter desert **ephemerals**, restrict all growth and flowering to periods when water is available. They are able to withstand droughts and high water stress because their underground rhizomes or bulbs remain **dormant** during the dry season. In extreme droughts, desert ephemerals may remain completely dormant, eliminate reproduction, or limit growth to the vegetative phase. Other species, such as the California poppy and other

---

MAJOR DESERTS OF THE WORLD

North America: Great Basin, Sonoran, Mojave, Baja California, Chihuahuan

South America: Patagonian, Puna, Monte, Chaco, Espinal, Peruvian-Chilean, Atacama

Asia: Gobi, Takla Makan, Iranian, Thar, Syrian, Arabian, Sinai, Negev

Africa: Sahara, Sahel, Somalian, Namib, Karoo, Kalahari, Madagascar

Australia: Great Sandy, Gibson, Great Victoria, Arunta, Stuart

---

soil horizon distinct layers of soil

gypsipherous containing the mineral gypsum

ephemerals plants that bloom and die back within a short period

dormant inactive, not growing

Sand dunes in the Gobi
Desert of Mongolia.

biomass the dry weight
of a living organism

morphology shape and
form

desert annuals, complete their entire life cycle during the rainy season. Their long-lived seeds germinate only under suitable environmental conditions. As a result, they respond to the pulse-reserve system of resource availability, showing high rates of primary production in favorable years and minimal, or no production, in drought years. Ephemerals and annuals, while showy, produce minimal **biomass**.

In deserts worldwide, perennial shrubs and subshrubs, such as the creosote bush and jojoba, produce most of the desert plant biomass. These species limit water loss and reduce heat loads at the leaf surface by limiting the surface area to many small single, dissected, or compound leaves covered with a waxy cuticle or leaf hairs. Most shrubs have canopies with a compact globe or inverted cone shape. This **morphology** allows water to funnel directly to the plant roots and reduces the amount of surface area that is exposed to sunlight. Perennials have a large root-to-shoot ratio, and most roots are distributed in the soil in one of two ways. The roots may be confined to the upper meter of the soil profile and fan out horizontally from the base of the shrub, enabling shrubs access to even the slightest rainfall. Alternatively, the roots may extend deep into the soil profile—up to 12 meters with mesquite—and allow plants to obtain water that is stored at these depths. As with other desert plants, perennials may also limit or suppress flowering and fruiting in years of extreme drought.

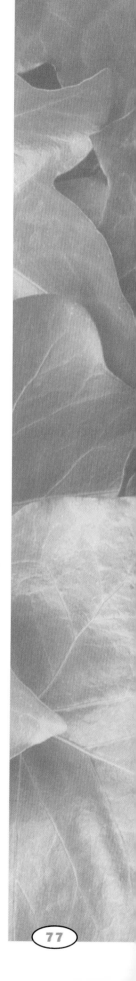

Perennials are able to remain metabolically active at very low soil- and plant-water potentials, high internal water deficits, and high temperatures. They have sensitive regulation of leaf **stomata** as a function of internal and external conditions, including water stress, temperature, atmospheric humidity, and light intensity. Most shrub species acquire carbon throughout the C_3 photosynthetic pathway, despite the fact that the alternative C_4 pathway is thought to increase the amount of carbon gain per unit of water used (water-use efficiency [WUE]). The only desert perennials that have the C_4 pathway are the halophytic (salt-tolerant) species, such as tamarisk, short-lived summer active perennials, and most grasses.

Cacti, common to deserts, show unique adaptations to the desert environment. They have shallow, horizontally extended root systems, an upright, ribbed trunk that reduces the midday heat and solar radiation load and water storage within their trunks. Saguaro cacti, located near Tucson, Arizona, expand and contract like an accordion depending on the moisture conditions. In wet years the cacti are plump and green, but in dry years they are slim and yellow-green in color. Because cacti lack typical broad leaves, the overall green coloring derives from the photosynthetic trunk. Over evolutionary time, cactus "leaves" have been reduced to hairlike spines that reflect solar radiation or spikelike spines that protect the plant from **herbivores**. Other noncactus species, such as ocotillo and the boojum trees native to Baja California, produce photosynthetically active leaves only in wet years and limit photosynthesis to the stems when drought prevails. Cacti and other **succulent** species obtain carbon through the **crassulacean acid metabolism (CAM)** photosynthetic pathway. CAM photosynthesis allows the cacti to open their stomata only at night in order to reduce water loss. SEE ALSO CACTI; DESERTIFICATION; PHOTOSYSTHESIS, CARBON FIXATION AND.

Anne Fernald Cross

stomata pores that open to allow gas exchange and close to prevent water loss

herbivore an organism that feeds on plant parts

succulent marked by fleshy, water-holding leaves or stems

crassulacean acid metabolism a water-conserving strategy used by several types of plants

Bibliography

Caldwell, M. M., J. H. Manwaring, and S. L. Durham. "The Microscale Distribution of Neighboring Plant Roots in Fertile Soil Microsites." *Functional Ecology* 5 (1991): 765–72.

Cross, A. F., and W. H. Schlesinger. "Plant Regulation of Soil Nutrient Distribution in the Northern Chihuahuan Desert." *Plant Ecology* 145 (1999): 11–25.

Fox, G. A. "Drought and the Evolution of Flowering Time in Desert Annuals." *American Journal of Botany* 77 (1990): 1508–18.

Le Houérou, H. N. "Climate, Flora and Fauna Changes in the Sahara Over the Past 500 Million Years." *Journal of Arid Environments* 37 (1997): 619–47.

Mahall, B. E., and R. M. Callaway. "Root Communication Mechanisms and Intracommunity Distributions of Two Mojave Desert Shrubs." *Ecology* 73 (1992): 2145–51.

Martinez–Meza, E., and W. G. Whitford. "Stemflow, Throughfall, and Channelization of Stemflow by Three Chihuahuan Desert Shrubs." *Journal of Arid Environments* 32 (1996): 271–87.

McAuliffe, J. R. "Markovian Dynamics of Simple and Complex Desert Plant Communities." *American Naturalist* 131 (1988): 459–90.

Nobel, P. S. *Environmental Biology of Agaves and Cacti.* Cambridge, UK: Cambridge University Press, 1988.

Schlesinger, W. H., J. F. Reynolds, G. L. Cunningham, L. F. Huenneke, W. M. Jarrell, R. A. Virginia, and W. G. Whitford. "Biological Feedbacks in Global Desertification." *Science* 247 (1990): 1043–48.

———, J. Raikes, A. E. Hartley, and A. F. Cross. "On the Spatial Pattern of Soil Nutrients in Desert Ecosystems." *Ecology* 77 (1996): 364–74.

Dicots

The dicots (short for dicotyledons) have long been recognized as one of two major groups or classes (class Magnoliopsida) of flowering plants (division Anthophyta or Magnoliophyta), the other major group being the monocots (monocotyledons; class Liliopsida). The dicots have traditionally been distinguished from monocots by a suite of **morphological** and anatomical features, all of which are subject to exception, however. For example, as the name of the group suggests, most dicots possess two seedling leaves, or cotyledons. In addition, dicots often possess netlike leaf venation, flower parts in fours or fives (or multiples thereof), vascular bundles in the stem arranged in a ring, with the potential for true secondary growth, and a root system of primary and **adventitious** roots. Monocots, in contrast, have one cotyledon, parallel leaf venation, flower parts in threes (or multiples thereof), scattered **vascular** bundles in the stem, lack true secondary growth, and have only an adventitious root system. As traditionally defined, the dicots comprise approximately 165,000 to 180,000 species; the monocots are the smaller of the two groups, consisting of about 60,000 species. The dicots include all the familiar **angiosperm** trees and shrubs (though not the conifers) and many herbaceous groups, including magnolias, roses, oaks, walnuts, **legumes**, sunflowers, snapdragons, mints, and mustards. Most recent classification schemes, such as those of Cronquist, Takhtajan, and Thorne, have divided the dicots into six subclasses: Magnoliidae, Hamamelidae, Caryophyllidae, Rosidae, Dilleniidae, and Asteridae.

Although the monocot-dicot division has been recognized since the late nineteenth century, recent **phylogenetic** studies demonstrate clearly that this split does not accurately reflect the evolutionary history of flowering plants. That is, phylogenetic trees depicting historical relationships have re-

morphological related to shape

adventitious arising from secondary buds, forming a fibrous root system

vascular related to transport of nutrients

angiosperm a flowering plant

legumes beans and other members of the Fabaceae family

phylogenetic related to phylogeny, the evolutionary development of a species

MAJOR DICOT FAMILIES

Family	Common Name	Number of Species (approximate)
Apiaceae	Parsley or carrot family	3,000
Asteraceae	Sunflower family	25,000
Betulaceae	Birch family	170
Brassicaceae	Mustard family	3,000
Cactaceae	Cactus family	2,000
Caryophyllaceae	Carnation family	2,000
Cornaceae	Dogwood family	100
Cucurbitaceae	Pumpkin family	700
Ericaceae	Heath family	3,000
Euphorbiaceae	Spurge family	5,000
Fabaceae	Pea or legume family	17,000
Fagaceae	Beech or oak family	1,000
Lamiaceae	Mint family	3,000
Lauraceae*	Cinnamon family	2,500
Magnoliaceae*	Magnolia family	200
Nymphaeaceae*	Water lily family	90
Papaveraceae*	Poppy family	650
Piperaceae*	Black pepper family	3,000
Ranunculaceae	Buttercup family	1,800
Rosaceae	Rose family	3,500

* Indicates families of traditional dicots that are now recognized as basal angiosperms, which are ancestral to both monocots and dicots.

cently been constructed for flowering plants (based on deoxyribonucleic acid [DNA] sequence data as well as morphological, anatomical, chemical, and other non-DNA characters). These diagrammatical trees indicate clearly that while the monocots form a **clade**, all of the dicots do not form a distinct group separate from the monocots. Instead, the monocots are imbedded in a clade of early branching **lineages** of flowering plants, usually referred to as magnoliids, all of which have the characteristics of the traditional dicots. These early branches of angiosperms, including the monocots, are characterized by pollen grains that have a single aperture (or line of weakness), or by pollen types that are derived from this single-aperture form.

The majority of angiosperms form a distinct clade and are referred to as the eudicots (or true dicots). Eudicots are characterized by pollen grains that typically possess three apertures; no other morphological or anatomical structures that mark this group have been identified, although the grouping of the eudicots is strongly supported by analyses based on DNA sequence data.

Thus, there is no monocot-dicot split in the angiosperms. Whereas *monocot* remains a useful term, *dicot* does not represent a natural group of flowering plants and should be abandoned. It is more useful to refer to eudicots, which represent a well-marked clade of flowering plants, and to specific groups of ancient dicotyledonous angiosperms (basal angiosperms). In many ways this conclusion is not surprising. Botanists long theorized that the monocots were derived from an ancient group of dicots during the early diversification of the angiosperms. Phylogenetic trees of relationship derived from molecular data confirm this longstanding hypothesis and pinpoint the possible close relatives of the monocots.

The eudicots, containing approximately 75 percent of all angiosperm species, comprise several distinct lineages. The earliest branches of eudicots are the Ranunculales, which include the Ranunculaceae (buttercup family) and Papaveraceae (poppy family), as well as the Buxaceae (boxwood family) and Platanaceae (sycamore family). Most eudicots form a large clade, composed of three main branches and several smaller ones. The main branches of eudicots are the eurosids (made up of members of the traditional subclasses Rosidae, Dilleniidae, and Asteridae), the asterids (containing members of subclasses Asteridae, Dilleniidae, and Rosidae), and the Caryophyllales; there is no clade that corresponds to subclass Dilleniidae.

The first angiosperms that appear in the fossil record possess those characteristics typically assigned to the dicots, and both the monocots and eudicots evolved later. The eudicots can be identified in the fossil record by their three-grooved pollen as early as 110 million years ago. Following the origin of this group, it diversified rapidly, and by 90 to 80 million years ago many of today's prominent families of angiosperms were established and are clearly recognizable in the fossil record. SEE ALSO ANGIOSPERMS; EVOLUTION OF PLANTS; MONOCOTS; SYSTEMATICS, PLANT.

Doug Soltis and Pam Soltis

Bibliography

Cronquist, A. *An Integrated System of Classification of Flowering Plants.* New York: Columbia University Press, 1981.

Soltis, P. S., and D. E. Soltis. "Angiosperm Phylogeny Inferred from Multiple Genes as a Tool for Comparative Biology." *Nature* 402 (1999): 402-04.

clade a group of organisms composed of an ancestor and all of its descendants

lineage ancestry; the line of evolutionary descent of an organism

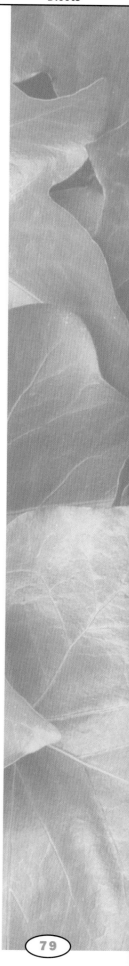

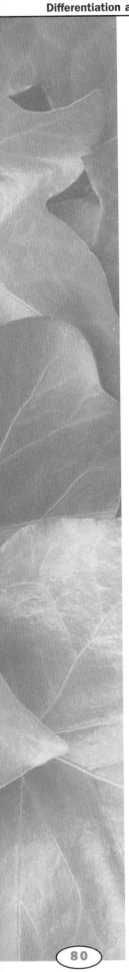

Differentiation and Development

Mitotic cell division in unicellular organisms such as bacteria or yeast produces identical sister cells that are also identical to the mother cell. But in multicellular plants, sister cells are different from each other and usually also from the mother cell that produced them. These differences result from variations of gene expression in cells that are genetically identical. (The alternative hypothesis, that differentiation depends on differences in gene content in different cell types, can be discounted because differentiated cells isolated from the plant and placed in sterile culture on suitable nutrient medium regenerate entire plants that contain all the expected cell types.) The fifty or so specialized cell types of higher plants result from the operation of three developmental processes: cell polarity, asymmetric cell divisions, and positional information.

Origin of Cell Polarity

Polarity is the condition in which opposite ends of a structure are different. In biology this can apply to a cell or a tissue or an organism. Polarity in a multicellular plant exists in the first cell, the **zygote**, with the consequence that the two sister cells produced by the first division have different developmental fates.

The best studied example is the origin of polarity in the zygote of *Fucus*, a brown alga of the marine **intertidal** zone. Eggs are released into the seawater and fertilized. Polarity is established initially by the site of sperm penetration, and in the absence of other disturbing factors the rhizoid emerges at this point. Numerous environmental gradients, however, including light, gravity, temperature, and pH, may act as final determinants of the polar axis. The zygote settles onto a **substrate**, and a rhizoidal outgrowth develops from one side of the cell. Following nuclear division, a new cell wall separates cells that have different developmental fates: a hemispherical cell that will form the **thallus**, and a rhizoidal cell that will form the holdfast.

The process of polar axis fixation involves a current of calcium ions moving into the cell at the site of future rhizoid emergence and the accumulation of calcium channels in the membrane at this site. Actin filaments then accumulate, and Golgi-derived **vesicles** containing cell wall precursors migrate through the cytoplasm and release their contents at the site of rhizoid formation. All these events precede division of the zygote into two cells, so that it is the zygote itself that becomes polarized.

In **angiosperms**, the egg is already polarized at the time of fertilization. The nucleus and most of the cytoplasmic **organelles** are located near the **apical** end of the cell and a large **vacuole** occupies much of the basal (lower) half. Division of the zygote is **transverse**, separating a small cytoplasmically rich apical cell that forms all or most of the embryo from a large vacuolated basal cell that forms the extraembryonic suspensor.

It has been proposed that auxin establishes the polar axis in angiosperm embryos, as it does in *Fucus* zygotes. Movement of **auxin** through plant cells and tissues is polar from apex to base. This one-way transport is thought to depend on differential or polarized localization of membrane-associated auxin binding and transport proteins.

zygote the egg immediately after it has been fertilized; the one-cell stage of a new individual

intertidal between the lines of high and low tide

substrate the physical structure to which an organism attaches

thallus simple, flattened, nonleafy plant body

vesicle a membrane-bound cell structure with specialized contents

angiosperm a flowering plant

organelle a membrane-bound structure within a cell

apical at the tip

vacuole the large fluid-filled sac that occupies most of the space in a plant cell. Use for storage and maintaining internal pressure

transverse across, or side to side

auxin a plant hormone

In the above examples, the result of cell division is the production of two cells that are visibly different and have different developmental fates. Such divisions are said to be asymmetric.

Asymmetric Cell Divisions

Asymmetric cell divisions are those in which there is unequal partitioning of cell components to the daughter cells. Examples are unequal distribution of cytoplasmic organelles, membrane components such as ion channels or pores, receptor molecules, or cell wall components. As a result of this differential inheritance of fate determinants from the mother cell, the daughter cells have different developmental fates, and this is the way that the term *asymmetric cell division* has been applied usually.

In the development of root epidermal cells of monocotyledons, cytoplasm accumulates at the end nearest the root tip, resulting in a polarized cell. This end is subsequently cut off by an asymmetric cell division, resulting in a small, cytoplasmically rich trichoblast ("hair precursor"), and a larger vacuolated epidermal cell. An outgrowth of the trichoblast develops as a root hair.

The formation of stomata, the pores that allow gas exchange between the atmosphere and internal tissues of leaves, involves both symmetric and asymmetric divisions. In most dicotyledons a developing epidermal cell divides asymmetrically to form a small triangular cell (when viewed from the surface). This cell, termed a meristemoid because it continues to divide after adjacent cells have ceased division, divides symmetrically to form two identical stomatal guard cells that form the pore, or in some species it may undergo several divisions before forming the guard cells.

Another important asymmetric division is the division of the microspore, separating a small, cytoplasmically rich generative cell that forms the male gametes from a larger vegetative cell. This is the first division in pollen development and separates two cells with different developmental fates. In mutants where this division is affected, either the division fails to occur or it is symmetric. In either case pollen development fails, indicating the importance of the asymmetric division to this process.

Positional Information in Cell Differentiation

The consequences of cell polarity and asymmetric divisions are to place sister cells of a mitotic division in different cellular environments, such as closer to or farther from the tip of the organ or to the inside or outside in a tissue. These cells, occupying different positions, may then be receptive to different external information, and this is the basis for the concept of positional information. Although the concept has a long history in developmental biology, it was Lewis Wolpert in 1971 who formalized it.

Positional information has been invoked to explain many developmental processes but there are relatively few in which it has been subjected to experimental analysis. One of the best examples is the development of root hairs in *Arabidopsis*. The root **epidermis** consists of files of root-hair-bearing trichoblasts alternating with files of hairless cells. Trichoblasts occupy predictable positions over the radial walls of underlying **cortical** cells. This suggests that the alternating pattern of trichoblast files is determined

epidermis outer layer of cells

cortical relating to the cortex of a plant

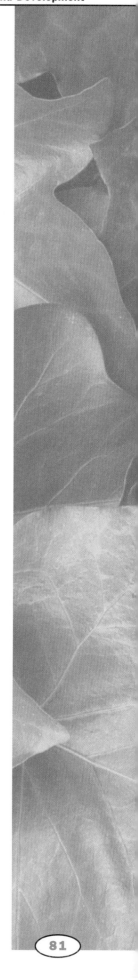

Stomata from a tulip leaf. The formation of stomata involves both symmetric and asymmetric divisions.

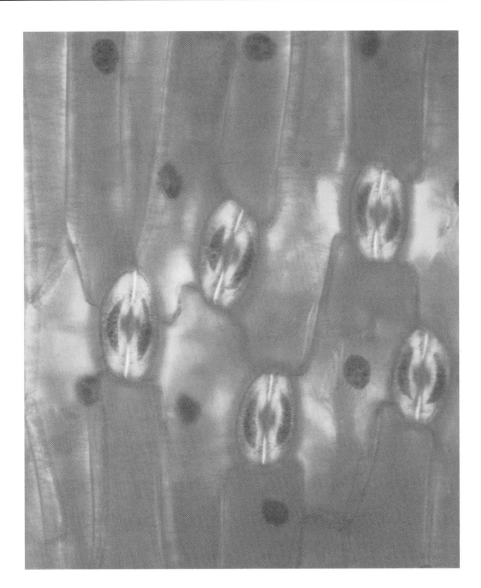

by the positions they occupy, and it has been proposed that the gaseous plant hormone ethylene is produced in the radial wall boundaries of cortical cells and activates root-hair formation. Mutants that vary in their response to ethylene confirm this suggestion, indicating that the molecular basis of positional information in this case had been identified. SEE ALSO ANATOMY OF PLANTS; EMBRYOGENESIS; GENETIC MECHANISMS AND DEVELOPMENT; GERMINATION AND GROWTH; HORMONAL CONTROL AND DEVELOPMENT; MERISTEMS; SENESCENCE; TISSUES.

Ian Sussex and Nancy Kerk

Bibliography

Gallagher, Kimberly, and Laurie G. Smith. "Asymmetric Cell Division and Cell Fate in Plants." *Current Opinion in Cell Biology* 9 (1997): 842–48.

Jürgens, Gerd, Markus Grebe, and Thomas Steinmann. "Establishment of Cell Polarity in Plant Development." *Current Opinion in Cell Biology* 9 (1997): 849–52.

Lyndon, Robert F. *Plant Development: The Cellular Basis.* London: Unwin Hyman, 1990.

Scheres, Ben. "Cell Signalling in Root Development." *Current Opinion in Genetics and Development* 7 (1997): 501–06.

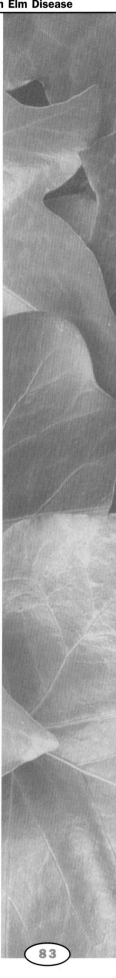

Wardlaw, Claude W. "A Commentary on Turing's Diffusion-Reaction Theory of Morphogenesis." *New Phytologist* 52 (1953): 40–47.

Wolpert, Lewis. "One Hundred Years of Positional Information." *Trends in Genetics* 12 (1996): 359–64.

Dioscorea

Second only to potatoes in terms of world tuber production, true yams (genus *Dioscorea*) are more closely related to tulips (both are monocots) than to the sweet potato (*Ipomoea batatas*), which is also often called a yam. The genus *Dioscorea* includes around eight hundred tuberous, annual species of **twining** or **rambling habit**, mostly found in tropical regions.

Cultivated for their starch-rich tubers, true yams were originally **domesticated** in three independent regions: Africa, Asia, and the New World. Today, yams, especially *D. rotundata*, are grown extensively throughout the tropics.

A number of *Dioscorea* species naturally produce saponins (a type of steroid). The most useful of these compounds, diosgenin, is very similar to the human sex hormones estrogen, progesterone, and testosterone. Present in the tubers at concentrations of up to 40 percent of its steroidal contents, *Dioscorea* represents a valuable source of diosgenin that is used to synthesize human sex hormones at low cost. This led to the development of the female contraceptive pill, which continues to be one of the most effective and widely used methods of birth control.

In 1952 researchers discovered that the fungus *Rhizopus* can convert diosgenin into the steroid cortisone, a human hormone. Along with hydrocortisone (also produced from diosgenin), cortisone plays an important role in medicine, particularly in the treatment of allergic reactions (such as those produced by insect bites and stings), and for reducing inflammation of the joints in patients suffering from arthritis. SEE ALSO ECONOMIC IMPORTANCE OF PLANTS; LIPIDS; MEDICINAL PLANTS; MONOCOTS.

Charles A. Butterworth

twining twisting around while climbing

rambling habit growing without obvious intended direction

domesticate to tame an organism to live with and to be of use to humans

Bibliography

Simpson, Beryl B., and Molly C. Ogorzaly. *Economic Botany: Plants in Our World.* New York: McGraw-Hill, 1986.

Dutch Elm Disease

Dutch elm disease is a fungal infection of the **vascular** system of elm trees. The fungus, *Ophiostoma ulmi*, is spread from diseased to healthy trees by elm bark beetles. Fungal spores adhering to the beetles are introduced to the tree through feeding wounds in young branches. In nonresistant elms, large portions of the vascular system are infected before the tree can defend itself against the invading **pathogen**. Water transport within the tree is blocked by the fungus and the tree eventually wilts and dies.

The fungus first appeared in the Netherlands about 1912; from there it spread across Europe, reaching the United States in 1930. At the time, the

vascular related to transport of nutrients

pathogen disease-causing organism

Bark beetle tunnels revealed beneath the bark of a tree infected with Dutch elm disease.

American elm, *Ulmus americana*, was the premier urban tree, planted for its beauty, shade, and durability. Across the Midwest, this hardy, quick-growing tree was used for windbreaks as well as on the streets of new towns. As the disease spread across the nation, streets once shaded by majestic, arching elms were soon barren of trees. It is estimated that over one hundred million trees have been lost to the disease.

vector carrier, usually a carrier who is not affected by the thing carried

hybrid a mix of two species

Early attempts at controlling the disease concentrated on killing the fungus and its **vector**. As tree spraying became frowned upon and injection of fungicides more costly, more effort has been made to breed disease-resistant elms. Several European cultivars that have been developed are not completely resistant to the disease or sufficiently cold-hardy for North America. **Hybrid** crosses of resistant Asian species with American species lack the height and characteristic form of the American elm. Selective breeding and testing of American elms has led to promising varieties such as American Liberty, Princeton, and Valley Forge, but whether any of these will be resistant to the disease as the fungus itself evolves remains to be seen. SEE ALSO BREEDING; INTERACTIONS, PLANT-FUNGAL; INTERACTIONS, PLANT-INSECT; PATHOGENS.

Craig Steely

Bibliography

Stipes, R. Jay, and Richard J. Campana, eds. *Compendium of Elm Diseases*. St. Paul, MN: American Phytopathological Society, 1981.

Ecology

Ecology is the study of organisms and their relationship to the environment. The field was born in 1866 when German biologist and philosopher Ernst Haeckel (1834–1919) created the precursor to the modern word "ecology" by combining the Greek words *oikos*, meaning "home," and *logos*, meaning "study," to create the word "oecology." Haeckel used this word to summarize the concept of natural selection and the struggle for existence that Eng-

lish naturalist Charles Darwin (1809–1882) had outlined in his ground-breaking work on evolution, *On the Origin of Species.*

In the early twentieth century, even before the modern word *ecology* had been invented, interest in what is now called plant ecology began to grow. American botanist and ecologist Frederic Clements (1874–1945) and others conceived the idea that plants would develop in an orderly succession of formations from pioneer species to a well-defined and stable group of species called a climax community. Clements believed that plant formations were like intact organisms with a predictable pattern of birth, growth, and death. Clements's ideas were quickly challenged. American botanist and plant ecologist Henry Allan Gleason (1882–1975) argued that the distribution of plants was the result of random events in the environment that combine to form an individual and possibly unique plant community. Partially in response to the rigid classification developed by Clements, British ecologist Arthur Tansley (1871–1955) in 1935 coined the word *ecosystem* to describe what he called a *quasi organism.* Tansley's concept of the ecosystem as a single physical unit containing both organisms and their environment is essentially the same to this day.

Plant Ecology

The concept of ecology may seem fairly simple, but in practice it is very complex. As the field developed, scientists soon found themselves unable to master the entire discipline, and even within the already narrowed field of plant ecology, subfields rapidly developed. Today, there are six major fields of plant ecology:

- **Population ecologists** study the relationship of individuals of one species in a given area to each other and to their environment. A population ecologist might be interested in what environmental conditions limit the northern range of black spruce trees in the Canadian boreal forest.

- **Community ecologists** study the distribution and abundance of groups of species and how they are influenced by biological and environmental factors. Community ecologists have studied the major associations of deciduous forests in the eastern United States and how the environment, in terms of climate, soils, and topography, controls this association.

- **Ecosystem ecologists** study energy and matter transport through organisms (see below). This includes studies of how nutrients, energy, and **biomass** are cycled through ecosystems. The study area for ecosystem ecologists depends on the defined ecosystem and can vary from small ponds or tiny forest plots to the entire globe. Ecosystem ecologists are today conducting politically and economically important research on the global carbon cycle.

biomass the total dry weight of an organism or group of organisms

- **Physiological ecologists** study how environmental factors such as light, temperature, and humidity influence the biochemical functioning of individual organisms. Physiological ecology and ecosystem ecology are very complementary; often ecologists have a hard time deciding if they are one or the other.

- **Landscape ecologists** study the biological and environmental factors that influence vegetation patterns observed in a landscape. Land-

Energy flow refers to the way that energy is transformed through a food chain (pictured here) containing a series of levels, including plants, consumers, predators, and decomposers.

scape ecologists may study the factors controlling the boundary between forests and grasslands.

- **Human ecologists** study the influence of human activity, both currently and historically, in controlling the distribution and abundance of organisms. Human ecology also examines the social and cultural factors that control the way humans exploit, alter, and manage the environment. Most ecological research has focused too much on natural ecosystems while pretending that humans do not exist. For example, an ecologist coming across the deciduous forest in New England today might assume that the forest always looked that way. In fact, the present pattern of forest distribution is the result of extensive human modifications by Native Americans, European colonists, and foresters.

Food Webs

In the 1950s the idea of the food web began to emerge in ecosystem ecology. Food webs and the related topics of **trophic** levels and energy flow are some of the most critical ecological concepts because they illustrate the connections between organisms that are required to maintain healthy ecosystems.

Energy flow refers to the way that energy is transformed through a food chain containing a series of levels, including plants, consumers, predators, and decomposers. Each step in the food chain is called a trophic level (from the Greek word *trophikos*, meaning "nutrition"). Primary producers (plants, algae, and photosynthetic microbes) are the base of food chains and are the lowest trophic level. They transform energy from the Sun into sugars. Primary producers thus make their own food and are called **autotrophs**; all other organisms ultimately use the energy produced by autotrophs and are called **heterotrophs**. At the next trophic level, primary consumers (**herbivores**) eat some of the sugars produced by primary producers. Secondary consumers (predators) consume primary consumers and other secondary

trophic related to feeding

autotroph "self-feeder"; any organism that uses sunlight or chemical energy

heterotroph an organism that derives its energy from consuming other organisms or their body parts

herbivore an organism that feeds on plant parts

consumers. Decomposers such as earthworms, maggots, fungi, and bacteria break down the carcasses of dead primary and secondary consumers and un-eaten primary producers.

The amount of living material (biomass) and energy in food chains has a specific ordering between trophic levels. Consider a simple example of an African savanna ecosystem consisting of trees and grasses (primary producers), gazelles and zebras (primary consumers), and lions (secondary consumers). If we check the trophic levels, we will find that primary producers have the most biomass, followed by primary consumers, and then secondary consumers. The amount of energy at each trophic level will follow the same pattern. This ordering of trophic levels forms a pyramid with primary producers at the bottom followed by primary consumers in the middle and secondary consumers on the top. More energy is required at the lower levels of the pyramid because during the transfer between trophic levels energy is lost through heat and waste products.

Most ecosystems on land follow the pyramid pattern. In the ocean or other aquatic systems, the opposite pattern may at times be true: at any one time, the biomass and energy of the primary and secondary consumers may exceed those of the primary producers. This is because photosynthetic algae have a very short life span. Even though they may have a low biomass at any one time, their biomass measured over the whole year will be larger than the biomass of the consumers.

The pyramid concept of trophic levels is consistent across many terrestrial ecosystems, but in reality the interactions among organisms are much more complex than in the African example. A food web is a network of connected food chains and is used to describe community interactions. Consider a food chain in the Rocky Mountains. Small aquatic plants are primary consumers in a stream ecosystem. Arthropods and fly larvae feed on the plants and are in turn consumed by trout. Bears eat the trout. But each part of this food chain is also connected to other food chains. Birds feed on plants and fish, while bears will also feed on roots, tubers, and rodents. The complete network of these connections forms an ecosystem food web.

Food webs are usually more complex in ecosystems that have not been disturbed for a long time. Food webs in coral reefs and tropical forests have thousands of highly specific food chains. In these ecosystems, many animals are adapted to feed on one or only a few food sources. Disruption of a few elements can have serious consequences for the entire food web. By contrast, the tundra ecosystem was covered in ice until about 8000 B.C.E. In this ecosystem, there has been less time to evolve complex and specific food webs. Species tend to be interchangeable. Removal of one species or interaction does not usually seriously damage the health of the entire food web.

Advances in Ecological Research

Advances in the ecology field happen frequently. The following four examples from the late twentieth century show the breadth of the field as well as the need for ecologists to reach across disciplines.

Leaf Design. There are thousands of kinds of leaves, ranging from tiny evergreen needles to enormous tropical leaves more than fifty centimeters wide. In spite of great diversity, leaves follow a strict set of rules. Long-lived

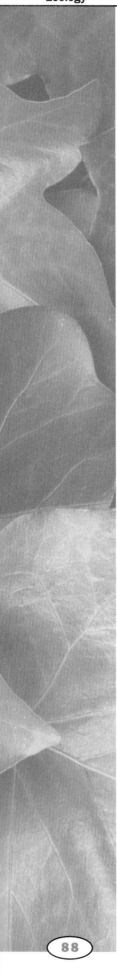

leaves, such as ten-year-old spruce needles, have a low nitrogen concentration (this means low rates of photosynthesis) and thick, dense leaves that are highly resistant to herbivores. Short-lived leaves, such as blades of grass lasting only weeks or a few months, have a very high nitrogen concentration and thin, light leaves. Almost all leaves follow this pattern and are either long-lived with low rates of photosynthesis and a high resistance to herbivores, or short-lived with high rates of photosynthesis and herbivory. Intermediate levels of all three traits are also possible. This finding, drawn from hundreds of plants all over the world, helps to explain the appearance and **physiology** of leaves and is one of the most important ecological findings in recent years.

Ecosystem Carbon Storage. Many ecologists wanted to know the total amount of carbon released or stored by ecosystems, but until recently, there was no way to accomplish this. Experimental meteorologists devised a method called eddy covariance to measure the amount of carbon dioxide entering or leaving an ecosystem. By adding up these numbers over the course of a day or year, ecologists can now determine if an ecosystem is storing more carbon through photosynthesis or releasing more carbon through respiration. They found that many forests are storing carbon, but that some, especially in the boreal forest, can release carbon due to slight changes in climate. This research is critical for understanding the carbon cycle and the potential for global climate change.

Impacts of Rising Carbon Dioxide. Scientists have published hundreds of research articles on the response of plants in greenhouses or special enclosures to increased carbon dioxide (CO_2) levels, but there had been no way to test the response of real ecosystems. Scientists at the Brookhaven National Laboratories developed the Free-Air CO_2 Enrichment (FACE) system. FACE uses a circle of instruments that pump CO_2 into the atmosphere to artificially increase the CO_2 levels of a real ecosystem. The increased CO_2 increased photosynthesis, supporting earlier greenhouse results showing that plants would respond to higher CO_2.

Ecology and Natural Resource Management

Beginning in the early twentieth century, ecological theories began to be seriously considered in natural resource management. Unfortunately, results were not always good. In an application of Darwinian theory, U.S. Forest Service managers believed that by clearing old, unproductive forests and replacing them with young, vigorously growing forests they would increase forest health and productivity. Instead, throughout much of the dry inland Rocky Mountains foresters created dense thickets of fire- and insect-susceptible forests. Today, guided by modern ecological research, this policy is changing to include a focus on returning fire to the ecosystem and managing forests for the health of the entire ecosystem, not just human economics. This is called ecosystem management. In large part, it was the legal, political, and social pressures exerted by nonscientist citizen activists that caused this shift in natural resource management policy.

Ecological research has been used in many other ways to improve natural resource management. Due to ecological research showing the catastrophic effects of cyanide on river ecosystems, **cyanide heap leach gold mining** is now being restricted. Ecologists showed how DDT, an insecti-

physiology the biochemical processes carried out by an organism

cyanide heap leach gold mining a technique used to extract gold by treating ore with cyanide

cide common in much of the world during the mid-1900s, was transferred through trophic levels until it reached toxic levels in secondary consumers. Millions of birds were killed before DDT was banned in most of the world. Ecologists found that large, interconnected populations of grizzly bears were required to ensure long-term breeding success of the species and natural resource managers are now designing migration corridors to link the remaining bear populations.

In short, there are very few areas of natural resource management that are unaffected by ecology. Critical developments include:

- ecosystem management for recreation, water quality, and protection of endangered species, not just economic development

- an increased awareness of public health consequences

- attempts to reintroduce elements of ecosystems that had been removed by humans

- consideration of the complex and sometimes fragile nature of food webs before making resource management decisions.

Role of Computer Modeling

Politicians, scientists, and natural resource managers are becoming more and more interested in complicated ecological questions over large regions. For example, the economically critical and politically sensitive issue of the global carbon cycle is being answered mostly by ecosystem ecologists. Clearly, it is impossible to measure the entire Earth. Another solution is required, and computer models have filled this need.

A computer model is a system of mathematical equations that ecologists use to represent the ecosystem or problem being assessed. Models do not duplicate reality; they are simplified systems that attempt to represent the most critical processes while ignoring all the details that are impossible to measure or extremely difficult to represent with mathematics. Ecological models range from detailed treatments of gas exchange for a single leaf to carbon cycle models for the entire globe. Developing a good model of the global carbon cycle is like trying to make the simplest possible car: you strip away everything you possibly can until the car stops running. Just as in a car you could probably remove the windows and the passenger seat but not the transmission or the engine, in a global carbon model, you can probably ignore individual species and hour-to-hour weather changes but not vegetation and climate.

Computer models have an extremely significant role in ecology. In fact, because so much in ecology is so difficult to measure except for the smallest plot, models are common in every field of ecology. Models are highly useful for testing scenarios. What will happen to stream flow and fish populations if 50 percent of trees are cut in a watershed? How will elk populations change if wolves are reintroduced to a particular area? How will the introduction of small controlled fires affect the potential for larger, highly destructive fires? How will forests respond if carbon dioxide levels double in the next one hundred years? These are just some of the ways that ecological models are used. SEE ALSO BIOME; CARBON CYCLE; CLEMENTS, FREDERIC; ECOLOGY, ENERGY FLOW; ECOLOGY, FIRE;

ECOLOGY, HISTORY OF; GLOBAL WARMING; INTERACTIONS, PLANT-FUNGAL; INTERACTIONS, PLANT-INSECT; INTERACTIONS, PLANT-PLANT; INTERACTIONS, PLANT-VERTEBRATE; PLANT COMMUNITY PROCESSES; SAVANNA; TUNDRA.

Michael A. White

Bibliography

Bailey, Robert G. *Ecosystem Geography*. New York: Springer-Verlag, 1996.

Colinvaux, Paul. *Ecology 2*. New York: John Wiley & Sons, 1993.

Crawley, Michael J., ed. *Plant Ecology*, 2nd ed. Cambridge, UK: Blackwell Science 1997.

Daily, Gretchen C., ed. *Nature's Services: Societal Dependence on Natural Ecosystems*. Washington, DC: Island Press, 1997.

Dickinson, Gordon, and Kevin Murphy. *Ecosystems: A Functional Approach*. New York: Routledge, 1998.

Dodson, Stanley. *Ecology*. New York: Oxford University Press, 1998.

Kohm, Kathryn A., and Jerry F. Franklin, eds. *Creating a Forestry for the 21st Century: The Science of Ecosystem Management*. Washington, DC: Island Press, 1997.

Morgan, Sally. *Ecology and Environment: The Cycles of Life*. New York: Oxford University Press, 1995.

Real, Leslie A., and James H. Brown, eds. *Foundations of Ecology: Classic Papers with Commentaries*. Chicago: University of Chicago Press, 1991.

Waring, Richard H., and Steven W. Running. *Forest Ecosystems: Analysis at Multiple Scales*, 2nd ed. San Diego: Academic Press, 1998.

Ecology, Energy Flow

Organisms are complex biochemical machines that require a constant consumption of energy to grow, reproduce, and maintain their biological integrity. The use of energy must obey physical principles: the laws of thermodynamics. Constraints imposed by these principles have profound influence in the flow and conservation of energy and therefore the structure of an ecological community.

Energy from the sun powers the world's ecological communities. Solar energy is channeled into an ecological community by way of photosynthesis in green plants and many other photosynthetic microorganisms. Energy harvested by photosynthesis is used to produce plant tissue where light energy is saved as chemical energy. This chemical energy is transferred when plants are eaten by herbivores (plant-eating animals). Energy stored in herbivores can further be transferred to carnivores (animal-eating animals). This sequence of energy transfer from plants to herbivores and then carnivores is called a food chain. Along the food chain, the number of transfers for the solar energy to reach an organism defines its **trophic** level. Plants therefore occupy the first trophic level, herbivores the second trophic level, and herbivore-eating carnivores the third trophic level. A species population can occupy more than one trophic level depending on the source of energy actually assimilated.

Organisms can be classified into **autotrophs** and **heterotrophs** depending on the nature of energy and nutrients they use. Autotrophs, which include all the higher plants and algae, use light as their energy source and

trophic related to feeding

autotroph "self-feeder"; any organism that uses sunlight or chemical energy

heterotroph an organism that derives its energy from consuming other organisms or their body parts

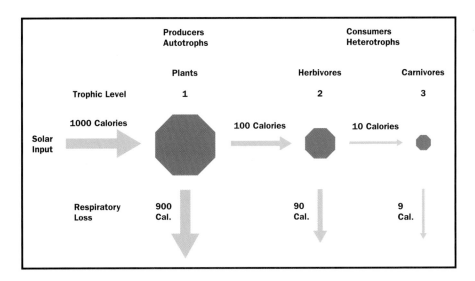

they depend completely on inorganic nutrients for their growth. Heterotrophs, which include all the animals, protocists, fungi, and many bacteria, use chemical energy for their needs and require organic compounds for their growth. Heterotrophs acquire both energy and organic carbon from their food. In an ecological community, autotrophs also are called producers for their roles in the harness of solar energy to convert inorganic nutrients into energy rich organic material. Heterotrophs are called consumers, for their dependence on autotrophs for energy and nutrients.

Laws of Thermodynamics

The laws of thermodynamics set stringent constraints on the use of energy by every organism. It is important to know what these constraints are and their ecological implications. The first law of thermodynamics states that energy is conserved and can neither be created nor destroyed. During photosynthesis, the energy in light is used to convert carbon dioxide and water into glucose and oxygen. Part of the light energy is harvested by the plant and stored in glucose with the rest of the energy **dissipated**. The amount of energy involved in photosynthesis remains the same before and after the process. The amount of energy that can be conserved by the process, the chemical energy stored in glucose, however, is constrained by the second law of thermodynamics.

dissipate to reduce by spreading out or scattering

Any natural process that involves the use, transformation, and conservation of energy is constrained by the second law of thermodynamics. The law requires that any **irreversible** process will result in the degradation of the energy involved. In other words, there is an energetic cost associated with every irreversible process. Each organism is a complex biochemical machine that is made up of a network of metabolic pathways. Every metabolic pathway amounts to a nonequilibrium chemical reaction and therefore is an irreversible process. Using photosynthesis as an example, for every one hundred calories of light energy absorbed by a plant, the amount of energy that can be harvested and stored in glucose will have to be less than one hundred calories. The second law, however, does not provide guidance on how much of the energy will have to be degraded during each irreversible process. Direct measurement is needed to determine the actual efficiency.

irreversible unable to be reversed

The Structure of an Ecological Community

Energy flow in an ecological community must obey the laws of thermodynamics. These constraints affect the flow of energy and therefore the structure of an ecological community. Using the grazing food chain as an example, let's see how these laws affect the flow of energy at each trophic level. For the harvest of solar energy by plants in the production of plant tissues, the first law of thermodynamics requires that the amount of solar energy captured by the plants remain the same before and after the transformation; the energy involved cannot be created nor destroyed. For every thousand calories of solar energy captured and transformed by plant, there remain a thousand calories afterward. The second law of thermodynamics, however, requires that the harvesting of solar energy cannot be 100 percent efficient; only a portion of the solar energy transformed by the plant can be conserved in the production of plant tissue. Measurements on various plant communities show that the actual efficiency is below 10 percent. Most of the light energy, over 90 percent, is degraded by respiration into nonusable form. The rate of production of plant tissue, a reflection of the net harvesting of solar energy, is defined as the net primary productivity.

The transformation of energy at the second trophic level, or any other trophic levels, follows the same pattern. As a rule of thumb, 90 percent of the energy involved is degraded at each trophic transfer and only 10 percent of the energy is conserved in the organism's tissue. With 1,000 calories of solar energy captured by the plant, 100 calories of plant tissue can be produced, which in turn can be used to produce 10 calories of herbivore tissue, and in turn 1 calorie of carnivore tissue. The amount of energy potentially available to a species population is greatly influenced by its position on the food chain; the lower its position the more its available energy. This energetic constraint is widely reflected in many ecological communities, as herbivores, whether they are zebras or deer, usually outnumber their predators, lions or wolves. Because of this rapid decrease in the amount of usable energy, the length of the food chain is usually limited to a maximum of four to five levels. SEE ALSO ECOLOGY; ECOLOGY, HISTORY OF; ODUM, EUGENE.

Charles J. Gwo

Bibliography

Lewis, Gilbert Newton, and Merle Randall. *Thermodynamics*, 2nd ed., rev. by Kenneth Sanborn Pitzer and Leo Brewer. New York: McGraw-Hill, 1961.

Odum, Eugene P. *Fundamentals of Ecology*, 3rd ed. Philadelphia: Saunders, 1971.

Schrödinger, Erwin. *What Is Life?: The Physical Aspect of the Living Cell*. Cambridge, UK: Cambridge University Press, 1944.

Ecology, Fire

Fire has been an agent of change in nearly every terrestrial vegetation type on Earth, shaping both the species composition and structure. The probability of occurrence and the effects of fire vary widely depending upon the amount of fuel present, topography, climate, sources of ignition, and present species composition of the area. Fires may be severe, causing great mortality of existing plants and significantly changing the species composition

The California Department of Forestry holds a prescribed burn of shrub-chaparral mix in the Mojave Desert.

of the burned area, or they may have little impact on the composition and consume only the dry dead plant material present. They may burn intensely as fast-moving fires with flame lengths greater than 25 meters, or they may occur as slow-moving fires with flame lengths less than 0.5 meter. These sources of variation influence the effects that fire has on the vegetation and the ecological role of fire.

Prior to human intervention, fires occurred very frequently in some vegetation types. Fire history studies in temperate grasslands in Africa and North America, some ponderosa pine forests of western North America, and longleaf pine forests of southeastern North America indicate that fires occurred at an average of less than every ten years. When fires occur frequently, the vegetation's composition becomes dominated by fire-adapted (tolerant) species. Consequently, when fires occur, there is only minor change in species composition and the vegetation quickly recovers to the preburn condition, often within five years or less. The more frequently fire occurs on an area, the more it becomes dominated by fire-adapted species.

In other vegetation types, the fires may occur many decades or even centuries apart. Fires were naturally very infrequent in many arid areas where the fuels are not sufficient to carry a fire, or in humid areas where the fuels are seldom adequately dry to burn. Very often the effects of fire in these areas is long lasting and the vegetation may not recover for many centuries. When fires occur infrequently, fire-intolerant species become established, and the effects of fire are much more lasting. Even in these communities,

ecosystem an ecological community together with its environment

biota the sum total of living organisms in a region of a given size

biomass the total dry weight of an organism or group of organisms

however, fire may play important ecological roles in the functioning of the **ecosystem**.

Ecologists are becoming increasingly aware of the importance of fire in the maintenance and functioning of ecosystems. Rather than focusing on a single fire event, it is useful to apply the concept of a fire regime when considering the effects of fire on large areas over a long time. A fire regime describes the typical fire characteristics when applied to a landscape over many burning cycles. Fire regimes include characteristics such as frequency (how often the fire occurs over time), size, intensity (the rate at which fire consumes fuel and releases heat), severity (the effects of fire on the **biota** and soil), continuity (the degree to which unburned areas remain within the fire's perimeter), pattern (where fire typically occurs on the landscape), and variability in the previous characteristics. Modern humans have changed the fire regimes for many areas of the world. When fire regimes change, ecosystems and fire effects change in ways that are often not desirable. For instance, when fires are less frequent, they burn more intensely.

Creation and Maintenance of Vegetation Composition and Diversity

Fire and other disturbances typically kill some plants and alter the competitive relationships between species. The initial postburn community is composed of those species that survive the fire and those that can efficiently migrate to the site. Community succession gradually modifies the postburn environment of the site and the composition changes in response to the changing environment. Species and, in some cases, the community may be replaced by later successional species and communities. Thus, fire plays a critical role in maintaining or creating new habitat for those species that are adapted to fire occurrence. For example, in many areas ponderosa pine-bunchgrass vegetation will gradually change to a forest dominated by other tree species, such as Douglas-fir, in the absence of fire. Periodic fires maintain the ponderosa pine-bunchgrass vegetation. A similar situation exists for many temperate grasslands, where in the absence of fire, grasslands are replaced through succession by forest or woodland vegetation.

In some instances, the vegetation itself must be removed by fire in order for the environment necessary for that vegetation to be maintained. For example, big sagebrush grassland often occurs in a fire-maintained mosaic with juniper woodland vegetation in western North America. In the absence of fire, the juniper woodland vegetation will replace the sagebrush grassland through community succession. Young juniper that are establishing within the sagebrush grassland can be readily killed by fire. Sagebrush will also be removed by the fire and a community composed of grasses and other herbaceous plants will become established initially. Sagebrush seedlings that cannot become established within a dense juniper woodland, however, will establish within the grassland and thus, over time, fire maintains the sagebrush grassland vegetation in the landscape.

Cycling of Organic Matter and Nutrients

In many areas of the world, the rates of plant **biomass** production exceed the rates of biomass decomposition. In these cold or dry areas, biomass tends to gradually increase over time as succession and plant growth occur. Accumulation of biomass, particularly dead biomass, has many effects on the ecosystem. The nutrients essential to plant growth become increasingly concentrated in plant tissue and unavailable for subsequent plant growth. This may result in deficiencies of some essential nutrients and the reduction in biomass production. Fire rapidly cycles these nutrients and makes them available for future plant growth. In this way fire may help maintain the productivity of the ecosystem. The combustion process, however, results in the volatilization of some elements such as nitrogen and carbon, and these are lost to the atmosphere. Nitrogen is replaced in the ecosystem through nitrogen fixation and other processes of the nitrogen cycle.

Aboriginal Humans and Fire

In addition to its use for heating, lighting, and cooking, fire was the first tool that primitive peoples had to manipulate the environment on a broad scale to better meet their purposes. Fire has been used by hunter-gatherer societies to promote the production of certain wild crops (such as seeds: wild rice, sunflower, balsamroot, and mesquite beans; tubers: camas and bracken; berries: blueberry and blackberry; and nuts: acorns and chestnuts), increase the nutritional quality of forage for wild animals, create desirable habitat for game species, decrease the natural migration rates of game species allowing for increased hunting possibilities, control problem tick and insect populations, open travel corridors, and reduce fire hazard and enemy hiding cover in the vicinity of campsites.

Aboriginal people have also used fire for driving game species into traps or to hunters, long-distance signaling, warfare, and ceremonial purposes. Some peoples had the tradition of setting large fires in hopes that it would induce rain. **Pastoralists** used fire to clear pastures of trees and shrubs, increase forage production, improve forage nutritional quality, and decrease parasites affecting their livestock. Early agricultural cultures used fire to clear natural vegetation to facilitate **cultivation**, remove organic crop residue, and fertilize fields by cycling nutrients. In addition, many fires were likely set by accident from cooking fires. Thus, human culture has had a long association and evolution with fire.

pastoralists farming people who keep animal flocks

cultivation growth of crop plants, or turning the soil for this purpose

Use of Fire as a Land Management Tool

The intentional use of fire to achieve a land management objective is often referred to as prescribed burning. The fire is prescribed in the sense that the specific area, burning conditions, and expected results are identified prior to ignition. In addition, specific land management objectives are developed that justify the use of fire. Weather conditions (such as wind, temperature, relative humidity, and fuel moisture) and ignition patterns are selected that allow the land manager to control fire spread and achieve desirable effects on the vegetation. The management objectives of today's prescribed burning remain very similar to many of the aboriginal people's uses. The most common objectives include: creating or maintaining habitat for wild and domestic plants and animals, controlling undesirable plants, increasing the nutritional quality of forage for wild and domestic **herbivores**, reducing fire hazard through fuel reduction, and increasing nutrient cycling rates. Fire continues to be extensively used as a land treatment by hunter-

herbivore an organism that feeds on plant parts

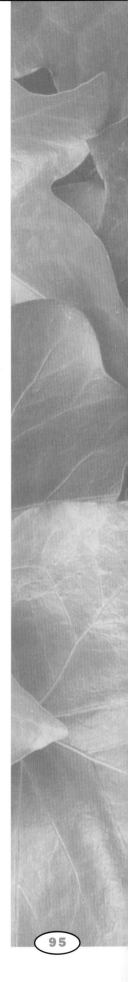

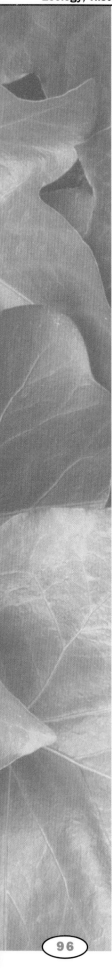

gatherer, pastoral, and agricultural peoples around the world to clear vegetation, improve pastures, and remove crop residue.

Natural fire programs are employed in some national parks and wilderness areas to maintain the ecosystem in nonhuman-affected conditions as much as possible. Natural fires are those that have a nonhuman ignition source, primarily lightning. Prior to initiating a natural fire program, land managers develop a plan that identifies the conditions under which lightning-ignited fires will be allowed to burn without direct fire suppression control measures being taken. Since the weather conditions or location of any specific fire cannot be precisely predicted, however, the expected results of fire are usually described in more general terms than for human-ignited fire. The objectives of these fires usually includes having fire play a natural role in the ecological processes of the ecosystem. SEE ALSO CHAPARRAL; CONIFEROUS FORESTS; ECOLOGY; GRASSLANDS.

Stephen C. Bunting

Bibliography

Agee, James K. *Fire Ecology of Pacific Northwest Forests.* Covello, CA: Island Press, 1993.

Biswell, Harold H. *Prescribed Burning in California Wildlands Vegetation Management.* Berkeley, CA: University of California Press, 1989.

Boyd, Robert, ed. *Indians, Fire and the Land in the Pacific Northwest.* Corvallis, OR: Oregon State University Press, 1999.

Bunting, Stephen C. "The Use and Role of Fire in Natural Areas." In *National Parks and Protected Areas: Their Role in Environmental Protection,* ed. R. Gerald Wright. Cambridge, UK: Blackwell Science, 1996.

Pyne, Stephen J. *Fire in America: A Cultural History of Wildland and Rural Fire.* Princeton: Princeton University Press, 1988.

———. *World Fire: The Culture of Fire on Earth.* Seattle, WA: University of Washington Press, 1995.

———, Patricia L. Andrews, and Richard D. Laven. *Introduction to Wildland Fire,* 2nd ed. New York: John Wiley & Sons, 1996.

Ecology, History of

Historians have debated the origins of ecology for decades. But there is no particular person or precise date or definite occurrence that marks the beginning of the science. Ecology gradually emerged as a distinct discipline during the latter part of the nineteenth century from a diverse array of different areas, including plant geography, plant **physiology**, taxonomy, and Charles Darwin's theory of evolution.

physiology the biochemical processes carried out by an organism

Linnaeus and Humboldt

One of the most important individuals in the early development of an ecological view of nature was Swedish botanist Carolus Linnaeus (1707–1778). Linnaeus was the father of modern taxonomy, the science of identifying and naming species. His great goal was to describe and catalog all known organisms. In 1749 Linnaeus published a book called *The Oeconomy of Nature.* In this book Linnaeus presented his view that nature, while seemingly chaotic and unpredictable, actually existed in a balanced state of order as designed by the creator. Linnaeus felt that if one looks closely at nature it is clear that even the simplest organisms have an important role to play in this natural economy; that no living thing is useless.

By the end of the eighteenth century, many scientists began to question Linnaeus's views. They felt that he had been far too descriptive in his approach to understanding nature. Rather than the static, harmonious world that Linnaeus envisioned, nature was dynamic and constantly changing. The chief proponent of these views was German explorer and scientist Alexander von Humboldt (1769–1859). Humboldt insisted that the only way to understand nature's complexity was to take accurate measurements in the field and then search for general laws. Influenced by German philosopher Immanuel Kant (1724–1804), von Humboldt believed that nothing in nature could be studied in isolation. All phenomena were connected.

Darwin and Haeckel

While some historians claim that von Humboldt single-handedly created the science of ecology, the true origins of modern ecology are found in English naturalist Charles Darwin's (1809–1882) *On the Origin of Species*, published in 1859. Darwin's theory of evolution by natural selection provided a mechanism, not only for understanding how species arose, but also for interpreting patterns in the distribution and abundance of species. A central insight of *Origin* was that plants and animals had the potential to reproduce very quickly and reach huge population densities. Darwin realized that this potential was rarely achieved because each species is subject to a series of natural checks and balances. "Look at a plant in the midst of its range," said Darwin, "Why does it not double in numbers? . . . To give the plant increasing numbers, we should have to give it some advantage over its competitors or the animals that prey upon it." While Darwin's work laid the foundation for the emergence of ecology thirty years later, there was no term that clearly defined the new area of biology that he had created.

The German biologist Ernst Haeckel (1834–1919) soon provided a name for the science that Darwin founded. Greatly influenced by Darwin, Haeckel published the *Morphology of Organisms* in 1866 with the aim of interpreting anatomy in the light of evolution. In this book, Haeckel provided the first definition of ecology: "By ecology we mean the body of knowledge concerning the economy of nature—the total relations of the animal to both to its inorganic and organic environment."

Thanks to Haeckel, ecology finally had a name. But for almost two decades no one seemed to notice. In the 1880s and 1890s, however, ecology experienced an explosion of interest. In Germany in 1885, Hans Reiter published the first book with the new term "oekology" in its title. In Denmark, the botanist Johannes Eugenius Warming (1841–1924) began to study plant physiology in relation to the environment and published the first textbook on plant ecology in 1895. In America, ecology gained almost instantaneous recognition amongst botanists and soon attracted a following of bright, young researchers. The first mention of Haeckel's term in the American press occurred on December 1, 1892, in the *Boston Globe*. A front-page article read "New Science. Mrs. Richards Names It Oekology." (Mrs. Richards was the leading conservationist of her day and the first director of the Water Quality Lab at the Massachusetts Institute of Technology.) In 1893 the first book in English with ecology in its title, *Flower Ecology* by L. H. Pammel, was published. Also in 1893, the Madison Botanical Congress adopted the term "ecology" as denoting a new branch of botany distinct from physiology and **morphology**.

morphology shape and form

The Twentieth Century

By the start of the twentieth century American plant ecologists had taken a leading role in the development of the new science. At the University of Chicago, Henry Chandler Cowles (1869–1939) began a series of classic studies on ecological succession in the dunes around Lake Michigan. At the University of Nebraska, Frederic Clements (1874–1945) developed new dynamic theories of plant associations and vegetational change. Other ecologists soon challenged the ideas of Cowles and Clements. The British ecologist Arthur Tansley (1871–1955) developed the concept of an ecosystem as an alternative to Clements's classification of plant communities. American botanist and plant ecologist Henry Allan Gleason (1882–1975) criticized Clements's idea of the plant community as a superorganism and proposed an alternative individualistic theory of plant associations.

holistic including all the parts or factors that relate to an object or idea

In the era following World War II, plant ecologists abandoned many of the central principles developed by Clements, including the idea of the stable climax association. They reexamined the central issue of community ecology: whether communities were simply chance associations of independent species or integrated, **holistic** entities that could not be understood by studying individual species. In the 1950s American botanist and ecologist Robert Whittaker (1920–1980) created a technique called gradient analysis that helped to resolve this question. Whittaker's pioneering studies indicated that plant species had unique and fairly independent distributions across physical gradients such as moisture and temperature. These studies led ecologists to reject Clements's theory of holistic plant communities composed of predictable associations of species that shared similar environmental constraints.

biotic involving or related to life

Under the influence of American ecologist and educator Eugene Odum (1913–), a whole new subdiscipline of ecosystems ecology grew to prominence during the latter half of the twentieth century. Ecosystems ecology emphasized both the **biotic** and physical aspects of the environment. In particular, ecosystems ecology was concerned with the large-scale flows of energy and nutrients through ecological communities. The International Biological Program, and studies by Gene Likens and E. Herbert Bormann of nutrient budgets in the Hubbard Brook Experimental Forest, helped to bring the ecosystem approach to plant ecology into the mainstream of ecological science. While ecosystems ecology has fostered new methods of understanding the complex dynamics of natural systems, it has remained largely separate from more traditional branches of ecology that emphasize populations and individual adaptations.

biodiversity degree of variety of life

In the 1990s plant ecologists became increasingly concerned with issues related to **biodiversity** and the loss of plant habitats due to human activities. Human beings have destroyed about half of the forests that once covered 40 percent of the planet. Each year over 150,000 km^2 of tropical rain forest are lost to logging, farming, and fire. At this rate there will be no rain forests left in fifty years or less. Earth's plant communities provide homes for millions of different species. They cleanse the air and water, protect against erosion, and replenish the soil. What are the ecological consequences of the continued destruction of forests and other plant habitats? How can what is left be preserved? These and other questions regarding the management and maintenance of the natural world will be the consuming issues for plant ecologists over the coming decade. SEE ALSO CLEMENTS, FRED-

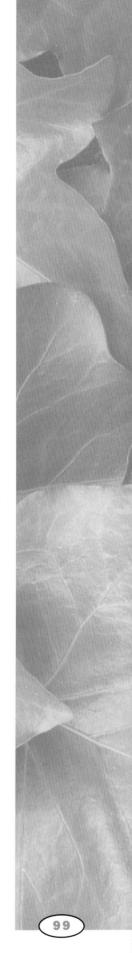

eric; Darwin, Charles; Ecology; Ecology, Energy Flow; Ecology, Fire; Humboldt, Alexander von; Linnaeus, Carolus; Odum, Eugene; Plant Community Processes; Warming, Johannes.

Bradford Carlton Lister

Bibliography

Kingsland, Sharon E. *Modeling Nature. Episodes in the History of Population Ecology.* Chicago: University of Chicago Press, 1985.

McIntosh, Robert P. *The Background of Ecology: Concept and Theory.* Cambridge, UK: Cambridge University Press, 1985.

Real, Leslie A., and James H. Brown, eds. *Foundations of Ecology Classic Papers with Commentaries.* Chicago: University of Chicago Press.

Economic Importance of Plants

Plants are extremely important in the lives of people throughout the world. People depend upon plants to satisfy such basic human needs as food, clothing, shelter, and health care. These needs are growing rapidly because of a growing world population, increasing incomes, and **urbanization**.

Plants provide food directly, of course, and also feed livestock that is then consumed itself. In addition, plants provide the raw materials for many types of pharmaceuticals, as well as tobacco, coffee, alcohol, and other drugs. The fiber industry depends heavily on the products of cotton, and the lumber products industry relies on wood from a wide variety of trees (wood fuel is used primarily in rural areas). Approximately 2.5 billion people in the world still rely on subsistence farming to satisfy their basic needs, while the rest are tied into increasingly complex production and distribution systems to provide food, fiber, fuel, and other plant-derived **commodities**. The capability of plants to satisfy these growing needs is not a new concern. The Reverend Thomas Malthus (1766–1834) in his *Essay on the Principle of Population* in 1798 argued that population growth would exceed nature's ability to provide subsistence. According to the U.S. Census Bureau, the world population was about one billion in 1800, doubled to two billion in 1930, doubled again to four billion in 1975, and reached six billion people in 2000. World population is expected to be nine billion by the year 2050. The challenge to satisfy human needs and wants still exists.

Income has also been increasing rapidly throughout most of the world at the same time. U.S. census estimates are that the gross national product reached $27,000 per person in 1997 and is expected to reach $69,000 in 2050 assuming a 1.8 percent annual rate of growth. Income per person in many countries of Asia, Latin America, and Africa has increased more rapidly, but continues to be less than in other areas such as Western Europe and the United States. As income grows, plants become more valuable because people want to buy more and higher-quality products to satisfy basic needs.

Increasing urbanization leads to an increase in demand for marketing services as populations relocate from rural areas to urban areas. According to the Census Bureau, the U.S. population, for example, changed from 60 percent rural in 1900 to less than 25 percent rural in 2000. This urbanization demands more marketing services to assemble, sort, transport, store, and package large quantities of foods from production centers to consumption centers.

urbanization increase in size or number of cities

commodities goods that are traded, especially agricultural goods

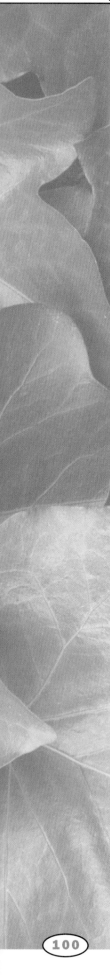

Value of Plants

According to the United Nations Food and Agriculture Organization, the estimated export value of major plant commodities traded in world markets for 1998 was: rice ($9.9 billion dollars), maize ($9.1 billion), wheat ($15.1 billion), soybeans ($9 billion), coffee greens and roast ($13.7 billion), sugar ($5.9 billion), tobacco ($24.1 billion), cigarettes ($15.4 billion), lint cotton ($8.2 billion), forest products ($123 billion), and forest pulp for paper ($13 billion).

Markets, a place where people buy and sell goods and services, determine the economic value of plants. The value depends on the expected uses and benefits provided. The economic value of plants is measured by their prices in a market economy. Demand and supply determine the price. In most countries, markets operate freely with little direct government interference in trading. In centrally planned economies such as China, however, the government frequently controls market operations, and buys and sells through government companies. In planned economies, governments may set prices administratively at levels that do not indicate true economic value to consumers and producers. As world economies become more open and market-oriented through trade agreements such as those that come from the World Trade Organization, the value of plants will likely become more equal among countries.

Two main types of markets set the value of plants: cash markets and future markets. The most common type is a cash market. Cash markets are very popular places throughout the world where buyers and sellers meet to exchange money for goods and services. Demand and supply in the cash market set the price at which buyers will exchange money with sellers for immediate possession of goods. In the simplest case, producers take goods to the market for immediate sale, and consumers arrive with cash to buy goods for immediate possession. In more complex cases, producers sell goods to one or more other buyers who in turn sell the goods to consumers.

Cash markets operate daily, weekly, or for other intervals all over the world. Consumers and producers trade in thousands of cash markets operating in the world today. These local cash markets in rural areas are linked to larger regional trading centers that in turn are linked to cash markets in the larger cities. Cash markets operate for all the major plant products.

Futures markets, a second major market to set the economic value of plants, operate very differently from cash markets. In cash markets buyers and sellers trade the physical good, whereas in futures markets buyers and sellers trade a futures contract. Futures contracts are standardized written documents calling for future delivery of a good at a particular time and place in the month of expiration. Futures markets attempt to discover the best value today for a good tomorrow based upon expected demand and supply in some future time period.

Futures markets have become increasingly popular around the world. Important futures exchanges include the Chicago Board of Trade for grains and oilseeds; the Chicago Mercantile Exchange for livestock, dairy products, and lumber; and the New York exchanges for cocoa, coffee, cotton, orange juice, and sugar. Futures contracts are traded on exchanges in Great

Britain, France, Japan, Australia, Singapore, and Canada. In addition, Brazil, China, Mexico, Italy, and Spain (to name a few) have futures exchanges.

It is interesting to note that futures markets do not trade contracts in fruits and vegetables and other highly perishable products. Futures trading is not possible for highly perishable products because of the difficulty of long-term storage.

Marketing Systems for Plants

The marketing system for most plants can be viewed as an hourglass shape that concentrates production from many farms into large quantities and fewer firms for processing and handling, followed by a distribution into smaller quantities and more firms for sale to many consumers. Marketing systems add value as the plants progress from the farmer to the consumer. The added value takes the form of marketing services that transform a raw commodity into a finished product for consumer use. Depending on the commodity, these services include cleaning, sorting, grading, packaging, storing, transporting, handling, processing, and financing until goods are sold to the consumer.

Farmers usually sell their goods at harvest time in local markets to buyers who may come from large urban or smaller regional trading centers, or farmers sell to agents of those buyers. The buyers assume the risks of ownership until they are able to sell the goods to consumers at a later time. The ownership risks include providing many valuable marketing services to assure that products will be available in the right quality, in the right place, at the right time, in the appropriate amount, and for a reasonable price.

The difference between the value paid by consumers for plants and the value received by producers is the marketing margin, which is the amount charged by the businesses for the services provided. For example, if the consumer pays one dollar for a product in the supermarket, and the producer receives forty cents, then the marketing margin is sixty cents.

Higher incomes and growing populations mean that consumers will demand more marketing services that increase convenience and reduce preparation time, such as slicing, freezing, packaging, and ready for microwaving. In addition, as per capita income increases, the composition of demand for food changes to increased consumption of higher-value products. These changes typically mean increased consumption of products such as fruits and vegetables, meat, dairy, and processed products, and decreased consumption of staples such as potatoes, cassava, and rice. More marketing services are required for high-valued products.

As consumers demand more marketing services, the marketing margin will increase, causing the farmers' share of the consumer food dollar to decline. In many countries, the farmers' share of consumer expenditures (about 40 to 50 percent) is already declining, as marketing margins increase. John Abbott in *Agricultural and Food Marketing in Developing Countries* indicated that margins also vary by country for the same commodity due to differences in income, geography, **infrastructure**, and marketing systems.

The farmers' share of consumer food expenditures has declined steadily through time in the United States to about 21 percent in 1993; ranging from

infrastructure roads, phone lines, and other utilities that allow commerce

25 percent for food consumed at home to 15 percent for away-from-home consumption. This declining farmers' share can be expected to continue as income increases. A declining farmers' share does not mean that the marketing system is inefficient or that farming is unprofitable. Technical progress that increases productivity generally will result in declining real prices per unit of output.

Farmers can increase their share of the consumer food expenditures by adding value to what they sell. Some examples of added value are direct sales to consumers at farmers' markets, roadside markets, and farmer-owned marketing and processing cooperatives. Paul Eck in *The American Cranberry* described Ocean Spray cranberry juice as a most successful story of farmers adding value to cranberries. Cranberry growers formed a cooperative to process and market Ocean Spray cranberry juice more profitably, a product that has great brand identification with consumers. SEE ALSO AGRICULTURE, HISTORY OF; AGRICULTURE, MODERN; ALCOHOLIC BEVERAGE INDUSTRY; ALCOHOLIC BEVERAGES; ALLIACEAE; CACAO; COFFEE; CORN; COTTON; FIBER AND FIBER PRODUCTS; FORESTRY; FRUITS; GRAINS; OILS, PLANT-DERIVED; PAPER; POTATO; POTATO BLIGHT; RICE; SUGAR; TEA; TOBACCO; VEGETABLES; WHEAT.

Donald W. Larson

Bibliography

Abbott, John C. *Agricultural and Food Marketing in Developing Countries: Selected Readings.* Tucson, AZ: University of Arizona Press, 1993.

Catlett, Lowell B., and James D. Libbin. *Investing in Futures and Options Markets.* Albany, NY: Delmar Publishers, 1999.

Eck, Paul. *The American Cranberry.* New Brunswick, NJ: Rutgers University Press, 1990.

Meyer, Richard L., and Donald W. Larson. "Issues in Providing Agricultural Services in Developing Countries." In *Promoting Third-World Development and Food Security*, eds. Luther G. Tweeten and Donald G. McClelland. Westport, CT: Praeger, 1997.

Rhodes, V. James, and Jan L. Dauve. *The Agricultural Marketing System*, 5th ed. Scottsdale, AZ: Holcomb Hathaway, 1998.

Ecosystems

Systems are assemblages of interacting objects that are linked by transfers of energy and matter, behave in specific ways under certain conditions, and are often governed by cybernetic controls that involve the flow of information through positive and **negative feedback**. In 1935 British ecologist Arthur Tansley (1871–1955) described functioning organisms and their physical environment as the "basic units of nature on the face of the Earth" and referred to them by the term "ecosystem." The components are both living (within the biotic realm) and nonliving (abiotic). The biotic components comprise the communities of organisms formed by interacting populations. While ecosystems are real, functioning places, they are also the abstractions, or models, that are developed to characterize the function and potentially predict the behavior of these real places.

One important aspect of ecosystems is the definition of their boundaries. In some cases this is superficially obvious. A pond can be thought of as an ecosystem with the boundaries between the water and the terrestrial

negative feedback a process in which a change in some variable leads to a system response that minimizes that change

Interior of Biosphere II, an enclosed ecosystem, at Oracle, Arizona.

environment forming a shoreline, the interface between the water surface and the atmosphere defining the top, and the lower extent of wet sediments in the ooze at its bottom as recognizable surfaces. Even these, however, are not quite as clear-cut as they may seem when viewed in closer detail. The shoreline is much longer when measured with centimeter segments than with a meter stick. The water surface boundary has a layer of air **saturated** by water vapor that may or may not be considered to be part of the ecosystem; and the bottom could be complicated by the presence of the inlet from an underground spring. Boundaries are even harder to define within an expanse of seemingly continuous grassland or forest, and are therefore at times assigned in an arbitrary manner by researchers.

saturated containing as much dissolved substance as possible

Size alone does not necessarily help resolve the question. In some cases the interactions within an ecosystem occur over many kilometers, and the boundaries are formed by decreasing probabilities of transfers of matter and energy with other parts of the system. On the other hand, sometimes very small units can be thought of as ecosystems. The moss-covered back of a sloth, a pile of bear dung, or the surface of your skin can be treated theoretically as a microcosm or miniature ecosystem. The frequent indistinctness of boundaries, and the fact that energy and matter enters and leaves the ecosystem, makes them open systems. Even if energy gains and losses are in balance, it is more appropriate to describe an ecosystem as a steady state rather than equilibrium, because equilibrium (which is only possible in a completely isolated, thermodynamically closed system), does not ade-

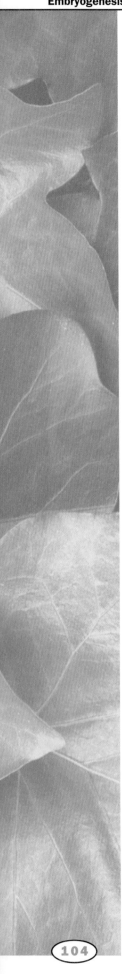

quately model ecosystems. They are always dynamically interacting with adjacent ecosystems to form a complex landscape.

One of the most powerful tools emerging from the ecosystem concept is the development of models that abstract the structure and function of the real world. Pictures and graphs describe physical arrangement of objects. Flow charts characterize highly probable pathways for energy or nutrients to pass through the system. In the case of energy, this flow is a one-way street with its ultimate dissipation outside of the boundaries as heat and entropy. Nutrients, however, can be retained and recycled within the ecosystem. The extent to which this happens is one measure of stability.

The beauty of ecosystem models is that they can be quantified. This allows them to be analyzed mathematically on computers and ultimately, if the models are based on real, natural behaviors, they can be used to predict the future of ecosystems. The rapidly developing field of general systems theory can be applied to ecosystems resulting in insights about how they function. These tools also allow ecologists to make predictions about the behavior of ecosystems when disturbed, stressed, or altered by evolutionary time, questions that society is finding pressing with increasing pollution, global warming, and other environmental threats. SEE ALSO AGRICULTURAL ECOSYSTEMS; AQUATIC ECOSYSTEMS; BIOME; COASTAL ECOSYSTEMS; ECOLOGY, ENERGY FLOW; ECOLOGY, FIRE; ECOLOGY, HISTORY OF; PLANT COMMUNITY PROCESSES.

W. Dean Cocking

Bibliography

Tansley, Arthur G. "The Use and Abuse of Vegetational Concepts and Terms." *Ecology* 16, no. 3 (1935): 284–307.

Embryogenesis

The development of the embryo, or embryogenesis, begins with the repeated divisions of the **zygote** to give rise to thousands of cells. These in turn form the various tissues and organs of the adult plant. In seed plants, embryogenesis occurs within the embryo sac of the ovule. Since the ovule is transformed into the seed, embryo development is intimately associated with seed formation.

Dicot and Monocot Embryos

The first division of the zygote is almost always asymmetric (uneven) and **transverse to** its long axis, producing a small **apical** cell and a large basal (bottom) cell. The apical cell then divides, forming a longitudinal wall, and then divides again, forming a second wall at right angles to the first, to generate a four-celled embryo; subsequent divisions give rise to a globular embryo of eight to thirty-two cells. By changes in shape, accompanied by tissue and organ formation, the globular embryo successively forms the heart-shaped, torpedo-shaped, walking-stick-shaped, and mature embryo.

In contrast, the basal cell divides by a series of transverse walls to form a **filamentous** structure known as the suspensor, which anchors the embryo to the embryo sac wall and aids in nutrient absorption from the

zygote the egg immediately after it has been fertilized; the one-cell stage of a new individual

transverse to across, or side to side

apical at the tip

filamentous thin and long

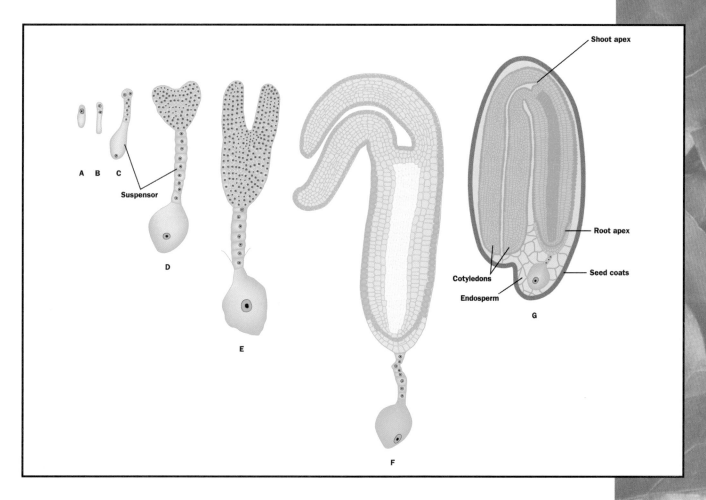

Diagrammatic representations of embryogenesis and seed formation in *Capsella bursa-pastoris*. A) Zygote. B) First zygote division producing a small apical cell and a large basal cell. C) Further divisions of the apical cells and basal cells to form the globular embryo and suspensor, respectively. D) A heart-shaped embryo. E) A torpedo-shaped embryo. The suspensor has attained its maximum development. F) A walking-stick-shaped embryo. Suspensor degeneration begins. G) A mature embryo enclosed inside the seed and covered by seed coats. Only a few endosperm cells are present; suspensor loses its connection with the embryo.

surrounding tissues. Typically in dicots, the mature embryo consists of the shoot apex, the two cotyledons (seed leaves), the hypocotyl (primitive stem), and the root. Together, these occupy most of the volume of the mature seed. Although the early division sequences of embryos of monocots appear somewhat similar to those of dicots, several organs not found in dicot embryos assume prominence in monocot embryos, especially in embryos of cereal grains. In the latter, the single cotyledon (known as the scutellum) functions to absorb nutrients from the endosperm. Sheathlike structures, known as the coleorhiza and coleoptile, cover the root and shoot, respectively. Finally, a flaplike outgrowth called the epiblast is found at the origin of the coleorhiza. The mature embryo is confined to a small part of the cereal grain, which is filled with the nutritive tissue of the endosperm.

Tissue Formation in the Early Embryo

Although embryos lack most organs of the adult plant, the characteristic body plan of the adult is nonetheless established during early embryogenesis. This involves the formation of an apico-basal (top-bottom) axis, constituting the body of the embryo, and a radial axis of differentiated tissues around the apico-basal axis. In dicots, the apico-basal axis is established as early as the four-celled stage of the embryo, when a transverse division gives rise to upper and lower tiers of four cells each. The shoot apical meristem and cotyledons are generated from the upper tier of cells, and the

Genetic and molecular studies of embryogenesis in *Arabidopsis thaliana* have shown that specific genes control the formation of both apico-basal and radial pattern elements in the embryo. Among the genes isolated and characterized are *Gnom*, *Monopteros*, and *Shoot Meristemless*, controlling the apico-basal pattern, and *Knolle*, controlling the radial pattern.

meristem the growing tip of a plant

epidermis outer layer of cells

primordial primitive or early

vascular related to transport of nutrients

lateral away from the center

hypocotyl and root are generated from the lower tier. Thus, the primary **meristems** of the shoot and root come to occupy positions at opposite poles of the embryo axis. In *Arabidopsis thaliana* and *Capsella bursa-pastoris*, two model species to study embryogenesis in dicots, the uppermost cell of the suspensor (known as the hypophysis) functions as the founder cell that generates parts of the embryonic root such as the root cap, cortex, quiescent center, and **epidermis**.

After the apico-basal axis is established, the radial pattern elements of the **primordial** tissue layers are laid down in the eight-celled embryo by a new round of divisions. These create an outer layer of eight cells (forming the protoderm) and an inner core of eight cells (forming the ground meristem and procambium). The protoderm and procambium become the epidermal and **vascular** tissues, respectively, of the mature embryo, whereas the cells of the ground meristem differentiate into a cortex or into both cortex and pith. In cereals such as maize, the globular embryo of sixteen to thirty-two cells attains a club-shaped stage when the scutellum appears as a vague elevation at the apico-basal region. The shoot apex and leaf primordia are formed as **lateral** outgrowths opposite the scutellum. Finally, the appearance of the coleorhiza and the differentiation of the root in the central zone of the embryo complete the process of embryogenesis. In both dicot and monocot embryos, the active life of the suspensor is terminated when the embryonic organs are formed. SEE ALSO CELLS, SPECIALIZED TYPES; DIFFERENTIATION AND DEVELOPMENT; GENETIC MECHANISMS AND DEVELOPMENT; GERMINATION; REPRODUCTION, FERTILIZATION AND; SEEDS; TISSUES.

V. Raghavan

Bibliography

Raghavan, V. *Molecular Embryology of Flowering Plants*. New York: Cambridge University Press, 1997.

Raven, Peter H., Ray F. Evert, and Susan E. Eichhorn. *Biology of Plants*, 6th ed. New York: W. H. Freeman and Company, 1999.

Endangered Species

An endangered species is a species that is in immediate danger of becoming extinct. The designation of *endangered* to a species means that there is still time to save it but once it is extinct it is gone forever. Also of concern are threatened species, species whose numbers are low or declining but not in immediate danger of extinction. A *threatened* species is likely to become endangered if it is not protected.

Most species that are endangered are found in only limited geographic areas. Because these plants or animals are not widespread to begin with, they are more likely to be affected by major or catastrophic changes in their environment. Widespread common species, while sometimes significantly hurt by a regional catastrophe, are more likely to survive because many individuals will escape the damage elsewhere. In contrast, species found only in small and unusual habitats can suddenly become endangered or extinct if their limited habitat disappears.

A leaf of the Presidio manzanita in San Francisco's Golden Gate Park. Only one such plant survives in the wild.

Processes That Threaten Endangered Species

Extinction can be part of the natural order. Only about one in a thousand of all of the species that have ever lived on Earth is still living today. The vast majority became extinct because of naturally changing physical and biological conditions. Changing climate such as that experienced during the Ice Age (which eliminated many plant species from very large areas of North America and Europe) and other natural events such as volcanic activity have caused localized plant extinctions. The slow movement of the continents (most notably Antarctica and Australia) into unsuitable climate zones caused many organisms to become extinct. Far more widespread and devastating natural extinctions have been caused by the rare impacts of asteroids and comets on the Earth. Some impacts have caused the extinction of even common species on a global scale.

The danger to plants and animals today is most often a direct result of human activities and human population increase. These activities have taken the form of habitat alteration, economic exploitation, the intentional elim-

The Beni Biosphere Reserve in Bolivia. Managing ecosystems or saving species collectively is the best known solution for protecting endangered species.

ination of pests, the introduction of exotic (nonnative) organisms, the increase of invasive native grazers, and the effects of environmental pollution.

Habitat alteration is the main factor endangering species throughout the world, from the American Midwest where the prairies have been converted to cropland to the equator where the tropical rain forests are being cut and burned. Wetlands filling and draining, agricultural expansion, and residential housing development are all significant factors in habitat destruction.

Trade in live plants and animals and the products made from them is the second greatest factor endangering species. The cutting of forests for wood and fuel, the digging of rare plants for sale, and the harvesting of medicinal plants for commerce is as common as the illegal hunting and poaching of animals for sport, food, products, or pets. Plant examples include such species as ginseng, which has been harvested in several states to the point of near extinction.

The intentional elimination of species is a third human factor endangering species. Many plants and animals have become endangered or extinct simply because people decided they were pests. Killing for the sake of elim-

inating an unwanted animal or plant has been common, as seen in the burning or clearing of forests for agriculture or other development, or in the killing of lions, wolves, sharks, or many snakes considered to be pests.

Invasions by exotic species (animal or plant species that have been introduced to an area where they did not naturally occur) threaten many endangered plants. When plants or animals are introduced into an area where they have no natural enemies, they may start to compete with the native plants and animals for food, water, shelter, and space and often replace them. Some plant examples include teasel and aggressive European pasture grasses that have invaded the few remaining tallgrass prairies or aquatic plants that have clogged streams and canals. The introduction of goats to tropical islands, for example, has caused the endangerment and extinction of many plant species that were not adapted to such grazing. A similar impact to plants can occur from locally overabundant or expanding native species such as beavers, rabbits, and deer that have altered many habitats because of the elimination of their former natural predators. For example, in many areas of the midwestern and eastern United States, heavy browsing by white-tailed deer is preventing the regeneration of the endangered components of native plant communities. Conservation biologists must be as effective in controlling invasive and destructive species as they are at saving endangered native species.

Environmental poisons and pollution are endangering numerous plants and animals worldwide as well. Examples of plants and animals today that are being poisoned by environmental **toxins** and solid wastes such as deadly chemicals, oils, and acids are numerous. Scientists learned long ago that groups of organisms in a limited environment can be killed by their own wastes.

toxin a poisonous substance

Many Plants Are Endangered

One in ten, or a total of about three thousand plants native to the United States is endangered. Many of these endangered plants include some of the most showy, such as the large-flowered orchids. Increasingly, many plants around the world no longer reseed and therefore remain as lone survivors of their species. For example, the Presidio manzanita is so rare that only one plant survives in the wild, at San Francisco's Golden Gate Park. While cuttings have been **propagated**, they cannot self-fertilize. Another example of a lone survivor can be found on the Indian Ocean's Mascarene Islands where a palm tree, the *Hyophorbe amaricaulis*, survives as a single individual. One severe storm could cause its extinction. More than two hundred other plant species have also stopped reproducing. Worldwide, an impressive one in eight plants is endangered, according to the *1997 IUCN Red List of Threatened Plants*.

propagate to create more of through sexual or asexual reproduction

Plant Extinctions Are Increasing

Although conservation efforts have begun in recent years, people are still exterminating entire species at an ever-increasing rate. Since the Pilgrims landed at Plymouth Rock, more than five hundred species, subspecies, and varieties of our nation's plants and animals have become lost forever. By contrast, during the three thousand years of the Pleistocene Ice Age, all of North America lost only about ninety species. The situation is even worse in many other parts of the world. Some scientists believe that if present

trends continue, two-thirds of the world's three hundred thousand plant species will disappear by the end of the twenty-first century.

Extinction is a difficult concept to fully grasp. We are very aware that dinosaurs no longer exist and that other animals (such as the mammoth, dodo, Carolina parakeet, passenger pigeon, and the Atlantic grey whale) are gone forever due to human activity. The Sexton Mountain mariposa lily, a flower of southwestern Oregon, was unintentionally exterminated by a road crew when Interstate 5 was built in the 1960s. The maidenhair (ginkgo) tree was planted by the Chinese in gardens many centuries ago before it became extinct in the wild. A few plants that have become extinct in the wild in recent times have been saved in some form in **cultivation**. The Franklin tree (*Franklinia*, named after Ben Franklin) was last seen in the wild in 1803 in Georgia. However, a few individuals were planted in gardens at that time and have been propagated, saving the species from total extinction. In the mid-1990s the Graves's beach plum, a seashore tree found only in Connecticut, became extinct in the wild when the only known individual died. A few cuttings have been saved in botanical gardens. Although cloning results in plants that are genetically identical, those that have become extinct in the wild but that have been saved in cultivation cannot effectively reproduce.

Mechanisms of Environmental Protection for Endangered Species

Enacted in 1973, the Endangered Species Act (ESA) is the principal tool in the United States for slowing or stopping what has become the greatest rate of extinction worldwide since the disappearance of the dinosaurs sixty-five million years ago. In adopting the Endangered Species Act, Congress found that "various species have been rendered extinct as a consequence of economic growth and development untempered by adequate concern and conservation." In addition, Congress recognized that threatened and endangered species "are of aesthetic, ecological, educational, historical, recreational, and scientific value to the Nation and its people." Congress enacted the ESA in order "to provide a means whereby the **ecosystems** upon which endangered species and threatened species depend may be conserved" and to provide a program for the conservation of the species themselves. Under the ESA, species are listed as endangered or threatened. The Interior Secretary is generally required to designate critical habitats (areas essential to the survival and recovery of a species) for threatened and endangered species. In addition, recovery plans (blueprints for bringing species back to a point where they are no longer threatened or endangered) must be developed and implemented. About one-third of listed species are now stable or improving as a result of the ESA Protections for Listed Species. Effective protection is limited by the degree of funding and enforcement of the law.

The Convention on International Trade in Endangered Species of Wild Fauna and Flora (CITES), convened in Washington, D.C., in 1973, has been signed by more than 120 countries. CITES was established for the purposes of controlling and monitoring international trade in plants and animals considered to be threatened or likely to be threatened through commercial exploitation. It states that flora and fauna comprise an "irreplaceable part of natural systems which must be protected for generations to

cultivation plant growth involving human intervention

ecosystem an ecological community together with its environment

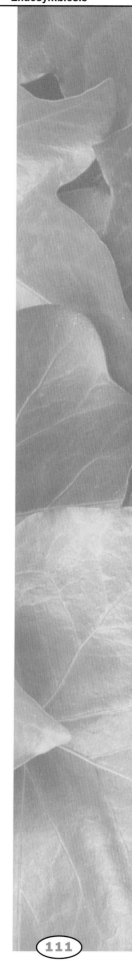

come" and "international cooperation is essential for the protection of certain species . . . [endangered by] over-exploitation through international trade." This treaty was one of the first to take account of the need for conservation of both plants and animals and provided the legal framework within which those in trade can be protected from extinction.

Conservation practices provide the only solution for protecting endangered species. Propagation centers, such as botanical gardens, are actively attempting to save some endangered plant species. Protected collections of seeds and plants can help stop species loss, but protection in the wild is much more desirable because propagating endangered species can be considered to be meaningless if they do not have a home. Managing ecosystems or saving species collectively is the best known solution. Around the world more than thirty-five hundred protected areas (with a total of about 2 million square miles [5 million square kilometers], or 3 percent of Earth's land area) exist in the form of parks, wildlife refuges, and other reserves. Three percent of the planet's area, however, can only protect a relatively small number of species. SEE ALSO BIODIVERSITY; BOTANICAL GARDENS; GINKGO; INVASIVE SPECIES; RAIN FORESTS; SEED PRESERVATION.

Steven R. Hill

Bibliography

Alvarez, L. W., W. Alvarez, F. Asaro, and H. V. Michel. "Extraterrestrial Cause for the Cretaceous-Tertiary Extinction." *Science* 208 (1980): 1095–1108.

Frankel, O. H., A. Brown, and J. J. Burdon. *The Conservation of Plant Biodiversity.* Cambridge, England: Cambridge University Press, 1995.

Garrott, R. A., and C. A. Vanderbilt White. "Overabundance: An Issue for Conservation Biologists?" *Conservation Biology* 7 (1993): 946–49.

Head, S., and R. Heinzman. *Lessons of the Rainforest.* New York: Random House, 1990.

Hecht, J. *Vanishing Life: The Mystery of Mass Extinctions.* New York: Charles Scribner's Sons, 1993.

Hunter, M. L., Jr. *Fundamentals of Conservation Biology.* Cambridge, MA: Blackwell Science, Inc., 1996.

Masters, L. L. "Assessing Threats and Setting Priorities for Conservation." *Conservation Biology* 5 (1991): 559–63.

Morse, L. E. "Rare Plant Protection, Conservancy Style." *Nature Conservancy Magazine* 37 (1987): 10–15.

Walter, K. S., and H. Gillett, eds. *1997 IUCN Red List of Threatened Plants.* Cambridge: International Union for Conservation of Nature and Natural Resources—World Conservation Union, 1998.

Endosymbiosis

Once considered a relative rarity, endosymbiosis, the living together of one organism inside another, has increasingly become recognized as a major factor in the evolution of life forms. The word *endosymbiosis* comes from Greek words meaning "inside," "with," and "living." Endosymbiosis in biology is a subdivision of the more general concept, symbiosis, which refers to living beings of different species living together for most of the life history of a member of at least one of those species. (In the case of the bacteria it suffices to say "living together of different types" because bacteria often cannot clearly be assigned to species.) Ectosymbiosis is a more familiar notion,

A micrograph of a leaf, showing chloroplasts (green). These plastids are believed to have once been free-living photosynthetic bacteria that became parts of plant cells by endosymbiosis.

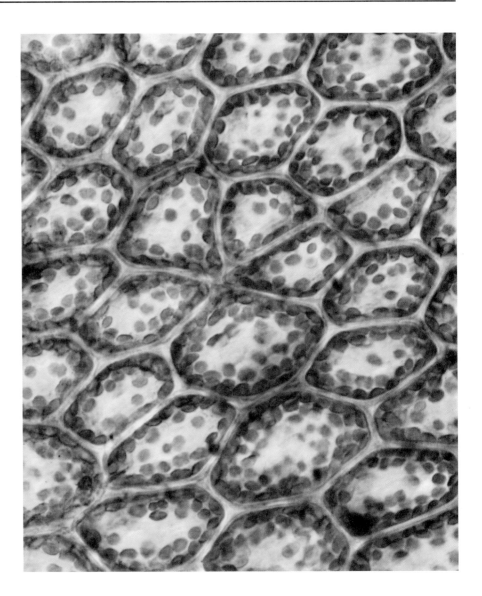

chloroplast the photo-synthetic organelle of plants and algae

an association between organisms of different species where one is attached in some way to the outside of the other. Barnacles adhere to the hairy, wet surfaces of whales where the pattern of barnacle distribution is used by whales to distinguish each other. This is one example of ectosymbiosis.

Endosymbiosis often takes symbiosis proper a step further. As in sexual reproduction, genes from two beings come together giving added abilities to the mutual organism. Unlike in sex, however, the two organisms do not necessarily come apart immediately after their fusion. They may dwell in the same body forever. Indeed, permanent symbiosis has been proven as a means of producing new organisms.

The most stunning and momentous example of endosymbiosis is per-haps that of the photosynthetic parts of algal and plant cells, called plastids, which are now believed to have once been free-living photosynthetic bac-teria. Red plastids of red algae are called rhodoplasts. The more familiar green plastids are called **chloroplasts**. The plastids that give plants and al-gae their metabolic ability to use light to produce chemical food and energy are the same size, shape, and composition as photosynthetic bacteria. They also divide to reproduce by a process of fission—distinct from the complex mitotic division found in all nonbacterial cells with nuclei, such as plant, algae, and fungal cells. Genetic similarities in long stretches of deoxyribonucleic acid (DNA) show definitively that rhodoplasts are very closely related to cyanobacteria (oxygen-producing, green-tinged bacteria). Therefore, the direct link between cyanobacteria and the plastids of algae and plants is one of ancestry. Free-living cyanobacteria merged with nonphotosynthetic ancestors of the algal cell, including the algae that evolved into plants. Ancestors of plant cells, in other words, acquired their plastids, once free-living cyanobacteria, by endosymbiosis.

Plastids are one of a class of membrane-bounded cell structures called organelles. Others include mitochondria, bodies that react with oxygen to produce energy for the rest of the cell in which they reside. Mitochondria also contain their own DNA and are thought to be the descendants of formerly free-living bacteria. The details of how plastids, mitochondria, and other organelles came to live in permanent endosymbiosis with cells are complicated. The original union leading to the origin of plastids, however, is easy to envision. Some hungry, translucent **protists** ate delicious photosynthetic cyanobacteria and failed to digest them. In the light the cyanobacteria could not help but continue its photosynthesis. Hence, the merger, now a green cell, evolved from its cyanobacterial and **translucent** ancestors. With the passage of time the association became permanent, and resulted in the evolution of algae. Genes between the two types of life were exchanged. Eventually plants evolved from the endosymbiotic union. SEE ALSO ALGAE; CHLOROPLASTS; CYANOBACTERIA; EUBACTERIA; EVOLUTION OF PLANTS; PLASTIDS.

Lynn Margulis and Dorion Sagan

protist usually a single-celled organism with a cell nucleus, of the kingdom Protista

translucent allowing the passage of light

Bibliography

Margulis, Lynn. *Symbiosis in Cell Evolution,* 2nd ed. New York: W. H. Freeman and Company, 1993.

Epiphytes

Epiphytes (*epi,* meaning "surface," and *phytes,* meaning "plants") are plants that live on host plants, usually in the treetops. They include a wide variety of growth forms, ranging from woody structures to herbs. Epiphytes are not parasites but simply rely on their host trees for support. In return, they collect enough light to manufacture energy and also provide food and shelter for many organisms living in the treetops, such as insects, birds, and other small animals. More than twenty-five species of epiphytes have been classified by botanists, and more are found each year as botanists continue to find new ways to climb into the treetops of the tallest, unexplored regions of tropical rain forests.

Epiphytes have unique ecological characteristics that enable them to survive in the forest canopy. Some of these special adaptations include:

- holdfasts or other ways of adhering to the bark or branches of trees, so that wind or other forces do not knock them down and so they can compete for sunlight in the canopy; epiphytes do not have conventional roots that extend into the soil

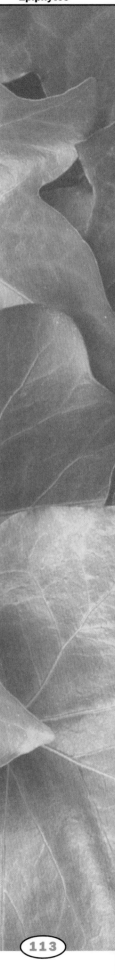

An epiphytic orchid on a tree trunk in Thailand.

herbivore an organism that feeds on plant parts

- evergreen foliage that is resistant to drying out in the hot, dry canopy and that is too tough to be chewed by insect **herbivores**

- plant shapes (e.g., cups or rosettes) that allow the collection of water, fallen leaves, and decomposing bodies of insects that together form a nutrient pool for the plant as well as for their aquatic animal inhabitants

- tiny seeds that are wind-dispersed and can lodge in tiny crevices in tree bark

- pollinators such as bees and flies that inhabit the canopy

- relationships with fungi (mycorrhizae) that aid the epiphyte in gathering additional nutrition for photosynthesis.

More than eighty families of plants contain species that are epiphytes, but only several have a significant number of species that are epiphytic in their habit. These include orchids (family Orchidaceae), bromeliads (family Bromeliaceae), cacti (family Cactaceae), ferns (family Pteridophyta), aroids (family Araceae), and several groups of ferns, mosses, and liverworts. Over

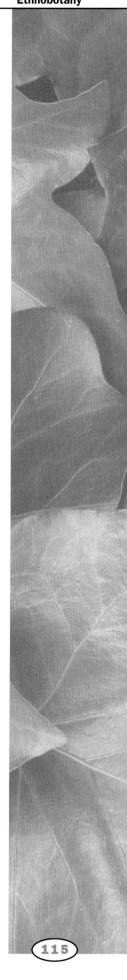

twenty-five thousand species of epiphytes exist, including approximately twenty-one thousand orchids and over one thousand species of bromeliads.

Many animals depend on epiphytes for their existence in the canopy. Tarantulas often live within the rosettes of bromeliads, while bats, birds, and insects serve as important pollinator groups for bromeliads; lizards and birds visit epiphytes for feeding and drinking; insects dominate as pollinators of orchids; and ant-nest garden epiphytes provide nesting cavities and shelter for their ant residents. Tank epiphytes, those plants that contain a pool of water formed by tightly pressed leaves in a rosette, provide a mini-aquatic ecosystem in the canopy that has been shown to support over fifty species of animals, including mosquito larvae, tadpoles, beetles, spiders, flies, and even lizards. Because epiphytes are plants and produce their own energy, they actually provide nutrients to other organisms and thereby enhance the diversity of life in the forest canopy.

Relatively little is known about epiphytes in contrast to the plants' terrestrial counterparts because of their location high above the forest floor. During the past decade, new methods for reaching the treetops have been developed that provide better access for the study of epiphytes. These techniques include the construction of canopy walkways, the use of ropes and technical climbing hardware, hot air balloons and inflatable canopy rafts, and even construction cranes. The challenge of reaching epiphytes and their inhabitants has been overcome, and in the future more information will be discovered about these unique plants that inhabit the treetops. SEE ALSO INTERACTIONS, PLANT-PLANT; MYCORRHIZAE; ORCHIDACEAE; RAIN FOREST CANOPY; RAIN FORESTS; SYMBIOSIS; TREES.

Margaret D. Lowman

Bibliography

Benzing, D. H. *Vascular Epiphytes.* Cambridge, England: Cambridge University Press, 1990.

Lowman, M. D. *Life in the Treetops.* New Haven, CT: Yale University Press, 1999.

Ethnobotany

Ethnobotany is generally defined as the scientific study of the relationships between plants and people. The fungi, while comprising a kingdom of life completely separate from plants, and, according to molecular evidence, are more closely related to animals than plants, have in practice been included within the scope of ethnobotanical research, although the term *ethnomycology* is sometimes employed to refer to the relationships between fungi and people. Additional terms are sometimes used to distinguish other subdisciplines of ethnobotany, such as *ethnopteridology* (the study of relationships between people and ferns and related plants), but for purposes of this encyclopedia, all such subdivisions are considered to be within the scope of ethnobotany. Sometimes a distinction is made between the term *economic botany*, referring to the study of the use of plants by industrialized society, and *ethnobotany*, referring to the study of plants used by nonindustrialized cultures, but this distinction is increasingly blurring. Sometimes economic botany is considered to be the broader discipline, encompassing all uses of plants by any people, from New York City to New Caledonia. For exam-

Shaman and healer Javier Zavala prepares the "rosa-risa" medicinal drink in Tarapoto, Peru. Made from the *Ayahuasca* plant and organic tobacco juice, the mixture is a hallucinogen that also serves to purge the stomach.

ple, the journal *Economic Botany* routinely contains research articles ranging from the use of fungi for medicinal purposes by Amazonian indigenous peoples to the chemical composition of palm seed oils with respect to potential industrial application. In this article, *economic botany* is considered to be synonymous with ethnobotany, and the latter term will be used hereafter.

Changing Approaches

The term "ethnobotany" was first used in a lecture by University of Pennsylvania botanist John W. Harshberger in 1895, but scholarly interest in the utility of plants goes back to the beginnings of botany, and practical interest goes back to the beginnings of civilization itself. Initially to survive, and then for civilization to develop, people needed to learn what plants were useful for foods, fuels, medicines, and fibers and how such plant resources could be mined or managed for human benefit. Harshberger's 1896 publication, *The Purposes of Ethnobotany*, marks the beginning of this academic discipline. Practitioners before and since have approached the subject from widely varying perspectives, resulting in a fluid and rapidly evolving discipline, but one with theoretical underpinnings that are still in their infancy.

Early in the twentieth century, two principal approaches to the study of plants and people developed, and it is not an oversimplification to state that one approach emphasized the "ethno" while the other focused on the "botany." Ethnobotanical studies conducted by botanists tended to be lists of plants arranged by scientific and common names with short commentary on the purpose for which the plants were used, but often with little or no information on how plant resources were managed or fit into people's lives. Anthropologists, on the other hand, were much more concerned with the cultural role of plants in people's lives, but generally only scant attention was paid to the botanical documentation of plant species being studied. One deficiency of some early ethnobotanical studies that did not cross-reference the name of a plant reported with a **specimen** deposited in an herbarium was that such studies were not reliable, as there was no way for subsequent researchers to confirm the identification or name of a plant cited. Not surprisingly, it was only when scientists of different disciplines began to col-

specimen object or organism under consideration

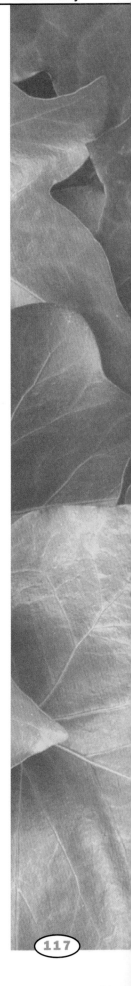

laborate with each other on ethnobotanical studies that more compete pictures began to emerge on the relationships between plants and people. In the twenty-first century, ethnobotany is characterized by being an interdisciplinary, dynamic endeavor, one that combines great intellectual challenge with tremendous practical urgency in terms of the conservation of biological and cultural diversity.

Aside from the great intellectual components to ethnobotany, the discipline is of more than academic interest. The contribution of plants to human welfare is beyond calculation. Suffice it to say, without plants there would be no people. It is impossible to overstate the importance of the contributions that ethnobotanists have made in collecting information about plants and fungi from indigenous peoples around the world. Dozens of modern medicines, such as pilocarpine, which is used for treating glaucoma, have active ingredients that came to light through ethnobotanical investigations. Hundreds of foods, fuels, fibers, and fragrances have been discovered by ethnobotanists through their investigations into the relationship between plants and people. It makes sense that indigenous people, who have experimented with using organisms in their natural environment for centuries, or even millennia, would never have survived to the present day if they had not figured out what components of the biosphere were useful, or, conversely, harmful. Ethnobotanists are basically studying the success stories in people's use and attempts to sustain nature, a topic of great and timely importance.

Great efforts are now being put into the prospecting for new commercial products from nature, and this activity, variously termed **biodiversity** prospecting or chemical prospecting, is now a major activity, supported by governments and industry. The activity is usually associated with the search for new patent medicines, but it applies equally to the search for new, naturally derived products of any sort; for example, a perfume company might undertake a program of searching for new fragrances from the rain forest, using indigenous people's knowledge of floral aromas as a starting point.

biodiversity degree of variety of life

Of equal importance are the activities of ethnobotanists that relate to understanding how local people manage their biotic resources; this research has great applicability to land use managers, conservation policymakers, and, of course, to local peoples themselves, as often the very act of documentation of resource use by scientists gives legitimacy to local people's tried-and-true management methods. This approach, when the conservation of biodiversity is factored into the equation, has been termed the "New Environmentalism" by renowned Harvard University biologist Professor Edward O. Wilson: "The race is on to develop methods, to draw more income from the wildlands without killing them, and so to give the invisible hand of free-market economics a green thumb." Ethnobotanists have a major role in developing the New Environmentalism as a strategy for managing biodiversity and maximizing its conservation, with efforts to make such efforts truly sustainable being the most elusive component.

Methods of Ethnobotany

Until the 1990s, there existed no widely available references on how ethnobotanical studies are conducted; students largely had to work under the supervision of an established researcher and/or figure out methodology through trial and error. This situation has now greatly improved, and aspiring ethnobotanists can consult Miguel N. Alexiades's *Selected Guidelines*

for Ethnobotanical Research: A Field Manual (1996) and Gary J. Martin's *Ethnobotany: A Methods Manual* (1995). Central to the conduct of ethnobotanical studies is the researcher's understanding of the professional ethics of the situation, and this involves openness and honesty in dealing with the people whose use of plants is being studied, collaborating scientists, government officials, project funding agencies, and all other stakeholders in the dynamic field research process. Ethnobotanists occupy a special position in the middle, serving as brokers of a sort, dealing on one hand with other scientists, policymakers, and funders, and on the other hand with people who may be among the least powerful in society, and for whom the ethnobotanist has a special responsibility in terms of respecting their confidentiality and trust.

Ethnobotanists tend to have their intellectual roots in one or more traditional academic discipline, such as botany or anthropology. Formal training equivalent to a double major in college is a good preparation. A graduate degree is practically required to secure employment as an ethnobotanist. As ethnobotany has become more interdisciplinary, the most interesting and vital studies are increasingly being done by researchers who have training in, for example, medicine and botany, or anthropology, economics, and botany, or informatics, botany, and geography. Obviously, no one individual can possibly encompass the range of disciplines represented in ethnobotany, but students should at least strive to be as broadly trained as possible, at least in the understanding of and appreciation for diverse approaches.

There are a number of practical considerations that an ethnobotanist should keep in mind in anticipation of conducting field research. It certainly helps to be in good physical condition, as fieldwork is often conducted in physically challenging locales and with local people who are fully adapted to those difficult conditions. Assuming the ethnobotanist can keep up with the people he or she wants to interview and learn from, the next consideration is linguistics. Ideally, the ethnobotanist will learn to speak as much of the relevant local language as possible. A less desirable but workable situation is to arrange for interpreters to assist with interviews, keeping in mind that the saying "things can get lost in the translation" has a basis in reality. Aside from the general trait of having a curious, analytic mind, which would describe most successful scientists, additional essential qualities that are required of ethnobotanists are those of patience, as information is usually gathered in a slow, methodical manner, and flexibility, as things rarely work out as planned. Ethnobotany has a large role in elucidating the information about the plant and fungal kingdoms that is needed by science and society. It is a dynamic, intellectually stimulating and rapidly evolving discipline, and one that holds much promise for shedding light on solutions to the crisis in biological diversity. SEE ALSO AGRICULTURE, HISTORY OF; MEDICINAL PLANTS; NATIVE FOOD CROPS; PLANT PROSPECTING; PSYCHOACTIVE PLANTS.

Brian M. Boom

Bibliography

Alexiades, M. N., ed. *Selected Guidelines for Ethnobotanical Research: A Field Manual.* New York: New York Botanical Garden Press, 1996.

Balick, M. J., and P. A. Cox. *Plants, People, and Culture: The Science of Ethnobotany.* New York: Scientific American Library, 1996.

Lewington, A. *Plants for People.* London: Natural History Museum, 1990.

Martin, Gary J. *Ethnobotany: A Methods Manual.* Staley Thornes, 1995.

Schultes, R. E., and S. von Reis, eds. *Ethnobotany: Evolution of a Discipline.* Portland, OR: Dioscorides Press, 1995.

Simpson, B. B., and M. C. Ogorzaly. *Economic Botany: Plants in Our World,* 2nd ed. New York: McGraw-Hill, Inc., 1995.

Ethylene *See Hormones.*

Eubacteria

Eubacteria (more commonly known as bacteria) are **prokaryotic** microorganisms that can be found almost everywhere on Earth. They are usually single cells but can also be found in chains, **filaments**, or multicellular clusters. Most are about 1 micron (1 μm), or one millionth of a meter in length, although some of the largest can be up to half a millimeter (500 μm). They come in a variety of shapes such as rods, filaments, spirals, vibrio (comma-shaped), and cocci (ball-shaped). Some have stalks that can be used for attachment. Many of them can move by gliding or by rotating small, pro-

prokaryotes single-celled organisms without nuclei, including Eubacteria and Archaea

filament a threadlike extension

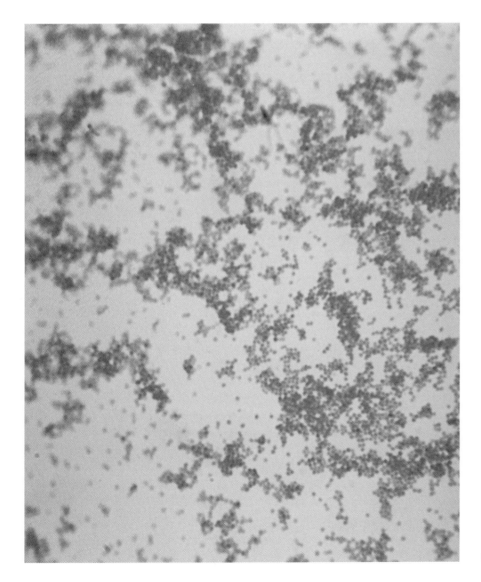

Cocci-shaped eubacteria.

flagella threadlike extension of the cell membrane, used for movement

mitosis the part of the cell cycle in which chromosomes are separated to give each daughter cell an identical chromosome set

eukaryotic a cell with a nucleus (*eu* means "true" and *karyo* means "nucleus"); includes protists, plants, animals, and fungi

protist usually a single-celled organism with a cell nucleus, of the kingdom Protista

organelle a membrane-bound structure within a cell

chloroplast the photosynthetic organelle of plants and algae

covalent held together by electron-sharing bonds

toxin a poisonous substance

jecting filaments called **flagella**. They lack the complex intracellular motility and **mitosis** found in **eukaryotic** cells.

Cellular Structure

Bacterial cells are fairly simple in structure when compared to the eukaryotic cells of fungi, **protists**, plants, and animals. As seen with an electron microscope, the majority of bacterial cell volume is filled with ribosomes, the sites of protein synthesis. Some bacteria, such as those that are photosynthetic, contain many internal membranes where metabolic processes take place. They contain no internal **organelles**, such as mitochondria and **chloroplasts**. Like archaea, bacteria have a prokaryotic cell organization: their deoxyribonucleic acid (DNA) is loosely gathered into a nucleoid and is not surrounded by a nuclear membrane, like that found in Eukaryotes. The DNA usually occurs as a single long circular strand, but some bacteria have linear chromosomes or divide their genetic material into several DNA molecules. Although they are different from the chromosomes of Eukaryotes, the large circular or linear prokaryotic DNA molecules are often termed chromosomes as well. Bacteria can also have smaller circles of DNA called plasmids, which usually carry a small number of genes used for specific metabolic functions—for example, to allow bacteria to metabolize certain compounds. Plasmids can easily be passed from cell to cell, allowing bacteria to rapidly pick up new metabolic functions, and are the basis for many advances in genetic engineering.

Like all living cells, bacteria are surrounded by lipid membranes. Most bacteria also have cell walls made up of a peptidoglycan called murein. The peptidoglycan layer is made up of a single kind of molecule from **covalently** linked sugar derivatives and amino acids. This molecule surrounds the bacterial cell like chain mail armor. Together with the osmotic pressure, the wall gives cells rigidity and shape. The cell wall structure and the presence or absence of a second lipid membrane surrounding the murein layer determine how bacteria react in a procedure called the Gram stain. Gram-positive organisms, which take up Gram stain, have a single membrane and a very thick outer peptidoglycan layer. Gram-negative organisms do not take up the stain and have two membranes in between which is a thin layer of peptidoglycan.

Distribution and Ecological Roles

Although bacteria may appear simple, they excel in the diversity and complexity of their metabolic capabilities and they are able to survive in many places. Bacteria are found everywhere on Earth where life is able to exist. They are plentiful in soils, bodies of water, on ice and snow, and are even found deep within Earth's crust. They often take advantage of living in and on other organisms in symbiotic relationships and can be found inhabiting the intestinal tracts and surfaces of animals, including humans. For the most part, the bacteria in and around us bring us more benefit than harm. Sometimes however, bacteria can be pathogenic, or disease causing. This can happen for a number of reasons, such as when the host has a compromised immune system or when a bacterium acquires genes that make it grow more aggressively or secrete **toxins** into its host environment.

Oxygen-producing photosynthesis, which is so familiar in plants, is actually a bacterial invention. Many bacteria are photosynthetic and use light energy to turn CO_2 from the atmosphere into cell material. Among these

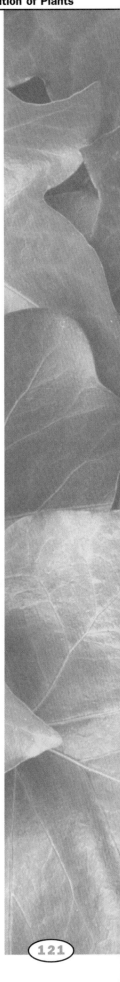

only the **cyanobacteria** produce oxygen during photosynthesis. Plastids, the photosynthetic organelles found in plants and algae, evolved from cyanobacteria through a process called endosymbiosis, in which cyanobacteria lived inside the cells of other organisms that were the ancestors of green algae. Mitochondria, found in most eukaryotic cells, also evolved from nonphotosynthetic respiring bacteria in this way.

Bacteria are crucial for the cycling of elements necessary for all life. Through various processes, which we generally call decomposition, bacteria break down the cell materials of dead organisms into simpler carbon-, phosphorus-, sulfur-, and nitrogen-containing nutrients that can be used again by other organisms for growth. Without bacteria to recycle these essential nutrients, they would remain within the dead organisms or sediments and would thus be unavailable for use by other organisms. SEE ALSO ARCHAEA; BIOGEOCHEMICAL CYCLES; CYANOBACTERIA; DECOMPOSERS; ENDOSYMBIOSIS; EVOLUTION OF PLANTS; NITROGEN FIXATION.

J. Peter Gogarten and Lorraine Olendzenski

Bibliography

Needham, Cynthia, Mahlon Hoagland, Kenneth McPherson, and Bert Dodson. *Intimate Strangers: Unseen Life on Earth*. Washington, DC: ASM Press, 2000.

Schlegel, H. G. *General Microbiology*, 7th ed., tr. M. Kogut. Cambridge: Cambridge University Press, 1993.

Evolution of Plants

Plants, descended from aquatic green algal ancestors, first appeared on land more than 450 million years ago during or prior to the Ordovician period. This event preceded the colonization of land by four-footed animals (tetrapods), which occurred considerably later in the Devonian period (408 to 360 million years ago). Understanding the origin of plants is important because early plants were essential to the development of favorable terrestrial environments and provided a source of food for animals. In addition, the earliest plants were ancestral to all of the food, fiber, and medicinal plants upon which modern humans depend. The hominid **lineage**, leading to modern humans, is only about 4 million years old; most modern plant community types are considerably older.

Ancient, microscopic fossils and deoxyribonucleic acid (DNA) evidence indicate that the earliest land plants resembled modern bryophytes, the liverworts, hornworts, and mosses. Bryophytes are smaller and simpler than other plants. Other larger and more complete fossils reveal that plants became increased in size, and their structure and reproduction became much more complex during the Silurian and Devonian periods (438 to 360 million years ago). The ancestors of today's **vascular** and seed plants appeared during this time. During the Carboniferous period (360 to 286 million years ago) the warm, moist climate favored the growth of extensive, lush forests of ferns and other tree-sized vascular plants. These forests had a dramatic effect on Earth's atmospheric chemistry, resulting in a large increase in oxygen and a drastic reduction in carbon dioxide. The consequent reduction in greenhouse warming caused the climate to change to cooler, drier conditions in the Permian (286 to 248 million years ago), and fostered the rise of the seed plants known as **gymnosperms**. The gymnosperms continued to dominate through the Mesozoic era (248 to 65 million years ago), provid-

cyanobacteria photosynthetic prokaryotic bacteria formerly known as blue-green algae

lineage ancestry; the line of evolutionary descent of an organism

vascular related to transport of nutrients

gymnosperm a major group of plants that includes the conifers

An example of a more complex charophycean green alga, *Coleochaete.* This alga is about the size of a pencil point and grows in shallow lakes and ponds, attached to rocks or higher plant stems and leaves. It has many plant-like features.

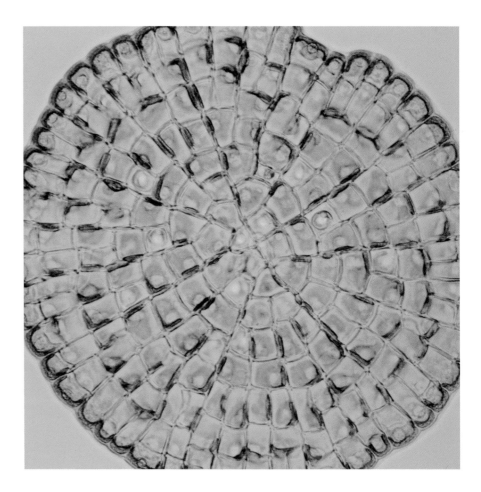

molecular systematics the analysis of DNA and other molecules to determine evolutionary relationships

phylogenetic related to phylogeny, the evolutionary development of a species

ing sustenance for giant, herbivorous dinosaurs. Although flowering plants, known as angiosperms, were present by the Cretaceous period (144 to 65 million years ago) and were quite diverse late in this time frame, they shared dominance with gymnosperms until the famously destructive Cretaceous/ Tertiary comet or asteroid impact about 65 million years ago. As a result of this event, many previously successful plant groups (as well as dinosaurs and other animals) became extinct. This created new opportunities for flowering plants, mammals, and birds, which consequently became very diverse.

Much of what we know about the origin and evolutionary diversification of plants comes from **molecular systematics**, the comparative study of DNA extracted from modern plants. This information allows botanists to construct phylogenetic trees, which are branched diagrams from which evolutionary events can be inferred. **Phylogenetic** trees can also be constructed from structural data, including information from fossils, in order to understand plant evolution. The study of fossils is important because many groups of extinct plants have left few or no close modern relatives from which DNA can be obtained.

The Origin of Land Plants

DNA, structural, and biochemical evidence has conclusively pinpointed a particular group of freshwater green algae known as the charophyceans as the modern organisms that are most closely related to the earliest plants, and have also revealed important steps in plant evolution. Bodies of the most basic charophyceans are either single-celled or form simple groups of cells. Other charophyceans more closely related to plants, according to DNA data, are more complex in their structure and reproduction. These include *Coleochaete* and Charales, a group that is commonly known as stoneworts. The comparison of simple to more complex charophyceans has revealed the origin of several important plant attributes, including: cellulose cell walls; intercellular connections known as **plasmodesmata**; and the **phragmoplast**, a specialized system of components necessary for plant cell division.

DNA evidence also marks liverworts as the modern land plants that appeared earliest; liverworts have the simplest plant bodies and reproduction of all plant groups. The ancient microfossils thought to represent the remains of the earliest plants are very similar to the components of modern liverworts. However, the order in which various bryophyte groups appeared is somewhat controversial; some experts argue that hornworts may have come first. Nonetheless, most experts are agreed that mosses are the latest-appearing group of bryophytes and that they are most closely related to vascular plants.

The balance of evidence strongly indicates that all of the modern land plants are derived from a single common ancestor (i.e., they are **monophyletic**), and that this ancestor resembled modern *Coleochaete* and Charales. DNA and other evidence do not support earlier ideas that various modern plant groups evolved independently from different charophycean ancestors. Because modern-day charophycean algae occupy primarily fresh waters, the direct ancestors of land plants are thought to have also been fresh water algae; plants did not arise from ocean seaweeds, as was once thought.

The comparison of *Coleochaete* and Charales to bryophytes, particularly liverworts, has revealed much about the evolutionary origin of plant features that contributed to the ability of the first plants to survive on land. These include reproductive spores that are covered with a resistant material known as sporopollenin, which allows them to be dispersed in the air without dying. An apical (top) region of young, dividing cells (**meristem**) that produces a body composed primarily of tissues, reduces the amount of plant surface area exposed to drying. A multicellular **sporophyte** (spore-producing) body enables plants to reproduce efficiently on land. In plants, sporophytes are always associated with parental gametophytes (the gamete-producing bodies) for at least some time in their early development, which is known as the embryonic stage. This combination of sporophyte and **gametophyte** in the life cycle is known as *alternation of generations*. Plant embryos are able to obtain food from the body of their female gametophytes via tissue known as placenta. A placenta is found at the junction of the embryonic sporophyte and gametophyte bodies in all plant groups. The plant placenta is analogous in location, structure, and function to the placenta of mammals. In both mammals and plants, the placenta increases the ability of the parent to produce more young.

Charophycean algae lack sporophytes, tissue-producing meristems, and walled spores. However, they do have precursor features: sporopollenin (though not produced around spores), regions formed of tissues (though these are not extensive and are not produced by an apical meristem), and a placenta (though this supports development of a unicellular **zygote** rather than a sporophyte). The plant sporophyte body is thought to have origi-

plasmodesmata intercellular connections that allow passage of small molecules between cells

phragmoplast the structure from which the cell plate forms during cell division in plants

monophyletic a group that includes an ancestral species and all its descendants

meristem the growing tip of a plant

sporophyte the diploid, spore-producing individual in the plant life cycle

gametophyte the haploid organism in the life cycle

zygote the egg immediately after it has been fertilized; the one-cell stage of a new individual

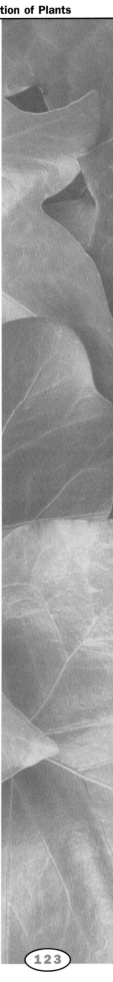

nated from the charophycean zygote. Comparison of charophyceans with bryophytes illustrates the evolutionary concept of *descent with modification*; features inherited by the first land plants from ancestral charophyceans became modified under the influence of terrestrial environments. Comparative studies of modern charophyceans and bryophytes are needed because no fossils are known that illuminate the algae-to-plant transition, which likely occurred in the early Ordovician or the Cambrian (590 to 505 million years ago) periods.

Plants, including bryophytes and vascular plants, are widely known by the term *embryophytes* because they all have a multicellular, nutritionally dependent embryo (young sporophyte). Synonyms for embryophytes include the term *metaphyta*, which corresponds to the term *metazoa* for members of the animal kingdom. The term *plant kingdom* has been used in a variety of ways by different experts; some restrict this term to embryophytes, some include green algae, and others include brown and red algae as well.

Diversification of Plants

Sometime after the origin of the first plants, bryophytes diversified into the three main modern lineages (liverworts, hornworts, and mosses) and possibly other groups that have since become extinct. Some experts think that bryophytes diversified during the Ordovician period (505 to 438 million years ago). Others are skeptical, because fossils of bryophytes that are sufficiently intact to be sure of their identity are much younger, occurring after the earliest fossils of vascular plants. This is usually explained as the result of the reduced ability of delicate bryophyte bodies to survive damage and decay after death, and the fact that Ordovician deposits are not as well studied as those of later periods. The DNA evidence that bryophytes appeared before vascular plants is very strong. It discounts earlier beliefs, based on the sparse early fossil record, that bryophytes might be descended from vascular plants.

Origin of vascular plants required three important evolutionary advances: (1) sporophytes became able to grow independently of their parents after the embryonic stage; (2) sporophytes were able to branch; and (3) sporophytes acquired lignin-walled vascular tissues. Lignin is a tough, plastic-like material that is deposited in the walls of vascular plant conducting cells, making them stronger and less likely to collapse.

In contrast to vascular plants, bryophyte sporophytes remain dependent on parental gametophytes throughout their lives. Bryophyte sporophytes are unable to branch, so they can produce only one organ that generates spores, the sporangium. Although many bryophytes possess conducting tissues, these lack lignin in their walls. Modern (and fossil) vascular plants, also known as tracheophytes, have branched sporophytes that at maturity are (were) able to grow independently of gametophytes. Independent growth allows tracheophyte sporophytes to live longer than those of bryophytes. Branching vastly increases reproductive potential because many more sporangia and spores can be produced. **Lignified** vascular tissues provide a more efficient water supply and greater mechanical strength, giving vascular plants the potential to grow much larger than bryophytes. Woody plants contain large amounts of lignified conducting tissues—the strength and durability of wood derives largely from its lignin content.

lignified composed of lignin, a tough and resistant plant compound

The hornwort *Anthoceros* has a very simple, flat inconspicuous gametophyte body, with more obvious elongate sporophytes growing from it. This plant commonly occurs in muddy places, but the sporophytes, which resemble clumps of small grass blades, are only visible in early spring.

The fossil record reveals that there were ancient plants that had many of the features of bryophytes, including absence of vascular tissues, but whose sporophytes were branched and capable of living independently at maturity like those of vascular plants. These plants lived in the late Silurian (about 420 million years ago) and into the Devonian period, then became extinct. Known only as fossils, these plants are described as *pretracheophyte* (meaning "before vascular plants") *polysporangiates* (meaning "producing many sporangia"). They are represented by fossils such as *Horneophyton* and are viewed as possible intermediates between bryophytes and vascular plants. They are also interesting because their sporophyte and gametophyte bodies were of similar size and complexity, in contrast to bryophytes (in which gametophytes are usually larger than sporophytes) and vascular plants (whose sporophytes are larger and more complex than gametophytes).

Fossils show that there were early vascular plants that had primitive lignified conducting cells. Later-appearing fossils and modern vascular plants are known as *eutracheophytes* because they have more complex conducting cells. Modern vascular plants are thought to be derived from a single common ancestor. The comparative study of fossil and modern vascular plants has been valuable in understanding the evolutionary origin of vascular tissues, leaves, and seeds.

Lycophytes. Fossil and DNA evidence indicates that the lycopsids were an early group of eutracheophytes; these include modern nonwoody (herbaceous) plants known as lycophytes (*Lycopodium*, *Selaginella*, and *Isoetes*) and extinct trees that dominated the coal swamps of the Carboniferous period (360 to 286 million years ago), producing extensive coal deposits. Modern and fossil lycopsids have (had) small leaves with just a single, unbranched vein, which are known as **microphylls**. It is amazing that the Carboniferous lycopsids were able to grow to such prodigious sizes and numbers since they only had tiny leaves with which to harvest sunlight energy. They did not produce seeds.

microphylls small leaves having a single, unbranched vein

Ferns and Horsetails. Later-appearing plants include ferns, the horsetail *Equisetum*, and seed plants; these plants have leaves with branched veins.

megaphylls large leaves having many veins or highly branched vein system

Leaves that have veins that branch, and thus are capable of supplying a larger area of photosynthetic cells, can become quite large and are consequently known as megaphylls. **Megaphylls** are an important adaptation that allow plants to harvest greater amounts of sunlight energy. Ferns, horsetails, and seed plants, as well as some extinct plants known only as fossils, are grouped together to form the *euphyllophytes* (meaning *plants with true or good leaves*). It is thought that megaphylls might have evolved separately in seed plants and ferns from separate ancestors that both had systems of branches called *megaphyll precursors*. The processes of planation (the compression of a branch system into a single plane) and webbing (the development of green, photosynthetic leaf tissue around such a branch system) are evolutionary stages in the origin of leaves that may have occurred independently in ferns and seed plants. This is another good example of *descent with modification*, and it illustrates the fact that similar changes often occur independently in different plant groups because they confer useful properties (convergent evolution). Leaves of one kind or another are thought to have evolved at least six times, in different plant groups.

Gymnosperms. Gymnosperms arose from a now-extinct group called the progymnosperms. Progymnosperms are represented by fossils such as *Archeopteris*, a large forest-forming tree that lived from about 370 to 340 million years ago and had megaphylls. Gymnosperms were dominant during the Permian period (286 to 248 million years ago), a time of cool, dry conditions for which gymnosperms were generally better adapted than many ferns and lycophytes. Adaptations that facilitate survival in cool, dry conditions include leaves that have reduced surface area (i.e., are needle or scale-shaped) and seeds. Reduced leaf surface area helps reduce the loss of water by evaporation. Having seeds reduces a plant's dependence on liquid water to accomplish fertilization during sexual reproduction and allows seed dormancy, the ability of the protected embryo to persist until conditions are favorable for germination. Today, gymnosperms are still quite successful in cool and dry environments, such as forests of high latitudes (taiga) and mountains. There were some ancient seed-producing ferns that do not seem to be related to any modern group. These ferns illustrate independent origin of seeds and the value of seeds as an adaptation.

The origin of modern seed plants was accompanied by the first appearance of embryonic roots (radicles). In contrast, nonseed plants lack an embryonic root, rather, roots arise from the adult stem, often from a kind of horizontal stem known as a rhizome.

Angiosperms. The origin of the first flowering plants is not well understood, and it is a topic of great interest to botanists. Progymnosperms and the Gnetales, an unusual group of modern gymnosperms, are thought by some experts to be closely related to angiosperms. However, DNA evidence has cast doubt on the connection to Gnetales. DNA evidence also indicates that the most primitive modern flowering plant is *Amborella*, a native of the Pacific island New Caledonia. Researchers are working to understand the origin of the unique and defining features of flowering plants, including flowers, fruits, and seeds with **endosperm**. The evolutionary radiation of flowering plants is associated with coevolution—the coordinated evolutionary divergence of many animal groups, including insects, bats, birds, and mammals. Animals depend on these plants as a source of food and play im-

endosperm the nutritive triploid tissue formed in angiosperm speeds during double fertilization

portant roles in carrying spores (pollen) between plants and transporting fruits and seeds to new locations. The extinction of any modern flowering plant could thus potentially cause animal extinctions, and vice versa.

There are at least 3,000 living species of charophyceans, primarily desmids living in peat bogs dominated by the moss *Sphagnum*. Species of living plants are estimated to include 6,000 liverworts, 100 hornworts, 9,500 mosses, 1,000 lycophytes, 11,000 ferns, 760 gymnosperms, and 230,000 angiosperms. New species are continuously being discovered. SEE ALSO ALGAE; ANGIOSPERMS; BRYOPHYTES; EVOLUTION OF PLANTS, HISTORY OF; GYMNOSPERMS; PHYLOGENY; SEEDLESS VASCULAR PLANTS; SYSTEMATICS, MOLECULAR; SYSTEMATICS, PLANT.

Linda E. Graham

Bibliography

Graham, Linda E. *Origin of Land Plants.* New York: John Wiley & Sons, Inc., 1993.

——, and Lee W. Wilcox. *Algae.* Upper Saddle River, NJ: Prentice-Hall, 2000.

Kenrick, Paul, and Peter R. Crane. *The Origin and Early Diversification of Land Plants. A Cladistic Study.* Washington, DC: Smithsonian Institution Press, 1997.

Raven, Peter R., Ray F. Evert, and Susan E. Eichhorn. *Biology of Plants*, 6th ed. New York: Worth Publishers, 1999.

Evolution of Plants, History of

The conception that living organisms are changing or mutable originated in the thoughts of Empedocles, an ancient Greek philosopher (c. 490–430 B.C.E.). He drew on the theories of Greek philosophers preceding him to suggest a unitary view of the world consisting of the four elements of earth, air, fire, and water, which interacted with each other according to the principles of love (attraction) and strife (repulsion). Organisms arose from varying combinations of the elements under the action of either love or strife. Thus organic (living) entities were thought to arise from inorganic (nonliving) materials, which then became adapted through a process of selection to their environment. Empedocles not only applied this theory to the origin of plants, but stated that they were the first living organisms.

From Aristotle to Lamarck

This evolutionary worldview was put on hold by the theories of the great Greek philosopher Aristotle (384–322 B.C.E.) and by his famous student Theophrastus (c. 372–287 B.C.E.), who is regarded as the father of scientific botany. They believed in a fixed or static universe, which saw all plants and animals as falling into discrete types or kinds organized in a well-defined, hierarchical scheme from lower to higher organisms. Aristotle called this organization of life, the *scala naturae*, or the ladder of creation. This view dominated natural philosophy and reached its fullest expression with the work of the great Swedish taxonomist, Carolus Linnaeus (1707–1778). His reform of the taxonomic system was built on the idea that organisms such as plants fall into well-defined types. The Linnaean system follows this typological or essentialistic approach to the natural world by adhering to the notion of the ideal type. This is seen in the pivotal taxonomic use of the type **specimen**, the technical taxonomic term for the first species of a new group described.

specimen object or organism under consideration

The return to a changing vision of life accompanied the new geological theories of the eighteenth century. These new theories were fueled by new fossil discoveries and the establishment of the view that fossils are organic in nature; that is, that they were remnants of once-living organisms. Plant fossils figured prominently in this. Geological theories were also informed by the revolutionary beliefs associated with the **Enlightenment,** especially the idea of progress. This idea implied a directionality to history and suggested that progress was in the natural order of things. It also suggested that the world, and Earth, were much older than previously thought, especially as revealed by Biblical scripture. Combined with developments in the comparatively new **morphology** of both plants and animals and the staggering diversity of new specimens of plants and animals flooding Europe from the voyages of discovery, the new geological theories began to uphold the view that Earth changed in a slow, gradual manner. Instead of accepting the view of unique, one-time, or catastrophic events—such as the flood of Noah—the view that uniform geological processes were responsible for creating Earth, or uniformitarianism, began to dominate geology. Soon, naturalists began to challenge the notion of the fixity of species as they realized that Earth itself was undergoing constant but uniform change.

The French naturalist Comte Georges-Louis Leclerc de Buffon (1707–1788), a contemporary of Linnaeus, was one of the first to suggest a **transmutationist** theory for living organisms. He made a famous speculative statement applying his belief in a constantly changing Earth to living organisms in volume three of his great compendium of the natural history of Earth, *Histoire naturelle* (1749–67). This statement paved the way for the first coherent transmutationist theory formulated by Jean Baptiste Lamarck (1744–1829), a botanist of some repute, and the first person to use the word "biology." This theory was clearly formulated in his *Philosophie zoologique* (1809). Despite its zoological title, the book drew on insights Lamarck had gleaned from his botanical background to explain the phenomenon of adaptation in all living organisms. According to Lamarck, favorable adaptations were originated by the effect of the environment acting directly on the organism. Lamarck therefore mistakenly thought that the environment directly induces permanent change in the genetic composition of organisms. This was what he meant by the "inheritance of acquired characters." The phenomenon of use and disuse, also associated with Lamarck, stated that prolonged use of an organ led to its modification, and disuse led to its elimination. Although Lamarck's theory was widely discussed and became especially popular in his native France, it did not provide a mechanism for how the environment induced such permanent modification, nor did it provide good scientific evidence.

Darwin, Mendel, and the Evolutionary Synthesis

These inadequacies were addressed by the individual who is most closely associated with the theory of organic evolution, Charles Darwin (1809–1882). Darwin did not explicitly reject Lamarck's explanation for adaptation, but instead suggested another mechanism he called natural selection. This was the process by which organisms with favorable variations survived to reproduce those favorable variations. Given enough time, he argued, subsequent generations would depart from the parental type under the action of selection until they formed a new species. This principle of di-

Enlightenment Eighteenth-century philosophical movement stressing rational critique of previously accepted doctrines in all areas of thought

morphology shape and form

transmutation change from one form to another

vergence supported and strengthened what Darwin formally called his "theory of descent with modification." This theory was set forth in *On the Origin of Species* (1859). Darwin drew heavily on examples from the distribution of plants and on knowledge of plant breeding to formulate his theory. In the last twenty years of his life, he studied the phenomenon of adaptation in plants such as orchids, which had evolved spectacular contrivances by which to attract pollinators such as bees. Plants were in fact to provide Darwin with some of the best evidence in support of his theory.

Darwin's theory of evolution transformed understanding of the origins of all life on planet Earth. Botanists such as Joseph Dalton Hooker (1817–1911) in England and Asa Gray (1810–1888) in the United States grew to accept and apply Darwinian evolution to the plant kingdom and to promote the theory further. Despite its success, a considerable number of botanists continued to uphold Lamarckian notions well into the twentieth century. One reason for this is that it is especially hard to distinguish between genotypical variation (variation due to genetics), and phenotypical variation (variation as the result of a direct response to the environment). Unlike animals, which have closed developmental systems, plants have open or indeterminate developmental systems that permit them to continue to "grow" and generate new tissue in regions such as the shoot and root. Plants are thus able to demonstrate the phenomenon of phenotypic plasticity, the ability to adapt readily to new environments and to generate especially complex variation patterns that appear to support Lamarckian inheritance.

It took the work of the geneticists such as Gregor Mendel (1822–1884), who formulated the modern theory of heredity, and Wilhelm Johansen (1857–1927), who first drew the distinction between phenotype and genotype, to begin to understand more complex aspects of plant evolution, such as plant **speciation**. It was not until 1950, however, that botanists were able to finally integrate Darwinian natural selection theory with Mendelian genetics, and finally dispelled notions of Lamarckian inheritance. Modern ideas of plant evolution and the science that is framed by the subject, plant evolutionary biology, appeared with the publication of *Variation and Evolution in Plants* (1950), by the American botanist George Ledyard Stebbins Jr. (1906–2000). With its appearance, botany and plant evolution are generally thought to have become part of the historical event termed "the evolutionary synthesis." This event finally saw the establishment of Darwinian evolution by means of natural selection synthesized with Mendelian genetics. It remains the overarching theoretical framework for explaining the evolution of plants. SEE ALSO DARWIN, CHARLES; EVOLUTION OF PLANTS; HOOKER, JOSEPH DALTON; MENDEL, GREGOR.

Vassiliki Betty Smocovitis

speciation creation of new species

Bibliography

Andrews, Henry N. *The Fossil Hunters: In Search of Ancient Plants.* Ithaca, NY: Cornell University Press, 1980.

Briggs, D., and S. M. Walters. *Plant Variation and Evolution*, 3rd ed. Cambridge, UK: Cambridge University Press, 1997.

Morton, A. G. *History of Botanical Science.* New York: Academic Press, 1981.

Stebbins, George Ledyard, Jr. *Variation and Evolution in Plants.* New York: Columbia University Press, 1950.

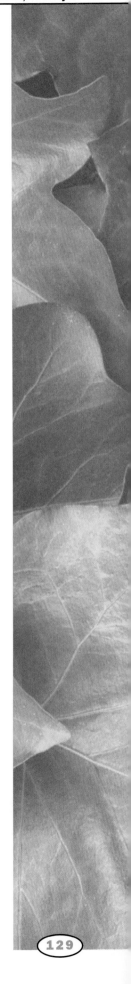

Fabaceae

The Fabaceae family, known as legumes, are one of the most important plant families in both ecological and economic terms. Legumes help increase soil nitrogen and provide rich sources of vegetable protein for humans, livestock, and wild animals.

Structure

The flowers of the legume family are diverse but uniformly bilaterally symmetric. Indeed, fifty-million-year-old fossil legume flowers provide the first instance of bilaterally symmetrical flowers in the fossil record of flowering plants. Most legumes have five petals and five **sepals**, with the sepals commonly fused at least at the base. The five petals commonly occur as one large upper petal, two lower petals that clasp the ovary and stamens, and two **lateral** petals that often act as a platform for a landing bee (or other insect). There are deviations to this pattern, including a common one where petals are all alike and arranged in a radially symmetric fashion even though the ovary or stamens always retain the bilateral symmetry.

The fruits of the legume family are also varied. Most commonly, one fruit (the pod) is produced per flower. The pod has two valves, each bearing a seed along the upper margin. The two valves together form the single compartment of most pods. When the fruit matures, the two valves often twist apart forcefully, catapulting the enclosed seeds. However, pods of many legume species remain intact and disperse with the mature seed. The seed then germinates from within the fallen pod. The pod may not have a single compartment, but rather can be transversely segmented such that each seed is enclosed in its own compartment. Pods can be small and contain one seed or linear to circular and contain dozens of seeds.

The distinctive aspect to the vegetative **morphology** of legumes is the compound leaf, mostly pinnately compound, but also palmately compound. Less common are simple legume leaves. Legume leaves are deciduous during the dry season in the tropics or during the winter in temperate regions. Deciduous leaves are considered an adaptation to habitats with seasonally varying moisture availability, which is especially the case in many tropical regions.

The morphology of the legume fruit is dependent upon how the pod disperses. Water-dispersed fruits have a thick buoyant outer covering that contains many air cells (e.g., *Andira*). Wind-dispersed fruits often bear wings of varying sizes and shapes (e.g., *Dalbergia*). Pods carried away on the fur of passing animals bear different kinds of hairs, ornaments, or glands to make them sticky (*Desmodium*, for example). The structure attaching the seed to the inside of the fruit is sometimes fleshy. This fleshy structure (the aril, as in *Pithecellobium*) is firmly attached to the seed and is often colorful and sweet and serves to disperse the seed (e.g., by birds). Legume seeds are highly variable but always include a preformed embryo with two large cotyledons. The cotyledons are rich in nitrogen compounds (such as alkaloids or nonprotein amino acids), most of which are toxic to animals. Selection during domestication has resulted in the loss of **toxins** while retaining the nitrogen-rich compounds. Legumes cultivated for their edible nitrogen rich seeds (e.g., beans, peas, and lentils) are referred to as pulses. Soybeans form an important part of the diet in Asia and are used as a protein-rich livestock feed in many countries.

sepals the outermost whorl of flower parts; usually green and leaf-like, they protect the inner parts of the flower

lateral away from the center

morphology shape and form

toxin a poisonous substance

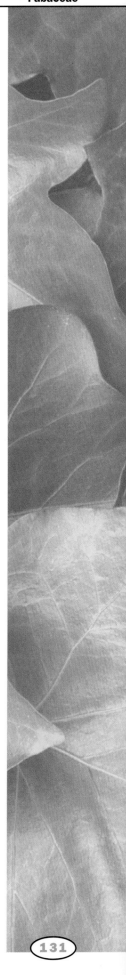

Distribution, Symbiosis, and Economic Importance

The Fabaceae predominate in most vegetation types of the world. Legume species are most abundant in seasonally dry, tropical forests, but they also abound in high deserts to lowland rain forests. They are notably uncommon in high alpine sites with abundant summer rains and in the southern beech forests of the Southern Hemisphere. Woody legume species are mostly confined to tropical and subtropical habitats, but herbaceous species occur from the tropics to cold temperate regions. Thus, many legume species are available for use in reforestation or revegetation projects worldwide. Their efficient ability to acquire nitrogen, phosphorus, and other essential nutrients, whether through nodulation or association with mycorrhizae (symbiotic root fungi), allows them to easily establish on abused lands where soils are eroded, leached, or acidic. Legumes can be found as pioneer species

ECONOMICALLY IMPORTANT LEGUMES

Common Name	Scientific Name	Uses
Edible (human or livestock)		
Alfalfa, lucerne	*Medicago sativa*	Forage, commercial source of chlorophyll
Alsike clover	*Trifolium hybridum*	Forage
Baked, navy, kidney bean	*Phaseolus vulgaris*	Edible seeds
Carob	*Ceratonia siliqua*	Pods with edible pulp, ornamental
Chick pea, garbanzo bean	*Cicer arietinum*	Edible seed
Faba bean	*Vicia faba*	Edible seeds
Fenugreek	*Trigonella foenum-graecum*	Edible and medicinal seeds, dye
Garden pea	*Pisum sativum*	Edible seed
Japanese clover	*Lespedeza stiata*	Forage, revegetation
Lentil	*Lens culinaris*	Edible seed
Licorice root	*Glycyrrhiza glabra*	Rhizomes a source of licorice
Lima bean	*Phaseolus lunatus*	Edible seeds
Mesquite	*Prosopis glandulosa*	Edible pods, forage, fuel
Mung bean	*Vigna radiata*	Edible seeds and pods
Peanut	*Arachis hypogaea*	Edible seeds
Potato bean, groundnut	*Apios tuberosa*	Edible tuber
Soybean	*Glycine max*	Edible seeds for oil and other products
Tamarind, Indian date	*Tamarindus indicus*	Pods with edible pulp
Vetch, tare	*Vicia sativa*	Forage or green manure
White clover	*Trifolium repens*	Forage
Yam bean, jicama	*Pachyrhizus erosus*	Edible tuber
Yellow sweetclover	*Melilotus officinalis*	Forage
Ornamental		
Black locust	*Robinia pseudoacacia*	Ornamental, timber, reforestation
Crown vetch	*Coronilla varia*	Ornamental, revegetation
Honey locust	*Gleditsia triacanthos*	Ornamental
Kentucky coffee tree	*Gymnocladus dioica*	Ornamental
Lupine	*Lupinus albus*	Ornamental, forage, edible seeds
Redbud	*Cercis canadensis*	Ornamental, edible flowers
Scarlet runner bean	*Phaseolus coccineus*	Ornamental, edible fruits and seeds
Sensitive plant	*Mimosa pudica*	Ornamental house plant
Silk tree	*Albizia julibrissin*	Ornamental
Sweet pea	*Lathyrus odoratus*	Ornamental
Other		
Acacia	*Acacia senegal*	Sap a source of gum arabic
African blackwood, Brazilan rosewood	*Dalbergia nigra*	Luxury timber
Cascolote	*Caesalpinia coriaria*	Source of tannins
Indigo	*Indigofera tinctoria*	Dye, forage
Kudzu vine	*Pueraria lobata*	Revegetation, forage
Peachwood, brasiletto	*Haematoxylum brasiletto*	Timber, dye, ornamental

or as major constituents in secondary vegetation. Disturbed lands characterized by high erosion, leaching of nutrients, or accumulation of salts can become readily inhabited by legume species. Notably, an association of mycorrhizae and legumes is just as important in this regard as is the legume-rhizobia association. This is especially true when soils are acidic. The nitrogen-rich metabolism of legumes is a desired property for revegetation because by killing the legume (naturally or intentionally), nitrogen is released for use by non-leguminous associates. Green manuring a worn-out field with clover, for instance, can help restore soil fertility.

A remarkable feature of the Fabaceae is the high nitrogen metabolism that occurs in all members of this family. Legumes are so nitrogen-demanding that they have evolved several mechanisms to efficiently scavenge organic and inorganic nitrogen from the soil. One of these is the formation of root nodules upon infection by rhizobia. Rhizobia is the collective name for bacteria that infect legume roots and fix atmospheric nitrogen, which then becomes available to the legume plant. Many legumes are susceptible to being infected by rhizobia, whereupon the rhizobia are localized by the legume plant in root, rarely stem, nodules.

Legumes and rhizobia have a symbiotic relationship, which benefits the legume but is not necessary for its growth. Legumes appear to acquire nitrogen by other means than nodulation first, and an influx of soil nitrogen, natural or otherwise, can cause a nodulating legume to cease its association with rhizobia.

Few if any other plant families have as many species that are so economically important worldwide as the Fabaceae. This is especially true for both industrial and nonindustrial economic species. Peas, beans, and lentils (the pulses) are probably the most important industrial species, but luxury timbers (e.g., rosewoods) are also important here. The most economically important nonindustrial species include multipurpose tree species, such as *Leucaena leucocaphala* or *Gliricidia sepium*, which are cultivated for shade in crop fields (as in coffee plantations), local timber, livestock forage, and cover for reforestation projects. Hundreds of herbaceous and woody legume species are cultivated regionally or globally as ornamentals, livestock forage, **green manure**, or as sources of gums, medicinal products, or secondary metabolites. SEE ALSO BIOGEOCHEMICAL CYCLES; KUDZU; NITROGEN FIXATION; PLANT COMMUNITY PROCESSES; SAVANNA; SOYBEAN; SYMBIOSIS.

Matt Lavin

green manure crop planted to be plowed under, to nourish the soil, especially with nitrogen

Family

Family is the taxonomic rank between order and genus. A number of related genera make up one family. A number of related families are then grouped into an order, a higher rank that therefore represents a larger group of plants. A family may include only one genus and one species or hundreds of genera and several thousand species. A large family may be further organized using the rank of subfamily, with related genera grouped into subfamilies, then subfamilies into families.

In the past, families and subfamilies were just groups of genera that shared some similar features, especially of the flower and fruit. Such groupings often omitted closely related plants that looked different. Beginning in the late twentieth century, botanists have come to think that families should be natural groups. A natural group, which includes all the descendants of some common ancestor, is based on evolutionary relationships, not just similar appearance.

Names of families can be recognized by the ending "-aceae." Each family has a type genus, a representative genus that defines that family, and the family's name is formed by adding -aceae to the name of that genus. For example, *Primulus* (primrose) is the type genus of the family Primulaceae, or primrose family. SEE ALSO PLANT SYSTEMATICS; TAXONOMY.

Wendy L. Applequist

Bibliography

Heywood, V. H., ed. *Flowering Plants of the World.* New York: Oxford University Press, 1993.

Zomlefer, W. B. *Guide to Flowering Plant Families.* Chapel Hill, NC: University of North Carolina Press, 1994.

Ferns

Ferns, like the more familiar seed plants, have stems, roots, and large, highly veined leaves. Ferns do not reproduce by seeds, however, and have several other distinctive features. The leaf of a fern is called a frond and, in many species, the green blade is divided into segments called pinnae. The leaves of most ferns have a distinctive juvenile stage called a fiddlehead, where all the segments are curled in a manner resembling the end of a violin's neck. Most ferns have underground stems called rhizomes and the only parts of the fern plant visible above ground are the leaves. Some tropical ferns, called tree ferns, have erect, unbranched stems up to 20 meters tall with all of the fronds arising from the tip. Ferns are perennial plants and some may grow for many years, but, as they lack annual growth rings, their age is not easily determined. However, in 1993, researchers using molecular genetic markers found some individual bracken fern (*Pteridium aquilinum*) plants more than 1 kilometer across. Researchers estimated that these ferns took more than 1,180 years to grow to this size, possibly putting them among the oldest living plants on Earth.

Ferns and seed plants are similar in having two kinds of plants present in their reproductive life cycle, but overall ferns reproduce very differently than seed plants. The familiar fern plant, described in the preceding paragraph, is the **sporophyte** (spore-bearing phase). Fern fronds bear organs known as sporangia. Inside each sporangium certain cells undergo reduction division, or meiosis, which yields haploid spores that have one set of genes for the fern. All of the cells in the sporophyte fern plant itself are diploid, having two sets of genes. The sporangia of most ferns are very small, scalelike, and contain only sixty-four spores, but some ferns have large sporangia containing hundreds of spores. A typical fern sporophyte plant may produce up to one billion spores per year. When the sporangia open, the spores are shed into the air and dispersed. While most fern spores land within one hundred meters of the fern producing them, some may be spread very far. Fern spores have been recovered from the upper atmosphere in samples collected by airplanes and weather balloons.

sporophyte the diploid, spore-producing individual in the plant life cycle

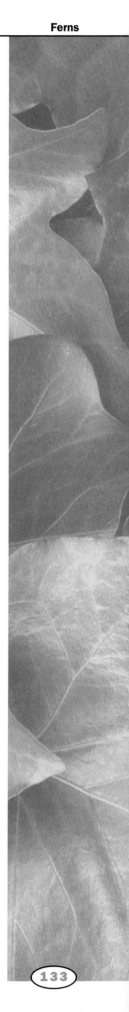

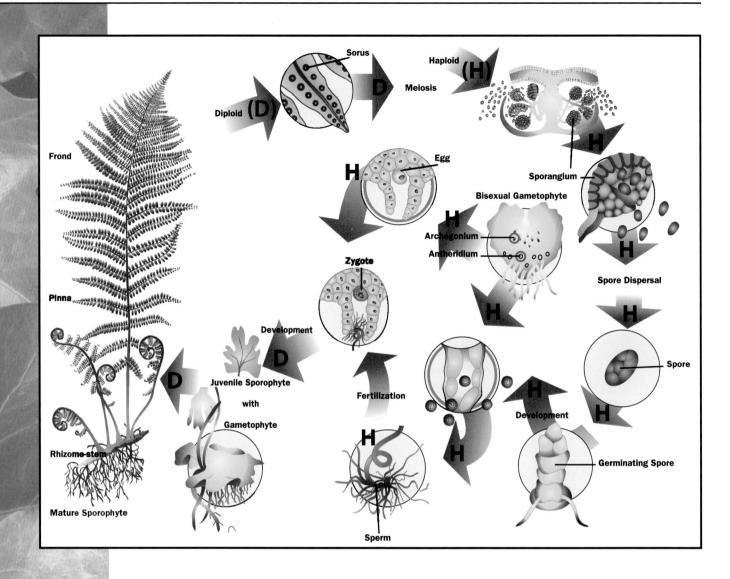

The life cycle of a fern.

substrate the physical structure to which an organism attaches

gametophyte the haploid organism in the life cycle

When the single-celled fern spore lands on a suitable **substrate**, it may undergo mitotic cell division and develop into a very different kind of plant. The plant that grows from a fern spore, called the prothallus, is barely visible to the naked eye. It resembles a tiny, heart-shaped ribbon and lacks any stems, roots, leaves, or internal food- or water-conducting tissues. Reproductively, this small, independent fern plant is critical because it bears the sex organs. Although the basics of sexual reproduction in ferns were discovered in the nineteenth century, many crucial details are still being clarified. A single fern **gametophyte** may produce both sperm-bearing sex organs, called antheridia, and egg-bearing sex organs, known as archegonia, but frequently an individual gametophyte has only one type of sex organ. Fertilization occurs when a sperm swims to unite with an egg to form a diploid zygote, which then develops into the sporophyte.

Whether the individual gametophyte plants in a population are bisexual or unisexual is very important because it is basic to determining the degree of genetic variation possible in the sporophyte generation produced. A single bisexual gametophyte can fertilize its own eggs and produce a new sporophyte plant, but such a sporophyte would be highly inbred because both the sperm and egg producing it would be genetically identical. Most ferns control the sexual expression of the individual plants in a gametophyte population so that each plant is either male or female. Thus, fertilization usually requires two gametophytes that are close enough for sperm to swim in water between them. Receptive archegonia secrete a sperm **attractant** to help the sperm find its way. When genetic material from two different gametophytes is mixed in the zygote, the sporophyte that develops has more genetic variation than one arising from a single gametophyte. If the entire fern sporophyte population is reproduced this way, it may be more likely to survive because some of its members may have inherited the traits needed to endure unforeseen changes in its environment. On the other hand, a distinct survival advantage arises when a single fern spore, dispersed a long distance, can produce a sporophyte from one gametophyte, because this permits rapid colonization of distant, favorable habitats.

attractant something that attracts

Although factors regulating fern spore germination and development are fairly well known from laboratory studies, relatively little is known about how ferns actually reproduce in their environments. Most fern spores germinate readily on moist soil. Germination often requires red light that is absorbed by a pigment in the spore. Calcium ions are important to germination, and red and blue light control the pattern of gametophyte development. Fern spores are known to persist in the soil, forming spore banks. These factors and many more interact in complex ways in the field. Ecologically, most fern species are found in habitats where moisture is readily available, permitting gametophytes to grow and sperm to swim to eggs in water. Those concerned with preserving a rare fern species at a site must understand that if the locality does not provide safe sites for the independent gametophytes, with their distinct ecological requirements, the species cannot reproduce and the sporophytes will eventually die off.

Moist, tropical mountain forest communities contain the largest number of fern species. Of the approximately 12,000 fern species worldwide, about 75 percent are tropical. The flora of North America, north of Mexico, contains about 350 fern species, whereas southern Mexico and Central America have about 900. A few ferns are occasionally eaten. However, some, like bracken fern, contain poisons or carcinogens. Ferns are present in most plant communities but dominant in few. SEE ALSO EPIPHYTES; SEEDLESS VASCULAR PLANTS.

James C. Parks

Bibliography

Burnie, David. *How Nature Works.* Pleasantville, NY: Reader's Digest, 1991.

Jones, David. *Encyclopaedia of Ferns.* Melbourne: Lothian Publishing Co., Ltd., 1987.

Raven, Peter H., Ray F. Evert, and Susan E. Eichhorn. *Biology of Plants,* 6th ed. New York: W. H. Freeman and Company, 1999.

Tryon, Rolla, and Alice Tryon. *Ferns and Allied Plants.* New York: Springer-Verlag, 1982.

Fertilizer

Adding nutrients to agricultural systems is essential to enhance crop yield, crop quality, and economic returns. Commercial fertilizers are typically used to supply needed nutrients to crops. Nitrogen (N), phosphorus (P), and

An Amish farmer uses a horse team to spread fertilizer on a field in Lancaster County, Pennsylvania.

potassium (K) fertilizers are used extensively. Other secondary and micronutrient fertilizers are generally required in small quantities to correct plant nutrient deficiencies.

Commercial fertilizers contain a guaranteed quantity of nutrients, expressed as fertilizer grade on a label showing the weight percentage of available N, P_2O_5, and K_2O equivalent (N-P-K) in the fertilizer. Additional nutrients in fertilizer formulations are listed at the end of the fertilizer grade with the nutrient identified. Commonly used commercial fertilizers include ammonium nitrate (fertilizer grade 33-0-0), urea (45-0-0), urea-ammonium nitrate (28-0-0), anhydrous ammonia (82-0-0), diammonium phosphate (18-46-0), monoammonium phosphate (10-52-0), ammonium polyphosphate (10-34-0), ammonium thiosulfate (12-0-0-26S), potassium chloride (0-0-60-45Cl), potassium sulfate (0-0-50-18S), and potassium-magnesium sulfate (0-0-22-22S-11Mg). The secondary plant nutrients sulfur (S) and magnesium (Mg) are often contained in the nitrogen, phosphorus, and potassium fertilizers as shown.

Fertilizers are available in several forms (solids, fluids, and gases), which makes their handling and precise application very compatible with planting and fertilizer application equipment. Fertilizers are applied in several ways; they can be broadcast over the soil surface or in narrow bands on or in the soil, as foliar applications to plants, or through irrigation systems. For more efficient use, fertilizer should normally be applied just prior to the time of greatest plant nutrient uptake. In contrast, organic sources, such as animal manures, need to be applied and incorporated into the soil prior to planting the crop to be most effective.

Management of crop nutrient requirements is easier with commercial fertilizers than with organic fertilizers such as animal manures, bio-solids, byproducts, and other organic waste products. Release of many of the plant nutrients from these sources requires the breakdown of organic material by soil microbes and release of plant nutrients through a process called mineralization. Many of the nutrients from organic sources are not available to plants until this process has occurred. Release of plant nutrients from organic sources may not correspond with the period of greatest crop need.

Organic fertilizers and **legumes** are good sources of nutrients for crop production. Balancing the quantity of nutrient application with organic sources to match crop need is more difficult than with commercial fertilizers. Application of sufficient animal manure to meet crop nitrogen needs will likely result in an overapplication of phosphorus. Conversely, application of sufficient manure to meet the phosphorus needs of crops could result in the under application of nitrogen. Nutrient content of most organic sources is highly variable and needs to be determined before application to soils to avoid overapplication of some nutrients.

legumes beans and other members of the Fabaceae family

Balancing crop nutrient needs using both inorganic commercial fertilizer and organic sources is an excellent way to avoid overapplication of plant nutrients. Soil and/or plant tissue testing should be used to determine crop nutrient needs before applying nutrients from any source. This will ensure efficient use of plant nutrients while maintaining high crop yields, crop quality and profitability, and preserving or enhancing environmental quality. SEE ALSO AGRICULTURE, MODERN; BIOCHEMICAL CYCLES; COMPOST; NUTRIENTS; ORGANIC AGRICULTURE; SOIL, CHEMISTRY OF; SOIL, PHYSICAL CHARACTERISTICS OF.

Ardell D. Halvorson

Bibliography

California Fertilizer Association. Soil Improvement Committee. *Western Fertilizer Handbook.* Danville, IL: Interstate Publishers, 1995.

United Nations Industrial Development Organization. *Fertilizer Manual.* Norwell, MA: Kluwer Academic, 1998.

Fiber and Fiber Products

Fibers are strands of cells that are characterized by an elongate shape and a thickened secondary cell wall composed of cellulose and hemicellulose. Dead at maturity, fiber cells possess tapered, overlapping ends that form long, multicellular fibers. These fibers impart elastic strength to stems, leaves, roots, fruits, and seeds of flowering plants. Most fiber cells arise from vascular tissues and are commonly found in association with phloem tissue, although fibers may also be found in xylem or independent of **vascular** tissue. Fiber cells typically incorporate lignin in their secondary wall, a substance that creates additional stiffness in fiber cells.

vascular related to transport of nutrients

In commerce, plant fibers are broadly defined to include materials that can be spun or twined to make fabrics and cordage, used directly as filling materials, or included in paper production. Plant fibers of commerce are

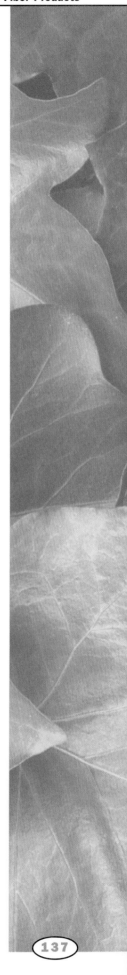

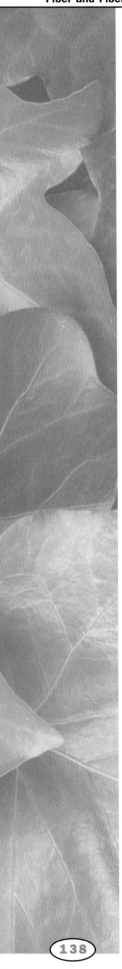

MAJOR FIBER PLANTS AND THEIR USES

Common Name	Scientific Name	Fiber	Family	Native Region	Uses
Flax	*Linum usitatissimum*	Bast (stem)	Linaceae	Eurasia	Linen fabrics, seed oil
Ramie	*Boehmeria nivea*	Bast (stem)	Urticaceae	Tropical Asia	Textiles (blended with cotton), paper, cordage
Hemp	*Cannabis sativa*	Bast (stem)	Cannabaceae	Eurasia	Cordage, nets, paper
Jute	*Corchorus capsularis, Corchorus olitorius*	Bast (stem)	Tiliaceae	Eurasia	Cordage, burlap bagging
Kenaf Roselle	*Hibiscus cannabinus Hibiscus sabdariffa*	Bast (stem)	Malvaceae	Africa, India	Paper, cordage, bagging, seed oil
Sunnhemp	*Crotalaria juncea*	Bast (stem)	Fabaceae	Central Asia	Cordage, high-grade paper, fire hoses, sandals
Urena	*Urena lobata, Urena sinuata*	Bast (stem)	Malvaceae	China	Paper, bagging, cordage, upholstery
Sisal Henequen	*Agave sisalana Agave fourcroydes*	Hard (leaf)	Agavaceae	Mexico	Cordage, bagging, coarse fabrics
Abacá	*Musa textilis*	Hard (leaf)	Musaceae	Philippines	Marine cordage, paper, mats
Upland cotton	*Gossypium hirsutum*	Seed trichome	Malvaceae	Central America	Textiles, paper, seed oil
Sea Island cotton	*Gossypium barbadense*			South America	
Tree cotton	*Gossypium arboreum, Gossypium herbaceum*			Africa	
Kapok	*Ceiba pentandra*	Fruit trichome	Bombacaceae	Pantropical	Upholstery padding, flotation devices
Coir	*Cocos nucifera*	Fruit fiber	Aracaceae	Pantropical	Rugs, mats, brushes

classified by the part of the plant from which they are obtained: (1) stem or bast fibers of dicotyledonous plants arise from phloem tissues and run the length of the plant between the bark and the phloem; (2) leaf or hard fibers of monocotyledonous plants arise from vascular tissue and run lengthwise along a leaf; and (3) seed or fruit fibers arise from seed hairs, seed pods, or fibrous fruit husks. Other minor sources of plant fibers include entire grass stems and strips of leaves or leaf sheaths from palms.

Bast Fibers. Bast fibers arise from phloem cells in the stems of a variety of dicotyledonous plant species. Fiber cells range from 1 millimeter in jute to more than 250 millimeters in ramie, and individual fibers may be comprised of thousands of cells extending up to 1 meter (3.3 feet) in length. Bast fibers from a number of plant species are employed in the weaving of fine textiles, the manufacture of cordage (rope and twine), and paper production. Bast fibers from flax (*Linum*) are used to make linen, the fabric used in wrapping Egyptian mummies more than four thousand years ago. Fibers from jute (*Corchorus*) have been used since biblical times, and it remains the world's most important source of bast fibers, yielding twice as much fiber as all other sources combined. Coarse cloths, rope, and twine are produced from hemp (*Cannabis*), ramie (*Boehmeria*), and sunnhemp (*Crotalaria*), while bast fibers from a number of plants such as hemp, sunnhemp, and *Urena* are important in paper production.

Bast fibers are localized inside the stem and are cemented to adjacent cells with pectins (a form of carbohydrate). Because of this intimate association, bast fibers are isolated from surrounding tissues using a combination of processes that incorporate bacterial decomposition (called retting), mechanical separation of fiber from wood and bark (scutching), and fine combing to separate individual fiber strands (hackling). In retting, stems are bundled after harvest and allowed to partially decompose in fields, ponds, streams, or tanks. This process of slow decomposition degrades pectins and allows fiber strands to dissociate from adjacent tissues. After retting, the stems are rinsed and dried, and the woody portion of the plant is removed from the fibers by scutching, a process that involves crushing stems in a series of fluted metal rollers. After scutching, bast fibers are hackled by drawing them through sets of progressively finer combs. This separates the long, fine fibers used for spinning and weaving from short fibers that are used in other applications.

Hard Fibers. Hard fibers are obtained from leaves of certain monocotyledonous plants. Individual hard fiber cells range from 1 millimeter in sisal to more than 12 millimeters in abacá. Although individual hard fiber cells are usually shorter than bast fiber cells, fiber strands from abacá can exceed 4.5 meters (15 feet) in length. Hard fibers possess thick, **lignified** secondary cell walls that impart additional stiffness and rigidity to the fibers. Hard fibers find their primary application in cordage, although they are also used in the manufacture of sacks, carpets, and specialty papers. The most important species for hard fibers include sisal (*Agave sisalana*), henequen (*A. fourcroydes*), and abacá or Manila hemp (*Musa textilis*). Sisal and henequen originated in Mexico and have been used extensively since the Mayan era. Present-day uses for sisal and henequen fibers include sacking, cordage, and mats. Abacá fiber comes from the leaves of *Musa textilis*, a member of the banana family. Abacá originates in the Philippines, and its fibers were used to make cloth prior to the arrival of explorer Ferdinand Magellan in 1521. Fibers from abacá are resistant to decay from salt water, making them the preferred source for marine cordage. In addition, abacá fiber is used to make mats, coarse fabrics, and paper stock for currency.

lignified composed of lignin, a tough and resistant plant compound

The extraction of hard fiber from leaves is a simple process, as entire leaves from sisal, henequen, or abacá are fed into a machine called a decorticator, which crushes the stalks and washes away the nonfiber pulp. The resulting ribbons of fiber are then washed and dried and can either be dyed or used directly.

Seed and Fruit Fibers. Only three seed and fruit fibers have commercial importance: cotton, kapok, and coir. Cotton is the most widely used of all fiber plants. Cotton fibers are unicellular hairs (trichomes) that emerge from the seed coat after fertilization. Cotton fibers exhibit two forms: the long "lint" fibers that are twisted into thread and woven into fabrics, and short "fuzz" fibers that are used for batting, felts, and paper production. Single-celled lint fibers grow rapidly and expand approximately 2,500-fold (from 0.020 to 50 millimeters) during maturation. Cultivated for over four thousand years, cotton fiber has historically been obtained from two diploid species (*G. arboreum*, *G. herbaceum*) native to Africa and Asia, and two **tetraploid** species (*G. barbadense*, *G. hirsutum*) native to the Americas. Presently, the tetraploid species account for nearly all of the worldwide production of cotton fiber.

tetraploid having four sets of chromosomes; a form of polyploidy.

Unlike the seed hair of cotton, kapok fibers are produced by the inner surface of fruit pods (capsules) from the silk cotton tree *Ceiba pentandra*. Kapok fibers reach 20 millimeters in length at maturity, and are waxier and one-sixth the weight of cotton fibers. These properties make kapok difficult to spin; however, its water resistance, light weight, and resilience make kapok an excellent waterproof material for upholstery and life-preservers. Coir fiber is made from the husk (mesocarp) of fruits from the coconut palm *Cocos*

nucifera. To produce coir, the husks are retted for up to a year, then beaten to separate individual fibers. The cleaned fibers can be spun into coarse yarns for use in ropes and matting, or for bristles in brushes and brooms. SEE ALSO CANNABIS; COTTON; ECONOMIC IMPORTANCE OF PLANTS; PAPER.

Richard Cronn

Bibliography

Esau, K. *Anatomy of Seed Plants*, 2nd ed. New York: John Wiley & Sons, 1977.

FAO Production Yearbook for 1998, vol. 52. Rome: Food and Agriculture Organization of the United Nations, 1999.

Simpson, B. B., and M. Conner-Ogorzaly. *Economic Botany: Plants in Our World*, 2nd ed. New York: McGraw-Hill, 1995.

Flavonoids

compound a substance formed from two or more elements

vascular related to transport of nutrients

gymnosperm a major group of plants that includes the conifers

angiosperm a flowering plant

epidermis outer layer of cells

herbivore an organism that feeds on plant parts

cortical relating to the cortex of a plant

tannins compounds produced by plants that usually serve protective functions; often colored and used for "tanning" and dyeing

Flavonoids are phenolic **compounds** composed of fifteen carbons that are found in land plants, including bryophytes (hornworts, liverworts, mosses) and **vascular** plants (ferns, **gymnosperms**, and **angiosperms**). There are five major types of flavonoids: anthocyanins, flavones, flavonols, isoflavonoids, and proanthocyanidins. They are synthesized in the cytoplasm and subsequently accumulated in small vacuoles that fuse with the central vacuole in both the **epidermis** and cortex. The original function of flavonoids in plant cells is thought to be defensive, providing protection against insect, fungal, and viral attacks and consumption by invertebrate and vertebrate **herbivores**. Over evolutionary time, their functions became diverse. Anthocyanins in floral and vegetative tissues range in colors from yellow to blue. Those found in petals and pollen grains of the flower attract pollinator insects and birds that visit for food. Visibly colorless flavonoids in the epidermal cells, such as flavones and flavonols, serve as ultraviolet shields for the underlying cells. Proanthocyanidins accumulate in vacuoles of **cortical** cells, seed coats, and secondary tissues such as bark, where they form mixtures of brown-black reddish pigments called condensed **tannins** in the walls. Isoflavonoids and flavones are secreted into the surrounding soil layers and function as signals in the interaction between plant roots and nitrogen-fixing bacteria to form nodules. SEE ALSO ANTHOCYANINS; PIGMENTS; VACUOLES.

Helen A. Stafford

Bibliography

Bohm, B. A. *Intoduction to Flavonoids*. India: Harwood Academy, 1998.

Dixon, R. A., and C. L. Steele. "Flavonoids and Isoflavonoids—A Gold Mine for Metabolic Engineering." *Trends in Plant Science* 4 (1999): 394–400.

Structure of flavonoids.

Stafford, H. A. "Flavonoid Evolution: An Enzymic Approach." *Plant Physiology* 96 (1991): 680–85.

———. "Teosinte to Maize—Some Aspects of Missing Biochemical and Physiological Data Concerning Regulation of Flavonoid Pathways." *Phytochemistry* 49 (1998): 285–93.

Flavor and Fragrance Chemist

Flavor and fragrance chemists are professionals engaged in the study and exploitation of materials capable of impacting the human senses of taste or smell. Flavor chemists work primarily with foods, beverages, and food/beverage ingredients; the latter comprise substances that are either derived (directly or indirectly) from plant or animal sources or are chemically synthesized from petrochemicals. Fragrance chemists work mostly with perfumes, fragranced personal care products, and scented household goods and the odoriferous ingredients used therein, which again may include materials of plant, animal, or petrochemical origin.

Research carried out by flavor and fragrance chemists is generally for the purpose of understanding, designing, or improving upon the sensory characteristics of the types of products and ingredients listed above. This often starts with the detailed chemical analysis of a specific target: a finished product or raw materials used in its manufacture. Creative flavorists or perfumers, respectively, with the help of product technologists, may then try to reconstitute flavors or fragrances that match or improve upon the sensory properties of the target. In the case of flavorists, matching a specific natural or processed food or beverage is usually the objective, while a perfumer often has more latitude in cases where the target fine perfume or household air freshener, for example, may be little more than a marketing concept. Product technologists help assure that flavors and fragrances are stable in products and are released and therefore perceivable at the time of consumption or use. Results of chemical analysis may alternatively be used, for example, to design better flavor or fragrance molecules; to make improvements in ingredient formulations or manufacturing processes; or even to provide direction in plant breeding or animal husbandry programs.

Most flavor and fragrance chemists are educated to Bachelor of Science (B.S.) level or higher, often in chemistry, perhaps with specialization in analytical, synthetic, organic, or physical chemistry. In the case of flavor chemists, a degree in food science and nutrition is also common. Additional training is frequently available through professional bodies and industry organizations such as (in the United States) the American Chemical Society, the Institute of Food Technologists, the Flavor and Extract Manufacturers Association, the Research Institute for Fragrance Materials, the Society of Flavor Chemists, and the American Society of Perfumers. Specialized training as a creative flavorist or perfumer, where a highly developed ability to distinguish and describe tastes and odors is absolutely vital, is generally received on the job and involves serving a lengthy apprenticeship.

Employment opportunities in the field of flavor and fragrance chemistry are widespread, especially in North America and Europe, and include university research departments, research institutes, consumer product companies as well as the flavor and fragrance industry. Career opportunities for

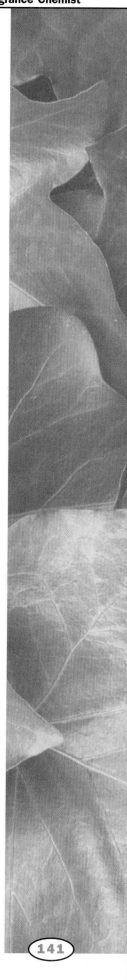

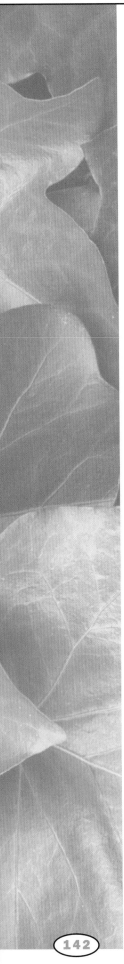

Perfumery research chemists from the Roure distillery near Plascassier, France, measure the strength of fragrance given off by roses.

a flavor or fragrance chemist can be extremely varied, including research, flavor/fragrance creation, product technology, quality control, regulatory, and so forth. Accordingly, the work environment is most often laboratory-based but, depending on the nature of the job, can include manufacturing facilities, visits to vendors and customers, and even time spent in remote locations such as African or Amazonian rain forests, searching for sources of novel and interesting flavor and fragrance materials. A career as a flavor/fragrance chemist offers the intriguing challenge of applying state-of-the-art technology to elucidate some of nature's best-kept secrets, involving a fascinating combination of science, creativity, and the use of our senses of taste and smell, in areas we can all readily identify with: namely, the food we enjoy and the odors we encounter on a daily basis. In 1999, salaries ranged from approximately $35,000 at entry level to more than $100,000 for the highly qualified and experienced flavor or fragrance chemist. SEE ALSO FOOD SCIENTIST; PLANT PROSPECTING.

Terry L. Peppard

Bibliography

Ashurst, P. R. *Food Flavourings.* New York: AVI, 1991.

Müller, P. M., and D. Lamparsky, eds. *Perfumes: Art, Science and Technology.* London: Elsevier Applied Science, 1991.

Flora

The word flora has two meanings in biology. One definition means all of the vegetation of a region, such as the flora of North America; the other means a book or other work that accounts for all of the plants of a region, such as *The Flora of the Great Plains* or *The Illustrated Flora of North Central Texas.* These books and others like them catalog the plants of a region and include information on distributions and habitat requirements, taxonomic keys for plant identification, and current nomenclature for the plants. The more sumptuous floras also include plant illustrations, distribution maps, and other sources of information. The flora of a region is a dynamic thing, and through time new plants are introduced, old plants change their distributions, some plants go extinct, botanical inaccuracies must be corrected, and new nomenclature must be accounted for. A flora is never truly completed. It is necessary for botanists to revise a regional flora periodically to bring its information up to date.

Systematic botany (or taxonomy) has two notable areas of study. One is monographic (or revisionary) study, with the goal of answering questions about evolutionary relationships, species delimitations, ecological matters, and other issues. The products of these studies are monographs or revisions that are based on field and laboratory studies and that account for a natural group of plants, regardless of where they occur. In the past emphasis was placed on understanding the biological nature of each species, and many research programs incorporated greenhouse and field studies and included studies of **hybridization**, chromosomal variations, and genetic differences associated with the plant's distribution. Such studies (termed *biosystematics*) continue to be important, but the recent past has seen the arrival of sophisticated techniques to analyze the molecular constituents of plant's genetic material, and there has been much effort spent on using molecular taxonomy to show natural relationships, that is, to untangle evolutionary history. The product of monographic or revisionary studies is an authoritative monograph, which reports the results of basic studies on a group of plants. One could say that plants do not come with their names on them. It is the monographer who works out the species and their biologies and puts the proper names on them.

Unlike monographic studies, which are concerned with the biological details of a group of related plants, a flora is concerned with all of the plants of a particular region. Floristicists (or floristicians) must have great field familiarity with their region, and they base their studies on the works of monographers, whose monographs are edited to make their data relevant to the region being studied. For plant groups that have never received monographic study, the flora writer must use his or her intuition as best as possible, based upon experience and the **specimens** at hand. Every floristic botanist can point out plant groups that need further study, either from an imperfect understanding of the plant's biological behavior or from inconsistent information about its ecology and distribution. Even though the knowledge of the plants in a region may be incomplete, there is still a need to communicate what is known to the other scientists in the field, who need to have accepted names for plants in hand, a means of identification for them, and readily accessible ecological information.

Systematic botanists sometimes speak of the "cascade" of botanical information, whereby the monographers do basic studies on natural plant groups. The writers of floras then synthesize these studies into books that are passed to the primary consumers of botanical information, such as applied scientists, including agronomists, foresters, environmentalists, land managers, and others. From these people, the information flows on to the ultimate consumers: farmers and ranchers, business and industrial people, and, finally, householders. SEE ALSO BIOGEOGRAPHY; HERBARIA; IDENTIFICATION OF PLANTS; SYSTEMATICS; TAXONOMIC KEYS; TAXONOMY.

Theodore M. Barkley

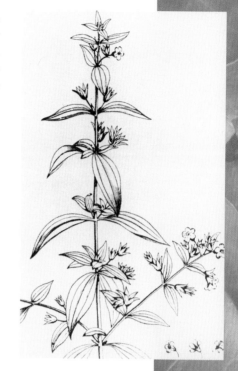

An illustration from the 1803 edition of *Flora Boreali-Americana,* the first book of American flora that was national in scope.

hybridization formation of a new individual from parents of different species or varieties

specimen object or organism under consideration

Bibliography

Diggs, G., B. Lipscomb, and R. O'Kennon. *Skinner's and Mahler's Illustrated Flora of North Central Texas*. Forth Worth, TX: Botanical Research Institute of Texas, 1999.

Great Plains Flora Association. *Flora of the Great Plains*. Lawrence, KS: University of Kansas Press, 1986.

Flowers

An enormous diversity of size, shape, and complexity exists among the flowers of the quarter-million species of **angiosperms**. Flower size varies over a thousandfold, with *Rafflesia* (Rafflesiaceae) flowers as large as 1 meter in diameter dwarfing the minuscule flowers of *Wolffia* (Lemnaceae), which measure less than 1 millimeter across. The number of floral organs also varies, with the complex flowers of the *Tambourissa* (Monimiaceae) species having more than one thousand organs while the simple flowers of the Chloranthaceae may consist of just a few. The coevolution of angiosperms with their animal pollinators is a driving force in the generation of flower diversity. The end product of pollination is the formation of a **viable** seed, therefore ensuring that the species will be perpetuated. Exclusive pollinator-flower relationships ensure that pollen will not be wasted by delivery to flowers of a different species.

Definition and Flower Parts

Despite the enormous diversity in the number, size, and shape of floral organs within the angiosperms, they all are built of four basic organ types (**sepals**, petals, stamens, and **carpels**) whose relative positions are invariant. The flower is an assemblage of **sterile** and fertile (reproductive) parts borne on a shoot or axis called the receptacle. The sterile parts include the sepals (collectively called the calyx) and the petals (collectively called the corolla). The sepals and petals together constitute the perianth. In a typical flower the sepals are green, and they enclose and protect the young flower before it opens. The petals, whose function is to attract pollinators, exhibit an assortment of colors, shapes, and sizes. In flowers in which the sepals and petals are indistinguishable from each other, such as tulips (Liliaceae), the perianth parts are called **tepals**.

The reproductive parts can be divided into the androecium and **gynoecium**. The androecium is composed of stamens, the male floral organs. Stamens usually have an apical anther, in which pollen develops, and a basal **filament** connecting the anther to the receptacle. One or more carpels constitute the gynoecium. Carpels are made of several functional tissues that facilitate pollination and protect developing ovules and seeds. The stigma on which the pollen germinates, and the style, through which the pollen tube grows toward the ovules, are examples of tissues that are intimately associated with pollination. The ovary, which houses the ovules, provides protection for both the developing ovules and seeds. In addition, the ovary often develops into a fruit that facilitates seed dispersal. The formation of a protected chamber in which the ovules and seeds develop is one of the defining features of angiosperms. The term angiosperm is derived from the Greek *angio* (a capsule-like covering) and *sperm* (seed).

angiosperm a flowering plant

viable able to live or to function

sepals the outermost whorl of flower parts; usually green and leaf-like, they protect the inner parts of the flower

carpels the innermost whorl of flower parts, including the egg-bearing ovules, plus the style and stigma attached to the ovules

sterile non-reproductive

tepal an undifferentiated sepal or petal

gynoecium the female reproductive organs as a whole

filament a threadlike extension

MAJOR ANIMAL POLLINATORS AND TARGETED FLOWERS

Animal	Flower Characteristics
Beetle	Open flower, white or dull coloring with strong odor (usually fruity, spicy, or similar to the foul odors of fermentation).
Bee	Any color but red; flower has nectar at the base of the flower that forces the bee to pass by the stigma and anthers on its way to the nectar.
Butterfly and some moths	Flowers tubular in shape, which precludes large insects from crawling into them but allows the long proboscis of the butterfly or moth to enter. Nectar contains amino acids that butterflies require; nectar is their sole food source.
Bird	Usually bright and showy flowers, the colors of which are red, orange, or yellow. Because of the bird's high rate of metabolism, bird-pollinated flowers usually produce large quantities of thin nectar. In the Western Hemisphere hummingbirds are the main bird pollinator; in other parts of the world representatives of other specialized bird families (e.g., sunbirds and honeyeaters) act as pollinators.
Bat	Large white flowers such as those of the saguaro cactus (Cactaceae), which are visible in dim light. Bats also require large amounts of nectar.

Function of Flowers

The function of the flower is to facilitate the reproduction of the organism. Cells within the pollen and embryo sac are **haploid** and are derived from the **diploid** cells that develop within the anthers and ovules, respectively. In angiosperms, pollination results in double fertilization. The egg cell nucleus fuses with a sperm nucleus to produce the zygote while the other sperm cell nucleus fuses with the two polar nuclei to form the triploid **endosperm**. The endosperm acts as a food supply for the developing embryo. After fertilization, the ovule with the developing embryo becomes a seed and the ovary becomes the fruit that houses the seed(s).

Diversity of Flowers

Among the quarter-million species of angiosperms, there are many variations of the generalized flower yielding an immense diversity of floral patterns. The diversity is due to variations in the number, symmetry, size, and fusion of floral parts. While most flowers contain both stamens and carpels (and are referred to as hermaphroditic), other flowers are unisexual. These may be either staminate flowers (missing the carpels) or carpellate flowers (missing the stamens). Species bearing both carpellate and staminate flowers on a single plant are referred to as monoecious ("one house"; maize [Gramineae] and oak trees [Fagaceae], for example). In contrast, dioecious ("two houses") species bear staminate and carpellate flowers on different plants (willow [Salicaceae], for example). Monoecism and dioecism, both of which have evolved multiple times within the angiosperms, provide a mechanism to promote outbreeding. Many other species have evolved more subtle mechanisms to promote cross-pollination. For example, plants may be self-incompatible; that is, they discriminate between self and nonself pollen and consequently reject their own pollen. Alternatively, a difference in the timing of maturation of the androecium and gynoecium in hermaphroditic flowers favors outbreeding.

Two conspicuous characters that contribute to floral diversity are the number and size of floral organs. Angiosperms are often divided into two groups based on their cotyledon number: monocotyledons (monocots, meaning one cotyledon) and dicotyledons (dicots, meaning two cotyledons). One of the characters that distinguish monocots from dicots is the

haploid having one set of chromosomes, versus having two (diploid)

diploid having two sets of chromosomes, versus having one (haploid)

endosperm the nutritive tissue in a seed, formed by fertilization of a diploid egg tissue by a sperm from pollen

A bleeding heart flower. Angiosperms, with a quarter-million species, display an enormous variety of flowers.

appendages parts that are attached to a central stalk or axis

whorl a ring

number of **appendages** within a **whorl**. Monocots usually have flowers with floral parts in multiples of three, whereas the dicots often have floral parts in multiples of four or five. Organ size can also vary enormously. For example, in the species *Lepidium* (Brassicaceae), the petals are microscopic, but in the genus *Camellia* (Theaceae), some species have petals 15 centimeters long.

Variations in fusion, arrangement, and symmetry of floral organs provide further diversity. Fusion between organs of the same whorl (coalescence) and fusion of organs from separate whorls (adnation) is common among many families of angiosperms. For instance, coalescence is seen in snapdragon (*Antirrhinum*, Scrophulariaceae) with the petals fused at the base, and adnation in tobacco (*Nicotiana*, Solanaceae) with stamens fused to the petals. Position of organ attachment to the receptacle also influences flower architecture. If the corolla and stamens attach to the receptacle below the ovary, the flower is referred to as having a superior ovary (e.g., *Liriodendron tulipifera*, Magnoliaceae). In contrast, having the corolla and stamens attach to the receptacle above the ovary produces a flower with an inferior ovary (e.g., *Iris*, Iridaceae). In radially symmetric flowers, termed actinomorphic, all organs within any particular whorl are identical and positioned equidistant from other organs within the whorl (e.g., California poppy *Eschscholzia californica*, Papaveraceae). Flowers in which organs in a particular whorl differ from other organs in the same whorl are referred to as zygomorphic (e.g., most orchids, Orchidaceae).

pheromone a chemical released by one organism to influence the behavior of another

While all of the mechanisms generating diversity contribute to their interactions with pollinators, the fusion and asymmetry of floral organs has allowed the evolution of fascinating and often bizarre plant-insect interactions. For example, some species of orchids attract potential pollinators with insect **pheromones**, luring the insect into a maze constructed of fused petals and stamens in which there is one entrance and one exit. In navigating the maze, the insect both delivers to the stigma of the gynoecium pollen from another flower and picks up a load of pollen to be distributed to another flower.

Evolution of Flowers

While angiosperms are prevalent in the fossil record from the mid-Cretaceous (approximately one hundred million years ago), it is thought that they may have evolved substantially earlier, perhaps as far back as two hundred million years ago. The closest extant relatives of the angiosperms are the gymnosperms, of which conifers are members. Conifers do not have flowers but rather produce female and male cones consisting of scales bearing exposed ovules and pollen sacs, respectively. It's intriguing to consider what evolutionary processes occurred to produce the complex assemblage of floral organs of extant angiosperms. Charles Darwin, upon thinking about this question, stated that flowers are an "abominable mystery." The answer to this question, however, may be found in comparative genetic studies. For example, some of the important regulatory genes promoting floral organ development are also found in conifers. Understanding their function in the cones of conifers may allow scientists to model evolutionary changes that occurred resulting in the formation of early flowers.

It is not clear which features were present in the flowers of the earliest angiosperms. Although by the mid-Cretaceous period angiosperm flowers were already quite diverse, a number of key features of extant flowers had not yet appeared. Fossil flowers from the Cretaceous often have organs that are spirally arranged, a perianth that does not have a distinct calyx and corolla, relatively few stamens, and multiple carpels that are not fused together. The attractiveness of the mainly fly- and beetle-pollinated flowers was due to the androceium, which was composed of anthers attached to showy, leaflike structures. The stigma and style of the early individually fused carpels ran down along the side of the ovary instead of being at the top, as seen in most extant carpels.

There are a number of major evolutionary trends when comparing these Cretaceous flowers to their modern counterparts. For example, in many modern flowers the perianth is differentiated into a distinct calyx and corolla. The evolution of the corolla facilitated the reduction in stature of the androecium such that the stamens are composed of anthers attached to slender filaments rather than large, leaflike appendages. In addition, fusion of organs occurred along with the establishment of zygomorphic flowers, creating flowers with deep, open, funnel-shaped flowers, both innovations allowing the evolution of elaborate pollination strategies. Another evolutionary trend is the formation of a gynoecium made up of multiple fused carpels that have only one stigma and style situated at the apical end of the ovary. This has been hypothesized to provide selection at the level of the male **gametophyte**, which must grow through these structures to effect fertilization.

Coevolution with Pollinators

The early seed-producing plants (such as conifers) utilize wind to move pollen from the staminate cones to the female ovule-bearing cones. To ensure that enough viable seeds are generated, copious quantities of pollen need to be produced. This process requires the expenditure of large amounts of stored resources and is not very efficient. Utilizing insects to transfer pollen to other flowers enables angiosperms to produce less pollen and still maintain a high fecundity in comparison with wind-pollinated plants. In

gametophyte the haploid organism in the life cycle

contrast to flowers of early angiosperms, extant flowers have evolved highly attractive characters to ensure that a specific pollinator continues to visit flowers from a specific species of plant. Flowers provide special sources of food for their pollinators to induce them to visit similar flowers. In addition to pollen and other edible floral parts, nectaries provide nectar, a high-energy food source for animals that can sometimes contain amino acids, proteins, lipids, **antioxidants**, and alkaloids.

antioxidant a substance that prevents damage from oxygen or other reactive substances

Many of the modifications that have evolved in angiosperm flowers are adaptations to promote constancy in pollinator visitation. However, not all angiosperm flowers require animal pollinators. The grasses, which evolved from insect-pollinated flowers, are wind-pollinated. The flowers of grasses are small with reduced or absent petals, and they produce large amounts of pollen.

The Development of Flowers

A basic floral ground plan exists that defines the relationship between organ type and position in all angiosperm species. Because of the constancy in the relative positions of floral organ types, it is hypothesized that a common genetic program to specify floral organ identity is utilized during the development of all flowers. Floral organs are ultimately derived from **primordia** that arise from the flanks of the flower **meristem**. It is thought that cells within the flower meristem assess their position relative to other cells and differentiate into the appropriate floral organ based on this positional information.

primordia the earliest and most primitive form

meristem the growing tip of a plant

To clarify how the identity of flower organ primordia is specified, researchers have taken a genetic approach. Mutations affecting flowers and their organs provide a powerful means for studying the genetic interactions involved in their development. Differences in the development of mutant versus normal (wild-type) plants reveal the function of the mutated gene. To carry out this work, researchers use two model plant systems, *Arabidopsis* (Brassicaceae) and *Antirrhinum* (Scrophulariaceae), and screen plants that have induced mutations in their **genome**. Studies have focused on a particular set of **homeotic** mutations. In homeotic mutants, normal organs develop in the positions where organs of another type are typically found. Specifically, the *Arabidopsis* floral homeotic mutations result in transformations of one floral organ type into another floral organ type.

genome the genetic material of an organism

homeotic relating to or being a gene producing a shift in structural development

It is of interest to note that several homeotic mutants exist in commonly cultivated garden plants. For example, a wild rose flower has five petals, and yet some of the hybrid tea roses have many times that number. Similar situations exist for camellias and carnations. These **hybrid** varieties represent changes in the genetic constitution of the plant to yield alterations in the floral architecture, which some people find attractive. SEE ALSO ANGIOSPERMS; GENETIC MECHANISMS AND DEVELOPMENT; IDENTIFICATION OF PLANTS; INFLORESCENCE; INTERACTIONS, PLANT-INSECT; POLLINATION BIOLOGY.

hybrid a mix of two species

Stuart F. Baum and John L. Bowman

Bibliography

Bentley, Barbara, and Thomas Elias, eds. *The Biology of Nectaries.* New York: Columbia University Press, 1983.

Campbell, Neil A. *Biology,* 3rd ed. Redwood City, CA: The Benjamin/Cummings Publishing Company, Inc., 1993.

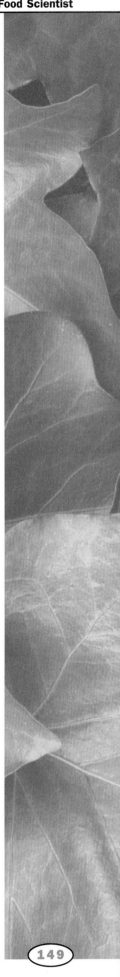

Crepet, W. L., and E. M. Friis. "The Evolution of Insect Pollination in Angiosperms." In *The Origins of Angiosperms and Their Biological Consequences*, eds. Else Marie Friis, William G. Chaloner, and Peter R. Crane. Cambridge: Cambridge University Press, 1987.

Heywood, V. H. *Flowering Plants of the World.* New York: Oxford University Press, 1993.

Meyerowitz, Elliot M. "The Genetics of Flower Development." *Scientific American* 271 (1994): 56–57, 60–65.

Raven, Peter H., Ray F. Evert, and Susan E. Eichhorn. *Biology of Plants.* New York: Worth Publishers, Inc., 1986.

Rost, Thomas L., Michael G. Barbour, C. Ralph Stocking, and Terence M. Murphy. *Plant Biology.* Belmont, CA: Wadsworth Publishing Co., 1998.

Food Scientist

A food scientist studies the science and technology of production, manufacturing, processing, product development, packaging, preparation, evaluation, distribution, utilization, and safety of food products. A food scientist can work and study in a wide range of areas, from meat science to dairy science to the science of fruit and vegetable products.

Food science plays a critical role in the health, welfare, and economic status of all individuals and nations. The food industry is one of the largest manufacturing industries in the United States, employing over two million people, with an additional fifteen million employed in other food-related fields and contributing more than $350 billion to the gross national product.

A food scientist must have an understanding of the basic sciences, which can include chemistry, biochemistry, biology, microbiology, toxicology, nutrition, engineering, marketing, economics, math, and physics. The scientist applies the principles of these basic sciences and engineering to the study of the physical, chemical, and biochemical nature of foods and food processing.

A food scientist tests samples of wine in a German laboratory.

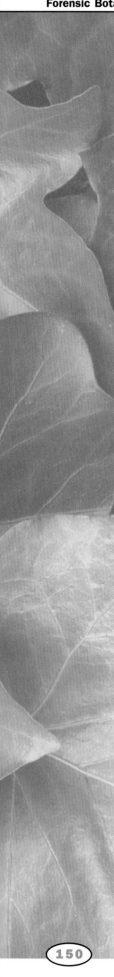

A food scientist with a specific interest in products of plant origin works primarily with fruit, vegetable, cereal grain, and oilseed products. In this work, the individual is concerned with the impacts of preharvest, postharvest, processing, and preservation variables and practices on the yield and quality of the processed product. For instance, a food scientist might monitor the impact of storage temperature on vitamin levels in wheat or the effect of a new oil extraction process on the shelf life of sunflower oil.

Degrees available to individuals desiring to study the food sciences include a Bachelor of Science (B.S.), a Master of Science (M.S.), and a Doctor of Philosophy (Ph.D.). A bachelor's degree in food science would qualify the individual for employment in such positions as a food processing production line supervisor; a laboratory technician with an industry, government, or independent research organization; or as a regulatory supervisor with a state or federal agency. With a master's degree, the food scientist would be eligible for positions such as quality control manager, process control supervisor, product development coordinator, or business manager. A doctoral degree would allow the individual to work in the areas of education, research, and outreach either with a university system, state or federal agency, or within the food science/food processing industry. The food industry is rapidly growing as population increases and with increasing demands for convenient, safe, and nutritious foods and beverages. The growth of the industry and its need for professionals make it possible to find a wide variety of careers.

The work environment for graduates in this career can be highly variable, ranging from outdoor fieldwork, including food production and raw product quality control, to processing plants, research laboratories, and classrooms. Employment is available in all fifty states and opportunities are available in basically all foreign countries. Because of the need for food scientists, salaries are often equal to or higher than those of other professions requiring equivalent levels of education. In 1999, food scientists with a bachelor's degree could expect a starting salary of $30,000 to $40,000. A master's degree earned a starting salary of $35,000 to $45,000, and a doctorate started at $50,000 or higher. SEE ALSO AGRONOMIST; ALCOHOLIC BEVERAGE INDUSTRY; FLAVOR AND FRAGRANCE CHEMIST; OILS, PLANT-DERIVED.

Donald L. Cawthon

Bibliography

Jelen, P. *Introduction to Food Processing.* Upper Saddle River, NJ: Prentice-Hall, 1985.

Potter, N. N., and J. H. Hotchkiss. *Food Science.* New York: Chapman and Hall, 1995.

Forensic Botany

Forensic botany is the application of the plant sciences to legal matters. Most often this means using clues from plants in order to aid in the solution of serious crimes such as murder, kidnapping, and the cause of death of a victim. Many aspects of plant science are employed, including plant anatomy, the study of plants cells; plant taxonomy, which deals with the identification of plants; plant systematics, focusing on plant relationships to other plants; plant ecology, which deals with plants and their environments; and palynology, which is the scientific study of plant pollen and spores.

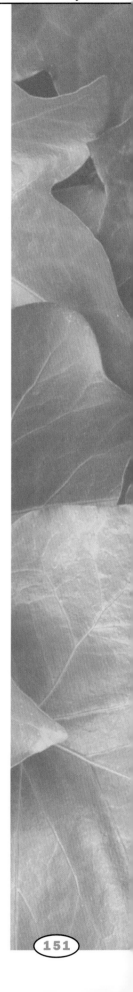

Plant cells possess cell walls made of cellulose, a complex carbohydrate **compound** that is virtually indestructible in comparison with most other natural compounds subject to decay. Plant cell walls can remain intact for thousands of years even though the cytoplasm long since has disappeared. The walls around pollen grains and spores also are made of different materials that are also resistant to decay. This allows plant parts to remain identifiable for long periods of time.

compound a substance formed from two or more elements

The plant foods we consume have distinctive cells within them. The tissues of food plants are made up of cells of distinctive shapes and sizes that are arranged in distinctive patterns. These characteristics are preserved all the way through the human digestive tract and beyond. This also is true for wood. This means it is possible to tell what a person's last meal was long after death. Also, if a person was stuck with a piece of wood, that piece often can be identified to species and/or matched to the larger wood piece from which it was obtained. Sometimes seeds, leaves, and plant fragments are associated with a crime. If the plant can be identified from these clues by a plant taxonomist, they may link the crime to a specific place (for example, one associated with a suspect). Also, taxonomists can be called upon to identify drug plants that are illegal in this country, such as coca.

Plant ecology has been found useful in the location of the graves of missing persons. It does not matter whether the grave is deep or shallow or whether the person was clothed, encased in plastic, or naked at the time of burial. The clues for the burial site come from the necessity of disturbing vegetation cover to dig a grave. A knowledge of plant **succession** patterns in the area is almost impossible to disguise from the eyes of a well-trained plant ecologist. They remain evident for at least a few years, and sometimes for a decade or more.

succession the pattern of changes in plant species that occurs after a soil disturbance

Palynological evidence can be used to suggest where a person was killed and to link a suspect to a crime scene. It also can be used to identify controlled (illegal) plant substances even if no other plant material is present.

Forensic botany is a new and growing field. Many criminal investigators, medical examiners, and attorneys are unaware of its usefulness because they have had little exposure to botany in their educational experiences. Most forensic botanists act as private consultants in crime matters. To be accepted to testify in a court case, forensic botanists must demonstrate that they are qualified to be expert witnesses. Their suitability for such testimony is judged by their experiences and educational credentials. SEE ALSO PALYNOLOGY; PLANT COMMUNITY PROCESSES.

Jane H. Bock and David O. Norris

Bibliography

Bock, Jane H., and David O. Norris. "Forensic Botany: An Underutilized Resource." *Journal of Forensic Sciences* 42, no. 3 (1997): 364–67.

France, D. L., T. J. Griffin, J. G. Swanberg, J. W. Lindemann, G. C. Davenport, and V. Trammell. "A Multidisciplinary Approach to the Detection of Clandestine Graves." *Journal of Forensic Sciences* 37 (1992): 1445–58.

Lane, M. A., L. C. Anderson, T. M. Barkley, J. H. Bock, E. M. Gifford, D. W. Hall, and D. O. Norris. "Plants, Perpetrators, Pests, Poisons, and Pot." *BioScience* 40 (1990): 34–39.

A forester with the Union Camp Corporation grafts a young pine bud onto an older plant that will someday be used for the manufacture of forest products.

Forester

Foresters practice and promote the art, science, technology, and profession of forestry. The field of forestry encompasses a diverse group of people working in many different areas. Foresters can be found in the woods, lumber mills, laboratories, classrooms, offices, urban areas, and even Congress.

The role of a forester can vary greatly, from technicians who focus mainly on forest inventory and management to urban foresters who focus on tree care in the urban setting. Other forestry jobs include consultants, who provide services to private landowners on how best to manage their lands to meet their objectives; rangers, who manage federal park and forest lands to meet specified goals; and professors, who teach the art, science, and technology of forestry. Foresters may also be nurserymen who produce tree seedlings; firefighters who work to extinguish uncontrolled forest fires; or lobbyists who provide vital forest-related information to policymakers, congressmen, and the public.

To become a professional forester, one must obtain a college degree from a school offering professional forestry education. Degrees include a two-year associate's degree, which qualifies the graduate to work as a forest technician, or a four-year bachelor's degree, after which the graduate typically starts in an entry-level position with the opportunity to advance to managerial positions. Graduates earning a master's or doctoral degree tend

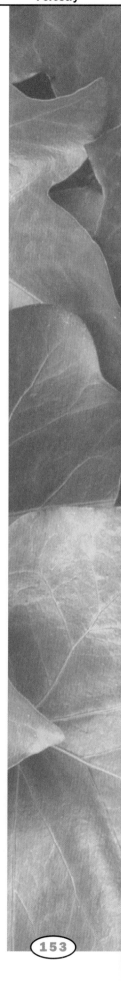

to focus on highly specialized areas of forestry, working as researchers, geneticists, and professors.

Foresters work in very diverse areas under varied conditions. From the old-growth forests in the northwest to the pine plantations in the southeast, foresters work hard to ensure that the land is managed properly. Foresters are also found in other parts of the world, such as Australia, Africa, Germany, Canada, and many other places.

From friendship to travel, the benefits of becoming a forester are numerous. The responsibility of quality land management rests in the hands of foresters, who take pride in the fact that they have the ability and scientific knowledge to improve forest health and productivity. Having fun is another great benefit of becoming a forester. Of all the rewards, though, one of the greatest may be found in teaching others about this great field. According to the *Occupational Outlook Handbook*, published by the Bureau of Labor Statistics and the U.S. Department of Labor, forester salaries ranged from $19,500 to $62,000 in 1997.

The job of a forester can encompass many different kinds of work. However, all foresters share one thing: the responsibility of managing a natural, renewable resource. Foresters take this job seriously and respect what the land has to offer, for it is the lifeblood of the profession. Without foresters and the science of forestry, forests would not be as healthy and productive as they are today. When you become a forester, you make a difference for generations to come. SEE ALSO CONIFEROUS FORESTS; DECIDUOUS FORESTS; RAIN FORESTS; TREES; WOOD PRODUCTS.

Sunburst Shell Crockett

Bibliography

Bureau of Labor Statistics, U. S. Department of Labor. *Occupational Outlook Handbook*, 1998–99 Edition. Washington, DC: U.S. Government Printing Office, 1998.

Forestry

Forestry is the discipline embracing the science, art, and practice of creating, managing, using, and conserving forests and associated wildlife, water, and other resources for human benefit and in a sustainable manner to meet desired goals, needs, and values. The broad field of forestry consists of those biological, quantitative, managerial, and social sciences that are applied to forest management and conservation. Forestry includes specialized fields, such as tree nursery management, forest genetics, forest soil science, silviculture (manipulating and tending forest stands), forest economics, forest engineering, and agroforestry (growing trees and food crops on the same land). Industrial forestry is focused on efficient and profitable production of trees for wood or fiber while meeting criteria of water and air quality, wildlife habitat, and esthetic values. In Oregon, Washington, California, and other states there are regulations governing forest management practices. Nonindustrial forestry (or small, private forestry) is practiced by many landowners to provide wood for income, recreational, and esthetic values and, often, a forest retreat from the bustle of urban life. Multiple-use forestry, practiced on many federal lands in the United States, includes considerations of potential wood

A logging camp on Okanagan Lake in British Columbia.

production, wildlife habitats, recreation opportunities, watershed protection, grazing opportunities for cattle or sheep, and special values such as nests of rare birds or areas of historical or spiritual significance. Wilderness and recreation areas of federal and state forest lands are managed with special considerations for maintaining pristine landscapes and providing opportunities for hiking, camping, boating, and other activities compatible with forests.

Foresters use a broad variety of technical skills, techniques, and equipment to tend, manipulate, and harvest forest trees and to evaluate and maintain water, wildlife habitat, recreation, and scenic values of forests. Foresters measure and evaluate resource values using aerial photographs, satellite images, global positioning systems, laser measuring devices, statistical sampling systems, field computers for data entry, and computer systems for data compilation, calculations, and simulation modeling (e.g., FORTOON, a gaming simulation by J. P. Kimmins of the University of British Columbia and associates). In harvesting trees and planning the next forest, foresters are concerned about tree sizes and the strength qualities of wood, disturbances to the remaining forest that may affect planting new trees, and maintaining water quality and wildlife habitat values. Regenerating a new forest, which may be expected to grow for twenty to one hundred or more years (depending on forest type and tree species), often involves planting seedlings, small trees grown in nurseries or greenhouses. These seedlings may be genetically improved, that is, grown from seeds from carefully selected and tended parent trees. New seedlings must often be protected from being eaten

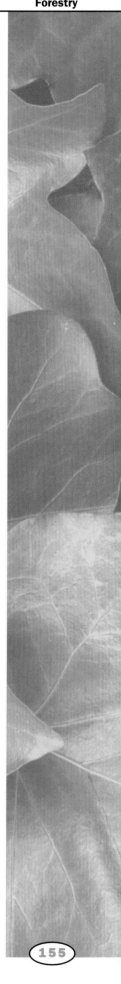

by deer, mice, or other forest dwellers, and competing vegetation (like weeds in a garden) must be controlled so the new trees can grow. Where the land is not too hilly or steep, trees can be planted from a plowlike machine pulled behind a tractor. In mountainous areas workers plant trees by hand using special hoes or shovels. In some forests, especially those of pines and other conifers, foresters often thin out some trees after a few years to leave more growing space for desired trees. And, on certain types of soils that are not so fertile, foresters may add fertilizers to improve tree growth (just as one might fertilize a lawn or garden).

Planning and management of forests must include consideration of the following matters:

- What kinds and amounts of wood can be cut, removed, and sold?

- Should all trees be cut (clearcut), only a few high-value trees (selection harvest) be cut, or should most trees be removed, leaving a few for shade and seed for the next forest (shelterwood)?

- What parts of a forest should or must be protected for the common good (e.g., streams and streamside zones; critical wildlife habitats, such as eagle nests; areas of special scenic beauty)?

- What can be kept as trees are cut (e.g., campsites; hiking trails; scenic vistas)?

- Operations planning: for instance, road building, timber harvest and transport, reforestation; forest stand tending (control of competing vegetation; thinning)

- Financial analysis: for instance, assessing where wood can be sold; costs, expenses, and potential profits; reinvestments needed for things such as road maintenance, tree nurseries, and pest controls.

For many state and all federal forest lands, and increasingly for private industrial forests, planning and management activities must involve informing neighbors and others of how the forest, including water, wildlife habitats, and recreation values will be changed. People care about *their* forests, whether they own them or not.

Forest scientists at universities and industrial, state, and federal research sites are constantly involved in seeking knowledge about how natural forests grow and change and how to grow better trees for human use. Today this research includes genetic engineering research with trees. An example of this is production of a tree that will not be killed by a weed-killing chemical (herbicide) used to control plants competing with desired tree growth. Research continues on basic wood structure and how to get more trees with desired wood strength or whiter paper-making fibers. Foresters and forest scientists are very knowledgeable about many aspects of how forests grow and change. But with increasing replacement of natural forests by managed plantations, and with urban areas expanding to forest edges, more detailed knowledge is needed about how trees use water and nutrients and interact with other plants, animals, and microorganisms in forests. Forest ecologists work in laboratories, large-scale research plots, and experimental forests to provide knowledge for better forest management for all forest products and values.

The forests of the world have many types of trees and wood, from black walnut and cherry of the midwest to spruces of the north, pines of the south

Loggers cut samples from a fallen giant sequoia. The tree rings will be studied to discover the sun cycles, amounts of rainfall, climate, and any fire incidences that occurred during the lifetime of the tree.

and Douglas-firs of the Pacific Northwest to eucalyptus trees of Australia. Forest engineers, wood products engineers, and wood scientists work on new ways of harvesting, transporting, and processing trees to make boards, beams, paper, plywood, and glued-together composite materials with very specific properties (e.g., strength), and other products such as the new fabric tencel. These people extend the work of foresters to our homes and everyday lives. SEE ALSO CONIFEROUS FORESTS; DECIDUOUS FORESTS; FORESTER; RAIN FORESTS; TREES; WOOD PRODUCTS.

James R. Boyle

Fruits

angiosperm a flowering plant

pistil the female reproduction organ

The fruit is the mature ovary and its associated parts. This unique covering of the seeds of flowering plants gives this group of plants their name: **angiosperms**. Fruits are formed by the enlargement and maturation of the **pistil**. Common examples of fruits include apples, oranges, grapefruits, lemons, grapes, peaches, plums, cherries, pineapples, and pears. Commonly, when people think about fruits, they think only of the fleshy and flavored fruits. In the botanical sense, however, any flowering plant that produces seeds also produces a fruit that contains the seed. Using the botanical definition, a number of so-called vegetables are actually fruits, including green peppers, tomatoes, cucumbers, squash, beans, and even such grains as corn, rice, and wheat. Fruits may also be hardened, such as walnuts, pecans, acorns, and coconuts. Horticulturalists define fruit crops as those that bear fleshy and flavored fruits. These fruit crops are grown on trees that require years of **cultivation**, but in some plants of the mustard family, the entire life cycle of the plant may be as brief as a month, including fruit formation.

Fruits are formed from the ovary alone in many plants, but in other plants, adjacent tissues that are not part of the pistil may become part of the fruit. These nonpistillate tissues form accessory parts of the fruit. In strawberries, the receptacle, which holds the tiny pistils, forms the fleshy part of the fruit. Pears and apples are two related examples of fruits formed by a floral cup located next to the ovary.

Function

The function of the fruit in flowering plants is to protect the seeds and to facilitate their dispersal. Fleshy fruits are usually edible and are dispersed after being eaten. Color changes in fruit often signal ripeness and make ripe fruit easy to see. When fruits are eaten, the seeds pass through the gut mostly unaffected. In fact, in some cases, the partial breakdown of the seed coat stimulates germination. Excreted seeds are surrounded by nutrients (including minerals and simple organic **compounds** in the dung) along with a **substrate** for early growth. Of course, this strategy fails if the seeds are actually digested. As a plant defense mechanism, some plants produce chemicals that can make an animal ill if too many are digested. Some of the plants modified by man no longer have such chemical defenses.

Dry fruits are characteristic of seeds dispersed by the wind and other natural agents or animals. These fruits may have barbs, hooks, or a sticky surface that catches the coat of a passing animal and disperses the seeds. Winged fruits or those with tufts of hair are designed to catch the wind (for example, dandelions). Fruits of seaside plants often float and are resistant to water damage. The occurrence of coconut palms on seashores around the world is evidence of the success of this strategy. A fibrous husk traps air and conveys the hard seed to the high-water mark on a beach where the plant can become established. Some plants, particularly those of the California chaparral, thrive after fire. Fire-adapted fruits not only withstand fire temperatures, but may need them to trigger seed release.

Dry fruits often have specific adaptations for seed release. Many dry fruits are dehiscent, forming openings at specific locations in the wall. How the fruit opens determines whether seed release occurs slowly or all at once. Some dry fruits are indehiscent and do not open at all prior to seed germination.

Fruit Development and Ripening

The formation of fruits is typically triggered by sexual fertilization. Many changes occur in the flower accompanying fertilization, including the loss of petals, anthers, and stigma, modification or shedding of the **sepals**, development of the ovules into seeds, and formation of the embryo and **endosperm** within the seed. As part of fruit formation, the walls of the ovary surrounding the seeds are stimulated to resume cell division and to expand. The differences in the size and shapes of fruits are limited to some extent by the structure of the flower, and to an even larger degree by later patterns of growth.

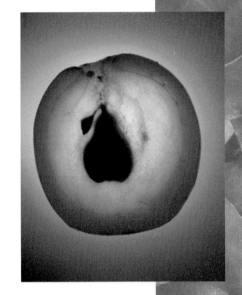

Cross section of a Chardonnay grape.

cultivation growth of crop plants, or turning the soil for this purpose

compound a substance formed from two or more elements

substrate the physical structure to which an organism attaches

sepals the outermost whorl of flower parts; usually green and leaf-like, they protect the inner parts of the flower

endosperm the nutritive tissue in a seed, formed by fertilization of a diploid egg tissue by a sperm from pollen

stimulus trigger

Some fruits do not form seeds, such as bananas and seedless grapes. Fruits produced without seeds are examples of so-called parthenocarpic fruits, in which ovules (precursors of seeds) are formed but do not successfully fertilize.

Plant hormones play an important role in the formation and maturation of fruit. Fleshy fruits grow and thicken in response to hormonal growth signals emitted by fertilized seeds. In strawberries, for example, seed formation is highly successful except for the tip of the fruit, which is poorly developed. Where seeds are underdeveloped, so is the fruit. The **stimulus** for fruit production in this plant can be replaced by a plant hormone known as auxin, which is often produced by developing seeds. Fruit maturation and the development of fruit color are triggered by a later-occurring hormonal signal, produced by the gas ethylene. For grocery stores, fruit is often picked before becoming ripe because unripe fruit is not as easily bruised. To ripen the fruits for sale, a human-made gas related to ethylene is used after harvest, causing the immature fruit to develop its characteristic color and texture.

Once the fruit is ripe, the pedicel or stem that holds the fruit begins to seal itself off from the plant, under the influence of the hormone abscisic acid (ABA). When this hormone is produced, fruit drop is stimulated. To prevent fruit drop, another hormone called cytokinin can be used to inhibit the production of ABA and delay overripening and fruit drop. Oranges and other citrus crops can be harvested yearlong by inhibiting fruit drop and senescence through the application of a cytokinin. Citrus fruits, which normally mature in the winter, can thus be harvested year round.

A careful examination of the fruit reveals how the tissues change during development. In citrus fruits, like grapefruits and oranges, the bulk of the fleshy fruit is formed by small juice sacs, which originate from small hairs lining the inside of the pistil. These juice sacs are simply hairs that swell at different positions along their length, filling the fruit. The nature of these hairs can be seen by gently teasing a few sacs from the center of the fruit. The fleshiness of the tomato fruit is the result of the swelling of the placenta, a tissue that connects the seeds to the walls. Frequently, the ovary wall itself forms most of the fruit, but the exact region of thickening differs in each plant group. In squash, cucumbers, and pumpkins for example, the middle of the ovary wall grows thicker than the inner and outer layers, whereas in grapes, the inner wall grows thicker, and in watermelons, the outer wall is particularly thick. In dry fruits, the thickening of the ovary wall is sometimes accompanied by cell hardening, which is caused by chemical changes in the cell walls. These hardened cells form the walls of nuts and other hard fruits. In dry fruits, the walls of the fruit are no longer living.

Types of Fruits

Fruits consist of three major types, depending on whether they are formed from a single flower with fused or unfused multiple simple pistils or from multiple flowers: (1) simple fruits consist of one simple or fused pistil, in which the pistil forms the simple fruit; (2) aggregate fruits consist of many unfused pistils as part of a single flower; and (3) multiple fruits consist of many flowers on the same floral stem fusing together during growth. Fruits formed with large areas of nonpistillate parts in the flower are known as accessory fruits, a term that may be used in combination with these other terms.

FRUIT CATEGORIES AND COMMON EXAMPLES

Major and Minor Categories of Fruit Types				Common Examples
Simple fruits (develop from one pistil and often include surrounding [accessory] ovary tissues)	**Fleshy fruits**	**Berry** (multi-seeded fruits with rind or skin-like covering)	**Typical berry** (fruits with skinlike covering)	Grape, tomato, gooseberry, cranberry
			Pepo (fruits with inseparable rind)	Cucumber, pumpkin, squash
			Hesperidium (fruits with separable rind)	Orange, grapefruit, lemon
		Drupe (single seeded with thin skin)		Peach, plum, cherry, olive
		Pome (multi-seeded fruit formed from floral tube [inferior ovary])		Apple, pear, quince
	Dry fruits	**Dehiscent fruits** (fruits that split at maturity)	**Legume** (single pistil forming two slits)	Peas, beans, locust
			Follicle (single pistil forming a single slit)	Milkweed, columbine, larkspur, magnolia
			Capsule (compound pistil opening variously)	Poppy, purslane, iris, Saint-John's-wort, morning glory
		Nondehiscent fruits (fruits that do not naturally split at maturity)	**Grain** (caryopsis; one-seeded with inseparable covering)	Corn, wheat, oats, rye, barley
			Achene (one-seeded with separable covering)	Sunflower, lettuce, buckwheat
			Samara (winged achene)	Ash, maple, elm, birch
			Nut (one-seeded, hard covered fruit with large embryo)	Chestnut, walnut, hazelnut, acorn, beechnut
Aggregate fruits (develop from one flower with multiple separate pistils)				Strawberry, raspberry, blackberry
Multiple fruits (develop from a flower cluster, multiple flowers of an inflorescence)				Pineapple, mulberry, osage orange, fig

Simple fleshy fruits are divided into three major types. Berries are multi-seeded fruits covered by a thinner skin (as in tomatoes) or a thickened rind (as in cucumbers). Some berries may be further divided into subtypes, including the pepo, characteristic of the cucumber family (e.g., cucumbers, squash, and pumpkins), and the hesperidium, characteristic of the citrus family (e.g., oranges, grapefruits, and lemons). Pomes are also multi-seeded fruits, but their fleshy body consists of largely nonfloral (accessory) parts. Since their body is not just pistil tissue, pomes can be regarded as accessory simple fruits. In pomes, the outer wall develops from the floral cup or hypanthium of the flower, as in apples, pears, and quinces. Drupes are single-seeded fruits that may contain a leathery or stonelike seed. Peaches and plums are examples of fruits with rock-hard seeds at their center, commonly classified as stone fruits.

Simple dry fruits include two types of fruits. Dehiscent dry fruits are those that normally open during the maturation process, releasing their seeds. Frequently, a line of dehiscence forms the opening in the fruit. **Legumes** are formed from single pistils that have two slits or lines of dehiscence on either side of the fruit. Legumes include peanuts and beans, and

legumes beans and other members of the Fabaceae family

suture line of attachment

are characteristic of the bean family. Follicles are dry fruits, often with vertical slits, which have a single dehiscence line. Capsules are formed from compound pistils and open through a variety of mechanisms. In poppies, these fruits have small pores at the top of their fruits. In contrast, irises form fruits that open along the **suture** lines of the compound pistil, splitting into their component pistils. The position of these openings is used to establish further subtypes (not mentioned here).

Nondehiscent dry fruits are those that do not normally open to release their seeds. Four types are commonly found. Grains, or caryopses, are small, one-seeded fruits that have fruit walls that are fused to the seed and are therefore inseparable, as in corn. Achenes are single-seeded indehiscent fruits in which the seed and fruit are readily separated, as in sunflowers. Samaras are winged fruits, such as those of maple, ash, and elm, which are readily dispersed by wind. Nuts are one-seeded fruits as well, but are characterized by their hard covering and often large and meaty embryos, as in walnuts, chestnuts, and acorns.

Aggregate fruits develop from single flowers with multiple separate pistils. Common examples composed mainly of pistillate tissues include raspberry and blackberry. The fleshy region of the strawberry originates from the receptacle of the former flower. Therefore, in addition to being an aggregate fruit, it is also called an accessory fruit.

Multiple fruits consist of the fused flowers of whole inflorescences (or flowering stalks). The most common of the multiple fruits is the pineapple, although the mulberry, Osage orange (or bois d'arc), and fig are also commonly encountered multiple fruits. SEE ALSO FRUITS, SEEDLESS; GRAINS; REPRODUCTION, SEXUAL; ROSACEAE; SEED DISPERSAL; SEEDS.

Scott D. Russell

Bibliography

Nicholson, B. E., C. Geissler, John G. Vaughan, Elizabeth Dowle. *The Oxford Book of Food Plants*, 2nd ed. Oxford University Press, 1998.

Schery, R. W. *Plants for Man.* New York: Prentice-Hall, 1959.

Simpson, B. B., and M. C. Ogorzaly. *Economic Botany.* New York: McGraw-Hill, 1995.

Whiteman, K. *Fruits of the World: A Comprehensive Guide to Choosing and Using.* Hermes House, 2000.

Fruits, Seedless

endosperm the nutritive tissue in a seed, formed by fertilization of a diploid egg tissue by a sperm from pollen

The absence of developed seeds in fruit improves its eating quality. Moreover, it may allow more uniform fruit production in different environments. Seedless fruit occurs when seed (embryo and **endosperm**) growth is inhibited or the seed dies early, while the remainder of the fruit continues to grow. Bananas and grapes are the most commonly available seedless fruits. Bananas are seedless because the parent banana tree is triploid (3X chromosome sets) even though pollination is normal. Generally, species with a chromosome set number divisible by two (e.g., 2X or 4X chromosome sets) are capable of seed production while uneven sets of chromosomes (e.g., 3X or 5X) are either **sterile** or do not produce seeds. After fer-

sterile non-reproductive

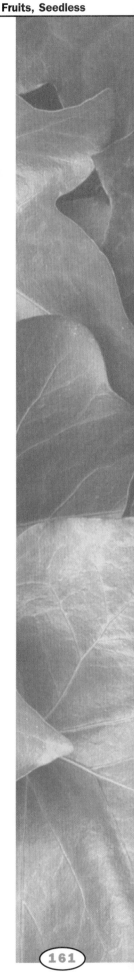

tilization, banana fruit development can proceed normally but seed development is arrested because of the genetic imbalance. Plant breeders have also produced seedless watermelons (*Citrullus lanatus*). The first practical system for producing seedless watermelons was the 4X-2X hybridization method. **Hybrid** seed is produced from crossing a **tetraploid** (4X) female and **diploid** (2X) male. Seedless fruit is produced on the resulting triploid (3X) hybrids. Pollination occurs, but just as in bananas, the fruit continues to grow while seed growth is reduced or absent because of uneven sets of chromosomes.

Parthenocarpy, fruit development without pollen fertilization and seed set, can result in seedless fruits such as grapes, squash (*Cucurbita pepo*), and eggplants (*Solanum melongena*). The majority of table grapes and raisins are seedless. Thompson seedless grapes have a normal chromosome constitution and pollination but have specific genes causing seedlessness. In addition, seedless grapes are treated with the hormone gibberellin, which is applied early in fruit development. The application of this hormone increases the size and consistency of the fruit.

Squash and eggplants can exhibit **facultative** parthenocarpy, that is, parthenocarpy that occurs under environmental conditions where pollination and seed would not occur normally. Cool weather (early spring or late fall) or greenhouse growth conditions are the most common environments where this type of parthenocarpy occurs. Commercial-quality fruit can be produced in cool environments or in greenhouse winter production locations where pollination is limiting. Under summer growth conditions, normal pollination, fruit production, and seed set occurs. Hormone treatments cannot be reliably used under these conditions to induce parthenocarpy or increase fruit size. Seedless summer squash, zucchini, has been obtained by crossing two varieties, DG4 and Striata. This parthenocarpic variety is stable and has been used to produce additional commercial squash hybrids.

Genetic engineering has been used to produce facultative parthenocarpic eggplants. A two-part gene transferred into eggplants consists of DefH9 from snapdragon (*Antirrhinum majus*) and iaaM from a fungus (*Pseudomonas syringae*). The iaaM gene produces the plant hormone auxin, while the DefH9 component restricts expression of the hormone gene to the immature fruit of the eggplants. Thus, the eggplants apply their own hormone treatment at the appropriate time and place. Conventional application of auxin on the surface of the fruit is ineffective in this case. Normal eggplant fruit are produced even when pollination does not occur, such as in winter greenhouse production. Fruit set and seed set are normal under favorable pollination conditions. In the future, this method could also be used for producing seedless fruits of many different species. SEE ALSO BREEDING; FRUITS; HORMONES; POLYPLOIDY; PROPAGATION; REPRODUCTION, SEXUAL.

Dwight T. Tomes

hybrid a mix of two varieties or species

tetraploid having four sets of chromosomes; a form of polyploidy

diploid having two sets of chromosomes, versus having one (haploid)

facultative capable of but not obligated to

Bibliography

Mohr, H. C. "Watermelon Breeding." In *Breeding Vegetable Crops.* Edited by Mark J. Bassett. Westport, CT: Avi Publishing Company, Inc., 1986.

Rotino, G. L., E. M. Perri, M. Zottini, H. Sommer, A. Spena. "Genetic Engineering of Parthenocarpic Plants." *Nature Biotechnology* 15 (1997): 1398–1401.

Fungi

Mycology is the study of fungi (*mykes*, Greek for "fungi," and *ology*, meaning "study of"). Most contemporary mycologists consider the fungi to be in two kingdoms: kingdom Fungi with five phyla and kingdom Stramenopila with three phyla. The total number of fungi in the world is estimated to be over 1.5 million with less than 5 percent of the species described. Some mycologists believe that the total number of fungi may be more than 2 million. Two other kingdoms are sometimes mistaken for fungi: the slime molds (kingdom Myxomycota), which have a creeping plasmodium, and the bacteria and **actinomycetes** (kingdom Monera).

Structure and Life Cycle

Fungi are nonphotosynthetic, lacking the chlorophyll of higher plants and algae, and are recognized by their fruiting bodies, which is the visible part of the fungus. Examples include mushrooms, puffballs, molds, cup fungi, and morels. The vegetative structure consists of minute **filamentous** cells called hyphae, which are microscopic in size, usually from 1 micron to 10 microns in diameter. An aggregate of hyphae is called a mycelium, which is the **thallus** or vegetative part of the fungus plant known as spawn in the mushroom industry. In the kingdom Fungi, the mycelium has one haploid nucleus per cell (only one set of chromosomes) or is dikaryotic (two **haploid** nuclei per cell). In contrast, in the kingdom Stramenopila, mycelium has diploid nuclei (one nucleus with chromosomes from both parents). In both kingdoms, the mycelium has rigid cell walls usually composed of chitin (a complex carbon **compound**), although it is infrequently made up of cellulose in kingdom Fungi.

In both kingdoms, fungi obtain their nutrition by excreting **enzymes** into the host or any organic material, which is then broken down and absorbed into the hyphal cell to provide the nutrition necessary for growth. Fungi function in the **ecosystem** as saprophytes, or decomposers. They break down dead organic matter as parasites by attacking living hosts or host cells, and as mycorrhizae (*mycor*, meaning "fungi," and *rhizae*, meaning "root") by forming jointly beneficial unions with the roots of higher plants. Fungi and algae combine to form a plant called a lichen. Only fungi and bacteria decompose various kinds of organic matter and change complex organic structures, such as plant cell walls containing lignin or the chitinous exoskeletons of insects, into simple carbohydrates that can then be assimilated by a wide variety of organisms.

The hyphae grow until they form an extensive mycelium of fungal tissue. At this point a young fruiting body initial (or button) begins to form and develops into a mature fruiting body. In some phyla fruiting bodies are large and variously recognized as mushrooms, boletes, puffballs, conks, cup fungi, morels, false morels, truffles, and witches' butter, to mention only a few. However, many of the aquatic fungi, molds, and other fungi (such as the yeasts) form minute fruiting structures that can only be seen with the aid of a magnifying glass or a microscope.

The function of the fruiting body is to form a tissue in or on which the spore-bearing surface is formed. The spore-bearing surface covers the gills of a mushroom, is inside the tubes of the bolete, or forms a spore mass inside the puffball and truffle. The spore of the fungus serves the same purpose as the seed of the green plants, but the spore is composed of only one or several simple cells. The spore forms following meiosis in sexual cells lo-

Stinkhorn, *Dictyophora indusiata*, whose greenish-gray fetid-smelling spore mass and skirtlike indusium are both attractants for insects.

actinomycetes common name for a group of Gram-positive bacteria that are filamentous and superficially similar to fungi

filamentous thin and long

thallus simple, flattened, nonleafy plant body

haploid having one set of chromosomes, versus having two (diploid)

compound a substance formed from two or more elements

enzyme a protein that controls a reaction in a cell

ecosystem an ecological community together with its environment

cated in the spore-bearing surface. In the mushrooms, boletes, cup fungi, and morels, for example, the nearly mature spores are forcibly discharged at maturity from the spore-bearing surface. If one blows over the surface of a cup fungus at maturity, a small cloud (the puffing or a discharge of the spores) can be seen. However, in other fungi such as the puffballs, stinkhorns, and truffles, no forcible discharge occurs. The powdery spore mass of the puffball is often discharged through a pore in the top that forms at maturity. The greenish-gray spore mass of the stinkhorn emits a strong odor, which attracts insects that eat, contact, and spread the spores. The truffle, which is found at the surface of or beneath the soil, gradually matures and produces strong smells that attract small rodents that dig up and eat the fruiting bodies and distribute the spores.

Molds, such as *Penicillium*, produce microscopic asexual fruiting bodies that in turn produce asexual spores called conidia on structures known as conidiophores. Some yeast cells bud and reproduce asexually. Other fungi, such as the bread mold *Rhizopus*, produce asexual fruiting structures known as sporangiophores that support sacs called sporangia in which asexual spores are produced. Aquatic fungi also produce a variety of asexual spores, some of which are **motile** (called **zoospores**). These spores swim to a potential host, retract their **flagella**, and enter the host producing an oval fruiting body with a feeding tube or minute root-like rhizoids. The zoospores of the kingdom Fungi have one whiplash flagellum, while in the kingdom Stramenopila the zoospores have two flagella, one whiplash and one tinsel type, that move rapidly to propel the zoospore. Spores, either sexual or asexual, motile or nonmotile, usually germinate to form thin cylindric hyphal cells that rapidly elongate and branch to form the mycelium of the new fungus plant.

Nutrition

The fungus cell must grow into the host plant or a bit of organic material in order to gain nutrition from it. This is achieved by discharging enzymes (called exoenzymes) from the cells. Complex carbohydrates and proteins are broken down by this process and then are absorbed by the hyphae. The nutrients can then be **translocated** from one cell to another. The growth of most fungi is indeterminate (that is, it never stops) because the fungus must continue to grow into new areas to seek new sources of food. The typical fairy ring represents a visible bright green grass ring where the active mycelium is, and it is along this ring that the mushrooms will fruit. Each year the diameter of the ring will increase while the mycelium dies out in the middle because the food base is exhausted.

Mycorrhizae

Mycorrhizal fungi invade the healthy outer cells of the tiny rootlets of higher plants. Ectomycorrhizae surround the rootlet with a sheath of fungal cells, and special hyphae penetrate between the **cortical** cells of the rootlet and exchange nutrients with the higher plant, usually a tree or a shrub. Endomycorrhizae called VA (vesicular arbuscular) mycorrhizae form oval storage cells (vesicles) and minute branchlike processes (arbuscules) in the root cells of the host where nutrients are exchanged. Because fungi do not carry out photosynthesis and cannot make their own sugar, the mycorrhizal fungus obtains moisture and carbohydrates from its green plant host and, in return, provides the host with nitrogen, phosphorus, zinc, and other es-

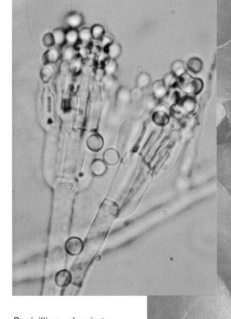

Penicillium, showing a conidiophore with asexual conidiospores.

motile capable of movement

zoospore a swimming spore

flagella threadlike extension of the cell membrane, used for movement

translocate to move materials from one region to another

cortical relating to the cortex of a plant

Amanita virosa, a deadly poisonous mushroom common in the United States.

sential compounds. It does this using the miles of tiny mycelium to successfully compete for phosphorus and nitrogen, which extends the root system of the green plant. Most of the woody plants such as the pine, oak, birch, and beech have ectomycorrhizae, and most herbaceous plants such as grass, corn, wheat, and rye have VA endomycorrhizae.

Food, Drugs, and Poisons

Fungi play a major role in the diet of humans. Yeasts (*Saccaromyces cerevisiae*) are used in the process of fermentation, in which they break down carbohydrates to liberate carbon dioxide and to produce alcohol. Gin is made when juniper berries are fermented, wine from grapes, beer from grains, bourbon from corn, and scotch from barley. Yeasts are also used in making Limburger cheese, yogurt, and Kombucha tea. Baker's yeast produces a high proportion of CO_2, which causes the dough to rise. Molds, generally species of *Penicillium*, are used to produce cheese such as blue, Roquefort, and Camembert.

The new age of antibiotics was ushered in with Sir Alexander Fleming's discovery of penicillin in 1929. It was first produced by the blue-green mold *Penicillium notatum.* Many other antibiotics are produced from Actinomycetes. On the other hand, aflatoxins produced by species of *Aspergillus* cause food spoilage and are carcinogenic. Mushrooms also produce **toxins** that only affect humans when they are eaten. Examples of these are the amatoxins and phallotoxins produced by a mushroom, *Amanita virosa,* that are often fatal to humans; muscarine and muscimol produced by the fly agaric, *Amanita muscaria,* are usually not fatal. **Hallucinogens** such as psilocybin and psilocin are produced by several species of mushrooms including *Psilocybe cubensis* and the protoplasmic poison monomethyhydrozine (MMH) by the false morel *Gyromitra esculenta.*

toxin a poisonous substance

hallucinogenic capable of inducing hallucinations

Fungal Diseases

Fungi that are parasitic on humans include the common **dermatophytes** on the skin, hair, and nails, causing such diseases as barber's itch and ath-

dermatophytes fungi that cause skin diseases

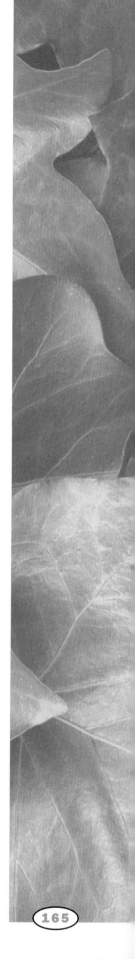

lete's foot (*Microsporium canis*). More serious diseases, such as *Histoplasma capsulatum* or histoplasmosis found in warm temperate climates and coccidiomycosis (*Coccidioides immitis*) in arid areas, grow in bird dung and soil, producing a respiratory infection in humans that is occasionally fatal. North and South American blastomycosis, sporotrichosis, and other diseases caused by fungi attack tissues and organs within the body and are incapacitating or fatal to their victims.

Diseases that affect major economic plants have historically impacted people. The ergot (*Claviceps purpurea*), which infects the grains of rye, produces deadly brown specks in bread and led to deformity and the death of thousands of people in the Middle Ages. The European grape was saved from the grips of the downy mildew (*Plasmopara viticola*) in the 1800s by the discovery of Bordeaux Mixture (copper sulfate and lime); the discovery gave birth to plant pathology as a science. The European potato famine, caused by the potato blight fungus (*Phytophthora infestans*), in the years 1845 to 1847 forced more than a million Irish to flee from Ireland. In the United States, the chestnut blight (*Cryphonectria parasitica*) has reduced the tall and highly valued American chestnut from the eastern forests to a rare shrub, while the Dutch elm disease (*Ceratocystis ulmi*) threatens to eliminate the American elm. Scientists struggle continually to produce resistant strains of wheat that will not be parasitized by the wheat rust (*Phytophthora infestans*) and corn that will be resistant to the corn smut (*Ustilago maydis*). Mexicans and Hispanic Americans cook the infected ears in many ways and consider them to be a delicacy.

The shelves of every supermarket have the meadow mushroom (*Agaricus bisporus*) and specialty mushrooms like Shiitake (*Lentinus edodes*), oyster shell (*Pleurotus ostreatus*), and the Portabello (*Agaricus* sp.) for sale. In fact, the leading agricultural crop in Pennsylvania is mushrooms. SEE ALSO CHESTNUT BLIGHT; DUTCH ELM DISEASE; INTERACTIONS, PLANT-FUNGAL; LICHEN; MYCORRHIZAE; PATHOGENS; PLANT SYSTEMATICS; POTATO BLIGHT; TAXONOMY; TAXONOMY, HISTORY OF.

Orson K. Miller Jr.

Bibliography

Alexopoulos, C. J., C. W. Mims, and M. Blackwell. *Introductory Mycology.* New York: John Wiley & Sons, 1996.

Kavaler, L. *Mushrooms Molds and Miracles.* New York: The New American Library, 1965.

Large, E. C. *The Advance of the Fungi.* New York: Henry Holt & Co., 1940.

Miller, O. K. *Mushrooms of North America.* New York: E. P. Dutton Inc., 1973.

Rolfe, R. T. and F. W. Rolfe. *The Romance of the Fungus World.* New York: Dover Publications Inc., 1925.

Schaechter, E. *In the Company of Mushrooms.* Cambridge, MA: Harvard University Press, 1997.

Stamets, P. *Growing Gourmet & Medicinal Mushrooms.* Berkeley, CA: Ten Speed Press, 1993.

haploid having one set of chromosomes, versus having two (diploid)

sporophyte the diploid, spore-producing individual in the plant life cycle

Gametophyte

A gametophyte, or gamete-bearing plant, is one of the two multicellular phases that occur in alternation of generations. The gametophyte is the **haploid** phase; that is, its cells contain only one set of chromosomes, in contrast to the **sporophyte** phase, where the cells contain two sets. The gametophyte

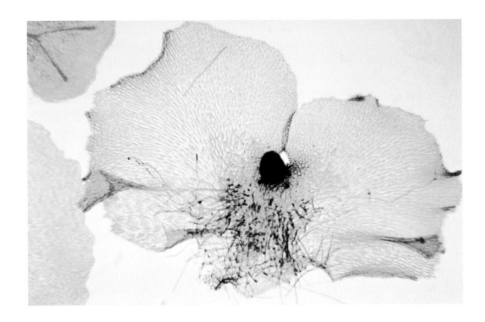

mitosis the part of the cell cycle in which chromosomes are separated to give each daughter cell an identical chromosome set

gametangia structure where gametes are formed

vascular related to transport of nutrients

thallus simple, flattened, nonleafy plant body

endosporic formation of a gametophyte inside the spore wall

heterosporous bearing spores of two types, large megaspores and small microspores

develops from the germinating, haploid spore, which was produced by meiosis in the sporangium of the sporophyte phase. Gametophytes produce sperm and egg cells by **mitosis**, often in multicellular **gametangia** known as antheridia and archegonia, respectively. Fertilization, which occurs in the female gametophyte, establishes a new sporophyte generation. In some algae, like sea lettuce, the vegetative gametophyte is identical in form to the vegetative sporophyte, but in most organisms the gametophyte has a very different appearance from the sporophyte. In bryophytes the gametophyte is the highly visible, persistent phase of the plant, but in **vascular** plants the gametophyte is short-lived and often much reduced in size. Among land plants, gametophytes are of four different types. These include: (1) the green, leafy shoot systems of mosses, and leafy liverworts; (2) the green, **thallus** to prothallus forms of thalloid liverworts, hornworts, horsetails, most ferns, and some lycopods; (3) the colorless, subterranean, mycorrhizal axes of psilophytes and some lycopods; and (4) the small, **endosporic** forms of **heterosporous** lycopods, some ferns, and all seed plants. The smallest and least complex gametophytes are those of the flowering plants. The male gametophyte is the two- or three-celled pollen grain that is released from the anther, and the female gametophyte is the seven-celled embryo sac that is located in the base of the pistil of the flower. SEE ALSO BRYOPHYTES; REPRODUCTION, ALTERNATION OF GENERATIONS AND; REPRODUCTION, FERTILIZATION AND; REPRODUCTION, SEXUAL; SPOROPHYTE.

Barbara Crandall-Stotler

Bibliography

Graham, Linda. "The Origin of the Life Cycle of Land Plants." *American Scientist* 73 (1985):178–186.

Genetic Engineer

Plant genetic engineers create new varieties of plants, including row crops, vegetables and berries, forest and fruit trees, and ornamentals. These new varieties contain any number of new or improved traits, such as resistance

A lab technician monitors the growth of a sunflower plant raised from an embryo in controlled conditions as a genetic engineering project at the Sungene Technologies Laboratory in Palo Alto, California.

to pests and diseases, resistance to poor growing conditions, resistance to herbicides, and improved nutrition, wood quality, storage characteristics, and horticultural traits. Plant genetic engineers are also modifying plants to produce industrial **enzymes**, biodegradable plastics, pharmaceutical products, and edible vaccines. Plant genetic engineers collaborate closely with molecular biologists to identify and clone the necessary genes, and with plant breeders, who breed these into improved plant varieties.

Genetic engineers are drawn to the discipline because of the power that creating new plant varieties has to help preserve crop yields, produce a better, healthier product for the consumer, and help safeguard the environment. Though some of the daily tasks can be routine and repetitive, the field is advancing rapidly, and mastering the new advances continuously provides challenges and prevents research and development from becoming routine.

Plant genetic engineers must have a strong background in biology, with an emphasis in botany, biochemistry, and genetics. An understanding of agriculture or forestry can be particularly helpful, especially for the selection of

enzyme a protein that controls a reaction in a cell

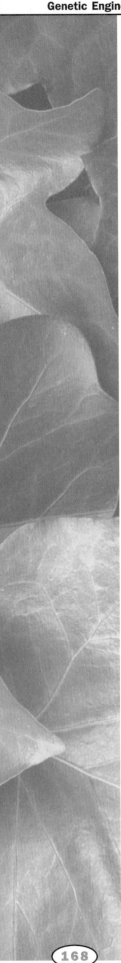

the traits to be modified. Plant genetic engineers begin with an undergraduate degree in one of the agricultural plant sciences, forestry, botany, genetics, biotechnology, or biochemistry, and many obtain an M.S. and/or a Ph.D. in these fields.

Those with B.S. and M.S. degrees usually work in a laboratory and handle the necessary deoxyribonucleic acid (DNA), plant cell cultures, and analytical work. Those with a Ph.D. set research goals and determine research directions. Salary range depends strongly on educational level. In 1999, people with a B.S. or M.S. may have earned $20,000 to $30,000 for an entry-level position, while entry positions for a Ph.D. degree were in the vicinity of $50,000. Senior-level Ph.D. positions may have earned $150,000. Chief areas of employment would be research universities, biotechnology companies, forest products companies, and international research centers. The greatest amount of genetic engineering takes place in the United States and Europe. However, because plant genetic engineering is taking place in many places of the world, there may be employment opportunities throughout the world.

toxin a poisonous substance

Very vocal groups of opponents to genetic engineering technology claim that genetic engineering will lead to genetic pollution, introduce **toxins** into the food supply, and damage the environment. Such opposition has led to bans on genetically engineered plants and food products in many countries, as well as an extensive patchwork of regulations. Sustained opposition to genetically engineered plants may limit employment opportunities in the future. SEE ALSO BREEDER; BREEDING; GENETIC ENGINEERING; MOLECULAR PLANT GENETICS; TRANSGENIC PLANTS.

Scott Merkle and Wayne Parrott

Genetic Engineering

Humans have been modifying the genetic constitution (genomes) of crop plants for thousands of years, since the very beginning of agriculture. In the past, modifying the genomes of crop plants was accomplished by selecting seeds from those individual plants that produced the most grain, were most resistant to diseases, or were most tolerant of environmental stresses (e.g., drought). These seeds were then used to plant the next year's crop. This approach is sometimes referred to as classical plant breeding, and it has been extraordinarily successful at producing improved crops. However, this approach is subject to a major limitation in that it only allows for the selection of genes (and the associated genetic traits) that are already present in the genome of the crop plant. Although many potentially useful genes are present in the genomes of other organisms, they are not always present in the genomes of crop plants.

The limitations of classical plant breeding can be partially addressed by facilitating sexual reproduction between a crop plant and a wild plant species. This approach can be used to introduce new genes into a crop plant genome (e.g., genes for disease resistance). Unfortunately, sexual reproduction between crop plants and other species is restricted to closely related plant species, limiting the pool of potential genes that could be added to the crop plant genome. For example, commercially grown tomatoes (*Ly-*

copersicon esculentum) may be able to reproduce sexually with wild tomato relatives (other members of the genus *Lycopersicon*), but they would not be able to reproduce sexually with any wild (or domestic) member of the grass family (species within the family Poaceae). In addition, no human-directed mechanism for introducing genes into plants from other types of organisms (e.g., bacteria, fungi, mammals, etc.) was available prior to the advent of genetic engineering.

Plant genetic engineering has been developed to circumvent the limitations of classical plant breeding, allowing the addition of genes (i.e., segments of deoxyribonucleic acid [DNA]) from any organism to the genomes of crop plants. Plants to which one or more genes have been added through a means other than sexual reproduction are called genetically modified organisms (GMOs) or transgenic plants. The genes that are introduced into the plants are referred to as transgenes.

The Process of Genetically Engineering Plants

In order to achieve genetic engineering of plants, a series of tools and technologies are necessary. The ability to identify, isolate, and replicate specific genes is required. This series of steps is referred to as gene (or DNA) cloning. (A complete description of cloning is beyond the scope of this entry, but may be found in most biology textbooks.) A method to insert the cloned gene(s) into the genome of the crop plant is required, as is a method for identifying those cells that have incorporated the gene. The ability to regenerate entire plants from transgenic cells is essential, as is a means of verifying the presence of the transgene in the GMO.

Once a target gene has been cloned it is typically introduced into the genome of a crop plant by one of two means: *Agrobacterium*-mediated transformation or particle bombardment (biolistic) transformation. *Agrobacterium tumefaciens* is a very interesting soil bacterium that is a nonhuman "genetic engineer." Under natural circumstances, *Agrobacterium* has the ability to cause crown gall disease in some plants. The cause of the disease stems from *Agrobacterium*'s ability to insert some of its own genes into the genome of the plant. This results in the formation of a gall (tumorlike growth) on the plant and in the production of a food source, of which only the bacteria can make use. Deletion of the gall-inducing genes has allowed *Agrobacterium* to be used to produce many types of transgenic crop plants, including tomato, potato, and cotton.

Unfortunately, many important crop species are not easily susceptible to *Agrobacterium*-mediated transformation. The globally important cereal grains (such as corn, wheat, and rice) are prime examples of such species. Therefore, other approaches for introducing genes were developed. The most widely used is the particle bombardment technique. This technique involves accelerating small DNA-coated gold particles to a high velocity such that they are able to penetrate the cell walls of plant cells. Once inside the cell wall, some of the DNA is able to separate from the gold particles and integrate into the genome of the plant cell.

Regardless of whether the new DNA (transgene) is introduced by *Agrobacterium* or by particle bombardment, it is essential to understand that not all of the plant cells will contain the new gene(s). Therefore, a means of screening for the presence of the new DNA is required. Com-

A geneticist holds a test tube containing a cloned flowering plant.

Corn tissues at various stages of growth used by genetic engineers at the Sungene Technologies Laboratory in Palo Alto, California, to cultivate desired traits.

toxin a poisonous substance

monly, this is accomplished by including additional genes in the introduced DNA whose protein products confer resistance to a **toxin** that would normally kill plant cells. For example, the phosphinothricin acetyltransferase (PAT) gene confers resistance to the herbicide Basta. If a population of plant cells is bombarded with DNA that includes the PAT gene, and subsequently the cells are grown on a medium containing Basta, only those cells that contain the newly introduced transgenes will be able to grow.

The transgenetic cells must then be able to be regenerated into entire plants. This is accomplished through a series of steps referred to as tissue culture and makes use of plant hormones to stimulate the production of roots and stems from the transgenic cells. Various methods can be used to verify the continued presence of the transgene(s) in the regenerated plants. One method is to specifically amplify (thereby allowing easy detection) the DNA of the transgene using a technique called polymerase chain reaction (PCR).

An Example of a Genetically Engineered Crop Plant

To see how genetic engineering may be used to improve crops, let's look at a specific example. In the United States corn (maize) is attacked by an introduced insect pest called the european corn borer (ECB). This pest is a moth, and it is during the larval stage (the caterpillar stage) that it actually feeds on corn plants. Under some circumstances this pest can cause major damage to corn crops. There is also a naturally occurring species of bacterium (*Bacillus thuringiensis*) that possesses a gene encoding a protein toxin (Bt-toxin) that is quite effective in killing many species of caterpillars. In addition, the Bt-toxin protein is not toxic to mammals, birds, and most other animals. Clearly, this Bt-toxin gene cannot be introduced into corn via sexual reproduction, as corn plants and bacteria are unable to reproduce sexually. However, genetic engineering provides an alternate approach to introduce the Bt-toxin gene into the genome of the corn plant.

The Bt-toxin gene has been cloned from *Bacillus thuringiensis* and introduced into the genome of corn plants using the particle bombardment approach. The resulting transgenic corn plants are resistant to ECB, and are, in fact, capable of killing ECB larvae that feed upon them. In essence, these transgenic corn plants are producing their own internal insecticide, allowing the farmer to plant corn without needing to subsequently apply chemical insecticides to prevent damage caused by ECB.

Potential Benefits and Concerns Regarding the Widespread Use of Genetically Engineered Crops

What are the potential benefits of planting transgenic corn producing the Bt-toxin? Potentially, the yield of corn may increase as corn plants are protected from ECB. Depending on market conditions and the cost of buying the Bt-toxin producing corn seed, this may or may not represent an economic benefit for corn growers. However, if the corn crop had been routinely sprayed with chemical insecticides to control ECB (true in some parts of the corn belt), then that economic cost to the farmer would be eliminated. In addition, the environmental costs of spraying a chemical pesticide, which can result in extensive killing of nontarget species, would be minimized. There have been, however, various concerns raised about the widespread use of Bt-toxin-containing corn, so we should also consider the potential dangers of applying this technology.

The potential concerns with widespread usage of Bt-toxin containing corn fall into three primary categories: direct health impacts of Bt-toxin on humans, selection for Bt-toxin resistant populations of ECB, and unintended environmental impacts. Bt-toxin-containing insecticides have been used for many years, and there have been no indications of direct toxic effects on humans. Nonetheless, there is the possibility that some individuals could develop allergic reactions to this protein. Widespread human use of transgenic corn containing Bt-toxin could potentially expose a much larger number of people to this protein.

Development of Bt-toxin-resistant populations of ECB is also certainly a major area of concern. Such insects would be able to feed on Bt-transgenic corn and could potentially lead to increased populations of ECB. Other insects have demonstrated a remarkable ability to develop resistance to various insecticides (DDT-resistant mosquitoes, for example). Current approaches to minimize development of Bt-resistant ECB include planting mixtures of Bt-toxin containing corn and nontransgenic corn. The idea is to allow those corn borers that are susceptible to Bt-toxin to continue to reproduce, maintaining the presence of the susceptibility gene(s) in the ECB

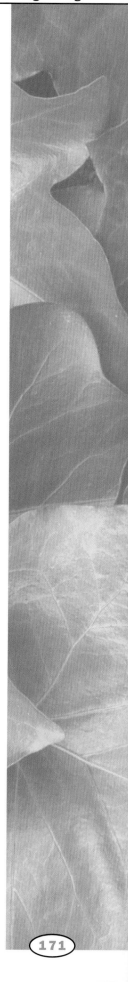

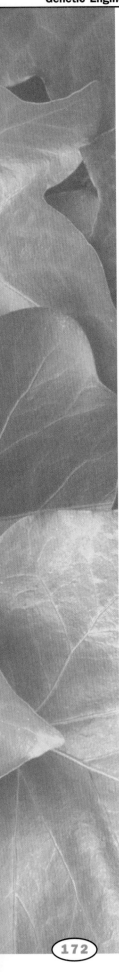

population. A related concern is that decreasing the population of ECB through widespread use of Bt-toxin-containing corn will result in a decline of the populations of other insects (principally types of wasps) that prey on ECB, reducing the potential for natural control of the ECB population.

The area of unintended environmental impacts is also of major concern. It is important to recognize that, while the Bt-toxin does not affect mammals or birds, it is toxic to many species of insects, not just ECB. Current commercially available Bt-toxin-containing corn varieties produce the toxin throughout the entire body of the plant, including the pollen grains. When a pollen grain is released from an anther it is dispersed by the wind in an attempt to reach the stigma (silk) of a female flower, but the vast majority of the pollen grains never reach a silk; they land somewhere else. If that somewhere else is a plant leaf that serves as a food source for another species of insect, that nontarget insect may be harmed or killed by the Bt-toxin. This concern has been specifically raised with regard to the monarch butterfly, whose caterpillars feed on milkweeds in and near corn fields; but there are, of course, many other species of moths or butterflies that could be potentially affected. Further studies are in progress to assess the impact of pollen-born Bt-toxin on monarch or other butterfly or moth species. One possibility to minimize this problem is to eliminate production of the Bt-toxin in the pollen grains, while continuing production in those plant parts most affected by ECB, principally the stems and ears. This approach will necessitate the development of new varieties of Bt-toxin-containing transgenic corn that include the appropriate gene-regulating elements.

Clearly, the use of genetic engineering to modify crop plants has the potential to greatly benefit humans. Increased crop productivity could be used to feed the still-increasing population of humans on our planet. Increased production might also allow preservation, or restoration, of some natural areas that would otherwise be required for agricultural purposes. Other plant genetic engineering strategies may allow production of crops with improved nutritional qualities, the ability to synthesize industrial feedstocks, resistance to various types of environmental stresses, or even the ability to produce drugs used in human medicine. However, as the Bt-toxin-containing corn example demonstrates, it is essential that we investigate, as thoroughly as possible, what unintended consequences may arise from use of the technology prior to widespread adoption of a particular type of transgenic crop plant. SEE ALSO BREEDING; GENETIC ENGINEER; TISSUE CULTURE; TRANSGENIC PLANTS.

James T. Colbert

Bibliography

Abelson, Philip H., and Pamela J. Hines. "The Plant Revolution." *Science* 285 (1999): 367–68.

Campbell, Neil A., Jane B. Reece, and Lawrence G. Mitchell. *Biology*, 5th ed. Menlo Park, CA: Benjamin Cummings, 1999.

DellaPenna, Dean. "Nutritional Genomics: Manipulating Plant Micronutrients to Improve Human Health." *Science* 285 (1999): 375–79.

Ferber, Dan. "GM Crops in the Cross Hairs." *Science* 286 (1999): 1662–66.

Moffat, Anne S. "Engineering Plants to Cope with Metals." *Science* 285 (1999): 369–370.

Raven, Peter H., Ray F. Evert, and Susan E. Eichhorn. *Biology of Plants*, 6th ed. New York: W. H. Freeman and Company, 1999.

Genetic Mechanisms and Development

Development in plants refers to the formation of shape and pattern in the multicellular organism. While development can be influenced by environmental factors such as light or temperature, the major factor controlling development of any plant is, of course, its genes. Genes determine the overall shape and size of the mature plant, its branching pattern and leaf type, the extent and arrangement of **vascular** tissue in root and shoot, and the timing of flowering and the form of flowers produced.

In plants the genetic mechanisms that control developmental events are best understood in the case of flower development. A normal (wild type) flower of most **angiosperms** (flowering plants) has four distinct types of organs that are arranged in four concentric rings (whorls). The outermost whorl has green, leaflike organs called **sepals**. The second whorl from outside consists of brightly colored organs called petals. The third whorl consists of stamens, which are male reproductive structures that make pollen. The innermost whorl consists of female reproductive structures called carpels. Although the number and shape of these organs differ from species to species, they are genetically determined and develop sequentially from outside to inside (sepals, petals, stamens, and carpels). All floral organs develop from a small group of undifferentiated cells known as the floral meristem.

The genetic basis for this pattern formation was not known until recently. During the 1990s enormous progress was made in identifying the genes that determine the floral organ identity. Much of this information came from genetic studies with *Arabidopsis thaliana* (mouse ear cress or thale cress), which belongs to the mustard family, and *Antirrhinum majus* (snapdragon). A normal flower of *Arabidopsis* has four sepals, four petals, six stamens, and two carpels. Genetic studies with *Arabidopsis* and snapdragon indicate that three classes of genes (called class A, B, and C) work together to determine the organ identity and are responsible for the development of the right floral organs in the right place.

Each class of genes acts in two adjacent whorls in a combinatorial fashion to specify organ identity. Whether the cells in the floral **meristem** develop into a particular organ will depend on the expression of one or two of these classes of genes. Class A genes are active in whorls 1 and 2, Class B genes function in whorls 2 and 3, and class C genes are active in whorls 3 and 4. The activity of class A genes alone leads to the development of sepals, expression of A and B in cells leads to petal development, B and C class genes are necessary for stamen development, and the activity of C class alone allows carpel development. In addition, A activity inhibits the expression of C class and vice versa such that C activity is found in all four whorls of A mutants whereas A activity is found in all four whorls in C mutants.

This model has been supported by several kinds of genetic tests by creating single, double, or triple mutations in ABC genes, expression analysis of these genes, and also by artificially expressing A, B, and/or C genes in wrong whorls. Because A inhibits C, inactivation of A results in expansion of C activity into the first and second whorls, and to the development of carpel-like structures in place of sepals (C acting alone) and stamens in place

vascular related to transport of nutrients

angiosperm a flowering plant

sepals the outermost whorl of flower parts; usually green and leaf-like, they protect the inner parts of the flower

In *Arabidopsis*, A-class genes include two genes (APETALA1, AP1; APETALA2, AP2); B-class has two genes (APETALA3, AP3; PISTILLATA, PI); and C-class has one gene (AGAMOUS, AG).

meristem the growing tip of a plant

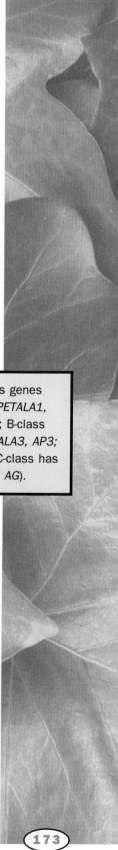

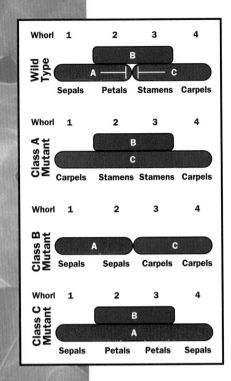

The "ABC" model, which explains the specification of floral organ identity by three classes of genes. Numbers on the top indicate four whorls in the flower. The activity of the A, B and C class genes in each whorl of the wild type is indicated in the top panel. The sign ⊢ indicates the inhibition of A activity by C and vice versa. Mutants affecting the A (class A mutant), B (class B mutant), or C (class C mutant) function result in changes in organ identity as shown in the figure.

transcription factors proteins that bind to a specific DNA sequence called the promoter to regulate the expression of a nearby gene.

endosperm the nutritive tissue in a seed, formed by fertilization of a diploid egg tissue by a sperm from pollen

solute a substance dissolved in a solution

enzyme a protein that controls a reaction in a cell

of petals (C acting with B). Where B is inactivated, stamens are converted to carpels and petals to sepals. When C is inactivated, the presence of A activity in the third and fourth whorls leads to conversion of stamens to petals and carpels to sepals. In plants lacking both B and C genes, class-A genes are expressed in all four whorls, leading to a flower with sepals in all four whorls. Overexpression of class-B genes in all four whorls results in a flower consisting of petals in the first and second whorls and stamens in third and fourth whorls. Inactivation of all three classes of genes results in a flower that has leaves in all four whorls, indicating that the floral organs are modified leaves consistent with theories of floral evolution.

Although the mechanisms through which the activity of ABC genes specifies the floral organ identity are not clear, it is likely that they regulate the expression of other genes that are involved in the development of a specific floral organ. This speculation is supported by the fact that four of the five genes that belong to ABC classes encode **transcription factors**. How these organ identity genes are turned on at the right time and in the right cells of the floral meristem is not completely understood. SEE ALSO DIFFERENTIATION AND DEVELOPMENT; EMBRYOGENESIS; FLOWERS; GERMINATION AND GROWTH; HORMONAL CONTROL AND DEVELOPMENT; HORMONES; MOLECULAR PLANT GENETICS; SENESCENCE.

A. S. N. Reddy

Bibliography

Clark, Steve E., and Elliot M. Meyerowitz. "Arabidopsis Flower Development." In *Arabidopsis*, eds. Elliot Meyerowitz and Chris Somerville. New York: Cold Spring Harbor Press, 1994.

Coen, Enrico S., and Elliot M. Meyerowitz. "The War of the Whorls: Genetic Interactions Controlling Flower Development." *Nature* 353 (1991): 31–37.

Meyerowitz, Elliot M. "The Genetics of Flower Development." *Scientific American* 271 (1994): 56–65.

Germination

Seeds are usually shed from their parent plant in a mature dry state. The dry seed contains an embryo that is the next generation of the plant in miniature. Before the seed can grow, however, it must first emerge from the seed and establish itself as an independent, photosynthetic seedling. Germination, by definition, starts when the seed takes up water, a process known as imbibition, and is completed when the embryonic root, the radicle, penetrates the outer structures of the seed (usually the seed coat and, in some species, the surrounding storage tissues of the **endosperm**).

In the mature dry state, the seed is metabolically inactive (quiescent) and can withstand environmental extremes of temperature and drought. When water enters the seed during imbibition there is a leakage of **solutes** (ions, sugars, and amino acids) because cell membranes are temporarily unstable during hydration. Cellular metabolism recommences within minutes after imbibition begins, using cell components and **enzymes** that were present in the dry seed. Respiration to provide energy and protein synthesis to produce new enzymes that support metabolism are important early events in germination.

A germinating corn kernel.

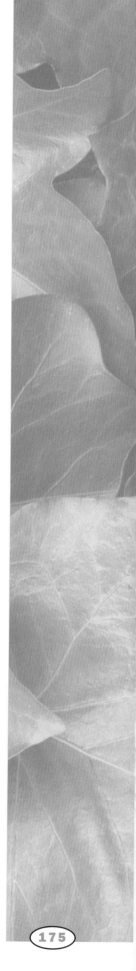

Following imbibition, there is a period when no further water is taken up (plateau phase) and during which metabolism proceeds to ready the seed to complete germination. Restitution of cellular damage resulting from drying and imbibition is completed (e.g., DNA and mitochondria are repaired), and new enzymes and other proteins are synthesized. Elongation of the cells of the radicle is responsible for its emergence from the seed. Their cell walls become more stretchable and the internal water pressure (turgor) of the cells causes them to expand. Cell division and deoxyribonucleic acid (DNA) synthesis occur after radicle emergence, and later the mobilization of food reserves occurs within the storage organs of the seed to provide nutrients for post-germinative growth.

In some seeds the embryo is surrounded by a storage tissue that is sufficiently rigid to prevent extension of the radicle and completion of germination. This tissue frequently has thickened hemicellulose-containing cell walls, and a reduction in their resistance is necessary to permit radicle penetration. This might be achieved by cell-wall hydrolases or cell-separating enzymes, perhaps induced in the storage tissue in response to hormones released from the embryo late during germination.

Seeds of many noncultivated species, such as weeds, are often **dormant** when mature. When imbibed, these seeds exhibit the same intense metabolic activity as non-dormant seeds but do not complete germination. Germination does not occur unless the seeds receive an external **stimulus** (e.g., low or fluctuating temperatures, or light) while in the imbibed state. The

dormant inactive, not growing

stimulus trigger

plant hormone abscisic acid plays some role in inducing dormancy during seed development, and its application to many seeds can prevent radicle emergence. Conversely, the plant hormone gibberellic acid, when applied in low concentrations to dormant seeds, will promote the completion of germination. How abscisic acid and gibberellic acid control germination is not known. SEE ALSO GERMINATION AND GROWTH; HORMONES; SEEDS.

J. Derek Bewley

Bibliography

Bewley, J. D. "Seed Germination and Dormancy." *The Plant Cell* 9 (1997): 1055–66.

————, and M. Black. *Seeds: Physiology of Development and Germination*, 2nd ed. New York: Plenum Press, 1994.

Germination and Growth

propagate to create more of through sexual or asexual reproduction

A seed is an enclosed, protected package of cells surrounding a miniature plant, the embryo, that can grow to form a copy of the plant bearing it. Seeds thus serve to spread and **propagate** plants, but they can also help the plant survive unfavorable climatic conditions, such as a freezing winter, in the form of the protected embryo.

A typical seed consists of three main parts. The outer layer, or seed coat, protects the interior contents against drying out, infection, attack by predators, and noxious chemicals in the environment; it may also bear hooks or other structures that attach the seed to passing animals, aiding dissemination. The innermost structure is the embryo, complete with root tip, stem tip, and specialized seed leaves called cotyledons. Between these two structures lies the endosperm, cells containing stored food that the embryo digests and uses as an energy source when it starts to grow. Sometimes, as in beans, the stored food is in the cotyledons of the embryo rather than in separate endosperm cells.

dormant inactive, not growing

Seeds are drier than growing plant cells, and as a result are **dormant**. Germination begins when the seed absorbs water and the cells of the embryo elongate, pushing the root tip beyond the seed coat. To accomplish this, the embryo mobilizes the food reserves of the endosperm by secreting the hormone gibberellin, which travels to the endosperm. When gibberellin reaches its target cells in the endosperm, it stimulates gene activity, causing the production of digestive enzymes that break down stored starch, proteins, and fats into simpler molecules that can be burned (oxidized), thus furnishing energy for growth.

Seeds are formed from ovules located in the ovary in the center of the flower. These highly hydrated cells become partially dehydrated and dormant in response to accumulation of another hormone, abscisic acid (ABA), produced by the mother plant and transported into the seed. Before becoming active and germinating, the seed must first destroy part of its ABA content. Without ABA to confer dormancy, the seed might germinate prematurely on the mother plant, negating its function of dissemination. Without the water-removing action of ABA, seeds could not withstand freezing temperatures and other unfavorable climatic conditions.

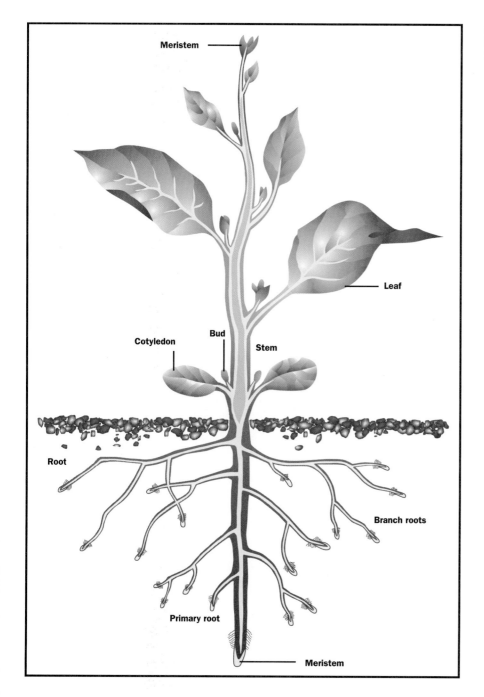

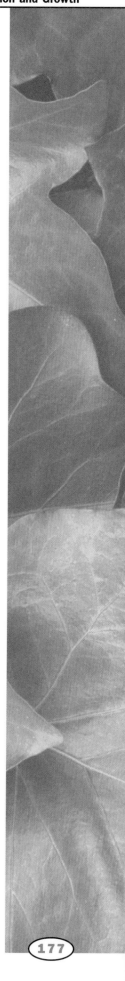

Areas of plant growth. Redrawn from Galston, 1994, p. 11.

Some seeds can lie dormant for years before germinating. A Chinese lotus seed is known to have germinated after at least three centuries of dormancy, and even longer dormancies have been claimed. Such deep dormancy requires an especially rugged and nonporous seed coat, made of hard, strong materials, and covered by water-resisting waxes, resins, and lacquerlike materials. Before such seeds can germinate, the coats must be made permeable, either by mechanical force or by chemical or microbial action. Some dormant seeds germinate when treated with gibberellin or another plant hormone, cytokinin; these hormones work against the effects of ABA. Certain seeds are sensitive to light, requiring some illumination before becoming active. This is due to activation of a pigment called phytochrome, which

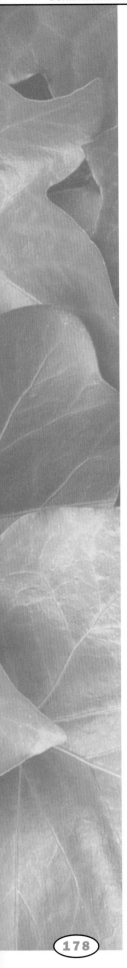

Broad bean *Vicia faba* germinates when suspended over water or in a medium of sodden paper.

also regulates seedling growth and development. The light requirement ensures that the seed will not germinate if it is buried too deeply in the soil to be able to reach the surface before its stored food supply runs out.

Germination occurs when the root protrudes from the seed coat. Root emergence is followed shortly by the emergence of the stem from the other end of the seed. The root grows downward, towards the center of gravity of Earth, while the stem grows upward. It is not yet understood why these organs behave oppositely toward gravity, but it appears that in both, gravity is sensed by the falling of heavy particles in the cells. Their opposite behavior toward gravity makes it likely that roots will find their way to water and minerals in the soil, while leaves will find the light needed for food synthesis. The orientation of plant organs is also affected by light, which generally causes stems to turn towards the light, roots away from the light, and leaf blades to become perpendicular to the source of light.

Growth and Development

The embryo has a bipolar axis, with a region of cell division retained at each end. These regions, called **meristems**, maintain this activity throughout the life of the plant. The meristem at the stem apex includes an outer layer, whose cells divide in only one plane to produce more surface area, and an inner layer whose cells divide in all directions to produce the interior bulk. From these layers are produced more stem, leaves, and ultimately flowers. By contrast, the root meristem produces only root tissue, covered

meristem the growing tip of a plant

at its apex by a root cap, whose hardy cells protect the delicate internal meristem region as the root pushes into the soil.

Whenever leaves are formed, **lateral** buds are also formed in the angle between leaf base and its insertion into the stem.

lateral away from the center

Each lateral bud contains a meristem, which is generally kept inactive by the downward diffusion of the hormone **auxin**, which is produced by the dominant bud at the apex. If this apical bud is injured or removed, or if there is an unusually large supply of cytokinin from the roots, a lateral bud may become active or even dominant.

auxin a plant hormone

When a seed germinates in darkness, the seedling stem is long, slender, and unpigmented, and may terminate in an apical hook that protects the delicate meristem during upward growth through the soil. The hook is formed in response to the gaseous hormone ethylene. When the seedling is illuminated, activation of phytochrome turns off ethylene production, opens the hook, inhibits further stem elongation, promotes leaf blade expansion, and initiates the synthesis of chlorophyll. In both stem and root, the area just behind the tip elongates the most, as a result of the elongation of young preexisting cells. SEE ALSO DIFFERENTIATION AND DEVELOPMENT; EMBRYO-GENESIS; GERMINATION; HORMONES; HORMONAL CONTROL AND DEVELOPMENT; MERISTEMS; PHYTOCHROME; SEED DISPERSAL; SEEDS; TROPISMS AND NASTIC MOVEMENTS.

Arthur W. Galston

Bibliography

Bewley, J. D., and M. Black. *Seeds: Physiology of Development and Germination*, 2nd ed. New York: Plenum Press, 1994.

Galston, A. W. *Life Processes of Plants*. New York: W. H. Freeman and Company, 1994.

Mayer, A. M., and A. Poljakoff-Mayber. *The Germination of Seeds*. Oxford: Pergamon Press, 1963.

Raven, P. H., R. F. Evert, and H. Curtis. *Biology of Plants*. New York: Worth Publishers, 1981.

Taiz, L., and E. Zeiger. *Plant Physiology*, 2nd ed. Sunderland, MA: Sinauer Associates, 1998.

Gibberelins *See Hormones.*

Ginkgo

Ginkgo biloba is a woody tree with a spreading form and a large trunk that reaches a height between fifty to eighty feet. The trees are sexually dimorphic (two-forms), and male trees typically have steep branching angles while female trees are broadly branched. Ginkgo grows in temperate climates and is long-lived, with trees up to one thousand years old having been reported.

Ginkgo is characterized by flattened, often bilobed leaves, with numerous fine veins that lack a midvein. Leaves are clustered on slow-growing, short shoots or spaced spirally on elongated shoots. Ginkgo trees are deciduous and the silhouettes of its bare branches make it easy to identify male and female trees. The pollen of Ginkgo is called prepollen because it pro-

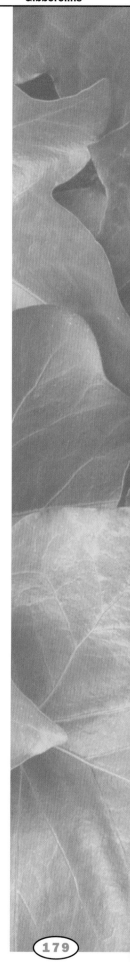

The leaves of a *Ginkgo biloba* tree.

haustorial related to a haustorium, or food-absorbing organ

duces a **haustorial** tube upon germination and only after several months releases a motile sperm cell that swims to fertilize the egg. Ginkgo is one of the most advanced land plants still fertilized by motile sperm cells. Ginkgo is a gymnosperm that produces specially modified plumlike seeds that, even though they look like fruits, botanically are seeds. The seed is surrounded by a thin papery inner seed coat, a middle shell-like hard seed coat, and a fleshy outer seed coat that ripens to a soft, pulpy, foul-smelling mass when the seeds are dropped from the female trees.

lineage ancestry; the line of evolutionary descent of an organism

Tertiary period geologic period from sixty-five to five million years ago

Ginkgo biloba has a long history, with ancestors extending back some 280 million years into the Permian. It is one of very few plants living today that has such a clear lineage dating back into the Paleozoic era. During the Mesozoic era the Ginkgo **lineage** diversified and spread to many parts of the world. During the Cretaceous, there were seven to ten species of Ginkgo trees living, and they would have been a common sight among the dinosaurs of the Northern Hemisphere. Fossil Ginkgo leaves and petrified trunks can be found during the **Tertiary period** in North America, Europe, and Asia where trees lived until less than five million years ago.

There is now only one living species in the family Ginkgoaceae, a once diverse and widespread group, and it is indigenous to only a small area in China. Although nearly extinct in the wild, it has been preserved as a living fossil because it was planted at the entrances to Chinese and Japanese temples. Ginkgo has commonly been planted as a street tree in temperate North American cities (such as Washington, D.C.). Male trees are often vegetatively **propagated** for this purpose because they lack the foul-smelling, fleshy fruitlike seeds. Ginkgo trees are quite tolerant of city pollution.

propagate to create more of through sexual or asexual reproduction

The cleaned seeds and leaves are reported to have beneficial health effects on the brain, hearing, eyes, lungs, kidneys, liver, and general circulation. The seeds are eaten and the leaves used to prepare tea. It is used for its antibacterial effects and benefits for nerves, asthma, vision, improving blood flow, and slowing aging. Several secondary metabolites such as **flavonoids**, terpenoids (e.g., ginkgolides A, B, and C, bilobalide, ginkgetin, and isoginkgetin), and organic acids are some of the chemicals isolated from

flavonoids aromatic compounds occurring in both seeds and young roots and involved in host-pathogen and host-symbiont interactions

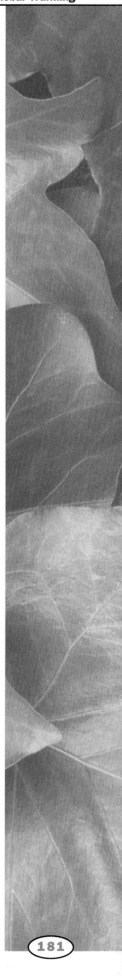

Ginkgo. Extracts of Ginkgo are sold as a health diet supplement. SEE ALSO EVOLUTION OF PLANTS; GYMNOSPERMS; SYSTEMATICS, PLANT; TAXONOMY; TREES.

David Dilcher

Bibliography

Hobbs, C. *Ginkgo, Elixir of Youth.* Loveland, CO: Botanica Press, 1991.

Hori, T., R. W. Ridge, W. Tulecke, P. Del Tredici, J. Tremouillaux-Guiller, and H. Tobe, eds. *Ginkgo Biloba—A Global Treasure.* Tokyo: Springer-Verlag, 1997.

Global Warming

The term *global warming* simply means that the global climate is warming. Humans are popularly assumed to be the cause of global warming. Further, global warming is usually assumed to be harmful to humans and to plant and animal life. Global warming is a commonly discussed and debated scientific topic both in the media and in the scientific community.

Scientific Debate: Existence, Extent, Causes, and Pace

Nearly all of the scientific community agrees that based on surface temperature observations, the global climate warmed by about 0.5° C in the twentieth century. Satellite observations of global temperatures show warming trends between 1970 and 1990 similar to those found in surface observations. Decreases in sea ice cover and global glacier retreat provide corroborating evidence of global warming. A few scientists believe that the warming at weather stations is due to the development of cities around weather stations, but analysis in the late 1990s has shown that warming is similar at urban and rural areas. Different areas of the world and different seasons have warmed more than others. Due to global atmospheric circulation patterns that transport heat from the tropics to the poles, warming has been greatest in high latitudes. In some areas of Alaska and Asia, average temperatures have warmed by over 4°C. Warming has also been greatest in spring months, particularly March, and in nighttime minimum temperatures much more than in daytime maximum temperatures.

While the presence of global warming is not seriously debated, its causes are. Greenhouse gases, including carbon dioxide, trap heat radiated from Earth and reemit some of it back to the ground. Without greenhouse gases, our planet would be uninhabitably cold. As shown by research on air bubbles trapped in ice cores, high temperatures have been associated with high levels of greenhouse gases during the geologic past. Most human-made carbon dioxide is produced by cars and industrial activity. As a result of fossil fuel burning, carbon dioxide levels have increased from 280 parts per million in preindustrial times to more than 360 parts per million by the late 1990s. Scientists believe that the pace of greenhouse gas emissions in the late twentieth century is partially responsible for the recorded temperature increases. This is called the enhanced greenhouse effect. A minority of scientists believe that natural processes, such as increased sun spot activity, account for the observed warming. However, statistical analysis shows that compared with the enhanced greenhouse effect, these other processes are highly unlikely causes of the observed warming.

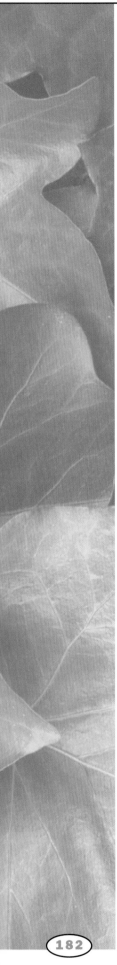

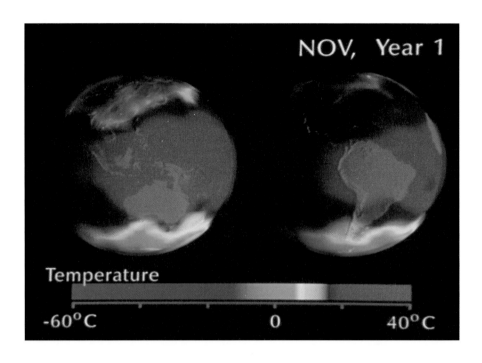

Year 1 of a simulated greenhouse effect. The temperature is coldest at the poles and graduates to the highest temperature around the equator.

negative feedback a process in which an increase in some variable causes a response that leads to a decrease in that variable

positive feedback a process in which an increase in some variable causes a response that leads to a further increase in that variable

ecosystem an ecological community together with its environment

Computer models called global circulation models (GCMs) predict that warming will continue to increase. Due to processes called **negative feedbacks** that reduce global warming, there is some uncertainty over how rapidly warming will occur. Clouds, for example, are a result of evaporation. In a warmer climate, more evaporation will occur, leading to more clouds. Most types of clouds reflect solar radiation; this would act to cool temperatures. Other processes can act as **positive feedbacks** that increase global warming. Sulfur particles emitted from factories block radiation and thus cool temperatures. In an ironic twist, making factories cleaner could actually increase global warming. Accurately considering the complex network of feedbacks is a critical field of global warming research. In spite of these uncertainties, GCMs consistently predict further global warming.

The pace at which record high temperatures are being broken is increasing. The years 1998, 1997, 1995, and 1990 were the warmest since at least 1400 C.E. The twentieth century was also the warmest century since at least 1000 C.E. The bulk of observational evidence shows that not only is warming occurring, but that it is occurring at a progressively more rapid pace. Scientists researching past climates have shown that during glacial and interglacial periods, global temperatures (and carbon dioxide levels) have changed by more than the 0.5 degree (and 25 percent) currently seen. If plants and animals have survived these past changes, why should we be concerned about present changes? The answer is that the rate of greenhouse gas and temperature increase appears to be unprecedented. There is no guarantee that **ecosystems** and the people that depend on them will be able to adjust to the predicted levels of global warming.

Plant-Atmosphere Interactions

Global warming effects on plants depend on the existing climate and vegetation, but in general, there are three main categories of potential effects. First, for plants existing in climatic extremes, global warming may have

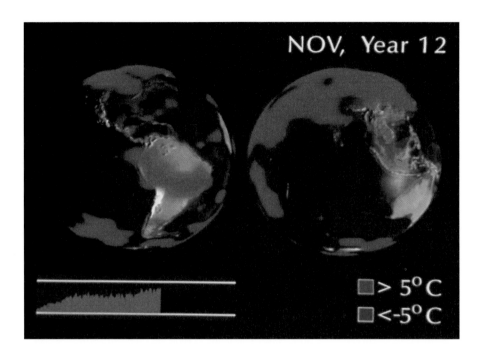

Year 12 of a simulated greenhouse effect. Note the irregularly shaped warm areas over Asia, North America, and Antarctica.

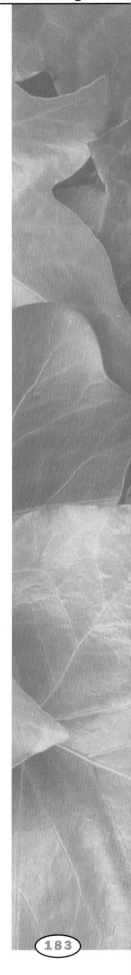

drastic impacts. For example, plants requiring cold temperatures may be forced off of mountain peak habitats. If this is their only habitat, extinction will occur. Second, global warming is likely to cause large shifts in biome distribution. Coniferous forests will shift farther north and grasslands and deserts will expand. Third, global warming can alter how plants function in their existing environment. For many areas, global warming is likely to lengthen the growing season, causing an increase in photosynthesis. Multiple observations show that the growing season has already significantly lengthened, especially in northern latitudes. For most plants, alteration in plant function without causing their extinction or displacement is the most likely consequence of global warming.

While people usually think about the effects of global warming on plants, plants can also moderate the effects of global warming. Only about half of the carbon dioxide put in the atmosphere remains there; the other half is taken up by Earth. Some of it is dissolved in the ocean, but plants take up some of it too. Plants are therefore acting to slow the pace of the enhanced greenhouse effect. Plants and especially trees are storing some of the carbon dioxide in wood. Unfortunately, this process is unlikely to continue forever. Eventually, when trees and shrubs die, the carbon stored in wood will enter the soil and will begin to decompose. Increased temperatures will cause high rates of decomposition, leading to an accelerated release of carbon dioxide from the soil. Consequently, it is likely that at a global level, ecosystems will begin to release carbon dioxide. Only by reducing fossil fuel emissions, a very difficult task both politically and economically, will we reduce greenhouse gasses. SEE ALSO ATMOSPHERE AND PLANTS; CARBON CYCLE; HUMAN IMPACTS.

Michael A. White

Bibliography

Houghton, J. *Global Warming: The Complete Briefing*, 2nd ed. New York: Cambridge University Press, 1997.

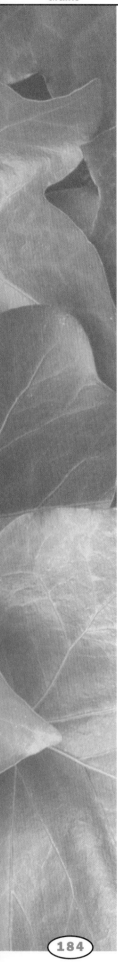

Intergovernmental Panel on Climate Change. *Climate Change 1995: The Science of Climate Change.* New York: Cambridge University Press, 1996.

Mann, M. E., R. S. Bradley, and M. K. Hughes. "Global-scale Temperature Patterns and Climate Forcing Over the Past Six Centuries." *Nature* 392 (1998): 779–87.

Philander, G. S. *Is the Temperature Rising?: The Uncertain Science of Global Warming.* Princeton, NJ: Princeton University Press, 1998.

Shugart, H. H. *Terrestrial Ecosystems in Changing Environments.* New York: Cambridge University Press, 1998.

Woodwell, G. M., and F. T. Mackenzie, eds. *Biotic Feedbacks in the Global Climate System: Will the Warming Feed the Warming?* New York: Oxford University Press, 1995.

Grains

Grain crops of the world include the food grains, the coarse or feed grains, and a few minor coarse grains. The food grains include rice (*Oryza sativa*) and wheat (*Triticum aestivum*); the coarse or feed grains are barley (*Hordeum vulgare*), maize (*Zea mays*), rye (*Secale cereale*), oats (*Avena sativa*), millets (*Pennisetum* and *Setaria* species), sorghum (*Sorghum vulgare*), buckwheat (*Fagopyrum esculentum*), and triticale X (*Triticosecale wittmack*). Except for buckwheat, virtually all of the grain crops are members of the grass family. The principal harvestable commodity of these crops is the grain. Grazing or hay production is a minor use of a few crops.

All of the grain crops now are distributed worldwide, although each crop generally originated in a specific region: rice in Asia; wheat, barley, oats, and rye in the Fertile Crescent of the Mideast; maize in Central America; sorghum and the *Pennisetum* millets in Africa. Triticale is a human-made grain produced within the twentieth century by hybridizing wheat and rye.

Total production of the two major food grains in 1999 was very similar: 589 Mmt (million metric tons) of rice from 153 Mha (million hectares) and 584 Mmt of wheat from 214 Mha. Much more rice is irrigated than wheat, which results in higher yields and accounts for the

Three different grains used in the manufacture of whiskey.

essentially equivalent production of rice from fewer hectares than wheat. Coarse grain production in 1999 was 900 Mmt, from 314 Mha. Maize, with 604 Mmt from 139 Mha, was by far the most prominent coarse grain.

Rice is typically consumed as whole grain boiled white rice, while wheat is ground into flour for bread making. Coarse grains are generally fed directly to animals as whole or cracked grains, but small amounts of these crops also are used for food, usually as a ground product or in porridges, especially in the respective regions of origin, for example, maize in Central America, and sorghum and millets in Africa. Barley is used worldwide in brewing, while oats, maize, and wheat are used in many processed cereals. Rye is still used in bread making in Europe and the United States, but food use consumption of this crop declined dramatically fifty years ago when it was recognized that the fungal disease ergot that infects rye grains caused the mysterious malady known as St. Anthony's fire, which can result in convulsions and death.

All of the grain crops are cultivated as annuals: rice, maize, sorghum, and *Pennisetum* millets as summer crops; while wheat, barley, oats, rye, and *Setaria* millets are cultivated both as winter crops and as spring crops. The winter versions are grown in mild climates while the spring versions are predominant in the northern regions, such as the former Soviet Union, the northern Great Plains of the United States, and northern China. Winter versions generally yield more than spring versions, because the growing season is much longer for the former.

The Green Revolution refers to the shortening of the stems of rice and wheat, which began in the 1960s and which has often led to doubling of yields. Shorter stemmed versions of the other grain crops have also been produced, especially in sorghum. SEE ALSO AGRICULTURE, MODERN; AGRONOMIST; BORLAUG, NORMAN; CORN; ECONOMIC IMPORTANCE OF PLANTS; GRASSES; GREEN REVOLUTION; RICE; SEEDS; WHEAT.

J. Neil Rutger

Bibliography

Food and Agricultural Organization of the United Nations. *FAO Statistical Databases.* [Online] Available at http://apps.fao.org.

Leonard, Warren H., and John H. Martin. *Cereal Crops.* New York: Macmillan, 1963.

Gramineae *See Grasses.*

Grasses

The grass family, known scientifically as either the Poaceae or Gramineae, is one of the four largest families of flowering plants, with approximately five hundred genera and ten thousand species. Grasses range from tiny inconspicuous herbs less than 5 centimeters tall to the giant bamboos, which grow to 40 meters tall. The family is undoubtedly the most important flowering plant family to humans, directly or indirectly providing more than three-quarters of our food. In addition, grasses are major producers of oxygen and a large component of environmental filtering processes due to the enormous geographic range, spatial coverage, and **biomass** of grasses on Earth. Grasses are the greatest single source of wealth in the world.

biomass the total dry weight of an organism or group of organisms

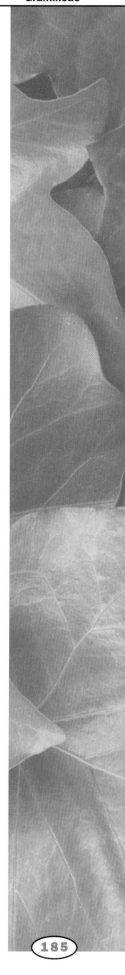

Grasses are the greatest single source of wealth in the world.

inflorescence an arrangement of flowers on a stalk

filament a threadlike extension

Morphology

All grasses have fibrous secondary roots (the primary root disappears early in development) and can be annual or perennial, in which case they usually have underground stems called rhizomes. These can be very short and knotty or very long. In some species the rhizomes can go for several meters. Sometimes these stems run horizontally above ground and are then called stolons. Grasses characteristically have stems that are round and usually hollow with a node (the swollen areas along the stem where the leaves and branches are attached) and internode (the part of the stem between the nodes) arrangement. Their leaves are attached at the nodes and consist of two parts. The sheath clasps the stem (also known as the culm) sometimes all the way up to or beyond the next node. The blade is the upper part of the leaf that is free from the stem. The fact that the top edges of the sheath may overlap each other around the stem but are not joined to each other is a defining characteristic of grasses. At the point where the blade joins the sheath, there may be a flap of tissue called a ligule. This structure keeps dirt and parasites from getting into the space between the sheath and the stem.

The tiny grass flower, called a spikelet, is actually a composite of one or more tiny flowers and is the most characteristic structure among grasses. It is generally composed of two bracts called glumes, with one to many tiny flowers called florets attached above them. Each floret consists of a bract called a lemma that generally wraps around a smaller and generally very thin bract called a palea. These two encase the nearly microscopic rudimentary petals called lodicules, the stamens (usually one to three), and the ovary, which can have two or three feathery stigmas at its apex. There may be only a few spikelets on a plant but usually there are many (sometimes hundreds) arranged variously in an **inflorescence**. The inflorescence is the plumelike structure that you see on sugarcane or the spike of a wheat plant. Corn is a special case, both the cob and the tassel are inflorescences, but the cob has only female flowers and the tassel only male. Some other grasses have separate male and female inflorescences and many have some of the spikelets with only male flowers, while other spikelets in the same inflorescence have hermaphrodite flowers. The grasses also have a very characteristic fruit (grain) called a caryopsis, which consists of the ovary with one or more of the floret bracts attached.

Pollination and Dispersal

Most grasses are wind-pollinated. Their anthers are versatile, meaning that they pivot on their stalk (or **filament**), and the stalks are very flexible, like a piece of string. At the appropriate time, usually early in the morning, the lodicules will swell with water and push the lemma and palea apart. The anthers will then pop out of the flower and dangle in the wind on their filaments, releasing their pollen as the breeze jostles them during the day. Most grass pollen is perfectly smooth and round with a single small hole in it. This is characteristic of many wind-pollinated plants. A few grasses—especially those that grow deep in the rain forest—are pollinated by insects, probably because there is no wind. Grasses have a myriad of dispersal mechanisms for their seeds. Some rain forest grasses shoot their seeds several feet across the forest floor and others have flowers that bloom underground on the tips of long rhizomes and may have an association with ants. Many grasses have smooth fruits that get blown by wind or carried either inside

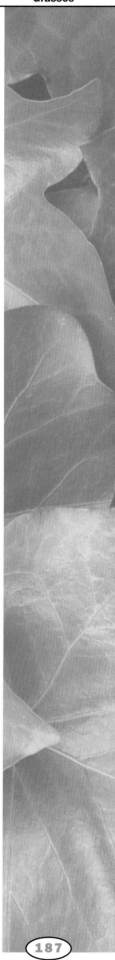

GRASSES CULTIVATED FOR FOOD

Common Name	Scientific Name	Geographic Origin and Area of Domestication	Area of Cultivation
Wheat	*Triticum aestivum*	Southwest Asia, especially Turkey and environs	Worldwide in temperate areas, especially in the Western Hemisphere
Maize or Corn	*Zea mays*	Mexico, Guatemala, Honduras	Primarily in the Western Hemisphere in both temperate and tropical areas
Rice	*Oryza sativa*	Asia, probably domesticated in China and southern Asia	Worldwide in mesic to wet tropical and warm temperate areas, especially in Asia
Sugarcane	*Saccharum officinarum*	New Guinea or Indonesia	Worldwide in wet tropical and subtropical areas
Barley	*Hordeum vulgare*	Southwest Asia	Primarily in temperate areas of the Western Hemisphere
Oats	*Avena sativa*	Probably Europe	Primarily in temperate areas of the Western Hemisphere
Rye	*Secale cereale*	Southwest Asia	Primarily in temperate areas of the Western Hemisphere
Millet	Finger millet (*Eleusine coracana*), proso millet (*Panicum miliaceum*), foxtail millet (*Setaria italica*), japanese barnyard millet (*Echinochola crusgalli*), teff millet (*Eragrostis tef*), pearl millet (*Pennisetum* glaucum), koda millet (*Paspalum scrobiculatum*)	Mostly in Europe and North America	Now important for food only in Asia and Africa although widely grown for birdseed in the United States and Europe
Sorghum	*Sorghum bicolor*	Africa	Most important in Africa and other dry regions of the tropics and subtropics

or on the outside of animals. Most have some kind of hooks or hairs to catch passing animals. Many have very specialized fruits that have a hard, drill-like point on one end and one or more long, pinlike awns on the other. An awn can catch the wind and vibrate the point like a jackhammer (e.g., the genus *Aristida*) or they can be twisted and sensitive to moisture (e.g., the genus *Heteropogon*) so that it turns the point like a drill bit into sweaty animal fur or feathers or into the soil. Stiff, back-pointing hairs on the awn and on the hard point of the fruit help by only allowing the fruit to burrow in, not out. Other grass fruits are completely covered with long hairs that allow them to catch the wind and float for several kilometers. Still others have an inflorescence that breaks off and blows across the ground like a tumbleweed unit (e.g., *Eragrostis spectabilis*), or is carried around by birds as nesting material (e.g., *Panicum maximum*). The sandburs (the genus *Cenchrus*) have a spiny bur around their seeds that sticks into your skin or an animal's fur while Job's Tears (*Coix lacryma-jobi*) have a hard, white, shiny flask around the seeds that is used in many tropical regions for beads. Several bamboos have thorns; a very few species of grass have irritating hairs and the leaf edges can be sharp, but other than the high levels of silica found in the leaves of many savanna grasses (which wear down the teeth of grazers), protective structures are rare in the grasses.

Where They Grow

Grasses are not only in your backyard. They are more geographically distributed than any other family of flowering plants. The southernmost recorded flowering plant is the Antarctic hair grass, *Deschampsia antarctica*, and several species of grasses are among the most northern growing tundra

Close-up of grass flower.

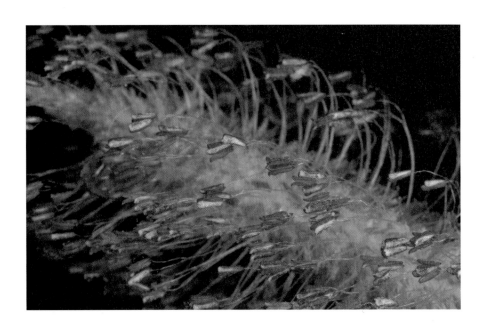

plants as well. They are very common in alpine areas and lowlands, in swamps, and in some deserts. When forest is cleared, grasses usually dominate the landscape. They bind the soil and prevent loss of topsoil all over the world. Grasses are planted as cover crops when land is cleared. Taken together, they cover more area on Earth than any other flowering plant family. They are the dominant plant in the savannas that ring Earth at the boundaries of the tropics, and they dominate the boreal steppe (cold temperate grasslands) and the prairies of North America. Tropical savannas currently cover some 23,000,000 square kilometers, or about 20 percent of Earth's land surface. Dominance of grasses in these habitats is usually maintained either because there is not enough water for trees to survive, there is heavy grazing pressure, or because there are fires frequently enough to keep the trees out. Grasses adapted to fire-prone areas have their growing tip either below ground or well protected within a tight clump of leaf bases. When they burn, only the leaves or the old flowerstalks are lost; the growing tip stays safe. They are also generally fast growers; for example, a bamboo has been measured growing 120 centimeters in twenty-four hours. Some grasses are actually stimulated to grow by grazing. The huge herds of more than a hundred different grazing animals in Africa, bison on the great plains of the United States, cattle all over the world, and billions of termites on the savannas of South America are all supported by grass.

There are two major photosynthetic pathways in grasses, C_3 and C_4 (with the exception of the bamboos, which are all C_3, and are common in the tropics and some temperate areas of Asia). Almost all grasses at high latitudes are C_3, while most of those at the equator are C_4. In general, C_4 grasses can work at higher temperatures and light levels than C_3 grasses but require higher temperatures and/or light levels to begin photosynthesizing.

Economic Importance

The economic importance of grasses can hardly be overstated. They provide the majority of food. Grasses provide much of the starch (e.g., rice, cornmeal, bread, cereal, pasta) and a certain amount of protein, in most hu-

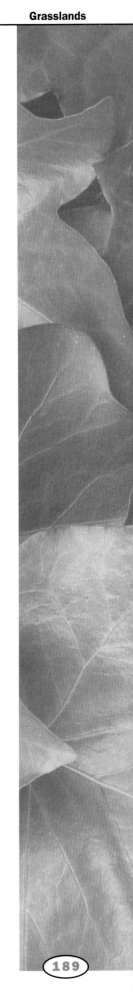

man diets. Although a few grasses absorb selenium and other harmful substances from the soil and others have potentially poisonous **cyanogenic** compounds in their shoots and leaves, most are not poisonous. The grains are naturally low in fat and rich in complex carbohydrates. Remember that most livestock eat primarily grass or grass products so leather, wool, meat, and milk also indirectly come from grass. Grasses sweeten what you drink and eat with cane sugar, molasses, and high fructose corn syrup. Corn byproducts also provide the raw material for many chemicals used in industry and everyday life. Grasses provide the raw material for most alcohol products (e.g., sake from rice, rum from sugarcane, beer from barley, bourbon from corn, and other whiskeys from barley, wheat, and rye). Although bamboo shoots are enormously important as a food crop in Asia, the real economic contribution of the bamboos is as a building material and a raw material for paper and furniture. More than three thousand uses have been listed for bamboos in Japan alone. There is even a bamboo culture in Honduras that is based on the giant *Guadua* bamboo. Of course, because corn and rice are the staple foods of many of the world's people, cultures can be defined by them as well. Rice is a sacred plant in many Asian cultures. In contrast to the enormous economic benefit of grasses, it must also be noted that they make up a large percentage of the world's worst weeds, which cost millions of dollars every year to manage. Cogon grass (*Imperata cylindrica*) and Bermuda grass (*Cynodon dactylon*) are two of the most common. Bermuda grass is also the most common grass on Earth. SEE ALSO BAMBOO; CORN; GRAINS; MONOCOTS; PHOTOSYNTHESIS, CARBON FIXATION AND; RICE; SAVANNA; SEED DISPERSAL; WHEAT.

Gerald F. Guala

cyanogenic giving rise to cyanide

Bibliography

Clark, L. G., and R. W. Pohl. *Agnes Chase's First Book of Grasses*, 4th ed. Washington, DC: Smithsonian Institution Press, 1996.

Cole, M. M. *The Savannas: Biogeography and Geobotany*. London: Academic Press, 1986.

Farrelly, D. *The Book of Bamboo*. San Francisco: Sierra Club Books, 1984.

Guinness Media. *The Guinness Book of World Records*. Stamford, CT: Guinness Media. 1996.

Heiser, C. B. *Seed to Civilization: The Story of Food*. Cambridge, MA: Harvard University Press, 1990.

Holm, L., J. Doll, E. Holm, J. Pancho, and J. Herberger. *World Weeds: Natural Histories and Distribution*. New York: Wiley & Sons, Inc., 1997.

Grasslands

Ecosystems in which grasses and grasslike plants such as sedges and rushes dominate the vegetation are termed grasslands. Grasslands occur on every continent except Antarctica. It is estimated that grasslands once covered as much as 25 to 40 percent of Earth's land surface, but much of this has been plowed and converted to crop production, such as corn, wheat, and soybeans. Prior to the European settlement of North America, the largest continuous grasslands in the United States stretched across the Great Plains from the Rocky Mountains and deserts of the southwestern states to the Mississippi River. Other extensive grasslands are (or were) found in Europe, South America, Asia, and Africa.

ecosystem an ecological community together with its environment

Cattle grazing on
grasslands in Spain.

Grasslands can be broadly categorized as temperate or tropical. Temperate grasslands have cold winters and warm-to-hot summers and often have deep fertile soils. Surprisingly, plant growth in temperate grasslands is often nutrient limited because much of the soil nitrogen is stored in forms unavailable for plant uptake. These nutrients, however, are made available to plants when plowing disrupts the structure of the soil. The combination of high soil fertility and relatively gentle topography made grasslands ideal candidates for conversion to crop production. Grasslands in the Midwestern United States that receive the most rainfall (75 to 90 centimeters) and are the most productive are termed tallgrass prairies. Historically, these prairies were most abundant in Iowa, Illinois, Minnesota, and Kansas. The driest grasslands (25 to 35 centimeters of rainfall) and least productive are termed shortgrass prairies or steppes. These grasslands are common in Texas, Colorado, Wyoming, and New Mexico. Grasslands that are intermediate between these extremes are termed midgrass prairies or mixed grass prairies. In tallgrass prairies, the grasses may grow to 3 meters tall in wet years. In shortgrass prairies, grasses seldom grow beyond 25 centimeters in height. In all temperate grasslands, production of root **biomass** belowground exceeds foliage production aboveground. Worldwide, other names for temperate grasslands include steppes, preferred for most of Europe and Asia, veld in Africa, and the pampas in South America. In North America, other names for temperate grasslands include prairies and steppes.

biomass the total dry weight of an organism or group of organisms

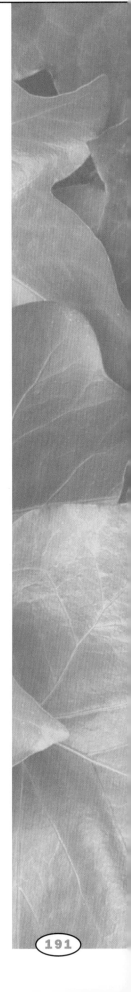

Tropical grasslands are warm throughout the year but have pronounced wet and dry seasons. Tropical grassland soils are often less fertile than temperate grassland soils, perhaps due to the high amount of rainfall (50 to 130 centimeters) that falls during the wet season and washes (or leaches) nutrients out of the soil. Most tropical grasslands have a greater density of woody shrubs and trees than temperate grasslands. Some tropical grasslands can be more productive than temperate grasslands. However, other tropical grasslands grow on soils that are quite infertile, or they may be periodically stressed by seasonal flooding. As a result, their productivity is reduced and may be similar to that of temperate grasslands. As noted for temperate grasslands, root production belowground far exceeds foliage production in all tropical grasslands. Other names for tropical grasslands include velds in Africa, and the compos and llanos in South America.

Although temperate and tropical grasslands encompass the most extensive grass-dominated ecosystems, grasses are present in most types of vegetation and regions of the world. Where grasses are locally dominant they may form desert grassland, Mediterranean grassland, **subalpine** and alpine grasslands (sometimes referred to as meadows or parks), and even coastal grassland. Most grasslands are dominated by perennial (long-lived) plants, but there are some annual grasslands in which the dominant species must reestablish each year by seed. Intensively managed, human-planted, and maintained grasslands occur worldwide as well.

subalpine a region less cold or elevated than alpine (mountain top)

It is generally recognized that climate, fire, and grazing are three primary factors that are responsible for the origin, maintenance, and structure of the most extensive natural grasslands. Although these factors will be described separately, their effects are not always independent of each other (e.g., grazing may reduce the fuel available for fire).

Climate

The climate of grasslands is best described as one of extremes. Average temperatures and yearly amounts of rainfall may not be much different from areas that are deserts or forested, but dry periods during which the plants suffer from water stress occur in most years in both temperate and tropical grasslands. The open nature of grasslands is accompanied by the presence of sustained high windspeeds. Windy conditions increase the evaporation of water from grasslands and this increases water stress in the plants and animals. Another factor that increases water stress is the high input of solar radiation in these open ecosystems. This leads to the **convective uplift** of moist air and results in intense thunderstorms. Rain falling in these intense storms may not be effectively captured by the soil, and the subsequent runoff of this water into streams reduces the moisture available to grassland plants and animals. In addition to periods of water stress within the growing season, consecutive years of extreme drought are more common in grassland than in adjacent forested areas. Such droughts may kill even mature trees, but the grasses and other grassland plants have extensive root systems and belowground buds that help them survive and regrow after drought periods.

convective uplift movement of air upwards due to heating from the sun

Fire

Historically, fires were a frequent occurrence in most large grasslands. Most grasslands are not harmed by fire. In fact, many benefit from fire

dormant inactive, not growing

and some depend on fire for their existence. When grasses are **dormant**, the moisture content of the foliage is low and the fine-textured fuel the grasses produce ignites easily and burns rapidly. The characteristic high windspeeds and lack of natural firebreaks in grasslands allows fires to cover large areas quickly. Fires may be started by lightning or set intentionally by humans in both tropical and temperate grasslands. Fires are most common in grasslands with high levels of plant productivity, such as tallgrass prairies, and in these grasslands fire is important for keeping trees and adjacent forests from encroaching into grasslands. Many tree species are killed by fire, or if they are not killed, they are damaged severely because their active growing points are aboveground. Grassland plants survive and even thrive after fire because their buds are belowground, where they are protected from lethal temperatures. In some highly productive grasslands, fire results in an increase in growth of the grasses and a greater production of plant biomass. This occurs because the buildup of dead biomass (mulch) from previous years inhibits growth, and fire removes this mulch layer. However, in drier grasslands, the burning of this dead plant material may cause the soil to become excessively dry due to high evaporation losses. As a result, plants become water-stressed, and growth is reduced after fire.

Most grassland animals are not harmed by fires, particularly if they occur during the dormant season. Animals living belowground are well protected, and most grassland birds and mammals are mobile enough to avoid direct contact with fire. Insects that live in and on the stems and leaves of the plants are the most affected by fire. But these animals have short generation times and populations recover quickly.

Grazing

herbivore an organism that feeds on plant parts

Grazing is a form of herbivory in which most of the plant (leaves aboveground) or specific plant parts (small roots and root hairs belowground) are consumed by **herbivores**. Grazing, both above and belowground, is an important process in all grasslands. Many formerly natural grasslands are now managed for the production of domestic livestock, primarily cattle in North America, as well as sheep in Europe, New Zealand, and other parts of the world.

Grazing aboveground by large herbivores alters grasslands in several ways. Grazers remove fuel aboveground and may lessen the frequency and intensity of fires. Most large grazers such as cattle or bison primarily consume the grasses, thus the less-abundant **forb** species may increase in abundance and new species may invade the space that is made available. As a result, plant species diversity may increase in grazed grasslands. However, this effect is strongly dependent on the amount of grazing that occurs. Overgrazing may rapidly degrade grasslands to systems dominated by weedy and nonnative plant species.

forb broad-leaved, herbaceous plants

Grazers may also accelerate the conversion of plant nutrients from forms that are unavailable for plant uptake to forms that can be readily used. Essential plant nutrients, such as nitrogen, are bound for long periods of time in unavailable (organic) forms in plant foliage, stems, and roots. Microbes slowly decompose these plant parts and the nutrients they contain are only gradually released in available (inorganic) forms. This decomposition process

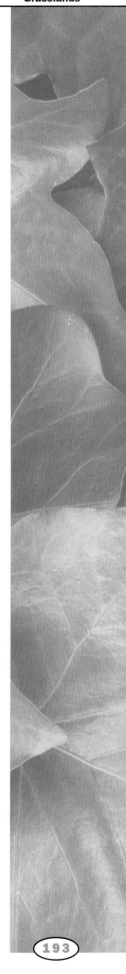

may take more than a year or two. Grazers consume these plant parts and excrete a portion of the nutrients they contain in plant-available forms. This happens very quickly compared to the slow decomposition process, and nutrients are excreted in high concentrations in small patches. Thus, grazers may increase the availability of potentially limiting nutrients to plants as well as alter the spatial distribution of these resources.

Some grasses and grassland plants can compensate for aboveground tissue lost to grazers by growing faster after grazing has occurred. Therefore, even though 50 percent of the grass foliage may be consumed by bison or wildebeest, when compared to ungrazed plants at the end of the season, the grazed grasses may be only slightly smaller, the same size, or even larger. This latter phenomenon, where grazed plants produce more growth than ungrazed plants, is called overcompensation and is somewhat controversial. However, the ability of grasses to compensate or make up partially or completely for foliage lost to grazers is well established. This compensation occurs for several reasons, including an increase in light available to growing shoots in grazed areas, greater nutrient availability (see above) to regrowing plants, and increased water availability. The latter occurs after grazing because the large roots system of the grasses is able to supply abundant water to a relatively small amount of regrowing leaf tissue.

Grassland Biota

By definition, grasses dominate grasslands in terms of plant numbers and biomass, but typically only a few species of grass account for most of the growth. By contrast, both temperate and tropical grasslands contain many more species of forbs than grasses. Forbs can be quite conspicuous when they have brightly colored flowers, and they are very important for maintaining high species diversity (biodiversity) in grasslands. The most conspicuous animals in grasslands are (or were) the large grazers, such as bison and antelope in North America and zebras, gazelles, and wildebeest in Africa. Although it may appear that the large herds of grazers in grasslands consume the most plant biomass, invertebrates such as grasshoppers aboveground can be important consumers of plants in some years, and nematodes and root-feeding invertebrates belowground are actually the most significant consumers of plant biomass.

Insect diversity can be great in grasslands. Even though most of the grasses are wind-pollinated, grassland forbs rely on a wide array of insect species for pollination. Grassland birds are unique in that many nest on the ground and some, such as the burrowing owl, nest belowground. Smaller mammals (e.g., mice, ground squirrels, prairie dogs, gophers) share the subterranean world and burrow extensively in some grasslands. These burrowing mammals may be important consumers of some plant parts and can alter soil nutrient availability to plants.

Conservation and Restoration

In North America, many grasslands are considered endangered ecosystems. For example, in some central Great Plains states that formerly had extensive tall grass prairies, up to 99 percent of these have been plowed and converted to agricultural use or lost due to **urbanization**. Similar but less dramatic losses of mixed and shortgrass prairies have occurred in other

urbanization increase in size or number of cities

areas. Because grasslands have tremendous economic value as grazing lands and also serve as critical habitats for many plant and animal species, efforts to conserve the remaining grasslands and restore grasslands on agricultural land are underway in many states and around the world. SEE ALSO BIOME; GRASSES; SAVANNA.

Alan K. Knapp

Bibliography

Archibold, O. W. *Ecology of World Vegetation*. New York: Chapman and Hall, 1995.

Borchert, J. R. "The Climate of the Central North American Grassland." *Annals of the Association of American Geographers* 40 (1950): 1–39.

Daubenmire, Rexford. *Plant Geography*. New York: Academic Press, 1978.

Frank, D. A., S. J. McNaughton, and B. F. Tracy. "The Ecology of the Earth's Grazing Ecosystems." *BioScience* 48 (1998): 513–21.

Knapp, A. K., J. M. Blair, J. M. Briggs, S. L. Collins, D. C. Hartnett, L. C. Johnson and E. G. Towne. "The Keystone Role of Bison in North American Tallgrass Prairie." *BioScience* 49 (1999): 39–50.

Samson, F., and F. Knopf. "Prairie Conservation in North America." *BioScience* 44 (1994): 418–21.

Weaver, J. E. *North American Prairie*. Lincoln, NE: Johnsen Publishing Co., 1954.

Gray, Asa

American Botanist
1810–1888

Asa Gray was the dominant force in botanical science in the United States throughout the mid-nineteenth century. He substantially advanced and influenced the study of North American flora and the dissemination of information about it. Gray's studies led to a reassessment of **floristic** plant geography in North America, and he was famous for the sheer volume of his knowledge and the way he used it to advance American botany. Gray won respect for American botany from abroad. Moreover, he played a critical role in the eventual acceptance of Darwin's theories in the United States.

Asa Gray was born in 1810 in Sauquoit Valley, New York, near Utica. As a youth he helped his father with farm and tannery work. He attended Fairfield Medical School, where he first became acquainted with basic botanical principles. Gray was awarded a medical degree in 1831, but then took a position as an instructor in chemistry, mineralogy, and botany in Utica, thus beginning his career in botany.

Gray corresponded with the famed botanist John Torrey (1796–1873), sending him **specimens** of local plants. In 1833 he joined Torrey in New York, first collecting plants for him, then as his assistant, and then shortly thereafter as his collaborator. Gray had a talent for investigation and scientific description, and even at this early stage of his career he was writing for publication. In 1835 he became curator and librarian at the Lyceum of Natural History in New York. He then accepted a position as botanist of the Wilkes Exploring Expedition, but various delays, coupled with his work on other projects, led to his resignation in 1837 before the expedition even began. Some time after the expedition, Gray was brought in to help publish its scientific results.

Asa Gray.

floristic related to plants

specimen object or organism under consideration

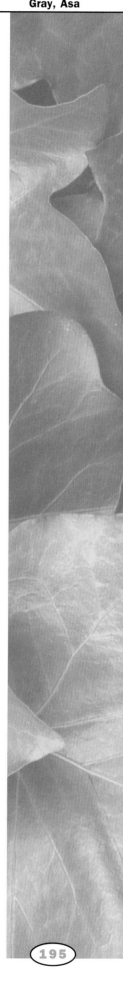

Gray began working with Torrey on a comprehensive flora of North America as early as 1835. This project eventually necessitated the study of American specimens located in European herbaria. Also at this time, Gray received a job offer as professor of botany and zoology at the not-yet-opened University of Michigan, and he was assigned the task of travelling to Europe to purchase books and equipment. He consequently went to Europe to study specimens and purchase resources, and while there he met prominent European scientists, including Charles Darwin (1809–1882). In 1839 Gray returned to the United States. Two volumes of the *Flora of North America* were published in 1838 and 1843; a third volume was never completed.

By 1842 the University of Michigan had still not yet opened, and so Gray accepted an invitation to become Fisher Professor of Natural History at Harvard University. In the course of his work and correspondence he built up a large herbarium and library, resources that enabled him to continue his botanical investigations and publications. Many specimens collected by others were given to Gray so that he could study, identify, and, if necessary, name them, publishing their descriptions and expanding botanical knowledge.

Gray published prolifically, including major studies such as the *Manual of the Botany of the Northern United States* (1848), the *Genera Florae Americae Boreali-Orientalis Illustrata* (1848–49), and various reports on botanical findings from expeditions and surveys. He also wrote a number of popular textbooks, held in high esteem by his peers and used widely in preparatory schools and colleges. These included *Elements of Botany* (1836), *First Lessons in Botany and Vegetable Physiology* (1857), and *How Plants Grow* (1858). He published two parts of a *Synoptical Flora of North America* before he died, and two more parts were published later by others.

The Flora of North America

Gray maintained an intense interest in the flora of North America throughout his career. This interest was fueled by various plant collection efforts, particularly in the American West, conducted as a result of mapping and surveying being done for the railroads and the geological surveys. Collectors also accompanied military expeditions, bringing back specimens from farther afield. Several new scientific institutions were formed, in part to accommodate the data and specimens being gathered.

Collectors brought new species to the attention of both Torrey and Gray, who influenced where plants were being collected and how the resulting information was processed and disseminated. Gray's extensive studies of collected specimens gave him an unparalleled working understanding of the North American landscape and the plants within it, including their distribution.

Evolution and Plant Geography

Gray also studied specimens collected from elsewhere, and he eventually demonstrated a direct relationship between certain Japanese and eastern North American plants. Many of the same species were found in both places but not elsewhere. Gray argued for a common ancestry for these species, reasoning that they must have grown all the way across the north-

ern continent at some time in the distant past, and that glaciers during the ice ages wiped out large sections of growth, so that the now-separated plants developed different characteristics. In 1859, this work led to a reassessment of plant geography in North America.

Gray expressed these ideas to Darwin, who also shared his own ideas with Gray before publishing them in *On the Origin of Species* in the same year. Gray became an advocate for Darwin's theories in the United States, helping to move the American scientific establishment further away from Linnaean ideas and toward those of Darwin. He demonstrated to scientists abroad that botany in North America was now being pursued with a professionalism comparable to that found in Europe. Gray was also a factor in the enhancement of scientific infrastructure in the United States, building an herbarium and library, influencing expeditions, and advising museums. These developments would persuade American collectors to entrust specimens to American institutions rather than sending them abroad to the great herbaria of Europe. Botany in the United States came of age with the work of Asa Gray. Gray received many honors during his lifetime and was a member of numerous academies and scholarly societies in America and Europe. He died in Cambridge, Massachusetts, in 1888. SEE ALSO FLORA; HERBARIA; TAXONOMIST; TAXONOMY; TAXONOMY, HISTORY OF; TORREY, JOHN.

Charlotte A. Tancin

Bibliography

Dupree, A. H. *Asa Gray, 1810–1888.* Cambridge, MA: Belknap Press of Harvard University Press, 1959.

Ewan, J. *A Short History of Botany in the United States.* New York: Hafner Publishing Co., 1969.

Humphrey, H. B. *Makers of North American Botany.* New York: Ronald Press Co., 1961.

Isely, D. *One Hundred and One Botanists.* Ames, IA: Iowa State University Press, 1994.

Kastner, J. *A Species of Eternity.* New York: Alfred A. Knopf, 1977.

Reed, H. S. *A Short History of the Plant Sciences.* New York: Ronald Press Co., 1942.

Reveal, J. L. *Gentle Conquest: The Botanical Discovery of North America.* Washington, DC: Starwood Publishing Co., 1992.

Spongberg, S. A. *A Reunion of Trees: The Discovery of Exotic Plants and Their Introduction into North American and European Landscapes.* Cambridge, MA: Harvard University Press, 1990.

Greenhouse Effect *See Global Warming.*

Green Revolution

Green revolution refers to the breeding and widespread use of new varieties of cereal grains, especially wheat and rice. These semidwarf varieties boost yields when grown with high inputs of fertilizer and water. Green revolution agriculture became widespread in less-industrialized countries in the 1960s when international aid agencies sponsored scientific and educational projects promoting the green revolution. These programs—including the adoption of new wheat varieties in India and Pakistan and new rice varieties in the Philippines and Indonesia—supported foreign policy objectives of the United States and were intended to alleviate hunger.

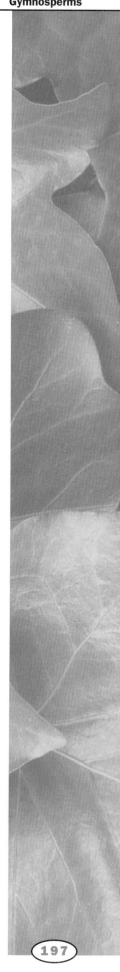

Supporters noted that the green revolution increased crop yields. India, for example, produced more wheat and rice, which helped avoid famines and save foreign exchange currency. Critics, however, charged that the green revolution increased inequalities: rich farmers became richer and poor farmers became poorer. Critics also complained that the green revolution encouraged increased environmental problems through the use of fertilizers, pesticides, and irrigation.

There were problems with both perspectives on the green revolution policies. Critics avoided providing realistic alternatives for solving national food deficits, and supporters avoided noting that poor individuals continued to be hungry, despite the increased supplies.

The green revolution was a change in agricultural practices with secondary social and political effects. Both industrialized and less-industrialized countries adopted the practices. Almost all wheat and rice grown today originated in the green revolution. SEE ALSO BORLAUG, NORMAN; ECONOMIC IMPORTANCE OF PLANTS; FERTILIZER; GRAINS; RICE; WHEAT.

John H. Perkins

Bibliography

Perkins, J. H. *Geopolitics and the Green Revolution: Wheat, Genes, and the Cold War.* New York: Oxford University Press, 1997.

Gymnosperms

Gymnosperms are seed plants that do not produce flowers. The term *gymnosperm* means "naked seed." However, usually when the seeds of gymnosperms are immature they are enclosed within and protected by modified leaves or a cone. In flowering plants (or *angiosperms*, which means "vessel seed") the ovary wall or fruit encloses the seeds, whereas in gymnosperms there is no equivalent structure; hence, the interpretation of the seeds as "naked" or not enclosed.

There are four groups of gymnosperms living today—Coniferophyta, Cycadophyta, Ginkgophyta, and Gnetophyta—but many additional groups are known from the fossil record. Seed plants evolved more than 350 million years ago and the first seed plants were gymnosperms. The relationship of the flowering plants to the gymnospermous seed plants remains a hotly contested issue within the scientific community.

Although each group of gymnosperms has its own specific characteristics, some features are shared throughout. For example, all gymnosperms produce at least some secondary growth, whereas secondary growth is lacking from most spore-bearing (nonseed) plants. Secondary growth is plant growth that does not occur directly from the tips of the plant; it is growth that occurs horizontally (or radially) rather than vertically. The most abundant product of secondary growth is the secondary xylem (xylem is the water-conducting tissue of plants), or wood.

Aspects of reproduction are also shared by all the gymnosperms. The ovule (the technical term for the seed prior to fertilization) consists of female nutritive tissue plus the female gamete, or egg, both enclosed by a

DISTINGUISHING CHARACTERS OF GYMNOSPERMS

Characters	Coniferophyta	Cycadophyta	Ginkgophyta	Gnetophyta
Extant members	50–60 genera, about 550 species	11 genera, about 160 species	1 species (*Ginkgo biloba*)	3 genera: *Ephedra* (35 species), *Gnetum* (30 species), *Welwitschia* (1 species)
Distribution	Worldwide, especially temperate regions	Tropics	Native to a small area of China	Isolated areas of temperate and tropical regions
Habit	Trees with branched woody trunk	Trees with unbranched fleshy trunk	Trees with branched woody trunk	Shrubs, vines, small trees, or weird tubers
Leaves	Simple, needlelike or broad	Large, compound (each leaf composed of many leaflets)	Simple, fan-shaped	Simple, needlelike or broad
Reproductive structure	Simple (unbranched) male, compound (branched) female cones	Simple cones (unbranched), male or female	Simple cones (unbranched), male or female	Compound (branched) male or female cones
Sex	Separate male and female cones on each plant (monoecious) or separate male and female plants (dioecious)	Individual plant male or female (dioecious)	Individual plant male or female (dioecious)	Individual plant male or female (dioecious)
Seeds	Small, without differentiated layers	Large, with outer fleshy layer and middle stony layer	Large, with outer fleshy layer and middle stony layer	Small, without differentiated layers
Sperm	No flagella; pollen tube delivers to egg	Swims using many flagella	Swims using many flagella	No flagella; pollen tube delivers to egg

layer of protective tissue (the integument). The male gamete is carried within the pollen. In most gymnosperms pollen is produced in great amounts, and the pollen grains are dispersed by the wind. Usually a small amount of sticky liquid (the pollination drop) is exuded at the tip of the ovule. Pollen grains become stuck in the pollination drop and, as the drop dries, the pollen is pulled into the ovule. Depending on the type of gymnosperm, the male gamete is released from the pollen and swims to the egg, or the male gamete is transported within a tube that grows to the egg. The fertilized egg then develops into the embryo of the seed. Ultimately, when the seed germinates, the embryo grows to produce the young seedling using the female nutritive tissue as a source of energy. An unusual attribute of the gymnosperms, except for the gnetophytes, is the long length of time—a year or more—that passes between the production of the egg and the sperm and the actual occurrence of fertilization.

Coniferophyta

The Coniferophyta, or conifers, are the most abundant group of living gymnosperms and the first of the living gymnosperm groups to appear in the fossil record. They have been important components of Earth's vegetation for almost three hundred million years. The oldest (bristlecone pine), the tallest (coast redwood), and the biggest (giant sequoia) organisms on the planet today are conifers. Most conifers are large trees that make abundant wood, have small evergreen leaves, and produce their seeds within woody cones.

Although most conifers fit that standard description, there are numerous exceptions. First, not all conifers are evergreen. A few types, such as the larch, are deciduous, losing all their leaves each fall and growing new leaves

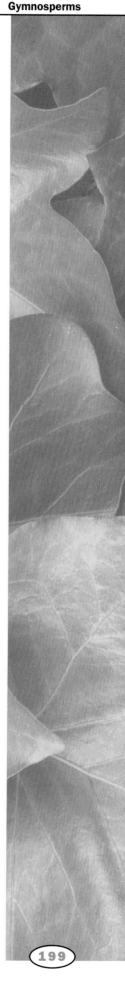

The female cones produced by most conifers are complex structures made of repeating units.

in the spring. Even the leaves of the evergreen type are not immortal; it is just that the senescence (aging and death) of leaves occurs individually rather than all at once. Second, not all conifers have small or needlelike leaves. Some conifers, native to the Southern Hemisphere, have broad leaves. Third, although all conifers are woody plants, not all conifers are large trees. A number are shrubs or small trees, and one is even a parasite on the roots of other coniferous trees. Finally, not all conifers have cones as people usually think of them. Some conifers, such as the yew, have solitary seeds covered with a fleshy, colorful tissue.

The female cones produced by most conifers are complex structures that are made of repeating units, each consisting of ovules on a woody platform (ovuliferous scale) beneath which is a bract (e.g., the "mouse tail" that peeks out of Douglas-fir cones). Cones of the other gymnosperms lack the equivalent of the ovuliferous scale. Conifers make rather small ovules and lack swimming sperm.

Cycadophyta

The Cycadophyta, or cycads, are restricted to tropical latitudes and were more abundant in the geologic past. These plants have unbranched, fleshy stems. The trunks of some species can grow fairly tall (15 to 18 meters), but all cycads lack extensive wood development. Because so much water is present in the stems, the plants are very vulnerable to damage from freezing (think of a soda can that explodes after you forget you have placed it in the freezer). Thus the cycads are restricted to parts of the world where freezing temperatures are rare or absent. A few types are found naturally in subtropical areas where mild freezing temperatures occasionally occur; these types of cycads have short, squat, subterranean stems. Some additional cycad species are hardy as ornamentals in similar subtropical to warm temperate areas. Excellent outdoor collections of cycads can be seen in the United States at Fairchild Botanical Garden in Miami, Florida, or at Huntington Botanical Garden east of Los Angeles, California.

A cycad, a gymnosperm that was more abundant in the geologic past.

The leaves of cycads occur as a crown at the top of the stem. Most often the leaves are very large (up to 1.5 meters in length), leathery, and compound; that is, the blade of the leaf is made of many separate leaflets. When the leaves fall off, usually the base of the leaf remains attached to the stem. Thus, the trunk is protected from herbivory and to some extent from freezing by the remnant bases.

Individual cycad plants are either male or female. At the tip of the trunk within the crown of leaves a cone develops that will either contain pollen or ovules, depending on the sex of the plant. Cycads make very large ovules and swimming sperm.

Ginkgophyta

Only one species of the Ginkgophyta group remains living today: the maidenhair tree, *Ginkgo biloba*. Twenty to thirty million years ago the ancestor of the modern species was found throughout the Northern Hemisphere. However, climatic changes have led to the plants gradually becoming reduced to a smaller and smaller territory. Since the last ice age, wild populations have been restricted to a small area in China. It is debated

whether or not any populations are truly wild. The tree still exists today because it was a sacred plant maintained in monasteries. Now the ginkgo tree is commonly used as a street tree and so has regained, in some sense, much of its earlier territory. Individual plants can live very long lives (more than one thousand years), and the species is unusually resistant to pollution and disease. The *Ginkgo* plant is a fairly tall (25 meters or more), much-branched tree with abundant wood, bearing fan-shaped leaves.

Individual ginkgo trees are either male or female. The sex of the plant does not become apparent until the tree is fifteen to twenty years old. Male plants are preferred as ornamentals. The ovule produced by the female is large with a stony interior and a fleshy outer covering that produces a smell usually equated with rotting butter. Ginkgo also produces swimming sperm.

Gnetophyta

The Gnetophyta are a small, odd group of living gymnosperms. Three types are known, each being somewhat different from the other gnetophytes and unusual among the seed plants in its own way. Species of the genus *Ephedra* are shrubby plants of arid temperate regions. They have tiny leaves and the stems are often green and photosynthetic. Species of the genus *Gnetum* are tropical plants that are small trees or, more usually, vines. The gnetums are unusual among the gymnosperms in that they produce broad leaves with netted venation similar to that found in flowering plants. The third group is represented by a single species, *Welwitschia mirabilis*. *Welwitschia* has been described as the "weirdest plant on Earth," a plant that has "lost its head" or a giant seedling that can reproduce. *Welwitschia* is native to the Namib Desert of southwest Africa and consists of a large tuber or taproot and two long, strap-shaped leaves that grow from their bases and are retained for the life of the plant.

Most gnetophytes produce separate female and male cones born on separate (male or female) plants. Each type of gnetophyte has a slightly different reproductive structure but all are variations on one theme: pairs of papery bracts (modified leaves) surround the ovule or pollen organs. Some botanists compare these bracts to the petals and **sepals** of angiosperm flowers, whereas others equate them to components of the cone found in conifers. Other aspects of the gnetophyte **morphology** are also ambiguous and, depending on their interpretation, suggests an evolutionary link to either the conifers or the angiosperms. For example, vessels, specialized water-conducting cells, occur in the wood of gnetophytes. These cells are dead at maturity, empty of any contents. Vessels lack any end walls; they are open-ended tubes that line up end to end and act as a pipe to transport water without any obstructions. Most flowering plants have vessels but most other types of plants lack this cell type. Some plant scientists see the gnetophyte vessels as evidence that gnetophytes and angiosperms share a common ancestor. However, because of differences in vessel cell anatomy and development between gnetophytes and flowering plants, other botanists consider the gnetophyte vessel to be an independent evolution of a water transport cell that lost an end wall. Molecular comparisons of the seed plants using different types of deoxyribonucleic acid (DNA) data have not settled this debate: gnetophytes remain a problematic group in terms of evolutionary placement and morphological interpretation.

sepals the outermost whorl of flower parts; usually green and leaf-like, they protect the inner parts of the flower

morphology shape and form

Ecological Significance

Conifers are the gymnospermous group with the most profound ecological role in Earth's vegetation. Conifers dominate some vegetation types, such as the taiga of high northern latitudes or boreal forests of lower latitudes. Some temperate forests, for example in Argentina, Australia, or northwestern North America, are also composed almost exclusively of coniferous trees.

Conifers can also be important as successional species or as the climax vegetation of odd environments in other temperate or tropical areas. For example, in environments prone to fire, with a long enough growing season and enough precipitation to support the growth of trees, conifers are often present. Conifer bark is thicker than most flowering plant tree bark and so coniferous trees are better able to survive ground fires. Some conifer cones open to release their seeds only after a fire.

Economic Significance

Conifers are also considered the most important gymnospermous group from an economic perspective. Coniferous trees are a very important source of timber for lumber and paper. They are harvested in North America, parts of Europe and Asia, and in Australia. In addition to timber, conifers provide Christmas trees, ornamental trees and shrubs, turpentine, and resin. Pine nuts (or pignoli), the seeds of some pine trees, are used as food. An important cancer-fighting drug, taxol, has been derived from the bark and leaves of the Pacific Coast yew (*Taxus*). Other gymnosperms also are the source of drugs and herbal medications. The powerful stimulant ephedrine derived from the gnetophyte *Ephedra* is often used in cold and allergy medications, and **compounds** shown to improve the mental capacities of the elderly have been discovered in *Ginkgo*. Ginkgo seeds are also quite nutritious and are used as food in Asia. Ginkgo and cycads are also important as ornamentals. SEE ALSO CONIFEROUS FORESTS; CONIFERS; EVOLUTION OF PLANTS; GINKGO; RECORD-HOLDING PLANTS; TREES; WOOD PRODUCTS.

Linda A. Raubeson

compound a substance formed from two or more elements

Bibliography

Burns, Russell M., and Barbara H. Honkala. *Silvics of North America*, Vol. 1: *Conifers.* Washington, DC: USDA Forest Service, Agriculture Handbook 654, 1990.

Homan, Dennis. *Biology of Seed Plants: A Laboratory Manual.* Dubuque, IA: Kendall/Hunt Publishing Co., 1997.

Hori, T., ed. *Ginkgo Biloba—A Global Treasure.* New York: Springer-Verlag, 1997.

Krussmann, Gerd. *Manual of Cultivated Conifers.* Portland, OR: Timber Press, 1985.

Nimsch, Hubertus. *A Reference Guide to the Gymnosperms of the World.* Champaign, IL: Balogh Scientific Books, 1995.

Norstog, Kurt J., and Trevor J. Nicholls. *The Biology of the Cycads.* Ithaca, NY: Cornell University Press, 1998.

Pielou, E. C. *The World of Northern Evergreens.* Ithaca, NY: Cornell University Press, 1988.

Photo and Illustration Credits

Volume 1

Ted Spiegel/Corbis: **2, 17, 96;** JLM Visuals: **4, 107;** Bojan Brecelj/Corbis: **6;** Tom Bean/ Corbis: **9, 49;** Thomas Del Brase/The Stock Market: **11;** Chinch Gryniewicz; Ecoscene/ Corbis: **13;** Charles O'Rear/Corbis: **19;** Steve Raymer/Corbis: **21;** Alex Rakoey/Custom Medical Stock Photo, Inc.: **28;** Wolfgang Kaehler/Corbis: **30, 100;** Field Mark Publications: **44;** Lester V. Bergman/Corbis: **50, 158;** Julie Meech; Ecoscene/Corbis: **53;** Raymond Gehman/Corbis: **55;** Dr. Kari Lounatmaa; Science Photo Library/Photo Researchers, Inc: **57;** Roger Tidman/Corbis: **58;** The Purcell Team/Corbis: **60;** David Muench/Corbis: **63, 114;** Adrian Arbib/ Corbis: **67;** Barry Griffiths; National Audubon Society Collection/Photo Researchers, Inc.: **76;** Kopp Illustration, 81; Prof. Jim Watson; Science Photo Library/ Photo Researchers, Inc: **85;** Michael S. Yamashita/Corbis: **87;** Pallava Bagla/Corbis: **88;** Bettmann/Corbis: **90, 116;** Richard T. Nowitz/Corbis: **92, 94;** UPI/Corbis– Bettmann: **109;** Owen Franken/Corbis: **112;** Bill Lisenby/Corbis: **119;** Hans & Cassady: **124, 136;** Fritz Polking; Frank Lane Picture Agency/Corbis: **128;** Ron Watts/Corbis: **130;** UPI/Bettmann Newsphotos: **131;** David Spears; Science Pictures Limited/Corbis: **138, 143;** Dr. Dennis Kunkel/Phototake NYC: **141;** Dr. Jeremy Burgess/Photo Researchers, Inc.: **146, 155;** Andrew Brown; Ecoscene/ Corbis: **148;** Richard Cummins/Corbis: **162.**

Volume 2

Arne Hodalic/Corbis: **2;** Gregory G. Dimijian/Photo Researchers, Inc.: **5;** Michael & Patricia Fogden/Corbis: **9;** Dean Conger/ Corbis: **11, 76;** Joseph Sohm; ChromoSohm, Inc./Corbis: **16;** Darrell Gulin/Corbis: **18, 61;** Galen Rowell/Corbis: **23;** Courtesy of the Library of Congress: **24, 40, 143;** Charles O'Rear/Corbis: **26, 157;** Liba Taylor/Corbis: **29;** Richard Hamilton Smith/Corbis: **31, 32;** Bojan Brecelj/Corbis: **35;** Lester V. Bergman/ Corbis: **39, 119, 166, 175;** Robert Estall/ Corbis: **48;** William A. Bake/Corbis: **52;** Rosemary Mayer/Photo Researchers, Inc.: **54;** George Lepp/Corbis: **56;** Michael S. Yamashita/Corbis: **58, 114;** Raymond Gehman/Corbis: **62, 93;** Wayne Lawler; Ecoscene/Corbis: **64;** Dr. William M. Harlow/Photo Researchers, Inc.: **66;** William Boyce/Corbis: **74;** David Spears; Science Pictures Limited/Corbis: **82;** Roger Tidman/ Corbis: **84;** Hans & Cassady: **86;** Roger Ressmeyer/Corbis: **103;** Susan Middleton and David Liitschwager/Corbis: **107;** Robin Foster/Conservation International: **108;** John Durham/Photo Researchers, Inc.: **112;** Jaime Razuri; AFP/Corbis: **116;** Courtesy of Linda E. Graham: **122, 125;** Buddy Mays/Corbis: **136;** Michael Freeman/Corbis: **142;** Field Mark Publications: **146, 186;** David Cumming; Eye Ubiquitous/Corbis: **149;** Bob Krist/Corbis: **152;** Gunter Marx/Corbis: **154;** Jim Sugar Photography/Corbis: **156;** Courtesy of Dr. Orson K. Miller, Jr.: **162, 163, 164;** Lowell Georgia/Corbis: **167, 170;** William James Warren/Corbis: **169;** Patrick Johns/Corbis: **178;** Eric and David Hosking/Corbis: **180;** Thomas Bettge,

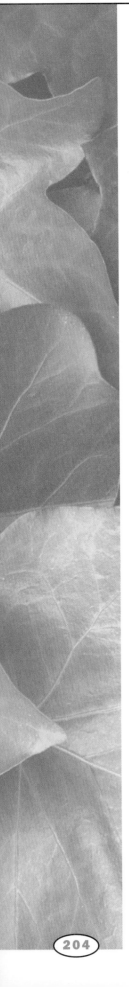

National Center for Atmospheric Research/ University Corporation for Atmospheric Research/National Science Foundation: **182, 183**; Philip Gould/Corbis: **184**; Roy Morsch/ The Stock Market: **188**; Tom Bean/Corbis: **190**; Archive Photos, Inc.: **194**; JLM Visuals: **199, 200**.

Volume 3

Courtesy of the Library of Congress: **1, 30, 61, 73**; JLM Visuals: **3, 49, 106**; Corbis: **4**; Anthony Cooper; Ecoscene/Corbis: **9**; Photo Researchers, Inc.: **11**; Archive Photos, Inc.: **12**; Ed Young/Corbis: **23, 147**; Kansas Division of Travel and Tourism: **26**; Asa Thoresen/Photo Researchers, Inc.: **28**; Ted Streshinsky/Corbis: **32**; Michael S. Yamashita/Corbis: **35**; Patrick Johns/Corbis: **38, 96, 104, 125, 187**; Cumego/Corbis/ Bettmann: **39**; David Spears; Science Pictures Limited/Corbis: **41, 54, 114, 129**; W. Wayne Lockwood, M.D./Corbis: **42**; Field Mark Publications: **44, 57, 71, 169, 171, 175**; Michael & Patricia Fogden/Corbis: **46**; Phil Schermeister/Corbis: **52**; Judyth Platt; Ecoscene/Corbis: **59**; Courtesy of Hunt Institute for Botanical Documentation, Carnegie Mellon University, Pittsburgh, PA: **62**; UPI/Bettmann: **66**; Eric Crichton/Corbis: **72**; Biophoto Associates; National Audubon Society Collection/Photo Researchers, Inc.: **88**; Adam Hart-Davis/Photo Researchers, Inc.: **92**; Lester V. Bergman/Corbis: **94, 108, 167**; Patrick Field; Eye Ubiquitous/Corbis: **103**; Michael Boys/Corbis: **105**; Sally A. Morgan; Ecoscene/Corbis: **110**; Kevin Schafer/Corbis: **112**; Jim Zipp; National Audubon Society Collection/Photo Researchers, Inc.: **117**; Richard T. Nowitz/ Corbis: **120**; Wayne Lawler; Ecoscene/ Corbis: **122**; Bob Krist/Corbis: **123**; Tom and

Pat Lesson/Photo Researchers, Inc.: **158**; Raymond Gehman/Corbis: **164**; George Lepp/Corbis: **177**; Richard Hamilton Smith/Corbis: **181**; Nigel Cattlin; Holt Studios International/Photo Researchers, Inc.: **185**; Owen Franken/Corbis: **189**; Alison Wright/Corbis: **193**.

Volume 4

Kevin Schafer/Corbis: **2, 42**; Wolfgang Kaehler/Corbis: **5, 7**; E. S. Ross: **9**; Galen Rowell/Corbis: **14, 127**; David Spears; Science Pictures Limited/Corbis: **17, 20, 79, 120, 161, 172**; Robert Pickett/Corbis: **19, 101**; Dr. Jeremy Burgess/Photo Researchers, Inc.: **21, 159**; Biophoto Associates/Photo Researchers, Inc.: **22, 142**; JLM Visuals: **25, 26, 40, 140, 155, 169**; Owen Franken/ Corbis: **27**; Philip Gould/Corbis: **30, 70**; Corbis: **39, 152**; Steve Raymer/Corbis: **49**; Mark Gibson/Corbis: **57**; James Lee Sikkema: **58**; Field Mark Publications: **62, 130, 167**; Wayne Lawler/Corbis: **63**; Richard T. Nowitz/Corbis: **66**; Photo Researchers, Inc.: **68**; Karen Tweedy-Holmes/Corbis: **73**; Lester V. Bergman/Corbis: **77, 147**; Craig Aurness/Corbis: **83**; John Holmes; Frank Lane Picture Agency/Corbis: **86**; Archivo Iconografico, S.A./Corbis: **92**; Paul Almasy/Corbis: **98**; Tiziana and Gianni Baldizzone/Corbis: **105**; Darrell Gulin/ Corbis: **108**; Lynda Richardson/Corbis: **110**; Courtesy of Thomas L. Rost and Deborah K. Canington: **112, 113, 114**; Laure Communications: **115**; Archive Photos, Inc.: **116**; Jim Sugar Photography/Corbis: **132**; Hugh Clark; Frank Lane Picture Agency/Corbis: **136, 137**; Ron Boardman; Frank Lane Picture Agency/ Corbis: **148**; Richard Hamilton Smith/Corbis: **165**; Joseph Sohm; ChromoSohm, Inc./ Corbis: **175**; Dave G. Houser/Corbis: **176**.

Glossary

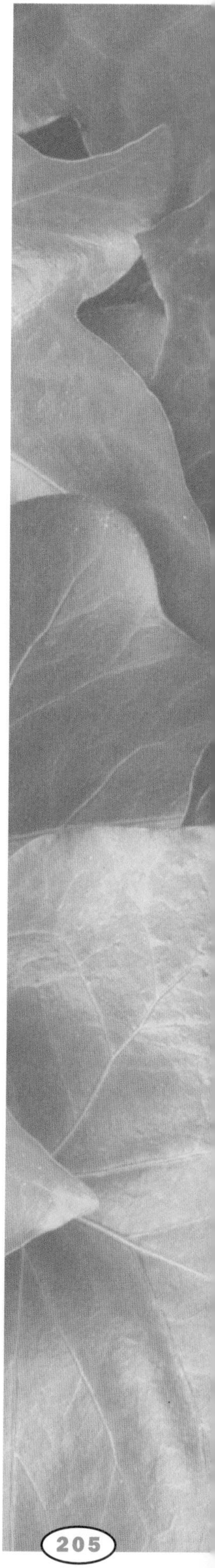

abiotic nonliving

abrade to wear away through contact

abrasive tending to wear away through contact

abscission dropping off or separating

accession a plant that has been acquired and catalogued

achene a small, dry, thin-walled type of fruit

actinomycetes common name for a group of Gram-positive bacteria that are filamentous and superficially similar to fungi

addictive capable of causing addiction or chemical dependence

adhesion sticking to the surface of

adventitious arising from secondary buds, or arising in an unusual position

aeration the introduction of air

albuminous gelatinous, or composed of the protein albumin

alkali chemically basic; the opposite of acidic

alkalinization increase in basicity or reduction in acidity

alkaloid bitter secondary plant compound, often used for defense

allele one form of a gene

allelopathy harmful action by one plant against another

allopolyploidy a polyploid organism formed by hybridization between two different species or varieties (*allo* = other)

alluvial plain broad area formed by the deposit of river sediment at its outlet

amended soils soils to which fertilizers or other growth aids have been added

amendment additive

anaerobic without oxygen

analgesic pain-relieving

analog a structure or thing, especially a chemical, similar to something else

angiosperm a flowering plant

anomalous unusual or out of place

anoxic without oxygen

antenna system a collection of protein complexes that harvests light energy and converts it to excitation energy that can migrate to a reaction center; the light is absorbed by pigment molecules (e.g., chlorophyll, carotenoids, phycobilin) that are attached to the protein

anthropogenic human-made; related to or produced by the influence of humans on nature

antibodies proteins produced to fight infection

antioxidant a substance that prevents damage from oxygen or other reactive substances

apical meristem region of dividing cells at the tips of growing plants

apical at the tip

apomixis asexual reproduction that may mimic sexual reproduction

appendages parts that are attached to a central stalk or axis

arable able to be cultivated for crops

Arcto-Tertiary geoflora the fossil flora discovered in Arctic areas dating back to the Tertiary period; this group contains magnolias (*Magnolia*), tulip trees (*Liriodendron*), maples (*Acer*), beech (*Fagus*), black gum (*Nyssa*), sweet gum (*Liquidambar*), dawn redwood (*Metasequoia*), cypress (*Taxodium*), and many other species

artifacts pots, tools, or other cultural objects

assayer one who performs chemical tests to determine the composition of a substance

ATP adenosine triphosphate, a small, water-soluble molecule that acts as an energy currency in cells

attractant something that attracts

autotroph "self-feeder"; any organism that uses sunlight or chemical energy

auxin a plant hormone

avian related to birds

axil the angle or crotch where a leaf stalk meets the stem

axillary bud the bud that forms in the angle between the stem and leaf

basipetal toward the base

belladonna the source of atropine; means "beautiful woman," and is so named because dilated pupils were thought to enhance a woman's beauty

binomial two-part

biodirected assays tests that examine some biological property

biodiversity degree of variety of life

biogeography the study of the reasons for the geographic distribution of organisms

biomass the total dry weight of an organism or group of organisms

biosphere the region of the Earth in which life exists

biosynthesis creation through biological pathways

biota the sum total of living organisms in a region of a given size

biotic involving or related to life

bryologist someone who studies bryophytes, a division of nonflowering plants

campanulate bell-shaped

capitulum the head of a compound flower, such as a dandelion

cardiotonic changing the contraction properties of the heart

carotenoid a yellow-colored molecule made by plants

carpels the innermost whorl of flower parts, including the egg-bearing ovules, plus the style and stigma attached to the ovules

catastrophism the geologic doctrine that sudden, violent changes mark the geologic history of Earth

cation positively charged particle

catkin a flowering structure used for wind pollination

centrifugation spinning at high speed in a centrifuge to separate components

chitin a cellulose-like molecule found in the cell wall of many fungi and arthropods

chloroplast the photosynthetic organelle of plants and algae

circadian "about a day"; related to a day

circumscription the definition of the boundaries surrounding an object or an idea

cisterna a fluid-containing sac or space

clade a group of organisms composed of an ancestor and all of its descendants

cladode a modified stem having the appearance and function of a leaf

coalescing roots roots that grow together

coleoptile the growing tip of a monocot seedling

collenchyma one of three cell types in ground tissue

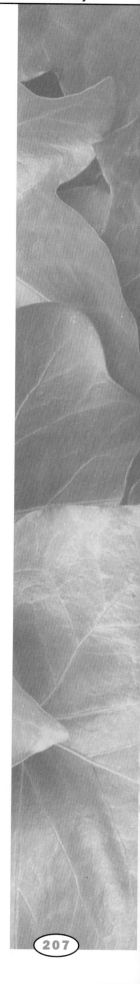

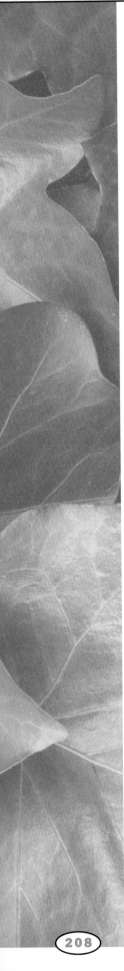

colonize to inhabit a new area

colony a group of organisms inhabiting a particular area, especially organisms descended from a common ancestor

commensalism a symbiotic association in which one organism benefits while the other is unaffected

commodities goods that are traded, especially agricultural goods

community a group of organisms of different species living in a region

compaction compacting of soil, leading to the loss of air spaces

complex hybrid hybridized plant having more than two parent plants

compound a substance formed from two or more elements

concentration gradient a difference in concentration between two areas

continental drift the movement of continental land masses due to plate tectonics

contractile capable of contracting

convective uplift the movement of air upwards due to heating from the sun

coppice growth the growth of many stems from a single trunk or root, following the removal of the main stem

cortical relating to the cortex of a plant

covalent held together by electron-sharing bonds

crassulacean acid metabolism water-conserving strategy used by several types of plants

crop rotation alternating crops from year to year in a particular field

cultivation growth of plants, or turning the soil for growth of crop plants

crystallography the use of x-rays on crystals to determine molecular structure

cuticle the waxy outer coating of a leaf or other structure, which provides protection against predators, infection, and water loss

cyanide heap leach gold mining a technique used to extract gold by treating ore with cyanide

cyanobacteria photosynthetic prokaryotic bacteria formerly known as blue-green algae

cyanogenic giving rise to cyanide

cytologist a scientist who studies cells

cytology the microscopic study of cells and cell structure

cytosol the fluid portion of a cell

cytostatic inhibiting cell division

deductive reasoning from facts to conclusion

dendrochronologist a scientist who uses tree rings to determine climate or other features of the past

dermatophytes fungi that cause skin diseases

desertification degradation of dry lands, reducing productivity

desiccation drying out

detritus material from decaying organisms

diatoms hard-shelled, single-celled marine organisms; a type of algae

dictyosome any one of the membranous or vesicular structures making up the Golgi apparatus

dioicous having male and female sexual parts on different plants

diploid having two sets of chromosomes, versus having one set (haploid)

dissipate to reduce by spreading out or scattering

distal further away from

diurnal daily, or by day

domestication the taming of an organism to live with and be of use to humans

dormant inactive, not growing

drupe a fruit with a leathery or stone-like seed

dynamical system theory the mathematical theory of change within a system

ecophysiological related to how an organism's physiology affects its function in an ecosystem

ecosystem an ecological community and its environment

elater an elongated, thickened filament

empirical formula the simplest whole number ratio of atoms in a compound

emulsifier a chemical used to suspend oils in water

encroachment moving in on

endemic belonging or native to a particular area or country

endophyte a fungus that lives within a plant

endoplasmic reticulum the membrane network inside a cell

endosperm the nutritive tissue in a seed, formed by the fertilization of a diploid egg tissue by a sperm from pollen

endosporic the formation of a gametophyte inside the spore wall

endosymbiosis a symbiosis in which one organism lives inside the other

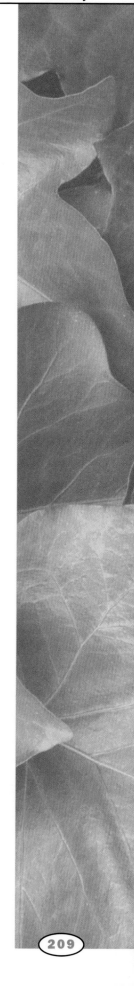

Enlightenment eighteenth-century philosophical movement stressing rational critique of previously accepted doctrines in all areas of thought

entomologist a scientist who studies insects

enzyme a protein that controls a reaction in a cell

ephemeral short-lived

epicuticle the waxy outer covering of a plant, produced by the epidermis

epidermis outer layer of cells

epiphytes plants that grow on other plants

escarpment a steep slope or cliff resulting from erosion

ethnobotanist a scientist who interacts with native peoples to learn more about the plants of a region

ethnobotany the study of traditional uses of plants within a culture

euglossine bees a group of bees that pollinate orchids and other rain-forest plants

eukaryotic a cell with a nucleus (*eu* means "true" and *karyo* means "nucleus"); includes protists, plants, animals, and fungi

extrafloral outside the flower

exudation the release of a liquid substance; oozing

facultative capable of but not obligated to

fertigation application of small amounts of fertilizer while irrigating

filament a threadlike extension

filamentous thin and long

flagella threadlike extension of the cell membrane, used for movement

flavonoids aromatic compounds occurring in both seeds and young roots and involved in host-pathogen and host-symbiont interactions

florigen a substance that promotes flowering

floristic related to plants

follicle sac or pouch

forbs broad-leaved, herbaceous plants

free radicals toxic molecular fragments

frugivous feeding on fruits

gametangia structure where gametes are formed

gametophyte the haploid organism in the life cycle

gel electrophoresis a technique for separating molecules based on size and electrical charge

genera plural of genus; a taxonomic level above species

genome the genetic material of an organism

genotype the genetic makeup of an organism

germplasm hereditary material, especially stored seed or other embryonic forms

globose rounded and swollen; globe-shaped

gradient difference in concentration between two places

green manure crop planted to be plowed under to nourish the soil, especially with nitrogen

gymnosperm a major group of plants that includes the conifers

gynoecium the female reproductive organs as a whole

gypsipherous containing the mineral gypsum

hallucinogenic capable of inducing hallucinations

haploid having one set of chromosomes, versus having two (diploid)

haustorial related to a haustorium, or food-absorbing organ

hemiterpene a half terpene

herbivore an organism that feeds on plant parts

heterocyclic a chemical ring structure composed of more than one type of atom, for instance carbon and nitrogen

heterosporous bearing spores of two types, large megaspores and small microspores

heterostylous having styles (female flower parts) of different lengths, to aid cross-pollination

heterotroph an organism that derives its energy from consuming other organisms or their body parts

holistic including all the parts or factors that relate to an object or idea

homeotic relating to or being a gene that produces a shift in structural development

homology a similarity in structure between anatomical parts due to descent from a common ancestor

humus the organic material in soil formed from decaying organisms

hybrid a mix of two varieties or species

hybridization formation of a new individual from parents of different species or varieties

hydrological cycle the movement of water through the biosphere

hydrophobic water repellent

hydroponic growing without soil, in a watery medium

hydroxyl the chemical group -OH

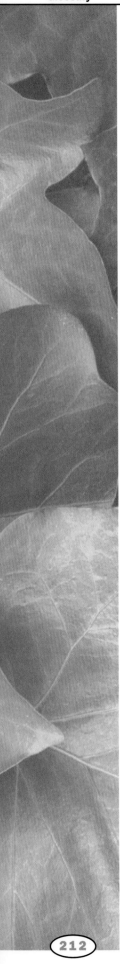

hyphae the threadlike body mass of a fungus

illicit illegal

impede to slow down or inhibit

inert incapable of reaction

inflorescence a group of flowers or arrangement of flowers in a flower head

infrastructure roads, phone lines, and other utilities that allow commerce

insectivorous insect-eating

intercalary inserted; between

interspecific hybridization hybridization between two species

intertidal between the lines of high and low tide

intracellular bacteria bacteria that live inside other cells

intraspecific taxa levels of classification below the species level

intuiting using intuition

ionic present as a charged particle

ions charged particles

irreversible unable to be reversed

juxtaposition contrast brought on by close positioning

lacerate cut

Lamarckian inheritance the hypothesis that acquired characteristics can be inherited

lamellae thin layers or plate-like structure

land-grant university a state university given land by the federal government on the condition that it offer courses in agriculture

landrace a variety of a cultivated plant, occurring in a particular region

lateral to the side of

legume beans and other members of the Fabaceae family

lignified composed of lignin, a tough and resistant plant compound

lineage ancestry; the line of evolutionary descent of an organism

loci (singular: locus) sites or locations

lodging falling over while still growing

lytic breaking apart by the action of enzymes

macromolecule a large molecule such as a protein, fat, nucleic acid, or carbohydrate

macroscopic large, visible

medulla middle part

megaphylls large leaves having many veins or a highly branched vein system

meiosis the division of chromosomes in which the resulting cells have half the original number of chromosomes

meristem the growing tip of a plant

mesic of medium wetness

microfibrils microscopic fibers in a cell

micron one millionth of a meter; also called micrometer

microphylls small leaves having a single unbranched vein

mitigation reduction of amount or effect

mitochondria cell organelles that produce adenosine triphosphate (ATP) to power cell reactions

mitosis the part of the cell cycle in which chromosomes are separated to give each daughter cell an identical chromosome set

molecular systematics the analysis of DNA and other molecules to determine evolutionary relationships

monoculture a large stand of a single crop species

monomer a single unit of a multi-unit structure

monophyletic a group that includes an ancestral species and all its descendants

montane growing in a mountainous region

morphology shape and form

motile capable of movement

mucilaginous sticky or gummy

murein a peptidoglycan, a molecule made up of sugar derivatives and amino acids

mutualism a symbiosis between two organisms in which both benefit

mycelium the vegetative body of a fungus, made up of threadlike hyphae

NADP$^+$ oxidized form of nicotinamide adenine dinucleotide phosphate

NADPH reduced form of nicotinamide adenine dinucleotide phosphate, a small, water-soluble molecule that acts as a hydrogen carrier in biochemical reactions

nanometer one billionth of a meter

nectaries organs in flowers that secrete nectar

negative feedback a process by which an increase in some variable causes a response that leads to a decrease in that variable

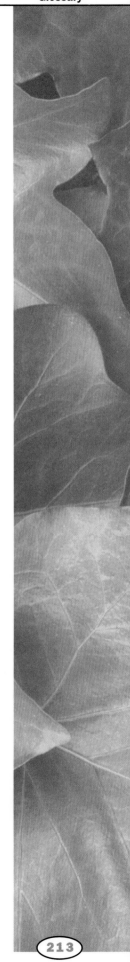

neuromuscular junction the place on the muscle surface where the muscle receives stimulus from the nervous system

neurotransmitter a chemical that passes messages between nerve cells

node branching site on a stem

nomenclature a naming system

nonmotile not moving

nonpolar not directed along the root-shoot axis, or not marked by separation of charge (unlike water and other polar substances)

nonsecretory not involved in secretion, or the release of materials

Northern Blot a technique for separating RNA molecules by electrophoresis and then identifying a target fragment with a DNA probe

nucleolar related to the nucleolus, a distinct region in the nucleus

nurseryman a worker in a plant nursery

obligate required, without another option

obligate parasite a parasite without a free-living stage in the life cycle

odorant a molecule with an odor

organelle a membrane-bound structure within a cell

osmosis the movement of water across a membrane to a region of high solute concentration

oviposition egg-laying

oxidation reaction with oxygen, or loss of electrons in a chemical reaction

paleobotany the study of ancient plants and plant communities

pangenesis the belief that acquired traits can be inherited by bodily influences on the reproductive cells

panicle a type of inflorescence (flower cluster) that is loosely packed and irregularly branched

paraphyletic group a taxonomic group that excludes one or more descendants of a common ancestor

parenchyma one of three types of cells found in ground tissue

pastoralists farming people who keep animal flocks

pathogen disease-causing organism

pedicel a plant stalk that supports a fruiting or spore-bearing organ

pentamerous composed of five parts

percolate to move through, as a fluid through a solid

peribacteroid a membrane surrounding individual or groups of rhizobia bacteria within the root cells of their host; in such situations the bacteria

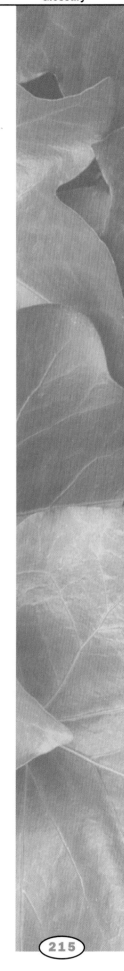

have frequently undergone some change in surface chemistry and are referred to as bacteroids

pericycle cell layer between the conducting tissue and the endodermis

permeability the property of being permeable, or open to the passage of other substances

petiole the stalk of a leaf, by which it attaches to the stem

pH a measure of acidity or alkalinity; the pH scale ranges from 0 to 14, with 7 being neutral. Low pH numbers indicate high acidity while high numbers indicate alkalinity

pharmacognosy the study of drugs derived from natural products

pharmacopeia a group of medicines

phenology seasonal or other time-related aspects of an organism's life

pheromone a chemical released by one organism to influence the behavior of another

photooxidize to react with oxygen under the influence of sunlight

photoperiod the period in which an organism is exposed to light or is sensitive to light exposure, causing flowering or other light-sensitive changes

photoprotectant molecules that protect against damage by sunlight

phylogenetic related to phylogeny, the evolutionary development of a species

physiology the biochemical processes carried out by an organism

phytogeographer a scientist who studies the distribution of plants

pigments colored molecules

pistil the female reproductive organ of a flower

plasmodesmata cell-cell junctions that allow passage of small molecules between cells

polyculture mixed species

polyhedral in the form of a polyhedron, a solid whose sides are polygons

polymer a large molecule made from many similar parts

polynomial "many-named"; a name composed of several individual parts

polyploidy having multiple sets of chromosomes

polysaccharide a linked chain of many sugar molecules

population a group of organisms of a single species that exist in the same region and interbreed

porosity openness

positive feedback a process by which an increase in some variable causes a response that leads to a further increase in that variable

precipitation rainfall; or the process of a substance separating from a solution

pre-Columbian before Columbus

precursor a substance from which another is made

predation the act of preying upon; consuming for food

primordial primitive or early

progenitor parent or ancestor

prokaryotes single-celled organisms without nuclei, including Eubacteria and Archaea

propagate to create more of through sexual or asexual reproduction

protist a usually single-celled organism with a cell nucleus, of the kingdom Protista

protoplasmic related to the protoplasm, cell material within the cell wall

protoplast the portion of a cell within the cell wall

psychoactive causing an effect on the brain

pubescence covered with short hairs

pyruvic acid a three-carbon compound that forms an important intermediate in many cellular processes

quadruple hybrid hybridized plant with four parents

quantitative numerical, especially as derived from measurement

quid a wad for chewing

quinone chemical compound found in plants, often used in making dyes

radii distance across, especially across a circle (singular = radius)

radioisotopes radioactive forms of an element

rambling habit growing without obvious intended direction

reaction center a protein complex that uses light energy to create a stable charge separation by transferring a single electron energetically uphill from a donor molecule to an acceptor molecule, both of which are located in the reaction center

redox oxidation and reduction

regurgitant material brought up from the stomach

Renaissance a period of artistic and intellectual expansion in Europe from the fourteenth to the sixteenth century

salinization increase in salt content

samara a winged seed

saprophytes plants that feed on decaying parts of other plants

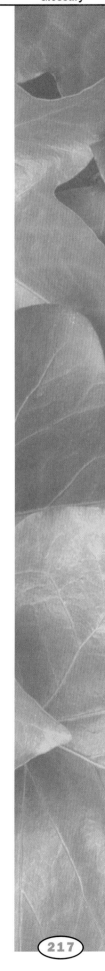

saturated containing as much dissolved substance as possible

sclerenchyma one of three cell types in ground tissue

sedimentation deposit of mud, sand, shell, or other material

semidwarf a variety that is intermediate in size between dwarf and full-size varieties

senescent aging or dying

sepals the outermost whorl of flower parts; usually green and leaf-like, they protect the inner parts of the flower

sequester to remove from circulation; lock up

serology the study of serum, the liquid, noncellular portion of blood

seta a stiff hair or bristle

silage livestock food produced by fermentation in a silo

siliceous composed of silica, a mineral

silicified composed of silicate minerals

soil horizon distinct layers of soil

solute a substance dissolved in a solution

Southern blot a technique for separating DNA fragments by electrophoresis and then identifying a target fragment with a DNA probe

spasticity abnormal muscle activity caused by damage to the nerve pathways controlling movement

speciation the creation of new species

specimen an object or organism under consideration

speciose marked by many species

sporophyte the diploid, spore-producing individual in the plant life cycle

sporulate to produce or release spores

sterile not capable or involved in reproduction, or unable to support life

sterols chemicals related to steroid hormones

stolons underground stems that may sprout and form new individuals

stomata openings between guard cells on the underside of leaves that allow gas exchange

stratification layering, or separation in space

stratigraphic geology the study of rock layers

stratigraphy the analysis of strata (layered rock)

strobili cone-like reproductive structures

subalpine a region less cold or elevated than alpine (mountaintop)

substrate the physical structure to which an organism attaches, or a molecule acted on by enzymes

succession the pattern of changes in plant species that occurs after a soil disturbance

succulent fleshy, moist

suckers naturally occuring adventitious shoots

suffrutescent a shrub-like plant with a woody base

sulfate a negatively charged particle combining sulfur and oxygen

surfaced smoothed for examination

susceptibility vulnerability

suture line of attachment

swidden agriculture the practice of farming an area until the soil has been depleted and then moving on

symbiont one member of a symbiotic association

symbiosis a relationship between organisms of two different species in which at least one benefits

systematists scientists who study systematics, the classification of species to reflect evolutionary relationships

systemic spread throughout the plant

tannins compounds produced by plants that usually serve protective functions, often colored and used for "tanning" and dyeing

taxa a type of organism, or a level of classification of organisms

tensile forces forces causing tension, or pulling apart; the opposite of compression

tepal an undifferentiated sepal or petal

Tertiary period geologic period from sixty-five to five million years ago

tetraploid having four sets of chromosomes; a form of polyploidy

thallus simple, flattened, nonleafy plant body

tilth soil structure characterized by open air spaces and high water storage capacity due to high levels of organic matter

tonoplast the membrane of the vacuole

topographic related to the shape or contours of the land

totipotent capable of forming entire plants from individual cells

toxin a poisonous substance

tracheid a type of xylem cell that conducts water from root to shoot

transcription factors proteins that bind to a specific DNA sequence called the promoter to regulate the expression of a nearby gene

translocate to move materials from one region to another

translucent allowing the passage of light

transmutation to change from one form to another

transpiration movement of water from soil to atmosphere through a plant

transverse across, or side to side

tribe a group of closely related genera

trophic related to feeding

turgor pressure the outward pressure exerted on the cell wall by the fluid within

twining twisting around while climbing

ultrastructural the level of structure visible with the electron microscope; very small details of structure

uniformitarian the geologic doctrine that formative processes on earth have proceeded at the same rate through time since earth's beginning

uplift raising up of rock layers, a geologic process caused by plate tectonics

urbanization increase in size or number of cities

vacuole the large fluid-filled sac that occupies most of the space in a plant cell. Used for storage and maintaining internal pressure

vascular plants plants with specialized transport cells; plants other than bryophytes

vascular related to the transport of nutrients, or related to blood vessels

vector a carrier, usually one that is not affected by the thing carried

vernal related to the spring season

vesicle a membrane-bound cell structure with specialized contents

viable able to live or to function

volatile easily released as a gas

volatilization the release of a gaseous substance

water table the level of water in the soil

whorl a ring

wort an old English term for plant; also an intermediate liquid in beer making

xenobiotics biomolecules from outside the plant, especially molecules that are potentially harmful

xeromorphic a form adapted for dry conditions

xerophytes plants adapted for growth in dry areas

zonation division into zones having different properties

zoospore a swimming spore

zygote the egg immediately after it has been fertilized; the one-cell stage of a new individual

Topic Outline

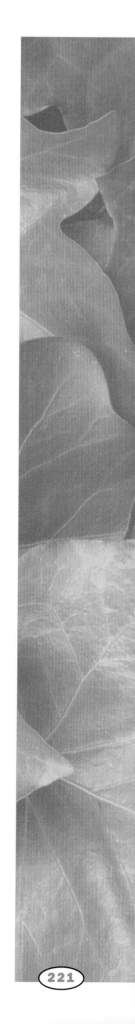

ADAPTATIONS

Alkaloids
Allelopathy
Cacti
Cells, Specialized Types
Clines and Ecotypes
Defenses, Chemical
Defenses, Physical
Halophytes
Lichens
Mycorrhizae
Nitrogen Fixation
Poisonous Plants
Seed Dispersal
Shape and Form of Plants
Symbiosis
Translocation
Trichomes

AGRICULTURE

Agriculture, History of
Agriculture, Modern
Agriculture, Organic
Agricultural Ecosystems
Agronomist
Alliaceae
Asteraceae
Biofuels
Borlaug, Norman
Breeder
Breeding
Burbank, Luther
Cacao
Carver, George W.
Coffee
Compost
Cork

Corn
Cotton
Economic Importance of Plants
Ethnobotany
Fertilizer
Fiber and Fiber Products
Food Scientist
Fruits
Fruits, Seedless
Genetic Engineer
Genetic Engineering
Grains
Grasslands
Green Revolution
Halophytes
Herbs and Spices
Herbicides
Horticulture
Horticulturist
Hydroponics
Native Food Crops
Nitrogen Fixation
Oils, Plant-Derived
Pathogens
Pathologist
Polyploidy
Potato
Potato Blight
Quantitative Trait Loci
Rice
Seed Preservation
Soil, Chemistry of
Soil, Physical Characteristics
Solanaceae
Soybeans
Sugar
Tea
Tissue Culture

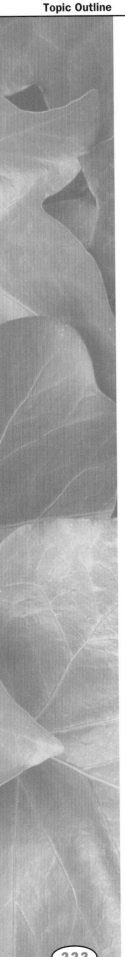

Tobacco
Transgenic Plants
Vavilov, N. I.
Vegetables
Weeds
Wheat
Wine and Beer Industry

ANATOMY

Anatomy of Plants
Bark
Botanical and Scientific Illustrator
Cell Walls
Cells
Cells, Specialized Types
Cork
Differentiation and Development
Fiber and Fiber Products
Flowers
Fruits
Inflorescence
Leaves
Meristems
Mycorrhizae
Phyllotaxis
Plants
Roots
Seeds
Shape and Form of Plants
Stems
Tissues
Tree Architecture
Trichomes
Vascular Tissues
Vegetables
Wood Anatomy

BIOCHEMISTRY/PHYSIOLOGY

Alcoholic Beverage Industry
Alkaloids
Anthocyanins
Biofuels
Biogeochemical Cycles
Bioremediation
Carbohydrates
Carbon Cycle
Cells
Cellulose
Chlorophyll
Chloroplasts

Cytokinins
Defenses, Chemical
Ecology, Energy Flow
Fertilizer
Flavonoids
Flavor and Fragrance Chemist
Halophytes
Herbicides
Hormones
Lipids
Medicinal Plants
Nitrogen Fixation
Nutrients
Oils, Plant-Derived
Pharmaceutical Scientist
Photoperiodism
Photosynthesis, Carbon Fixation
Photosynthesis, Light Reactions
Physiologist
Pigments
Poisonous Plants
Psychoactive Plants
Soil, Chemistry of
Terpenes
Translocation
Vacuoles
Water Movement

BIODIVERSITY

Agricultural Ecosystems
Aquatic Ecosystems
Biodiversity
Biogeography
Biome
Botanical Gardens and Arboreta
Chapparal
Clines and Ecotypes
Coastal Ecosystems
Coniferous Forests
Curator of a Botanical Garden
Curator of an Herbarium
Deciduous Forests
Deforestation
Desertification
Deserts
Ecology
Ethnobotany
Global Warning
Herbaria
Human Impacts
Invasive Species

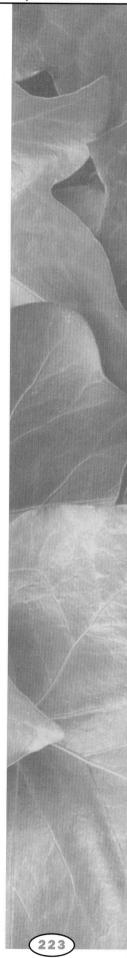

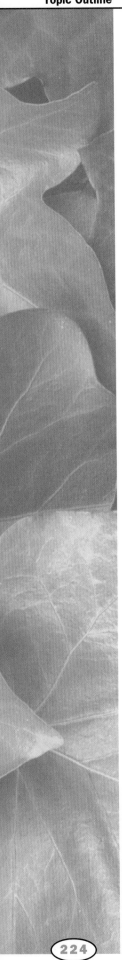

Desertification
Deserts
Ecosystem
Halophytes
Native Food Crops
Photosynthesis, Carbon Fixation and
Tundra

DISEASES OF PLANTS

Acid Rain
Chestnut Blight
Deforestation
Dutch Elm Disease
Fungi
Interactions, Plant-Fungal
Interactions, Plant-Insect
Nutrients
Pathogens
Pathologist
Potato Blight

DRUGS AND POISONS

Alcoholic Beverage Industry
Alcoholic Beverages
Alkaloids
Cacao
Cannabis
Coca
Coffee
Defenses, Chemical
Dioscorea
Economic Importance of Plants
Ethnobotany
Flavonoids
Medicinal Plants
Pharmaceutical Scientist
Plant Prospecting
Poison Ivy
Poisonous Plants
Psychoactive Plants
Solanaceae
Tea
Tobacco

ECOLOGY

Acid Rain
Agricultural Ecosystems
Aquatic Ecosystems
Atmosphere and Plants
Biodiversity
Biogeochemical Cycles

Biogeography
Biome
Carbon Cycle
Chapparal
Clines and Ecotypes
Coastal Ecosystems
Coniferous Forests
Deciduous Forests
Decomposers
Defenses, Chemical
Defenses, Physical
Deforestation
Desertification
Deserts
Ecology
Ecology, Energy Flow
Ecology, Fire
Ecosystem
Endangered Species
Global Warning
Grasslands
Human Impacts
Interactions, Plant-Fungal
Interactions, Plant-Insect
Interactions, Plant-Plant
Interactions, Plant-Vertebrate
Invasive Species
Mycorrhizae
Nutrients
Pathogens
Peat Bogs
Pollination Biology
Rain Forest Canopy
Rain Forests
Savanna
Seed Dispersal
Shape and Form of Plants
Soil, Chemistry of
Soil, Physical Characteristics
Symbiosis
Terpenes
Tundra
Wetlands

ECONOMIC IMPORTANCE OF PLANTS

Acid Rain
Agricultural Ecosystems
Arborist
Agriculture, History of
Agriculture, Modern
Agriculture, Organic

Alcoholic Beverage Industry
Alcoholic Beverages
Bamboo
Biofuels
Bioremediation
Breeder
Cacao
Cannabis
Chestnut Blight
Coffee
Coniferous Forests
Cork
Corn
Cotton
Deciduous Forests
Deforestation
Economic Importance of Plants
Fiber and Fiber Products
Flavor and Fragrance Chemist
Fruits
Fruits, Seedless
Food Scientist
Forensic Botany
Forester
Forestry
Genetic Engineer
Global Warning
Grains
Green Revolution
Herbs and Spices
Horticulture
Horticulturist
Human Impacts
Hydroponics
Landscape Architect
Medicinal Plants
Oils, Plant-Derived
Ornamental Plants
Paper
Peat Bogs
Pharmaceutical Scientist
Plant Prospecting
Potato Blight
Rice
Soybeans
Sugar
Tea
Turf Management
Wheat
Wood Products
Vegetables

EVOLUTION

Algae
Angiosperms
Archaea
Biodiversity
Biogeography
Breeding Systems
Bryophytes
Clines and Ecotypes
Curator of an Herbarium
Darwin, Charles
Defenses, Chemical
Defenses, Physical
Endangered Species
Endosymbiosis
Evolution of Plants, History of
Eubacteria
Ferns
Flora
Fungi
Global Warming
Hybrids and Hybridization
Interactions, Plant-Fungal
Interactions, Plant-Insect
Interactions, Plant-Plant
Interactions, Plant-Vertebrate
McClintock, Barbara
Molecular Plant Genetics
Mycorrhizae
Palynology
Phylogeny
Poisonous Plants
Pollination Biology
Polyploidy
Reproduction, Alternation of Generations
Seed Dispersal
Speciation
Symbiosis
Systematics, Molecular
Systematics, Plant
Warming, Johannes

FOODS

Alcoholic Beverage Industry
Alliaceae
Bamboo
Cacao
Cacti
Carbohydrates
Coffee
Corn

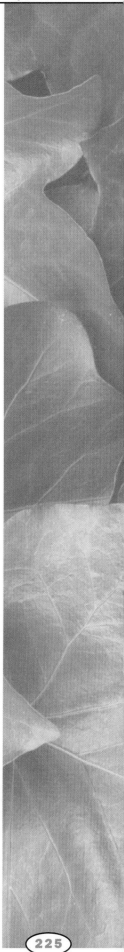

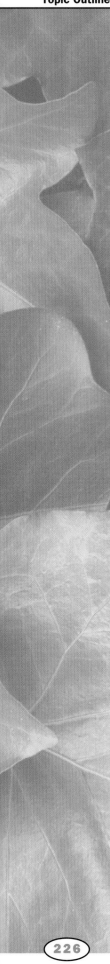

HORTICULTURE

Alliaceae
Asteraceae
Bonsai
Botanical Gardens and Arboreta
Breeder
Breeding
Cacti
Curator of a Botanical Garden
Horticulture
Horticulturist
Hybrids and Hybridization
Hydroponics
Landscape Architect
Ornamental Plants
Polyploidy
Propagation
Turf Management

INDIVIDUAL PLANTS AND PLANT FAMILIES

Alliaceae
Asteraceae
Bamboo
Cacao
Cacti
Cannabis
Coca
Coffee
Corn
Cotton
Dioscorea
Fabaceae
Ginkgo
Grasses
Kudzu
Opium Poppy
Orchidaceae
Palms
Poison Ivy
Potato
Rice
Rosaceae
Sequoia
Solanaceae
Soybeans
Tobacco
Wheat

LIFE CYCLE

Breeder
Breeding Systems
Cell Cycle
Differentiation and Development
Embryogenesis
Flowers
Fruits
Gametophyte
Genetic Mechanisms and Development
Germination
Germination and Growth
Hormonal Control and Development
Meristems
Pollination Biology
Reproduction, Alternation of Generations
Reproduction, Asexual
Reproduction, Fertilization
Reproduction, Sexual
Rhythms in Plant Life
Seed Dispersal
Seed Preservation
Seeds
Senescence
Sporophyte
Tissue Culture

NUTRITION

Acid Rain
Biogeochemical Cycles
Carbon Cycle
Carnivorous Plants
Compost
Decomposers
Ecology, Fire
Epiphytes
Fertilizer
Germination and Growth
Hydroponics
Mycorrhizae
Nitrogen Fixation
Nutrients
Peat Bogs
Physiologist
Roots
Soil, Chemistry of
Soil, Physical Characteristics
Translocation
Water Movement

Volume 2 Index

*Page numbers in **boldface** indicate article titles. Those in italics indicate illustrations. A cumulative index, which combines the terms in all volumes of Plant Sciences, can be found in volume 4 of this series.*

A

ABA. *See* Abscisic acid
Abacá *(Musa textilis)*, *138*, 139
Abbott, John, 101
ABC genes, 173–174, *174*
Abies (fir), 19, *22*
Abrade, defined, 74
Abrasion, defined, 26
Abscisic acid (ABA), 57, 158, 176, 177
Abscission, defined, 49
Abscission layer, abscission zone, 49, 51–52
Acacia, 60
caven, 48
Accelerated growth, 61
Accession, defined, 36
Accessory fruits, 158, 160
Acer. See Maple
Achenes, *159*, 160
Acidity. *See* pH
Acorns, 160
Acquired characters, 128
Actinomorphic flowers, 146
Actinomycetes, 162, 164
defined, 162
Adaptations
Darwin's studies of, 45, 129
deciduous habit, 49, 130
epiphytes, 113–114
fire, 93
Lamarck's theory of, 128
leaves, 52, 126
physical defenses, **60–62**
xerophytic. *See* Xerophytic adaptations
Adhesion, defined, 60
Adnation, flowers, 146
Adventitious, defined, 78
Adventitious root systems, 78
Aeration, defined, 15

Aflatoxins, 164
Africa
deserts, 64, *71*, *72*, 74, 75
See also specific countries
Agathis (kauri), 1–2
Agave
fourcroydes (henequen), *138*, 139
sisalana (sisal), *138*, 139
Aggregate fruits, 158, *159*, 160
Agricultural ecosystems, 12–13
Agriculture
desertification of agricultural lands, 72
fiber crops. *See* Fiber and fiber products
food crops. *See* Food crops; Grains; *specific crop plants*
forest conversion, 50, 63
grasslands conversion, 189, 193–194
marketing of agricultural products, 100–102
organic, 16, 33
permaculture, 65
soil impacts, 71
subsistence farming, 99
swidden, defined, 63
swidden/slash-and-burn, 63
yields, Green Revolution and, 197
See also Agricultural ecosystems; Breeding; Crop plants; Fertilizers; Forestry; Green Revolution; *specific crops*
Agrobacterium, 169
Agroecosystems. *See* Agricultural ecosystems
Agroforestry, 65, 153
See also Forestry
Alcoholic beverages, 30, 164, 189
beer, 164, 189
spirits, 164, 189
wine, 59, 164
Alerce *(Fitzroya)*, 21–22, *23*
Alexiades, Miguel N., 117–118
Algae
blue-green. *See* Cyanobacteria
brown, 80
charophycean, *122*, 122–124, 127

evolution, 113
in food web, 86, 87
green. *See* Green algae
phytoplankton, 2
plastids in, 112–113
red, 112
reproduction, 166
seaweeds, 2, 123
symbioses. *See* Corals; Lichens
See also Aquatic plants
Alien species. *See* Exotic species; Invasive species
Alkalinity. *See* pH
Alkaloids, 55
caffeine, 59
cocaine, 4–6, 59
codeine, 59
human uses, 59
in legumes, 55, 130
mescaline, 59
in nectar, 148
nicotine, 59
quinine, 10
synthesis and structure, 55, 58
taxol, 24, 202
Allelopathy, 7–8
See also Chemical defenses
Alternation of generations, 123
See also Gametophytes; Sporophytes; *specific plant groups*
Amanita
muscaria (fly agaric), 164
virosa, *163*, 164
Amatoxins, 164
Amborella, 126
Ambrosia beetles, 61
American Association for the Advancement of Science, 34
American Chemical Society, 141
American Society of Perfumers, 141
Amino acids, 30, 130, 148
Ammonia, anhydrous, 136
Ammonium nitrate, 136
Ammonium polyphosphate, 136
Ammonium thiosulfate, 136
Anabaena, 39
Analog, defined, 59
Androecium, 144, 145, 147
Angiosperms, 127, 156

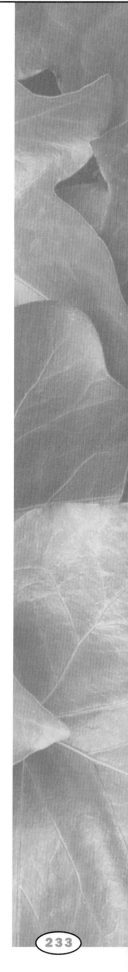

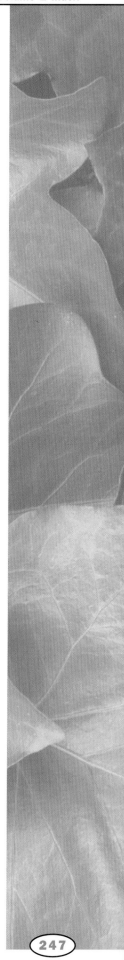